Degrees of Allegiance

Ohio University Press Series on Law, Society, and Politics in the Midwest

SERIES EDITORS: PAUL FINKELMAN AND L. DIANE BARNES

The History of Ohio Law, edited by Michael Les Benedict and John F. Winkler

Frontiers of Freedom: Cincinnati's Black Community, 1802–1868, by Nikki M. Taylor

A Place of Recourse: A History of the U.S. District Court for the Southern District of Ohio, 1803–2003, by Roberta Sue Alexander

The Black Laws: Race and the Legal Process in Early Ohio, by Stephen Middleton

The History of Indiana Law, edited by David J. Bodenhamer and Hon. Randall T. Shepard

The History of Michigan Law, edited by Paul Finkelman and Martin J. Hershock

The Rescue of Joshua Glover: A Fugitive Slave, the Constitution, and the Coming of the Civil War, by H. Robert Baker

The History of Nebraska Law, edited by Alan G. Gless

American Pogrom: The East St. Louis Race Riot and Black Politics, by Charles L. Lumpkins

No Winners Here Tonight: Race, Politics, and Geography in One of the Country's Busiest Death Penalty States, by Andrew Welsh-Huggins

The Dred Scott *Case: Historical and Contemporary Perspectives on Race and Law,* edited by David Thomas Konig, Paul Finkelman, and Christopher Alan Bracey

The Jury in Lincoln's America, by Stacy Pratt McDermott

Degrees of Allegiance: Harassment and Loyalty in Missouri's German-American Community during World War I, by Petra DeWitt

PETRA DEWITT

Degrees of Allegiance

HARASSMENT AND LOYALTY IN MISSOURI'S
GERMAN-AMERICAN COMMUNITY DURING WORLD WAR I

Ohio University Press – Athens

Ohio University Press, Athens, Ohio 45701
ohioswallow.com
© 2012 by Ohio University Press
All rights reserved

To obtain permission to quote, reprint, or otherwise reproduce or distribute
material from Ohio University Press publications, please contact our rights and
permissions department at (740) 593-1154 or (740) 593-4536 (fax).

Printed in the United States of America
Ohio University Press books are printed on acid-free paper ⊗ ™

20 19 18 17 16 15 14 13 12   5 4 3 2 1

Library of Congress Cataloging-in-Publication Data
DeWitt, Petra, 1961–
 Degrees of allegiance : harassment and loyalty in Missouri's German-American
community during World War I / Petra DeWitt.
    p. cm. — (Ohio University Press series on law, society, and politics in the
Midwest)
 Includes bibliographical references and index.
 ISBN 978-0-8214-2003-4 (hc : acid-free paper) — ISBN 978-0-8214-4419-1
(electronic)
 1. German Americans—Missouri—History—20th century. 2. World War, 1914–
1918—German-Americans. 3. World War, 1914–1918—Missouri. 4. Germans—
Missouri—History—20th century. 5. German Americans—Legal status, laws,
etc.—United States—History—20th century. I. Title.
 F475.G3D49 2012
 940.4'03—dc23

2011053208

CONTENTS

ILLUSTRATIONS

Figures

Maps

ACKNOWLEDGMENTS

Completing a project on the scale of this book, from the initial idea to the revised manuscript, would have been impossible without the assistance and support of many individuals along the way whom I wish to thank.

At the University of Missouri in Columbia, I had the pleasure of working with outstanding scholars who freely shared their knowledge and gave advice. Susan Flader, Mary Neth, John Bullion, Linda Reeder, Kirby Miller, and Walter Schroeder lent their support, expertise, and guidance and offered invaluable advice as this book took shape. Walter Kamphoefner, a leading scholar in the field of German immigration, added invaluable insight during several conferences. At the Missouri University of Science & Technology I also benefited from the advice of Larry Gragg. As a former mentor and now colleague, he willingly read and criticized my work as it grew.

During my lengthy research I had the help of many. The assistance of David Moore, John Konzal, and William Stolz at the Western Historical Manuscript Collection, University of Missouri–Columbia, has been very important over the years. The newspaper library at the State Historical Society of Missouri in Columbia houses the largest collection of newspapers of any state and is invaluable to anyone conducting research in regional history. Thank you also to Kimberlee Reid and the staff as well as to the volunteers at the National Archives, Central Plains Region, in Kansas City for their assistance during my search for Selective Service records and cases prosecuted under the Espionage Act in the Eastern District Court of Missouri. Members of the staff at the Missouri State Archives in Jefferson City were kind and efficient in responding to my requests for documents and microfilms. John Viessman, the curator of the State Museum at the Capitol in Jefferson City, provided access to his research, helped me find a survivor from the World War I era, and assisted during the resulting interview.

I thank all the dedicated staff, volunteers, and taxpayers who support numerous local libraries and county historical societies. Thank you, Claudia Baker and Mary Lou Schulte, for allowing me free access to the documents and family histories located at the Osage County Historical Society. My most heartfelt appreciation goes to Art Draper, Missy Frank, and Lois Puchta at the Gasconade County Historical Society. You graciously offered assistance, advice, and firsthand knowledge of the German culture in Hermann and Gasconade County. You have made me feel at home in Hermann, and your interest in my work, your contacts, and your personal knowledge of the area's history have helped tremendously.

I am grateful to several other individuals for their advice and inspiration. Father Joe Welschmeyer supplied me with his personal knowledge of Osage County and gave me a tour of Rich Fountain, Missouri. Phyllis Garstang, Marylin Shaw Smith, and Ralph Sellenschutter through their correspondence offered additional personal insight into the events during the war and the preservation of German culture. The editors at Ohio University Press, including Gillian Berchowitz and Nancy Basmajian, were very patient through the lengthy revision process, and their editorial suggestions made this a better book.

Not last, I wish to thank the women in my life who have served as shining examples of success despite the continued limits placed upon the female gender. Many thanks to my mother, Marlene Wagner, who still lives in Germany, for teaching me perseverance, patience, and organization. She, as I, was a migrant; only she took a greater and more difficult step when she, as a single person, packed a suitcase in 1957 and left her family in East Germany for a better future in West Germany. Her courage and determination have been an inspiration to me throughout my life. Ibby, you allowed me to come into your life as a transcriber of family letters and convinced me to continue the struggle when I was ready to throw in the towel. Your friendship and wisdom are precious to me.

Finally, I thank my husband of nearly thirty years, Melvin Clay DeWitt, for his support and acceptance of a weekend marriage for several years so that I could fulfill a dream. He patiently and proudly accompanied me to many conferences, lent an ear to new ideas and interpretations, and countless times thought of the right word or phrase. Not once did his faith in my ability to balance marriage, two homes, and full-time work falter or waver, not even after his diagnosis with Parkinson's disease, debilitating automobile accident, and forced retirement. Without his support and tolerance, this end product of many years simply could not have been possible. I dedicate this book to him.

Introduction

DURING THE early spring in 1918, Fritz Monat, a forty-two-year-old coal miner from Staunton, Illinois, was visiting family near St. Thomas in Cole County, Missouri. For several days, primarily during stops at taverns in Jefferson City, he boasted about having been born in Germany and expressed the hope that his birth country would win the Great War. A "Committee of Citizens" followed his movements throughout the city for several days to gather evidence of his disloyal behavior. On April 5, 1918, twenty-five committee members decided that Monat had expressed enough unpatriotic thoughts and that he should be punished. The incensed committee members nabbed him, took him to McClung Park, removed his shirt, threw several buckets of cold water on his back, and then "whipped [him] with a rawhide" until he apologized for his expressions and agreed to kiss the American flag. The group then took him to the Jefferson Theater and compelled him to kneel before a large audience, to apologize again for his remarks, and to kiss the flag. Members of the audience, who initially thought the incident funny and part of an act, quickly realized its seriousness when committee members warned the audience that they would deal in the same manner with other "disloyal utterances."[1]

Local and regional newspapers reinforced this warning. The editor of the *Missouri Volksfreund,* the German-language newspaper in Jefferson City, suggested that people should not express opposition to the government during times of emergency and that the government would punish such actions more severely in the future. The *Tipton Times,* in neighboring Moniteau County, stated that Monat would realize now that "fealty to the Fatherland with an utter disregard for his adopted state and everything that a true American should hold dear is not in keeping with good citizenship."[2]

At first glance this incident appears no different from any other incident in the widespread frenzy directed against German speakers living in heavily German-populated communities of the Midwest during the First World War. Frederick C. Luebke, still recognized as the leading historian on the subject, argued that during the "strong wave of anti-German hysteria" of World War I "citizens of German origin" experienced persecution and confronted "serious efforts . . . to eliminate German language and culture in the United States."[3] Chicagoans, for example, "spied on, terrorized, investigated, jailed and discharged [German-Americans] from their jobs in an effort to produce '100% Americanism.'" Iowa's governor W. L. Harding proclaimed that no person could speak German in public or on the telephone. Indiana's State Teachers' Association urged the elimination of German in elementary schools.[4] According to several historians this "hatred and persecution of German cultural manifestations" during the war struck a "sharp and powerful blow" at the German-American community by erasing its distinct culture from the nation.[5]

The analysis of social, economic, and political relationships at the local level in Missouri, however, reveals a much more complex truth that does not fit well with the bleak portrayal of the German-American experience during the Great War. This case study of Missouri in the context of the Midwest demonstrates that aggression toward German-Americans during World War I occurred in communities where personal relationships and emphasis on local enforcement of national war effort guidelines, not ethnicity itself, created suspicions. (By "German-Americans" I mean those persons, whether U.S. citizens or not, who were born in Germany and those whose heritage included a parent or grandparent born in Germany. By "Americans" and "Missourians" I mean persons whose heritage is other than German.)[6] In-depth evaluation of anti-German sentiment in Missouri, such as accusations of unpatriotic behavior, arrests under the Espionage Act, job loss, property destruction, and renaming of businesses or streets, evidenced in public documents and newspapers, revealed that Missouri Germans did not entirely escape charges of disloyalty. Nevertheless, they were not the subject of widespread hate crimes and ethnically targeted legislation German-Americans experienced in midwestern states such as Illinois, Iowa, Minnesota, Ohio, and Wisconsin.[7]

Missouri was unique in several ways. Its legislature did not meet during the war, and its governor did not perceive the need for an emergency session. Missouri's political culture, or "Show-Me" attitude, also encouraged individualism as well as minimal government interference in traditional social and economic structures.[8] Therefore, the Missouri Council of Defense, the organization in charge of the war effort, advocated volunteerism, opposed any form of mob violence, and appealed to German speakers to turn hesitant German-Americans into enthusiastic patriots. At the same time, strong labor union and socialist traditions in St. Louis and a social and religious culture opposed to government interference in Missouri resulted in pockets of anti-war sentiment. Consequently, appearance of loyalty based on local expectations or definitions shaped behavior. For example, less than enthusiastic individuals, whom zealous supporters viewed with suspicion, often diverted attention from themselves by harassing persons who openly criticized the government and the war. Complicating the situation was the desire by several Americans of German extraction to impress their sense of patriotism upon their neighbors even if that meant reporting fellow German-Americans for disloyal behavior to the authorities. German-Americans in Missouri thus experienced harassment, not persecution, during the war, at times at the hands of descendants of German immigrants. Physical violence was limited to individuals, such as Fritz Monat, who flaunted disloyal behavior.

This work also revises the conventional wisdom that the so-called persecution of everything German resulted in the eradication of German culture. Evidence indicates that the acculturation process varied by locality and German-Americans in several Missouri communities were able to preserve aspects of their ethnic culture despite the war. In Missouri the war thus did not have the same devastating impact on German culture as historians argue it had in other midwestern states. Recent studies about Germans in Texas and New England found similar experience and results.[9]

This book not only offers new insight into the history of Missouri, the debate over the intensity of the anti-German sentiment and its impact on German culture in the United States, but it also encourages more nuanced community studies in the Midwest to better understand the events during the Great War and the treatment of minority groups in general. For example, Katja Wüstenbecker's recent study evaluates the German-American experience in several midwestern states by concentrating on urban centers, including Cincinnati, Chicago, Milwaukee, and St. Louis, but takes little note of events in rural areas.[10] Historians should recognize that Americans and immigrants interact with each other everywhere on the local level—at work, during recreation, while shopping—and construct perceptions of themselves and each other through these interactions. Minorities are not homogeneous or united groups; instead, we need to understand relationships at the local level, within the ethnic group, and with the dominant culture before we can draw sweeping conclusions and apply them to the larger picture. Studies of ethnic soldiers in the United States military during the Great War, for example, have demonstrated that the military for pragmatic reasons was ethnically pluralistic and more tolerant than civilian authorities.[11] Such studies are also pertinent to the discussion of the legitimacy of dissent and its effectiveness during wartime, a subject that has resurfaced alongside ethnic scapegoating in recent years.[12]

Missouri is the perfect setting for a detailed study of the German-American experience during the Great War because it has many different German settlements, ranging from a large urban population in St. Louis to rural homogeneous town clusters such as Hermann in Gasconade County and Westphalia in Osage County. This allows the historian to compare and contrast various relationships among Germans, interactions between Germans, various ethnic groups, and the dominant culture, urban versus rural life, the complexities that informed the definition of loyalty, the reasons for distrust, and the multifaceted and complicated factors that contributed to the demise of German culture in some areas and its preservation in others.

The phenomenon of being one-hundred-percent American, that is, being absolutely loyal and devoted to the United States and no other country, had its roots in the years before World War I. German immigrants had been coming to the United States since the late seventeenth century, and the majority of those arriving in the nineteenth century settled in the Midwest, including Illinois, Iowa, Minnesota, Ohio, Wisconsin, and Missouri. Although German immigrants and their children had experienced a brief period of nativism in the 1850s, Americans in general accepted them into society without opposition. Changes in migration patterns, however, changed that favorable pattern.

From 1897 through 1914, immigration numbers rose rapidly and so did the numbers of immigrants from southern and eastern European nations who settled in America. Americans were not willing to overlook these strangers because they differed in ethnic and religious backgrounds from the White Anglo-Saxon Protestants from northern and western Europe who had built the nation. In their minds, these "new" immigrants were not the independent-minded individuals who established businesses or the rugged farmers who subdued the soil in the West. Instead, they were unskilled laborers who worked for lower wages, settled in tenement districts in industrial areas, and competed for jobs with the native born. American nativists singled out these foreigners as the causes for disruptive worker strikes, corrupt urban political machines, consumption of alcohol, and increasing squalor and poverty.[13] Progressive reformers thought that curtailing immigration and Americanizing foreigners would end alcoholism, corruption, poverty, and unemployment. Factories and cities throughout the nation established evening adult education classes to teach newcomers English, prepare them for citizenship, and Americanize them. Immigrants had to forsake the traditions of their homelands and adopt the language, ideals, and customs of their new country, the United States. By 1914, however, nativism had not yet been strong enough to influence immigration legislation and eliminate dual allegiance to the homeland and the United States.[14]

World War I and the fear that the enemy would destroy American democracy and liberty increased the anxieties and suspicions nativists harbored toward foreigners. The unprecedented mobilization of material and human resources demanded total loyalty and devotion to the nation and its higher purpose of ridding the world of German militarism. The slightest opposition seemed to hamper the war effort and to support the enemy. Nationalistic, or paranoid, citizens thought the only way to gain some sense of security was to make sure that everyone thought alike. Patriotism became a duty, and an individual had to subordinate personal rights and needs to the welfare and survival of the country.[15] In this context, Germans, who by 1917 still constituted the largest single nationality among the foreign born and who were related to the enemy, attracted what John Higham called "the plain and simple accusation in which every type of xenophobia culminated: the charge of disloyalty, the gravest sin in the morality of nationalism."[16] Americans demanded an end to divided loyalties to assure America's safety.

Searching for the roots of harassment and the meaning of loyalty during World War I in Missouri reveals how the language of patriotism and ethnic disloyalty concealed the real factors that contributed to mistrust and hostility during that war. Personal relationships and local circumstances, rather than ethnicity itself, were the factors that generated suspicions and superpatriotic activities such as the Monat incident. The event occurred in Jefferson City, the capital and seat of government of the state of Missouri. Because the Missouri legislature did not meet during U.S. participation in World War I, the governor and the Missouri Council of Defense, whom the governor had appointed upon the instructions of the National Council of Defense, represented authority in the state during this period. Governor Gardner, in order to mobilize the state, called for "one people, one sentiment, and one flag; ready to cooperate, ready to sacrifice, ready to suffer."[17] The council attempted to use the powers granted to it by federal officials to whip up support for the war. Impromptu rallies expressing community support for the war, financially successful Liberty Loan drives, and high membership numbers for the Red Cross indeed demonstrated patriotism and loyalty during the early weeks of the war.[18] As the number of complaints about disloyal behavior sent to the Council of Defense increased by late 1917 council members became aware of a "widespread lack of popular sentiment for the war."[19] Consequently, they reacted to problems within the state and encouraged more forceful approaches to preserve the state's patriotic image.

The evidence also illustrates that council members, including Chairman Frederick Mumford and Secretary William Saunders, recognized that they were not all-powerful and knew their limitations. Council officials in their correspondence with county council members admitted that legally they could not force compliance with mobilization guidelines but had to rely instead on volunteerism, friendly coercion, and intimidation as tools to maintain the state's patriotic image. The governor's public announcements also informed county officials that they were in charge of ensuring compliance with government guidelines for the home front. Thus, local enforcement power relationships shaped the reaction to real and suspected disloyalty. Consequently, citizens of Jefferson City were likely to hear or read about the government's task to unite public opinion in favor of the war and the council's mission to carry out the war effort in Missouri. They also thought that it was their responsibility to assure patriotism at the local level because the state council had delegated such power to county councils.

Fritz Monat was born in Germany but so were many residents of Jefferson City, a community with a sizable second and third generation German-American population, and they did not experience public flogging.[20] Instead, his public and disloyal expressions marked him as a supporter of the enemy. Furthermore, he was a union member and suspected socialist from Staunton, Illinois. Residents of Jefferson City read St. Louis newspapers and probably knew about the mob activities directed against union workers in Staunton during the winter and spring months of 1918, that resulted in the tarring and feathering of two members of the Industrial Workers of the World (IWW) and hundreds of workers kissing the American flag.[21] "Loyalist vigilantes" there used war anxieties, the perceived need to silence pro-Germans, and the language of patriotism to justify this violent treatment of workers while covering up factionalism in the union and a long history of mistrust between labor and management as the real reasons to eliminate the IWW and socialists in the coal-mining region of southwestern Illinois.[22]

On February 22, 1918, Jefferson City experienced its "first I.W.W. experience" when police had to save W. H. Edwards, a suspected "I.W.W. agitator," from an angry mob after he gave a speech criticizing the work of the Red Cross, the YMCA and the government.[23] Consequently, six weeks later, concerned citizens viewed Monat not only as a bragging German but also as a union member from Staunton and thus as a real threat to the harmony and reputation of the seat of government for Missouri. They decided to act quickly and decisively to preserve peace and coerce conformity during the upcoming Third Liberty Loan campaign.[24] Monat's punishment thus had dual purpose. Residents of Jefferson City, including German-Americans, saved the city from potentially violent labor or mob unrest and, at the same time, eliminated charges of disloyalty for the entire community. This one violent act, which newspaper editors including German-American editors supported, was enough to silence opposition. The relative tranquility during the remaining months of the war as well as the maintenance of local control also allowed German-Americans to weather the storm and preserve many aspects of their German culture in the city despite the war.

ONE

American yet German

The State of German-American Culture and the Relationship between Germans and Non-Germans in Missouri on the Eve of World War I

> Those who would meanly and coldly forget their old mother could not be expected to be faithful to their young bride.
>
> *Carl Schurz, Senate speech, 1872*

CARL SCHURZ, one of the most famous German immigrants who called Missouri his home for several years, said in a speech before the United States Senate that he and other German immigrants who came to America to begin a new life should not "entirely forget their old fatherland." He was "proud to be an American," but he did not believe he should be "ashamed of being a son of Germany," a nation that "has sent abroad thousands . . . of her children upon foreign shores with their intelligence, their industry, and their spirit of good citizenship."[1] Schurz embraced this philosophy throughout his distinguished career as a journalist and politician. He co-owned and co-edited the *Westliche Post,* the premier German-language newspaper of the Midwest, in St. Louis, served as a U.S. senator from Missouri between 1868 and 1874, and accepted the appointment as President Rutherford B. Hayes's secretary of the interior in 1877.[2] He became successful by learning English and embracing the American political system; but he also continued to speak and write in German. In short, he merged his foreign heritage with American ideals of freedom and prosperity and forged a new identity. Thus, Carl Schurz serves as an excellent example of the German-American identity most German immigrants and their descendants had created by the eve of World War I as they

8

adopted American economic and political principles while retaining German cultural traditions such as language and religious practices. Yet, several of the factors that contributed to the creation of the German-American identity also shaped relationships with non-Germans that would influence the treatment of German-Americans during World War I.

During the nineteenth century, five million German settlers came as groups, families, or individuals to the United States, including Missouri, where they represented the majority among the foreign-born population for many decades.[3] Motives for leaving the homeland varied. Some aimed to evade military duty or left for religious or political reasons. Inheritance patterns that splintered land into small economically unfeasible holdings and "economic misery" after series of failed harvests convinced others to look for a better life elsewhere. The end of the cottage textile industry, changes in the labor market, and reduced standards of living through the industrial revolution encouraged many Germans to migrate between German principalities, within Europe, and across the Atlantic Ocean.[4] What drove most was the dream for improved economic conditions and a new life.

Missouri became a popular destination for German immigrants in part because early nineteenth-century travelers to the territory, including Gottfried Duden, had written glowing reports about its land, waterways, and climate, and described a free society and accessible government that stood in stark contrast to Germany's closed and privileged society.[5] Additional elements that contributed to immigration to Missouri were the growing efficiency of emigration societies, improved accommodations aboard steamships, and the expanding rail networks that eased travel worries and expenses.[6] By midcentury the most important factor shaping the decision to cross the Atlantic was that more and more Germans had relatives in America who wrote letters to the old country. Their correspondence advised where land or employment opportunity was available, explained institutions and culture, and made suggestions about whom one could trust or whose assistance one should avoid along the way. Furthermore, relatives often sent money for others to undertake the voyage, provided shelter until the newly arrived could establish their own households, and secured work.[7]

The first sizable wave of German immigrants to Missouri during the early 1830s included a few noblemen, lower-middle-class scholars, preachers, artisans, and shopkeepers, as well as farmers and farm laborers from southwestern and northwestern German regions, who settled in St. Charles and Warren Counties. "Poor but not destitute," most of them had struggled to maintain their economic independence in the old country and had enough savings to pay the passage and to buy land.[8] Several of these early settlers were liberal intellectuals who fled repressive measures after the unsuccessful revolutions against the undemocratic governments in a number of German states during the early 1830s. As "Latin Farmers" they knew more about Greek and Latin than about farm implements; most failed as gentlemen farmers, became teachers or journalists, or moved to cities, including St. Louis.[9]

A sizable number of these settlers arrived through the assistance of well-organized emigration societies. For example, Friedrich Münch, a Lutheran pastor, writer, farmer, and later state senator, and Paul Fellonius, a lawyer and 1830 revolutionary, brought a group of settlers from the city of Gießen in the grand duchy of Hesse-Darmstadt. They had established the Gießener Auswanderungs-Gesellschaft, or Gießen Emigration Society, with the dream of creating new German republics in America, which would be used as stepping-stones toward future revolution in the homeland. However, cholera killed many of its members before they reached Missouri, and disappointed survivors soon scattered and settled in St. Louis and Warren County along the Missouri River.[10]

German immigrants who made present-day Gasconade County their home arrived under similar circumstances. The Deutsche Ansiedlungs-Gesellschaft, or German Settlement Society of Philadelphia, established the city of Hermann in 1837 with the purpose of uniting Germans in America into a colony or state where they could preserve German language, customs, and culture. The society purchased land along the Missouri and Gasconade rivers suitable for agricultural and manufacturing pursuits. Although aspects of German culture have survived in Gasconade County to the present, the founders of the society were not able to preserve unity and harmony because many settlers mistrusted society officers, desired local control, and separated from the society in 1839.[11]

Several of the early immigrants to Missouri followed their religious leaders, who not only hoped for economic betterment but also desired to establish utopian communities and secure greater freedom of worship. Martin Stephan and the Saxon Settlement Society brought a group of Lutheran clergymen to Missouri in 1839 to establish a religious community according to orthodox Lutheran principles in the vicinity of St. Louis. By the time this group reached Missouri, internal dissent had developed, and the majority of Saxons established settlements in Altenburg, Wittenberg, and Dresden in Perry County along the Mississippi River to the south of the city. Their dreams, however, were not dashed. Under the leadership of C. F. W. Walther, these Saxons established congregations that eventually united into the conservative German Evangelical Lutheran Synod of Missouri, Ohio and Other States, now the Lutheran Church—Missouri Synod. Education-minded leaders in Perry County also established the "log cabin college," a German gymnasium and theological college, which they moved to St. Louis in 1850 and renamed Concordia Seminary.[12] In 1844, William Keil founded the communal society of Bethel in Shelby County in northeast Missouri, and Low German speakers from the Kingdom of Hanover founded Cole Camp in Benton County and Concordia in Lafayette County. While agriculture and economic improvement were the primary reasons for settlement, these communities soon became centers for the preservation of the Lutheran faith and German traits, including *Plattdeutsch,* or the Low German dialect.[13]

German Catholics came to Missouri for economic reasons as well as religious freedom. Many settled along the Mississippi River in Zell, New Offenburg, Weingarten, and Coffman in Ste. Genevieve County during the 1840s. In central Missouri, Father Ferdinand M. Helias, a Belgian-born Jesuit who devoted his life to preserving the Catholic faith among German immigrants, established seventeen parishes for that purpose during the 1830s and 1840s, including Taos in Cole County, and Westphalia, Rich Fountain, and Loose Creek in Osage County.[14]

The majority of German immigrants who came to Missouri before the Civil War arrived between 1845 and 1854. So steady was their influx that by 1860 Missouri ranked sixth among the states in the size of its foreign-born German population. This diverse group of German immigrants included farmers, journalists, physicians, skilled craftsmen, merchants, and unskilled laborers who escaped economic crisis and looked for economic and social improvement, as well as the "Forty-Eighters" such as the famous political "refugees" Carl Schurz and Franz Sigel.[15]

The number of German immigrants briefly declined during the Civil War but rose again afterward and peaked during the 1880s. The drive to improve one's economic situation continued to shape migration decisions, and most utilized chain migration networks to move to already established neighborhoods or villages. Those who left Germany for Missouri during the 1870s and 1880s still came disproportionately from northern German provinces and predominantly from rural areas where the effects of industrialization changed accustomed living and working relationships. By the 1890s, however, single persons leaving Germany outnumbered those migrating as families; they were mostly urban workers and came from industrialized areas rather than specific geographic regions. German women also traveled independently and in increasing numbers to find work and husbands.[16] Immigration from Germany began to decline by the late 1880s because continuous industrial growth absorbed unemployed farm laborers and rural population and Bismarck's social programs and industrial codes improved wages and working conditions.[17]

On the eve of World War I, Germans formed the largest ethnic group in the United States as well as in Missouri, representing 8.7 percent of the entire population in the nation and 11.2 percent in the state.[18] The size of the German-born and German-speaking population would be reason enough to attract attention and resentment during World War I, but settlement patterns, the construction of a German-American identity, and the ability to preserve many aspects of the German culture also contributed to tensions during the war.

Slightly more than half of German immigrants who came to Missouri chose urban areas, especially St. Louis, as their primary destination. By 1910, 20 percent of St. Louis's population was either born in Germany or claimed that both parents had been born there; that is proportionately about half as many as in Milwaukee and about the same as in Cincinnati and Chicago.[19] These German immigrants were not destitute peasants but professionals, skilled craftsmen, and unskilled workers who moved to St. Louis in search of economic improvement, better wages, and business ownership. Carpenters, coopers, shoemakers, tailors, bakers, merchants, brewers, stonemasons, and bricklayers applied their trades and filled the high demand for skilled labor in the rapidly growing city. Displaced farm laborers and urban workers pursued manufacturing and mechanical occupations and added to the city's diversity of economic and social classes.[20] St. Louis and its rich farming hinterland also provided temporary employment for needy newcomers who had had enough savings to pay for the voyage across the Atlantic but not enough to purchase land. Single travelers or newlywed couples often lived in the city on the way to the farm. German settlers who had arrived earlier responded to the needs of those who reached St. Louis short of funds through mutual aid societies, such as the Deutsche Unterstützungs Bund (German Aid Society) and the Deutsche Gesellschaft (German Society) of St. Louis. These organizations assisted with finding work, provided access to hospital care, aided with burials, educated about American institutions, and assisted with arrangements for those who wished to continue their journey further west.[21]

German immigrants initially moved to the first, second, eighth, and tenth wards in the northern and southern sections of St. Louis, and by 1858, these four wards accounted for 64 percent of the German-born inhabitants of St. Louis.[22] As occurred in Chicago, Cincinnati, and Milwaukee, these well-defined German areas within the city were not permanent ethnic enclaves, as for example Italians established. Comparison of population distribution and occupational patterns demonstrates that by 1900 many German immigrants in St. Louis experienced economic success, took advantage of the social and geographic mobility of an open society and bought property in the form of a home, business, or land for development in the city's more affluent middle-class neighborhoods.[23]

Although the city of St. Louis may have attracted the highest concentration of German immigrants, Germans also accounted for a sizable proportion of the total population and a majority of the foreign-born population in several rural counties outside of St. Louis. As map 1.1 illustrates, Germans chose Chariton, Cole, Cooper, Franklin, Gasconade, Howard, Lafayette, Moniteau, Montgomery, Osage, St. Charles, St. Louis, Saline, and Warren Counties along the Missouri River, as well as Ste. Genevieve, Perry, and Cape Girardeau Counties on the Mississippi River as the primary areas for settlement. They preferred this particular area, known as the northern and eastern border region of the Ozarks, because it offered fertile land and easily accessible waterways and reminded many of the Rhine Valley in Germany.[24] Here, "poor but not destitute" Germans with an occupational background in agriculture including small-scale farmers, farm laborers, and cottagers, could purchase small farms, prosper within a few years, and pass the dream of land ownership on to their children. Even artisans and professionals, including blacksmiths and doctors, could prosper in these rural areas.[25]

MAP 1.1. German settlement patterns in Missouri. Reprinted from Russel L. Gerlach, *Settlement Patterns in Missouri: A Study of Population Origins,* by permission of the University of Missouri Press. Copyright © 1986 by the Curators of the University of Missouri.

However, plotting the numbers of German immigrants who settled in Missouri by counties can be misleading because Germans were not evenly distributed in this so-called German belt. Instead, they established ethnic communities within this geographic region, such as Washington in Franklin County, where 44.7 percent of its residents claimed German birth or parentage, while in the entire county only 19 percent claimed German parentage.[26] German immigrants also established isolated ethnic communities elsewhere in the state that remained German in character into the third and fourth generations. These islands of *Deutschtum,* or Germanism, included Dresden in Pettis County, Cole Camp in Benton County, and Freistatt in Lawrence County.[27] Provincial origin and dialect often influenced where Germans settled in these rural areas. For example, people from Osnabrück established Washington in Franklin County, Hanoverians moved to Concordia in Lafayette County, and Oldenburgers settled Augusta and Dutzow in Warren County.[28]

The same was true for Gasconade and Osage Counties. While both had a sizable German population, settlement patterns at the township level reveal that German speakers established ethnic clusters in specific geographic locations within these counties. In Gasconade County, German immigrants made Roark Township, including the city of Hermann, and Richland, Boef, and Boulware townships in the northern half of the county their home where they and their Missouri-born children owned most of the land, dominated the population, and operated most businesses (see map 1.2).[29] Although the city of Hermann because of its location on the Mississippi River and the Missouri Pacific Railroad provided opportunity to achieve economic success through non-farming work, the majority of German settlers in Gasconade County were farmers and maintained farmland within the same family for generations.

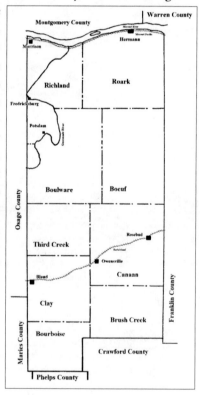

MAP 1.2. Township map of Gasconade County, redrawn to show railroads and additional communities. *Standard Atlas of Gasconade County, Missouri* (Chicago: George A. Ogle, 1913).

By the turn of the century, the children and grandchildren of the early German settlers contributed to the perpetuation of the German influence because they stayed in Gasconade County. They also spread that influence as they moved within the county and into the previously American-dominated areas of Bourboise, Canaan, Clay, and Third Creek townships. The arrival of the St. Louis and Chicago Railroad, also known as the Rock Island, in 1902 through the southern county brought additional opportunities for laborers, skilled craftsmen, and merchants. Missouri-born children and grandchildren of German immigrants sought these opportunities and seriously competed with non-Germans for land and economic opportunity. Second- and third-generation German-Americans in all of Gasconade County dominated the farming, professions, and skilled trades by 1910. As successful middle-class German-Americans, they wanted to preserve their economic, social, and political status. During a national emergency this environment of what one historian called "status anxiety" could lead to conflict between German-Americans as well as between German speakers and non-Germans.[30]

German immigrants created similar settlement patterns in Osage County where they established ethnic clusters in the three southwestern townships of Washington, Linn, and Jackson, including the towns of Westphalia, Rich Fountain, and Loose Creek between 1830 and 1860 (see map 1.3). Here German influence remained the strongest because Germans bought land, stayed on it, and passed it on to later generations in the same family. Advertisements, such as realtors Castrop and Swanson promoting as late as 1914 "three beautiful farms for sale on the Osage River" at "$30 and $25 dollars per acre" that would represent a *"gute Gelegenheit für Deutsche-Deutsche Nachbarschaft"* (good opportunity for a German-German neighborhood), confirmed that German-Americans preferred German-speaking neighbors. Consequently, German-Americans in the western townships of Osage County had consolidated land holdings, and nine out of ten farmers were either German-born or of German heritage.[31] By contrast, Americans settled the northern and eastern townships of Benton, Crawford, and Jefferson. However, by 1880 German immigrants and German-Americans also moved into Benton Township, where valuable river-bottom land along the Missouri River, fertile loess in the hill country just south of the river, and the divisional headquarters for the Missouri Pacific Railroad in Chamois offered economic opportunity for farmers, unskilled laborers, skilled professionals, and merchants.[32] Thus, by 1910, German immigrants not only established ethnic communities in specific geographic regions where they and their Missouri-born children dominated for several decades, but they also spread the German influence to an otherwise American-dominated area. That is significant because the

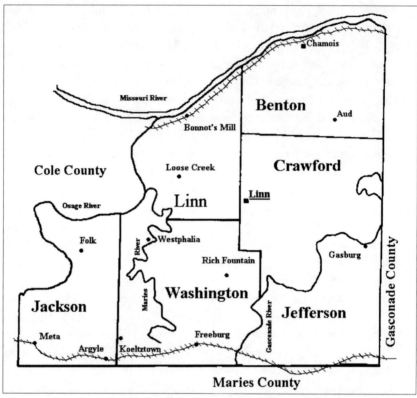

MAP 1.3. Township map of Osage County, redrawn to show railroad lines and additional communities. *Standard Atlas of Osage County, Missouri* (Chicago: George A. Ogle, 1913).

most violent anti-German expression in Osage County during the Great War occurred in Benton Township.

As in other midwestern states, German immigrants established "ethnic cocoons," or ethnically cohesive communities, in rural Missouri because the chains of the migration network were longer and stronger than in urban areas.[33] German immigrants informed relatives and friends in the old country about economic opportunities, and many then came to rural Missouri, including Gasconade and Osage Counties, to settle in the same villages or buy land nearby. These chain migrations sustained ethnic communities such as Westphalia in Osage County where the dialect from a particular region in Germany survived for several decades.[34] Agricultural occupations perpetuated homogeneity because the preservation of land within the family and the maintenance of old and creation of new family ties through land ownership lessened the possibility that children would leave.[35]

Religion was crucial to the establishment and maintenance of these ethnic communities because it "nurtured and was nurtured by ethnic consciousness" and outlasted "most if not all other ties with the Old World." Indeed, German settlements without a central church were more likely to decline than those with one.[36] In Osage County, religion was so important to the German community that villages literally grew around a church. For example, in Rich Fountain German immigrants from the lower Rhineland and Bavaria, who arrived in the area during the early 1830s, maintained self-sufficient farms, and few perceived an immediate need for a village or town. However, since most were Catholic and could not travel regularly to distant Westphalia to attend mass, the need for a priest and church grew. In 1840, Johann Theodore Struempf donated four acres for the building of Sacred Heart Church, and the community grew into a thriving village that included a tailor shop, blacksmith, cobbler store, wagon maker, hotel, flour mill, and sawmill by 1860.[37] Religion also cemented communities together through festivals such as Fronleichnam (Corpus Christi) that included traditional processions through decorated towns. As in many German communities in the Midwest, church organizations and societies provided opportunities to socialize during the week, especially for women. For example, the monthly Kaffeekranz (coffee social) of the Frauen Verein (women's association) from St. Paul Evangelische Kirche (St. Paul Evangelical Church) in Hermann fostered female fellowship as well as promoted missionary work, aided the sick and poor in Gasconade County, and supported the Red Cross and the armed services.[38]

A common faith also contributed to ethnic cohesion through marriage ties because when it came to religion and marriage, Germans preferred to stay among their own kind, especially in the rural areas. The same was true for one-church communities such as Westphalia and Rich Fountain, where Catholic Germans married within their faith as well as their ethnic group.[39] Thus the combination of similar regional origin, common dialects, a shared faith, and widespread consolidation of landholdings within families in a geographic area promoted the homogeneity of German settlements in rural Missouri. These communities were relatively sheltered from American influence, assimilative pressures, and conflicts with other ethnic groups; thus German immigrants and their children preserved many aspects of their German heritage with little interference.[40]

Historians, who describe how immigrants left homes in Europe, settled in the United States, and gradually changed their lives and identities, agree that acculturation is a complex, multifaceted, and individual process of discarding old traditions, adopting new customs, and fusing several old and new traits into a new identity. For the immigrant, transformation of his or her identity began as early as the decision to leave the homeland and continued during the journey as well as during the adjustment to social, political, and economic circumstances in the new environment. Immigrants, during their travels, carried along customs, dialects, life philosophies, and religious beliefs that defined their identity. This baggage influenced how they related to their new environment and interacted with fellow immigrants and Americans. Relationships between immigrants and Americans, whether based on competition, cooperation, or conflict, shaped the adaptation process as well as the creation of the ethnic identity. Although they and especially their American-born descendants could no longer claim their entire original regional identity, aspects of cultural practices characteristic of the old homeland persisted alongside the adaptations to the new country.[41]

In the Midwest, including Missouri, Germans and their American-born children molded and transformed their ethnic consciousness according to their individual circumstances and needs. Settlement choices, religion, occupation, class mobility, and interaction within the ethnic group, with Americans, and with other ethnic groups were the most important factors that contributed to their becoming German-American or Americans of German descent in Missouri. Based on individual decisions, they constructed a distinct identity in which being German did not conflict with being American. Although some quickly accepted Memorial Day to commemorate Germans and Americans who died during the Civil War and celebrated the Fourth of July and Thanksgiving as national holidays, others maintained the custom of children collecting *Fett Küchle* (deep-fried dumplings) just prior to Ash Wednesday and the German New Year's Eve tradition of "Shooting in the New Year."[42] Traditional religious holidays, such as *Maria Licht Mess,* that coincided with an American secular celebration, in this case Groundhog Day, melded into one and became part of the new identity. Children born in America to German parents began to look forward to Santa Claus, but for most German-Americans Christmas remained very German and often distinct according to regional or religious custom in the old country. For some, St. Nicholas or Knecht Ruprecht delivered gifts to children on December 6, others celebrated only the birth of Christ or the arrival of Christkindel (Christ child) on December 24.[43] Although several communities maintained traditional German sports associations such as the Schützenverein (Rifle Association), they also embraced American sports. For example, Hermannites celebrated the Schützenfest and crowned a Schützenkönig every year as well as adopted baseball with enthusiasm, and several German organizations sponsored the local amateur baseball team.[44]

Individuals represented this German-American identity as well. Martin Schulte, who grew up during the 1910s near Freeburg in Osage County, did not learn to speak English until seventh grade. He recalled traditional German customs such as St. Nickolaus and the "Devil" coming for a visit on December 6, and young men using chains to scare children during New Year's Eve revels. He was proud to be the grandson of German immigrants and to have been born in a "free country." For that same reason, neither he nor his parents before him saw a contradiction between being American and speaking German at the same time. William Wilke, the son of German-born farmers in Franklin County, called himself a "full-blooded American" although he spoke German and read the *Mississippi Blätter*, the Sunday edition of the *Westliche Post*.[45] In short, both held a truly German-American identity, an identity that many Americans would interpret as representing divided loyalty during the Great War.

In rural farming communities and villages, acculturation and adoption of English was relatively slow. The isolation of farming life facilitated the creation of so-called language islands relatively sheltered from American influence. Here German speakers served on school boards and as elders in church congregations and held on to their language well into the twentieth century. German women in particular through their seclusion from the outside world maintained language and dialects in the family. For example, Jetta Bruns, one of the pioneer women of Osage County, often lamented her isolation on the farm near Westphalia and her inability to speak English.[46] Ethnically homogeneous communities based on church, family, and agriculture such as Westphalia could also fulfill nearly all economic and cultural needs of their members; hence individuals Americanized more slowly than their counterparts in St. Louis.[47] Kathleen Conzen recognized a similar "institutional completeness" for German-Americans in Milwaukee that did not require them to go outside of the community for essential services.[48] In this environment several German business practices survived for many years. For example, Hermannites preserved the now long-forgotten tradition in Germany of opening businesses for a few hours on Sunday morning, until the arrival of the Sunday-closing laws in 1905.[49]

Yet, acculturation occurred in rural towns as well because their close proximity to major transportation arteries such as rivers, railroads, and paved roads brought even isolated ethnic communities into greater contact with the outside world and encouraged bilingualism. Shopkeepers and artisans also interacted increasingly with Americans in the marketplace. The local economy supplied the goods and labor necessary for such typical German products as beer and wine, but even the beer and wine industry sold to non-Germans and used English as the language of business and to transport these goods.[50] Although German remained the primary language in public and in the home for several decades, children in towns learned English, and by 1900 several schools, including the public school in Hermann and the parochial school in Westphalia, offered bilingual education.[51] Germans living in towns in rural Missouri because of their occupations and location thus acculturated sooner than those living on isolated farms.

Still, these German farmers, although more isolated than those living in towns, also acculturated in the economic realm and adapted to the environment by using their knowledge of soils, particularly the fertility of loess. They purchased land that settlers from Kentucky, Tennessee, and Virginia deemed as marginal for farming purposes and quickly gave up the production of rye and planted crops appropriate for the Missouri climate and soil quality, such as small grains, corn, and grapes. In Jefferson Township, Osage County, enterprising German farmers began to grow tobacco, owing to high demand.[52] Hard work, adjustment of agricultural habits to the American environment, preservation of several German farming habits, such as tilling methods to reduce erosion, and conservation to improve marginal land, steadily improved yields and crops and contributed to the prosperity of German immigrants in Missouri.[53]

In urban settings such as St. Louis acculturation occurred more rapidly because Germans mingled freely and interacted with other ethnic groups and native-born Americans in the urban market on an almost daily basis. German professionals and businessmen, in particular, had to adjust to and adhere to American regulations and business practices to prosper. Although some merchants succeeded by satisfying ethnic tastes, German goods were not always in high demand, and it was often more profitable to ship or purchase materials from within the United States. Consequently, in order to survive German entrepreneurs had to be businessmen first and Germans second. As German immigrants in St. Louis improved their economic status, they moved to more affluent neighborhoods, and their class interests often became more important than their ethnic interests.[54]

The most rapid acculturation occurred in the political realm. Contrary to expectations, Germans did not always support the Republican Party or vote as an ethnic block. Instead, Germans in Missouri, as those elsewhere in the Midwest, adapted to the two-party system and based their party affiliation on religious beliefs and personal, local, and economic interests, rather than ethnic unity. Although many middle-class Germans, including Hermannites, voted Republican, most Catholics, especially those in the rural areas, such as Osage County, supported the Democratic Party, and some Germans, particularly urban factory workers such as Ludwig Dilger, became members of the Socialist Party.[55]

At times, German-Americans united throughout Missouri when personal and business interests required, as was the case in the 1860 presidential election when a majority of German voters supported the Republican Party to stop the expansion of slavery and preserve the Union. And in 1897 middle-class German-Americans, Lutherans, and Catholics in St. Louis, dissatisfied with elitist rule and Edward Butler's city machine, united to elect one of their own, Henry Ziegenhein, as mayor.[56] Yet, if local issues or special interests warranted, German-Americans could also cross party lines. For example, German-Americans in St. Louis had a love-hate relationship with Democrat Joseph W. Folk. In 1904, many middle- and working-class German-Americans, who had previously voted for Republican candidates, helped elect Folk as governor because his reform tactics had succeeded in ridding city hall of corruption. However, during the 1908 senatorial primary election, they again crossed party lines, this time to support Senator William J. Stone and vote against Joseph W. Folk because, as governor, Folk had zealously enforced the Sunday laws that prohibited the consumption and sale of liquor on Sundays.[57]

The German-language press, although a tool to preserve Germanness, also contributed to acculturation. Weekly essays explaining holiday and social practices in Germany, columns reporting local news from various German provinces, and letters describing daily life nurtured ethnic consciousness and connected German readers to the fatherland.[58] At the same time, these papers had to cater to the needs and wants of their readers in order to survive. Depending on time of arrival, religious belief, and employment situation, Germans had different interests and read various publications. Catholics and many Democrats read the *Central Blatt* and the *Amerika,* freethinkers and many radicals subscribed to the *Anzeiger des Westens,* and Germans with a Republican inclination subscribed to the *Westliche Post.*[59] Workers read the German-language *Arbeiter-Zeitung* or its English-language counterpart, *St. Louis Labor,* which conveyed information about the Socialist Party as well as social organizations, worker benefits, and employment opportunities for all workers regardless of ethnicity.[60] Several of the German socialist editors, including Adolph Hepner, who published the short-lived St. Louis *Tageblatt* and had escaped antisocialist persecution and legislation in Germany, often incorporated material from the German labor press, and sent their original material to German Social-Democratic papers, thus maintaining a strong connection to the home country. Competition with socialist papers in the United States, however, also forced these German-language papers to cross ethnic lines and offer articles in English. The radical press thus also became a voice of acculturation for the second and third generations of German-American workers.[61]

The same was true for the rural weekly or daily German-language papers. Articles reported on agricultural, political, and social happenings and yet also explained American institutions, laws, and ideals to readers who did not yet understand the new language. Several publications, including the *Argyle Banner* in Osage County, listened to the demands by second- and third-generation German-Americans for more articles in English. Announcements and advertisements often interspersed English words with German expressions, such as Westphalia printing in its city directory the phrase "Stadt Mayor" rather than *Bürgermeister* or its English translation, city mayor, and thus created what language professor Marc Shell called "Germerican."[62] The *Deutsche Volksfreund,* published in Jackson, increased its readership in Cape Girardeau, Perry, and Scott Counties in southeast Missouri from 900 in 1910 to 1,170 in 1920 after it adopted English as its publication language. The widely read *Westliche Post* also printed and sold a small booklet titled "Wie werde ich Bürger?" (How do I become a citizen?), which instructed the reader about the naturalization process and the rudiments of American history and government.[63]

The German-language press, thus, eased the transition to the new country and aided in the acculturation process and the transition to English. Indeed, by the turn of the century, most English- and German-language newspapers in Missouri were so similar in format that one can assume that German-Americans had adjusted quite well to the American way of life and that they hung on to their German language for emotional reasons. Daily economic and social interaction with Americans and other ethnic groups required adoption of English; the perseverance of three daily, twenty-five weekly, and twelve monthly German-language publications in Missouri in 1914, however, indicates that many German-Americans continued to speak and read in German well into the twentieth century.[64] This is significant because during the Great War this particular remnant of German culture attracted negative attention.

The German Evangelical Lutheran Synod of Missouri, Ohio and Other States reinforced the preservation of both the German language and Lutheran faith through *Der Lutheraner,* the Synod's publication, the *Lehre und Wehre,* a professional theological journal, the *Kinder und Jugendblatt,* a magazine for Lutheran youth, and the *Evangelische-Lutheranische Schulblatt,* a magazine for schoolteachers. Articles did not just address theological matters but preserved German cultural characteristics by encouraging readers to not adopt all American traits such as charging interest or buying insurance, to not align with the labor movement, to limit American social practices such as dancing or theatergoing, and to preserve separation of church and state by limiting political activity. Use of German thus allowed the Synod and its members to practice separation from most cultural and religious groups, even other Lutherans.[65]

Indeed, German survived the longest in both rural and urban churches because religion and ethnic identity were closely intertwined, and preservation of the language often had religious ends.[66] Many pastors, especially Lutheran clergymen, believed that parishioners could learn spiritual truth only through the German language and, according to historian Frederick Luebke, used the language "to perpetuate the religious conservatism" and "religious identity of the group." Others believed that continued use of German would discourage members from leaving the faith because common religious belief defined how a person related to the rest of the community, and if one left the "old way" then one would also leave God.[67] In order to maintain knowledge of German and assure survival of the faith, Catholic and Protestant churches hired German-educated clergymen, established seminaries such as Concordia Seminary in St. Louis to train pastors in German, and established parochial schools where German was not just a subject but "the sole medium of instruction."[68]

By the turn of the century, however, German churches also had to adjust to reality because children and grandchildren of immigrants spoke English and began to demand sermons in English. This internal drive to gradually change to English as part of a natural progression, despite the opposition of elders, occurred throughout Missouri and within the several faiths in which Missourians of German birth believed. St. Paul Evangelical Church in Hermann decided to hold one English service per month in 1910. Priests in St. Peter Church in Jefferson City, Cole County, and St. George Church in Linn, Osage County, offered German and English sermons, and parishioners confessed in the language with which they felt most comfortable.[69] Even the conservative Lutherans had to adjust. English-speaking Lutherans of German birth or extraction in the Midwest had created the English Evangelical Lutheran Synod of Missouri and Other States and published the *Lutheran Witness*. Subsiding immigration from Germany and a declining retention rate among third-generation German-Americans who often chose the English synod contributed to reduction in membership for the German synod. Leaders of the German synod, such as August L. Graebner and his son Theodore Graebner, began to agitate for change, including English services and English classes to reverse the trend. Consequently, the Concordia Publishing House introduced the *Concordia Magazine* in 1895 and the *Theoretical Quarterly* in 1897 for English-reading members of the German synod. Although German remained the language of instruction of Concordia Seminary, the German Lutheran Holy Cross Church in St. Louis initiated English evening services on the second and fourth Sunday of every month in 1909.[70]

Despite these efforts, by 1914, nationwide two hundred Roman Catholic parishes continued to exclusively use the German language and another two thousand used it partially. Nearly half of all German Lutherans still worshipped in the German language. The Missouri Synod maintained more than two thousand parochial schools; other Lutheran synods operated one thousand additional schools, and the German Evangelical Synod of North America maintained three hundred schools at which a variation of German instruction and English instruction with German as a foreign language existed.[71]

Ethnocentric Americans in Missouri, as in most midwestern states, questioned the loyalty of clergymen who continued to conduct church services and parochial schools in German and thus preserved distinct cultural values and religious beliefs. Many nativists feared that the transmission of "unwholesome and dangerous ideas" hindered the creation of a common American culture and interrelated democracy, patriotism, and assimilation. In reaction, several midwestern states introduced compulsory public school attendance laws and teacher certification regulations that reflected the belief that only public education institutions could properly "instill patriotism and democratic ideals," especially for the "foreign element." Illinois initiated the Edwards Law, and Wisconsin initiated the Bennett Law in 1889, which also required the instruction of basic subjects—reading, writing, and math—in English for public as well as parochial elementary schools. German Lutherans answered with a well-organized campaign against such legislation. The 1890 Missouri Synod convention agreed that public schools "endangered and impaired" the spirituality of Christian children, resolved that the synod would "submit to no law of the state" regarding forced attendance in public schools, and promised to "combat" each compulsory law through legitimate means in order to preserve separation of church and state. Lobbying efforts contributed to the repeal of the Bennett Law in 1891 and the Edwards Law in 1892.[72]

When Missouri passed its first compulsory attendance law in 1905, German Lutherans were not alone in their opposition. Attendance in public schools did not reach 70 percent until 1917 because Baptists, Methodists, Catholics, and Missourians in general did not compel their children to attend school. Parents opposed the increase in taxes that came with the establishment of more schools, the teaching of curriculum that differed from the morals they wanted to instill, and the loss of personal authority over their children.[73] In Missouri, therefore, Germans and non-Germans alike resented this government interference into their lives, a mind-set that would also shape actions and expressions during World War I, as well as influence how nationalist Americans would interpret these actions and expressions.

Indeed, just before the war, Germans in St. Louis attracted particular attention through a campaign to revive the teaching of German. In 1887, the Missouri legislature had virtually eliminated the German language from the city's public schools by redrawing school districts so that Germans were in as few districts as possible, a process called gerrymandering.[74] In response, a group of German-Americans created the Deutsche Schulverein (German School Society) in 1909 and, with the agreement of the St. Louis Board of Education, provided free German classes on Saturday mornings in public school buildings for those who wished to learn the "mother tongue and German ideas." Between 1912 and 1915, 459 members attended classes and 332 nonmembers supported them financially.[75] Mayor Henry W. Kiel's apology during the German Day festivities in the city in June 1913 that he, as a second-generation German-American, could no longer address his fellow German-Americans in his parents' native language, may have served as evidence that they were Americanizing.[76] However, renewed interest in the German language through the Schulverein that coincided with the beginning of the Great War also served as evidence to nativists that German-Americans held divided loyalties.

Indeed, speaking a common language and socializing through ethnic organizations gave the public the impression that German immigrants and their children represented a united ethnic group intent on preserving every aspect of German life in the new homeland. Sängerbünde (singing societies), Turnvereine (gymnastic societies), Biergärten (beer gardens), and Schützenvereine (rifle associations) not only provided *Geselligkeit* (sociability) but also encouraged *Bildung* (intellectual cultivation) and preservation of German *Volkstum* (folk traditions).[77] These associations and the festivals they supported also increasingly emphasized the Germanness of members rather than the regionalism that initially identified German immigrants. For example, the *Hermanner Volksblatt* argued that the annual German Day celebrations offered all German speakers in the vicinity the opportunity to celebrate the contributions of Germans to American society and to demonstrate the unity of all Germans in Gasconade County and surrounding areas.[78]

This ethnic unity and pride became even more pronounced through the establishment of the Deutsche römisch-katholische central Verein in 1855 and the Deutschamerikanische Nationalbund, or National German-American Alliance, in 1901. The central verein, headquartered in St. Louis, had evolved from a collection of mutual benefit societies into a national federation of Catholic benevolent and social reform societies. However, efforts to reform American society, a determination to maintain an independent identity within the American Catholic Church, and arguments that members would be better

Catholics and Americans if they remained German created an image of ethnic separatism and the idea that all German Catholics in St. Louis thought alike. The Missouri chapter of the National Alliance received its charter from Congress and the state legislature in 1907. As the largest organization of any single ethnic group in American history, it aimed to unite all Germans, stimulate the teaching of German in public schools, celebrate the achievements of Germans in America, protect the German element against nativist attacks, and promote friendly relations between the United States and Germany. Although the alliance encouraged naturalization and required proof of American citizenship for membership, the joining together of German societies into the alliance to cultivate German culture promoted the perception of ethnic pride and unity rather than acculturation.[79]

Such oneness, however, is deceiving because Germans throughout the Midwest were never a united ethnic group, and fragmentation and disagreements existed from the early days of immigration. Germans were diverse in geographical origin, intellectual background, religion, social class, education, and attitudes, and most, especially those arriving before 1860, would not have held a national German identity. Germany as a nation did not yet exist and identity remained regional.[80] Although division was more pronounced in cities and towns than in rural communities, each group aimed to preserve its own religion, dialect, and regional customs and sought to maintain a separate identity and preserve special interests by restricting membership in social clubs to regional origin, social status, or occupation. For example, German singing societies in St. Louis included the Schwäbischer Sängerbund (Swabian Singers Union), Bayerische Männerchor (Bavarian Men's Choir), and Rheinischer Frohsinn (Rhenish Cheerfulness). Class status limited membership in the Liederkranz to affluent members such as bankers, merchants, or others with positions of eminence. By contrast, the Vorwaerts (Forward) singing society included men and women of the working class.[81]

Equally important are the differences in ideology between German-American workers over how to address the challenges of the Industrial Revolution, including de-skilling of work and the at times stubborn resistance by business owners to recognize worker rights and unions. As elsewhere in the Midwest, workers in Missouri, including those of German birth or ancestry, unionized to gain recognition and decent wages and working conditions. Slightly more than half of the 114,000 organized workers in Missouri lived in the St. Louis area by 1914. In 1887 more than thirty individual unions represented through the Central Labor Union, St. Louis Trades Assembly, and the German Arbeiter Verband merged into the St. Louis Central Trades and Labor

Union (CTLU). It had an approximate membership of 45,000 by 1912. Gottlieb Hoehn, German-born socialist and member of the Typographical Union, edited the German-language *Arbeiter Zeitung* and its English counterpart *St. Louis Labor*, the organs for the CTLU as well as the city's Socialist Party. Both the CTLU and the Socialist Party in St. Louis retained German traits because members conducted meetings at times in German, often met at the Turner Hall, and generally elected German-Americans to leadership positions.[82]

Statewide, the United Brewery Workmen and the United Mine Workers were Missouri's largest industrial unions. In contrast to Ohio, Wisconsin, and Illinois, in Missouri the Industrial Workers of the World were not significant. In 1891, the unions combined into the Missouri State Federation of Labor (MFL) to aid in organization, assistance, and leadership during strikes and to lobby the state legislature. Although associated with the national American Federation of Labor (AFL), these unions and their leaders in Missouri did not strictly adhere to AFL ideology. Workers, especially German-Americans who dominated the state's MFL and Socialist Party, were both trade unionists and socialists. They supported the socialist ideology of worker ownership of business and public ownership of municipal services, but they usually opposed violent revolution. Influenced by German social-democratic ideology, they instead advocated a return to true democratic principles by using "accepted institutional channels to promote their sense of social republicanism." In other words, they viewed polls and unions as legitimate venues within the established political order to affect social change. This approach did not necessarily upset many Missourians, which would have importance during World War I.[83]

Although German socialists dominated elected positions in the CTLU and the MFL, they were never powerful enough to absolutely control either or both. Unlike their counterparts in Chicago and Detroit, where radical socialists merged with trade unions to form the Chicago Federation of Labor and Detroit Council of Trade and Labor Unions as third labor parties, socialists in St. Louis did not present a united front. For example, David Kreyling, a cigar maker, a long-term secretary-organizer for the CTLU, and first president of the MFL, insisted on nonpartisanship. Consequently the CTLU did not endorse any candidates for public office regardless of party affiliation and required members running for office to resign any elected or appointed positions within their unions. Therefore, not all socialists were members of the CTLU, and those who were did not always agree with each other. For example, German socialists William Brandt, member of the CTLU and Cigar Makers Union, who ran for mayor in 1905, urged more political activism to effect true social reform. The CTLU, nevertheless, endorsed political issues such as the direct election of senators, federal judges, vice president, and president, the initiative and referendum, an end to convict and child labor, and regulation of work hours. Socialist candidates running on these issues in St. Louis by 1911 often received more votes than Democrat opponents but could never defeat Republican candidates. Consequently, German-American socialists in St. Louis were never as powerful as their counterparts in Milwaukee because they never held municipal offices.[84]

In contrast to German-American socialists, German Catholic workers and their leaders opposed socialism. They feared the "menace of the immigrant-led radical element" and argued that godless unions could only lead to anarchy. Therefore, as immigrants or descendants thereof, German Catholics used the rhetoric of American opponents to the Socialist Party to distinguish themselves from other immigrants and radicals. Instead of joining unions, they became members of parish workmen's associations, which priests had established to limit socialist influence. Under the leadership of Frederick Kenkel and Father Albert Mayer, these associations federated into the citywide Workingmen's Welfare Society and became members of the central verein. Catholic leaders and Verein members supported progressive social reform, such as the creation of employment bureaus in St. Louis, Louisville, and Milwaukee that maintained records of open jobs and available workers, investigation and reduction of occupational diseases, and establishment of St. Elizabeth Settlement House in St. Louis in 1915. Although it addressed worker issues and advocated social reform, the central verein opposed the liberal reforms the American Federation of Catholic Societies advocated in 1906, thus intricately linking religious distinctiveness and class interests with a German ethnic consciousness. This distinctiveness may have contributed to increased membership in the central verein and subscription to its bilingual *Central Blatt and Social Reform,* but it also reflected division within the working class of St. Louis.[85]

This lack of class solidarity within the ethnic group expressed itself at times at the workplace through conflict. Preservation of employment became more important than ethnic cohesion during economic hard times. For example, Germans who dominated the Local Brewers and Maltsters Union No. 6 would get into fistfights with fellow German maltsters and brewers and report any evidence of *faulenzen* (be lazy) on the part of their coworkers during the 1910s, a time when the prohibition movement was growing and the labor market was tightening.[86]

German-American educated intellectuals experienced class conflict as they struggled with adjustment to an unfamiliar environment and searched for suitable employment in the new homeland. They expected the same respect and status they had received in the old Vaterland and often resented the fact that farmers, artisans, and laborers, although rude and primitive in education, achieved financial security much sooner through their sheer physical effort and determination. Conversely, Germans who made a living through their own sweat and muscles looked upon their educated countrymen as pompous and proud. Others, primarily for economic reasons, insisted on Americanization and criticized the preservation of German habits as being backward and hindering progress. At times economic differences exacerbated resentments based on traditional regional misconceptions, especially between Bavarians and Westphalians. Specifically, farmers of Rich Fountain in Osage County perceived the "gentlemen" farmers in neighboring Westphalia as arrogant and snobbish.[87] The presence of this mind-set is significant because during the Great War it would again contribute to resentment within the ethnic group toward middle-class German-Americans who tried to create the perception of patriotism by urging fellow German-Americans to give up aspects of their German culture.

Even though divisions existed in the ethnic group, German culture and identity still existed in Missouri on the eve of World War I. Most churches still offered German services, an interested person could still learn the German language and apply it by reading German-language newspapers, and German clubs and organizations offered ample opportunity for intellectual stimulation and *Gemütlichkeit,* or socializing. Yet, despite their sentimental and cultural attachment to the old German *Heimat* (home country), German immigrants and their descendants had also become Americanized, especially in the economic and political sense. Indeed, many German-Americans in Missouri held an image of themselves as *wahre Amerikaner* (true Americans). As immigrants they believed they had a unique understanding of American values and citizenship, and they did not hesitate to remind Americans about their contributions to the nation. Germans, for example, helped George Washington create the union and during the Civil War placed their lives on the line to defend it. As members of the Radical Republican Party they also agitated for the recognition that all citizens, including former slaves and naturalized immigrants, should have civil rights.[88]

To dispel any lingering doubts about their loyalty to their adopted country, German-Americans pointed out to native-born Americans that they were deserving of recognition as citizens. They fully participated in Fourth of July festivities and other celebrations that honored aspects of their new homeland. Clubs and organizations, created to preserve German traditions, began to celebrate American history as well. For example, the 1902 Liederkranz masked ball in St. Louis memorialized the Louisiana Purchase. German Day festivities while commemorating German culture also praised American liberty and honored German immigrants who had helped preserve American ideals during the Revolutionary and Civil Wars.[89] Germans, like the Irish and other European immigrants, also used blackface minstrel shows, including "A Raid on the Chinese Laundry" and Zulu warriors exercising in a coconut grove, during social seasons to demonstrate that German-Americans were neither Chinese nor black but white, good immigrants and equals in American citizenship.[90]

English-language newspapers in St. Louis did not always oppose the German element in the city and celebrated the contributions to Missouri history by such notable German-Americans as Carl Schurz, Franz Sigel, Emil Preetorious, Carl Dänzer, and Adolphus Busch. The *Missouri Republican,* despite its strong opposition to the use of German in classrooms, congratulated the Liederkranz on its "graceful" opening of the 1887 social season and good taste in choosing music by "great German composers." The *St. Louis Republic,* usually an outspoken critic of Germanness, commented in a May 1910 article that German Turnvereine and other social organizations portrayed the best that German culture could offer to Americans, including "thoroughness, docility, and the 'scientific spirit that characterizes the Teutonic spirit.'" The *Encyclopedia of St. Louis* also praised the "virtues" of beer gardens as places where families could go for "clean, simple and wholesome . . . diversion, among pleasant and health giving surroundings."[91]

Indeed, Americans and Germans often found reason to celebrate the best of each other's cultures. Germans commemorated President Lincoln and Washington's birthdays with poetry and memorials. Thousands of prominent non-German and German St. Louisans attended the unveiling of the Alexander von Humboldt Statue in Tower Grove Park in November 1878 and celebrated the German scientist's views of tolerance and democratic openness. The much-celebrated yearly German Day activities in St. Louis and Hermann provided all Missourians, not just those of German heritage, with a chance to "march in or watch a good parade, enjoy a picnic and singing, the Turnerdrills, and the food and drink."[92]

Although it appears that non-Germans and Germans seemed to get along quite well on the eve of the World War I, beneath the surface of peaceful integration there also existed tensions. Economic and residential expansion beyond the boundaries of a clearly defined ethnic enclave in urban and rural areas led to increased levels of competition for land and employment and thus tensions with non-Germans. Although most Missourians praised the German work ethic, their agricultural skills, and their willingness to produce crops for which Americans would not waste time or effort, some criticized Germans for their conservatism and lack of modernization. Americans also perceived cultural activities, such as the drilling corps of the Turnvereine, singing societies or zither clubs, as different from American traditions, as a way to preserve European life, and as an attempt by Germans to isolate themselves from the rest of the population and thus limit Americanization.[93]

The maintenance and teaching of the German language for religious purposes could fuel anti-German sentiment. For example, Lutherans in St. Louis through their creation of the seminary and isolation from mainstream Protestantism easily became targets for the accusation that they were not being willing to become true Americans. In Osage County, German-Americans established St. Peter's Church, a German Methodist church, in 1865 near Deer in Crawford Township and St. Johannes German Evangelical Church in 1885 in Chamois, in previously American-dominated areas. Presiding ministers, including Hermann Walz, insisted on using the German language in these congregations. This could explain why Erwin Walz, the son of Reverend Walz, became the target of anti-German sentiment during World War I.[94]

Resentment also existed in the political realm. German-Americans throughout the Midwest, including Missouri, heartily adopted the American ideal of popular participation in government and became active in city and county governments because they wanted to influence community decisions such as location and improvement of roads and establishment of churches and schools. Most believed that it was the obligation of every American citizen of German birth or ancestry to fulfill the duties of citizenship, including party organization, nomination of candidates from the ethnic group, and voting.[95] German immigrants, if sufficiently acculturated and proficient in English, had opportunities to gain political offices, even in American-dominated communities. Henry Ernstmeyer, born and educated in Prussia and a small-business owner for more than twenty years in Osage County, was elected county judge in 1886 and served four terms as mayor of Chamois from 1900 to 1901 and from 1904 to 1910.[96] In St. Louis several German-born men, including Henry C. Overstolz and Henry Ziegenhein, and sons of German immigrants, such as Frederick Kreismann, served as mayors. Henry W. Kiel, a bricklayer turned politician, whose parents had been born in Germany, was elected to his first term as mayor of St. Louis on April 1, 1913. His fight against corruption and his progressive administration turned him into such a popular executive that voters returned him to office in April 1917, at the height of the excitement over the American declaration of war against Germany and despite attempts to question his loyalty as a German-American. And he was elected to a consecutive third term in 1921.[97]

Notwithstanding such political success stories, German-American leaders also received much criticism. During the Progressive Era, Folk's probe into corruption and the Butler machine revealed that several German politicians were involved in illegal activities. For example, Henry Ziegenhein had embezzled city funds and pocketed interest from illegal loans while serving as city collector; brewer Otto Stifel served as director to the Commonwealth Trust Company that became involved in extralegal real estate activities; and Councilman Emil Meysenberg received a guilty verdict in 1902 and a five-year sentence for bribery.[98] Such activities must have created suspicion about other German-Americans.

The Socialist Party, which drew heavily on German-born and German-American workers for its membership, also contributed to mistrust. Although the party never posed a serious threat to the two-party system in the state or in St. Louis, election results in the German wards in St. Louis indicated sizable support for Socialist Party candidates.[99] The *Westliche Post* provided space for the respectable Central Trades and Labor Union, published the proceedings, minutes, and announcements of the festivities of the local chapter of the Socialist Party, and defended workers' right to strike. This endorsement for Socialist, or what some would call un-American, ideals and activities by a newspaper recognized as representing the entire German-speaking community in the city and state contributed to growing resentment, especially during the Progressive Era when reformers viewed such activities with suspicions.[100]

German-Americans and Americans of other heritages also disagreed on many political issues. Before the Civil War, Germans in St. Louis fought Know-Nothings and other nativist elements over slavery, at the ballot box, and at times in fistfights. Most Germans opposed slavery and fought on the side of the Union, thus attracting the ire of pro-southern Americans.[101] The Civil War and postwar measures that limited the political clout of Confederates also allowed German immigrants to become more deeply involved in local and state politics and may have spawned resentment and suspicions of protecting special interests. During the Spanish-American War, several German-American leaders and newspapers were quite outspoken in their opposition to imperialism. German newspaper editors from throughout Missouri, many of whom had experienced imperialism firsthand in Germany and were now afraid that the economic competition over access to markets in the Pacific region might develop into war between Germany and the United States, met in St. Louis to discuss the issue. They issued a proclamation denouncing military imperialism as endangering the survival of the Republic and opposing the annexation of the Philippines, Cuba, and Puerto Rico. During a period of heightened nationalism such as the Spanish-American War, expressions of opposition increased antagonism toward German publishers in Missouri.[102] This might also explain why German leaders in Westphalia, who remembered that the editor of the *Osage County Volksblatt* had scathingly critiqued McKinley's imperialist policies, censored and subsequently shut down his paper after he opposed American entry into World War I.[103]

The prohibition movement and discussion over Sunday closing laws, in particular, drew Germans into political battles with Americans for decades. German-Americans in the United States and Missouri viewed prohibition as an attack on agelong German as well as American traditions and social customs, as an infringement on individual rights and detrimental to the local and state economy.[104] Thus, while trying to preserve a German tradition, Germans also interpreted the issue from an American viewpoint and as preserving Americanism, and they did not shy away from using their political power to protect their personal and economic interests. For example, during the 1910 election, when statewide prohibition came to a vote for the first time, the German-American Alliance used its political influence successfully in St. Louis where it defeated the efforts of the "Dry League" to unite several civic and labor organizations behind the push to end the sale of alcohol. Although concern over the economic impact of prohibition convinced St. Louis voters from all twenty-eight wards to soundly defeated prohibition, German-Americans had also turned one of their societies into a political lobbying organization.[105]

Osage County officials enforced Sunday closing laws throughout the county by 1905, but election results in 1910 demonstrate that a majority of voters, even in Chamois, opposed all-out prohibition. The temperance and prohibition movement had its largest following in the northern, less German townships, which only added to the already strained relationship between German-Americans and non-Germans in that area.[106] In 1905 several tavern owners in Hermann aimed to preserve the customary consumption and sale of alcohol in association with leisure or Gemütlichkeit on Sunday by first decrying Governor Folk's strict enforcement of the Sunday laws and then by defiantly opening establishments and selling alcohol on Sunday. Although officials in Hermann cited these offenders and threatened to deny the extension of their dramshop licenses, Missourians had read about this defiance of the law in newspapers and would remain on the alert for similar activities during the upcoming war.[107]

In addition to prohibition, German-Americans, including Mayor Kiel, socialists, and former members of the Radical Republican Party, also opposed the initiative petition that briefly established segregated housing in St. Louis by popular vote in 1916. The actions of two prominent men, however, made the law ineffective. They were Charles Nagel, former secretary of commerce under Taft and well-known German-American lawyer, who would defend the Busch family during the war, and federal judge David P. Dyer, who would soon oversee the prosecution of German-Americans and Socialists for violating the Espionage and Sedition Act. Such activism on behalf of special interests, in this case an ethnic group, created resentment not only among proponents of prohibition but also among segregationists, resentment that would reemerge during the upcoming crisis of war.[108]

Thus, by 1914 native-born Americans and Missourians viewed the German-born and their descendants as one homogeneous group with a common or single will despite differences in regional origin, variations in dialects, and distinctions in culture. At the same time they did not always object to German social organizations or the usage of German because German-Americans had adapted to American culture. But rather than adopting the dominant American culture wholesale, Germans in Missouri constructed a distinct German-American identity that was flexible, one that fit best with their local circumstances and in which being German did not conflict with being American. Many second- and third-generation German-Americans were indistinguishable in manner from other native-born Americans, with the exception of names and language. Otherwise, they wore the same clothes, conducted business in the same ways, and were just as passionate over political issues as fellow Americans.

Nativists during the early years of the twentieth century instead turned their attention to Catholics, Jews, and immigrants from southeastern Europe, who held radical ideas and competed for jobs with native-born Americans. The growing immigration restriction movement targeted so-called undesirable immigrants by calling for literacy tests as requirements for admittance to the United States. Germans, by contrast, had been part of the so-called old immigration group. Whereas nativists had attacked them in the past, most Americans did not perceive German-Americans as a threat to the United States on the eve of the Great War.[109] There existed little indication that German immigrants and their Missouri-born children could easily become targets of hateful nativism, persecution, and suspension of civil liberties. However, by the time the United States entered World War I, Americans widely distrusted German immigrants and their descendants. Preexisting tensions between Germans and non-Germans and within the German ethnic group would make it easier during the war to believe government assertions that German-Americans represented the enemy within. To understand this transition we need to first survey American, Missourian, and German-American reaction to the arrival of the Great War in Europe.

TWO

Divided Opinions and Growing Suspicions

Missourians and German-Americans during the Neutrality Period

> When they call themselves German-American,
> they mean that they are anti-American. . . .
> The German-American Alliance is, in practice,
> an anti-American Alliance.
>
> *Theodore Roosevelt, St. Louis, May 1916*

ON THE eve of the Great War, Missourians did not yet perceive German-Americans as the enemy within. The American neutrality period from August 1914, the beginning of the conflict in Europe, to April 1917, American entry into the global war, began to transform that mind-set. British propaganda, popular support for the Allies, the presidential campaign in 1916, and the actions of German-American individuals or organizations changed the opinions of many Americans and Missourians and began to create an image of German-Americans as less than loyal, especially in St. Louis. As Theodore Roosevelt asserted in a speech before the City Club of St. Louis on May 31, 1916, quoted in the epigraph, people who insisted on the usage of the hyphen or held divided identities were not true Americans.[1] German-Americans became conscious of this changing mind-set, and by the time the United States entered the war many had adopted measures to reduce the possibility of being accused of disloyalty.

When the Great War broke out in Europe during the summer months of 1914, President Woodrow Wilson asked Americans, including Missourians, for unbiased neutrality in both thought and action. However, too many cultural and political ties connecting them to either the Allies or Germany made compliance with such a request nearly impossible. Furthermore, Great Britain, once it cut the transatlantic cable and controlled the flow of information to the Western Hemisphere, promoted and sold the war "as a holy crusade against evil."[2] Sensational reports created the perception of Germany's war guilt, militarism, and inhumanity and molded American public opinion to support the Entente and to hate the Central Powers, especially Germany. The majority of Americans, as a result, supported the Allies and began to fear the distant enemy, Germany. Ludwig Dilger from St. Louis noted in a letter to his brother on December 6, 1914, that it was nearly "impossible to find out anything definite about the war in Europe"; so he asked, "Please, dear brother, write me the real truth, because the English newspapers only write about German defeats. . . . The American people, with only a few exceptions, are anti-German and openly show their friendship for the English."[3] Any attempts by Germany or German-Americans to counter such biased propaganda met with criticism and accusations of trying to subvert American public opinion. Instead, overwhelmed by rumors and outrageous newspaper accounts about intrigues and sabotage activity at home, Americans became increasingly frightened and suspected a German spy around every corner.[4]

Such accounts and interpretations of the propaganda battle during the American neutrality period could lead one to believe that all Americans learned to hate anything associated with Germany, including their German-American neighbors, before the nation entered the global conflict. Those who read national newspapers, such as the *New York Times,* might indeed have been convinced that Germany was evil incarnate. Not all Missourians, however, read such sensational stories as the Bryce Report, which depicted Belgium as a defenseless neutral country, mercilessly run over by hordes of German barbarians who committed reprehensible atrocities. With the exception of those in Kansas City and St. Louis, Missouri papers did not publish blatantly anti-German articles or reports that associated German saboteurs with every industrial mishap, such as an explosion at a munitions factory in Alton, Illinois, in March 1915.[5] Indeed, after the initial flurry of headlines, the war often received scant coverage in most newspapers.

Reading the occasional one or two "War News" or "*Kriegsnachrichten*" columns, usually in the form of preset type plates that government agencies sent to newspapers, leads the researcher to the initial impression that few editors had opinions on war-related subjects. By the fall of 1914 "the war had lost its attraction," the distance to Europe gave Missourians a false sense of security, and they were more concerned with local events, such as the planting, growing, and harvesting seasons. The *Franklin County Tribune* made the conscious decision to print only unbiased and fair news after Great Britain monopolized the Atlantic cable and telegraph stations, censored war news, and dispatched pro-Allied and anti-German propaganda. Editors in areas with substantial German populations, including Jefferson City and Hermann, most of whom were also owners of papers and active in local affairs, chose to limit coverage of the war and printed only enough information to satisfy local demand. Others, including several editors of German-language papers such as the *Chariton Courier,* were torn between personal and local sentiment and preferred to ignore the war so as to avoid criticism and economic repercussions.[6]

Nevertheless, whether they spoke English or German, Missourians, like the nation, were split in their opinions about the war and did not necessarily support the Allies. Senator William J. Stone often expressed anti-British thoughts and criticized the Wilson administration for its lack of neutrality. Despite being Democrats, Congressmen Dorsey W. Shackleford, Walter L. Hensley and Perl D. Decker often voted against the administration in order to preserve neutrality and to keep the nation out of war. German-born Republican Congressman Richard Barthold from St. Louis expressed his support for strict neutrality by co-authoring a measure in the House of Representatives that would have established a weapons embargo for all European countries involved in the war. This bill received widespread support in the Midwest not just among German-Americans but also among Irish- and Scandinavian-Americans, Pacifists and Socialists.[7]

Analysis of English- and German-language newspapers, generally considered a reflection of the mind-set of their readers, confirms the varied interpretations of the war's origin, American neutrality, submarine warfare, and preparedness for potential war. During the national discussion regarding the origin of the war and whom Americans should or should not support, several Missouri English-language newspapers, including the *Kansas City Journal,* endorsed the Allied point of view and placed responsibility for the war on Germany and Austria. These papers, in general, also defended American bankers who loaned millions of dollars to Britain and France in the form of the Anglo-French loan in 1915 on the grounds that it did not violate neutrality because Germany had been allowed to sell its own treasury notes in America and the loan would also benefit Missouri's economy.[8] By contrast, the *Springfield Leader, St. Louis Globe-Democrat,* and *St. Louis Post-Dispatch* saw fault in all the European powers, including England. They took a very neutral stand and insisted on fair coverage, such as providing the German in addition to the Allied view of the war, and adhering strictly to neutrality and the preservation of peace. Whereas the *Globe-Democrat* consistently criticized British naval practices, including the stoppage and confiscation of neutral ships, the *Post-Dispatch* found little fault with Britain's seizure of neutral ships as long as it reimbursed owners for lost cargo. Several, including the *Moberly Democrat,* also opposed the loan to the Allies because extending credit to any belligerent violated the concept of neutrality, gave the United States an interest in who would win the war, and presented the nation with an unnecessary economic risk.[9]

Missouri's German press was less divided on these war issues. The *Missouri Thalbote* in Higginsville and the *Sedalia Journal* were extremely pro-German and quite outspoken in their criticism of Great Britain and President Wilson's pro-British bias. The *Journal,* for example, scolded Wilson for talking about humanity, honor, and patriotism while acting contrary to such rhetoric and openly supporting a belligerent. The editor called such deception *Elende Heuchelei* (wretched hypocrisy). The *Deutsche Volksfreund* in Jackson throughout the fall of 1914 lauded the greatness of the German people and accused English politicians of lying and entering the war under false pretenses; but it also recognized the crucial role of the alliances that pulled most of Europe into military conflict. Others, such as the *Missouri Volksfreund* in Jefferson City, initially called for true neutrality because they feared that shortsightedness and sympathies would pull the United States into this brutal conflict. Yet, they, too, defended the side of Germany in the conflict and praised the kaiser's organizational talent, determination, and love for the Fatherland.[10]

The *Westliche Post* and *Amerika,* the two daily German-language newspapers in St. Louis, insisted on fair play, called for strict neutrality, warned about the dangers of British propaganda, and defended Germany's stand in the war, but did not always support its actions.[11] The *Westliche Post,* horrified that some of the rumors of German soldiers committing atrocities were true, nevertheless argued that Britain should not revel in the enemy's faults because it had committed similar acts of violence in India and Ireland. *Amerika* published letters sent from Germany to demonstrate that Belgium and France also committed atrocities and mistreated Catholic priests and German soldiers.[12] Although St. Louis firms, including the Wagner Electric Manufacturing Company, benefited from trade with Britain and France, the *Westliche Post* opposed the Anglo-French loan in the fall of 1915 because it was an unsecured loan.[13]

Surprisingly, the newspapers in Missouri, whether written in English or German, reacted almost in unity to the issue of submarine warfare. German-language papers argued that it was a legitimate tool to break the stronghold the British naval blockade inflicted on Germany, that passengers had been warned not to travel on the ships of belligerents to the war-torn area, and that England chartered foreign ships to disguise transportation of war materials.[14]

With the exception of a few ultra pro-Allied papers such as the *St. Louis Republic, St. Joseph News Press,* and the *Columbia Daily Tribune,* that denounced the sinking of ships as "wanton, wholesale murder" and "barbaric atrocity," the majority of English-language papers thought submarine warfare regrettable but necessary for Germany to fight the equally barbaric British naval blockade. These papers were outraged that Great Britain had not provided escorts, and editors were saddened that not more lives had been saved after the sinking of the *Lusitania* in May 1915, but they did not believe that the incident should draw the United States into the war. They also stated, in agreement with the *Westliche Post,* that passengers had been warned not to travel to the war-torn area on the ships of belligerents. Several urged calmness until officials evaluated all the facts, and the majority agreed that the United States must be cautious about this new tactic of warfare, avoid pro-British and pro-German rhetoric, and thus avert the possibility of destruction to American ships. Most congratulated Wilson for his ability to maintain peace and to eventually work out a compromise with Germany through diplomatic means that would mean that the United States would not enter the conflict.[15]

Individual German-Americans, including Louis Benecke, reflected this mind-set as well. The successful attorney argued that Germany had the right to torpedo the *Lusitania* but must have also expected more passengers to be saved. Nevertheless, Wilson was correct in demanding respect for American rights. The primary concern German-Americans such as Benecke expressed throughout the neutrality period and the submarine warfare debate was the preservation of peace by any honorable means possible.[16] Several prominent German-Americans, nonetheless, recognized the growing anti-German sentiment in the nation and in a *New York Times* interview expressed their support for President Wilson's diplomacy.[17]

Missouri's English- and German-language newspapers agreed on another subject, the preparedness movement, but supported it for slightly different reasons than the major eastern papers. They did not argue that the United States had to protect itself from an almost inescapable German invasion. They, instead, believed that the expansion of the army and navy would preserve the nation's honor, defend its border from Mexican rebels such as Pancho Villa, and protect the country from nations such as Great Britain that threatened America's security and abused her rights of the seas. Others feared that if the United States was not prepared for war, especially a conflict with a mighty military power such as Britain or Germany, untrained soldiers equipped with outmoded weapons would die needlessly in the battlefield. A few opposed preparedness because a standing army would make it easier to become involved in a military conflict.[18]

Public opinion as reflected in English- and German-language newspapers thus indicates that Missourians, especially those in rural areas, remained relatively neutral during the early months of the war. Furthermore, not all Missourians learned to immediately hate Germany or Germans because they did not always read about supposedly negative German traits, alleged atrocities, spy activities, and sabotage. Indeed, the *St. Louis Republic,* despite its pro-Allied viewpoint, did not yet associate the enemy Germany with German-Americans who lived in St. Louis. For example, the paper advertised *Alpen Brau,* a bottled beer produced by the local Independent Breweries Company, and the sale of Imperial German Government Treasury Notes through the local Central Trust Company representative. It even printed a German advertisement from its competitor the *Westliche Post* urging Germans who still valued their language to subscribe to the *Post* or *Mississippi Blätter.*[19] The creation of anti-German sentiment was thus delayed in many areas, and this played a crucial role in the treatment of German immigrants and their American-born children once the United States entered the War.

The outbreak of war in Europe, however, placed German-Americans and other immigrants in the Midwest, including Missouri, in a difficult situation, as the conflict reawakened old and sometimes forgotten feelings for a distant fatherland, and most fought individual battles over loyalty to their birth country or their adopted country. Several immigrants chose to return to Europe to fight. For example, Paul Chanoit, president of the International Sales Company of St. Louis, although happily married and already in possession of his first naturalization papers, returned to his beloved France despite his family and business ties in America. Several Germans also returned to serve the old fatherland. For example, Heinrich W. von Heinrichshofen, who had resigned from the German Army, came to St. Louis in 1890, worked as an insurance agent, became a naturalized citizen in 1896, and returned to Germany in October 1914 to serve again in the kaiser's army.[20]

German-Americans, whether they lived in Chicago, Cincinnati, Milwaukee, or St. Louis, reacted in two somewhat contradictory ways. Despite strong connections to the old homeland, the majority did not leave because they had become Americans, called the United States their home, and did not wish to become involved in a military conflict that might require that they fight distant relatives. Ludwig Dilger, for example, was convinced that if he still lived in the home country he would have gladly volunteered, but if the United States were attacked, "I wouldn't hesitate long to shoulder a gun" because this was "my new homeland."[21] At the same time German-Americans found it difficult to comply with President Woodrow Wilson's request to remain neutral in thought and deed. Most, including Mrs. E. Schumann Heinzt, had remained loyal to their *alte geliebte Heimat* (old beloved home country) but not to the German government. In fact, many had left their homeland for political reasons or to escape military service. Yet, they continued to believe in the greatness of the German people or the mystical land of their parents and cultivated close ties with their native country. A few St. Louis families, including the Busch family, continued to maintain connections with their native country because their American-born daughters were married to German nationals and had made Germany their home.[22]

The presence of family ties and emotional connection to the fatherland encouraged most German-Americans, whether they lived in Missouri or elsewhere in the Midwest, to express their feelings through mass demonstrations and fund-raisers. During a rally held at the St. Louis Turnhalle (Turner Hall) in August 1914, German-Americans sang *Die Wacht am Rhein* (The Watch on the Rhine) and *Deutschland über Alles* (Germany above Everything). Prominent German-American women created a Red Cross chapter in the city. They sewed and distributed garments, sheets, and bandages for Germany and Austria.[23] Like most ethnic societies in the United States, German-American societies in Missouri also turned their attentions to collecting money for relief funds to aid their distant countrymen, including the Relief of Widows and Orphans, the Hilfsverein Deutscher Frauen (Aid Society of German Women), the German Red Cross, the Blind Soldiers' Relief, and the German and Austro-Hungarian Prisoners of War in Siberia Fund. To boost contributions, clubs organized special festivals and bazaars and sold replicas of the Iron Cross. Missouri German-Americans, however, did not support these efforts as enthusiastically as hoped. The $100,000 sent from Missouri to Germany and Austria in January 1916 fell far short of the $1,000,000 goal and indicated a less than enthusiastic support for the fund-raiser.[24] Although German-Americans expressed support for the old home country they were not quite willing to support it with their pocketbooks. Possibly, they also realized that contributions could be held against them in the future should the unthinkable happen and the United States enter the conflict. Despite lackluster support, the cooperation between the elite, middle-, and working-class societies for these fund-raising efforts contributed to an image of ethnic unity and Germanism. In fact, advertisements, such as the invitation for a fund-raising rally for the Widows and Orphans of Fallen Soldiers at Delmar Gardens in October 1914, appealed to unity between all German speakers, including Austrians and Hungarians.[25] Interestingly, Missourians must not have objected to such fund-raising activities. English-language newspapers in Kansas City, for example, advertised the events and listed the names of donors and the amounts of their contributions.[26]

Nevertheless, this behavior of calling for neutrality while supporting the fatherland also contributed to questioning the loyalty of Germans and German-Americans. Nationwide, the National German-American Alliance scanned daily and weekly English-language newspapers for anti-German material to enforce neutrality in America. This assertive or negative approach often resulted in resentment toward the alliance. In contrast, organizations such as the Jackson chapter of the German-American Alliance and German-language newspapers in Missouri used the more positive approach of educating Americans about the reasons why Germans, although among the best of American citizens, still held sympathies for Germany. They argued that to be a German did not mean instinctive support or servitude to the kaiser. Germans who came to the United States embraced freedom and were loyal to the Stars and Stripes, but they also had a right to celebrate the culture and history of their forefathers. That did not make them any less American than those who honored their ties to the mother country, England.[27]

St. Louis, with its diverse ethnic population, like the rest of the nation, was divided over the many issues Americans debated during the neutrality period, and German-Americans soon gained attention for their thoughts on the issues. Unlike Chicago, however, the city did not experience many altercations between German speakers and immigrants of Slavic heritage who had left the oppressive Austro-Hungarian Empire and now used the war to call for the creation of independent countries in their homelands. One major reason for this difference was that the ratio of immigrants from German states to that from the Austrian Empire was much smaller in Chicago than in St. Louis.[28]

As elsewhere in America, workers, labor unions, and the Socialist Party in St. Louis also could not remain neutral. The Central Trades and Labor Union adopted a resolution on August 9, 1914 that opposed the war in general and accused the ruling European powers of recklessly and irresponsibly throwing the continent into a campaign of murder. The Socialist Party endorsed this resolution as well and held an Anti-War and Peace Demonstration on August 16, 1914. Speakers, representing workers from all the countries engulfed in the European conflict, called upon President Wilson to maintain true neutrality and prevent the shipment of foodstuffs and other materials that might prolong the senseless war. Since many members of these labor unions were Germans, St. Louisans interpreted such arguments as pro-German.[29]

The St. Louis Businessmen's League created the city's chapter of the National Security League to debate the nation's defense. Influential leaders, including

Mayor Henry Kiel, Archbishop John J. Glennon, the pharmaceutical manufacturer Albert B. Lambert, the banker Festus J. Wade, and the beer manufacturer August A. Busch, served in the league and called for a stronger army and navy. The huge crowd that attended a rally at the Coliseum in February 1916 to hear President Wilson make his case for preparedness indicated that many St. Louisans agreed. However, several German-Americans, including the editors of the *Westliche Post* and *Amerika,* although not opposed to preparedness in principle, also argued that financial and industrial businessmen supported this movement not to protect the United States but to enrich themselves. The German-American Alliance and labor organizations, including the St. Louis Central Trades and Labor Union, echoed this sentiment and refused to participate in any preparedness activities, arguing that capitalists (although several were German-Americans) controlled these events.[30]

In December 1914, Irish and German residents established the American Neutrality League of St. Louis to support Bartholdt's embargo bill that would have prohibited the sale of munitions to any participants in the war. Although the league's membership included Americans, the majority of speakers addressing an audience of over twelve thousand at a mass meeting at the Coliseum in January 1915 were well-known German- and Irish-Americans, and it appeared to many that this was a pro-German event. This intense mobilization of German-American political influence did not persuade St. Louisans to support this embargo bill but forged an image that all German-Americans in St. Louis held anti-administration views. Despite Bartholdt's protestations that all members were Americans at heart, public opinion began to question the purpose of the Neutrality League, and only seven thousand attended the second rally in April 1915.[31]

At the same time, articles in German-language publications and festivals also presented a pro-German image in St. Louis. The Lutheran Synod's *Abendschule* and *Der Lutheraner,* as well as its English-language *Lutheran Witness,* represented war news from the German perspective. The central verein expressed its support for Germany through a resolution drafted during its annual conference in August 1914 and published it in the *Central Blatt.* The Catholic *Amerika,* whose editor was a member of the central verein as well, also conveyed pro-German sympathies. In fact, the *Westliche Post* pointed out that the war succeeded in creating German unity in the United States, a feat that not even Bismarck with the creation of the German Reich had accomplished.[32] Speakers and banners during the Bavarian Festival in September 1916 commemorated a united Germanness in St. Louis, asserted that *Einigkeit macht stark* (unity brings strength) and predicted that a united German people would surely dictate the peace accords that would soon end the war. The publication of letters arguing that cannons or grenades could not destroy the German people but that they would always triumph over any obstacle also contributed to the perception of pro-Germanism by 1916.[33]

The actions of the St. Louis alliance chapter only confirmed those suspicions. Alliance members attacked the one-sided British propaganda and demanded a fair hearing for Germany's view of the conflict in the press. Accustomed to expressing opinions freely, the alliance opposed the Anglo-French loan and criticized the Wilson administration for not abiding by strict neutrality. Despite expressions of patriotism and assertions that German-Americans were not instruments of the German government, the alliance's portrayal of Wilson as a pawn of Great Britain or money trusts soon resulted in questions about its loyalty to the United States.[34]

In reality, however, the alliance in St. Louis did not present a united front. Several members accused each other of going too far in their stipulations for neutrality, thus actually favoring Germany and its autocratic government. Others in turn accused fellow German-Americans of being supporters of Great Britain and no longer remembering their German heritage. German- and English-language newspapers in St. Louis printed these internal squabbles, and the public must have realized that German-Americans were not united and that the alliance did not speak for all Americans of German heritage.[35] Indeed, most were not yet willing to question the loyalty of average German-Americans or to associate them with the autocracy of Germany or with the alliance. Both the *Republic* and the *Post-Dispatch* argued it was understandable that German-Americans in St. Louis would have certain sympathetic feelings toward Germany during the war. But, as the *Republic* argued, no one should confuse these individual German-Americans with those, like the *Westliche Post* or the alliance, who were under the direct influence of German propagandists and slandered President Wilson.[36]

In this context, the 1916 election campaign gains importance because it turned Americanism and loyalty into nationally debated issues. In fact, the debates resulted in the unprecedented registration of 173,760 voters in St. Louis.[37] Unlike in previous elections, where nativism based on economic competition with immigrants and anti-Catholic sentiment informed campaign rhetoric and influenced voting habits, growing anti-German sentiment now singled out German-Americans and their perceived lack of patriotism.[38] German-American organizations, especially in St. Louis, were also very vocal; they attracted attention and created an image of ethnic unity that, although contrary to reality, influenced how Missourians perceived German-Americans.

In the presidential campaign, Republicans and their candidate, former New York governor and United States Supreme Court justice Charles Evans Hughes, vied for the German-American vote in the nation and in Missouri as a peace candidate. Although Hughes did not denounce German-Americans, he and his party were associated with former president Theodore Roosevelt, who regularly condemned immigrants for holding divided loyalties and attacked German-Americans, their persistent call for neutrality, and their suspected pro-Germanism.[39] Woodrow Wilson and the Democratic Party, in contrast, posed as the party of prosperity, peace, and true Americanism. They painted Republicans as warmongers, repudiated the vote of "hyphenates," used Hughes's German-American support to discredit him, and asserted that those questioning Wilson's foreign policy were un-American and supported Germany. They demanded that German-Americans decide whether they were American or German; they could no longer be something in between.[40]

Few English-language newspapers in rural Missouri printed editorials about the hyphen or divided loyalty, and the Americanization issue failed to gain widespread attention in rural areas. Nor did such rhetoric deter prominent German-American politicians, such as Missouri congressman Richard Bartholdt, and several newspapers from speaking out on behalf of an arms embargo or a negotiated peace.[41] The Democratic Party held its national convention in St. Louis. Nationally known politicians and candidates came to the city. Thus St. Louis attracted national attention, and the election campaign frequently graced the front pages of both English- and German-language newspapers. Representatives from both parties argued that the financial and emotional support German-Americans had sent to Germany and their critique of Wilson represented lack of neutrality and thus disloyalty. Republicans, especially Theodore Roosevelt in a speech in St. Louis in May 1916, denounced so-called hyphenated Americans, particularly German-Americans, who allegedly held divided loyalties. Democrats, during their national convention in St. Louis, also included an Americanization plank in their platform that asserted that all Americans must be patriots regardless of birth and charged that those who criticized the administration advanced the interests of Germany.[42] St. Louisans, therefore, heard and read about the suspected pro-Germanism of immigrants and learned to associate it with disloyalty.

The German-American Alliance received the most attention because it attempted to sway voters and defeat Wilson during the campaign although its constitution prohibited political activism. The *Post-Dispatch,* the most outspoken critic of the alliance in St. Louis, interpreted this political activism as an alien conspiracy to subordinate American interests to German dominance.[43]

Several German-Americans reacted and defended the alliance's lobbying activities as following traditional American political practices. Henry Kersting, the president of the city alliance chapter, argued that Roosevelt had no right to define disloyal behavior or to determine who was loyal, and several prominent German-Americans pointed out that Roosevelt had been happy to receive the organization's financial support during his presidential campaign. Nevertheless, the former president's campaign rhetoric turned any association with the alliance into evidence of pro-Germanism.[44]

German-Americans in Missouri were united in their resentment of the Democratic platform's emphasis on Americanism, proclaimed their loyalty to the United States, and argued that neither birth nor use of language should serve as a barometer of loyalty. The *Westliche Post* also participated in the hyphen debate and argued that the subject of loyalty was moot because the United States was not involved in the war. Indeed, the *Westliche Post* reminded its readers that German-Americans, who had defended and upheld the Constitution in past wars, understood true Americanism much better than Wilson, whose neutrality was biased toward Britain. Nativists who applied the hyphen to Germans sh5ould instead bestow its negative meaning on other immigrant groups, such as Serbians, Croats, and Slovenians who were known for their militarism and oppression but hid behind pretentious patriotism.[45]

German-Americans, however, were not united in their support for Hughes or Wilson. Several, such as John Folz, editor of the *Kansas City Presse,* wholeheartedly supported Hughes because he was a Republican, a true American, and not pro-British.[46] As a Republican paper, the *Westliche Post* also enthusiastically endorsed Charles Evans Hughes for president. It dissociated the judge from Roosevelt by pointing out that vice presidential candidate Charles Fairbanks in several speeches had spoken out against racial and ethnic stereotyping and thus indicated that Hughes's presidency would represent true Americanism.[47]

Yet, many German-Americans, such as Louis Benecke, a lifelong Republican and German-born politician from Brunswick, Missouri, left the Republican Party to support Wilson because Hughes did not distance himself from Theodore Roosevelt's anti-German and anti-immigrant sentiments. For others, the promise of prosperity, progressive reform, and peace was enough to vote for Wilson.[48] By contrast, not all German-American Democrats could easily support Wilson, his pro-British bias, and his stand on Americanism.[49] For example, the Democratic *Amerika* hesitantly endorsed Woodrow Wilson, because anyone associated with Theodore Roosevelt, who had expressed anti-German thoughts, did not deserve the German-American vote. Disagreeing with his foreign policy, the paper nevertheless encouraged its readers to vote for Woodrow Wilson because he was a progressive, who had supported the eight-hour day for railroad employees and child-labor reform.[50]

Interestingly, despite the anti-immigrant rhetoric, both parties also tried to persuade German-Americans in St. Louis to vote for their candidate. Democratic Senators James A. Reed and William J. Stone, sent to the city to appeal to German-Americans in particular, argued that Wilson had proven his dedication to preserving peace, but that Roosevelt's influence in the Republican Party would certainly lead to war for America. Republicans brought Hughes to St. Louis in high hopes that all Republicans, including German-Americans, would unite behind him.[51]

The election results, however, provide a more complex reality. Wilson carried Missouri with a vote of 397,016 to 369,167 for Hughes, and several newspapers in Missouri agreed with national papers that the slogan "He kept us out of war" was the reason for his victory.[52] Analysis of voting habits in Missouri's 114 counties between 1908 and 1916 supports these assertions because Wilson gained two or more percentage points over the Democratic candidate in 1908 and his own election in 1912 in fifty-four counties, including Cole County, a heavily German-American-populated area. Of course, any evaluation of results has to take into consideration that in contrast to the 1912 campaign when candidates from three major parties vied for the presidency, the 1916 election was a contest between two major party candidates. Wilson, nevertheless, lost percentage points in several counties containing sizable German-American populations when compared to results in 1908. Wilson lost the highest proportion of votes in Gasconade, Osage, and Perry counties. In Lincoln and Osage counties voters also cast decidedly fewer votes for Wilson than for fellow Democrats such as Senator James A. Reed and the gubernatorial candidate Frederick D. Gardner.[53] In St. Louis Wilson lost to Hughes by over nine thousand votes, but the Alliance was not able to mobilize a united German-American vote for Hughes because a considerable number voted for Wilson despite the Americanization plank in the Democratic platform. Voter returns show that although Wilson carried only ten of the twenty-eight wards, he gained four or more percentage points over his previous election in 1912 in fifteen wards, including in seven of the eleven German wards.[54] This illustrates that German-Americans in Missouri were just as divided as the nation over who represented the best interests of the nation.

The big loser in 1916 in St. Louis was the Socialist Party; it experienced a dramatic decline from 1912 in the German wards. Sally Miller, the historian of the Socialist Party in St. Louis, argues that the city charter of 1914 sounded the "death knell of the Socialist movement" in St. Louis because the new at-large electoral system for aldermen virtually eliminated any opportunity for Socialists to hold offices on the city council. German-American leadership also did not always appeal to a large number of American members. More likely, the party, in coordination with the local CTLU, had placed too much emphasis on democratization and social reform rather than radicalism, and any success in St. Louis required cooperation with progressive city leaders who were not inclined to work with Socialists. Consequently, the two established parties, especially the Democrats, could easily co-opt or implement reforms the Socialists had advocated, such as direct election of senators, initiative-referendum, and compulsory education laws. Wilson may have received more votes in these working-class neighborhoods because as a progressive Democrat he supported several of these issues.[55]

One additional issue that brought many voters, including German-American voters, to the polls was the prohibition amendment that the Democratic-controlled legislature placed on the November 1916 ballot. The primary argument German-Americans and other "wets" used against prohibition asserted that it would result in higher taxes, especially for farmers, less revenue for roads and schools and thus a decline in the economy, and would not lower but increase drunkenness, divorce rates, and crime.[56] While Labor supported temperance and regulation of liquor transportation, it also opposed prohibition arguing that it violated civil rights. To create a more effective opposition to the prohibition movement, brewery workers, most of whom were German-Americans, created the Trades Union Liberty League of Missouri in 1915.[57] The German-American Alliance also became very active in organizing the so-called German vote to prevent statewide prohibition. In previous elections the alliance, despite strong activism, had not been able to prevent the enactment of the Sunday laws that prohibited the consumption and sale of liquor on Sundays. But now in 1916, its registration efforts were instrumental in defeating the amendment. However, the enlistment of a German-born businessman from Indianapolis to help with local fund-raisers again contributed to the perception that the alliance operated under the influence of German propagandists. This political activism during the prohibition campaign created the impression that all German-speakers were united, would do anything to protect their ethnic interests, and indicated to nativists the power of the ethnic vote.[58]

Voters in Missouri turned down the attempt to bring statewide prohibition to the state by a vote of 416,826 to 294,288, although seventy-two counties voted for the amendment. The city of St. Louis and forty-two counties voted against it. The majority of these held large German-American populations and opposed prohibition by a sizable margin. Although the effort to turn Missouri dry failed, the campaign brought ethnic differences in opinion to the foreground and created suspicion toward German-Americans in the minds of many Missourians.[59]

Although not as hotly debated, the governor's race in 1916 is of particular interest because the campaign indicates that speaking positively about Germany or Germans in Missouri did not necessarily lead to political repercussions. Henry Lamm from Sedalia, a former state supreme court justice, was the Republican candidate, and Frederick D. Gardner, president of the St. Louis Coffin Company and a political unknown, was the Democratic candidate for governor.[60] The gubernatorial campaign concentrated on eliminating the state's debt, reform of the penal system, improvement of roads, and Gardner's land-bank plan, a low-interest loan system for farmers. Republicans asserted that Democrats had bankrupted the state and accused Gardner of cheating on his taxes and using the land-bank bill to lure farmer votes.[61] Surprisingly, Americanism was not a primary concern despite Gardner's previously expressed positive views about Germany.

One year before the election, during the annual picnic of the Cape Girardeau chapter of the National German-American Alliance, Gardner had given a speech that praised Germany's industrial development and German traits. He had visited Germany during the summer of 1914 to research the progress of Germany's economy, industry, and science, and he published articles on the subject in several magazines. He explained that during his travels he had become convinced that Germany fought the Great War to defend its existence, and he called upon German-Americans to use their political power to keep the United States out of the war.[62] With the exception of a few German-language newspapers, not many Missourians learned about this speech, and it did not resurface during the gubernatorial campaign. But Germans and German-Americans in Missouri looked upon Gardner as a "great friend" of the German Reich and the German people. Gardner-for-Governor clubs sprang up in many German towns, and several German-language newspapers proudly endorsed Gardner for governor, despite his being a Democrat, because he opposed prohibition and held characteristics dear to Germans, such as honesty, liberal principles, and hard work. It also helped that he had fashioned his suggestion for the Missouri land-bank plan after the German land-credit system.[63]

Gardner won the election because Democrats swept the state and national elections, but he defeated Lamm by only 2,263 votes, a much smaller margin of victory than either Reed or Wilson, who won by 24,456 and 28,693 votes, respectively. Analysis of election results at the county level demonstrates that Gardner did not carry the German counties and received fewer votes than Wilson in all but four counties in Missouri. His being a businessman and political unknown may have been the reason for this narrow win. Perhaps, in counties with sizable German populations, such as Chariton, Cole, Gasconade, Lafayette, Morgan, and Pettis counties, where newspapers noted his speech, non-German Democrats consciously voted against him because of his pro-German rhetoric in 1915.[64]

Gardner's election as governor is important for several reasons. Missourians were not yet concerned with hatred of everything German because they did not use his pro-German speech in 1915 against him. That would also explain why Missourians did not immediately harass all German-Americans once the United States entered the war. However, Gardner's narrow victory also suggests that in the future this politician would have to be careful about his association with the enemy. This is significant because the election of Gardner as governor would affect Missourians, and especially German-Americans, in a way that few could have predicted in November 1916.

The 1916 election demonstrated that German-Americans did not necessarily vote as an ethnic block. The Americanization campaign and activism of German-American leaders during the campaign, however, had increased mistrust and the sense that immigrants were not one hundred percent American, especially in St. Louis. Events between November 1916 and April 1917 only confirmed this impression.

Workers became increasingly militant in their demands for union recognition and humane treatment. Although opportunities for steady and good-paying jobs had increased during the neutrality period, inflation had diminished the standard of living. The streetcar worker strike in Springfield, Missouri, against Springfield Traction Company, which began in October 1916, also inspired streetcar workers in St. Louis to organize. Wagner Electric experienced several walkouts during 1916 despite the introduction of welfare capitalism such as recreation and sports programs as well as sick and death benefits. These gains did not make up for management's determination to preserve the open shop, lower wage standards, and hire workers, including women, from rural areas outside the city who worked for less and were less likely to organize.[65] In the minds of many Missourians and St. Louisans, however, this growing militancy among workers, many of whom were German-Americans and Socialists, no longer just represented class conflict but a loyalty issue.

In this context, even the leader of all Catholics in St. Louis, Archbishop John Glennon, disappointed many, who wondered whether he was a true American.

During a speech at Jefferson Barracks in November 1916 he expressed the hope that the nation would not enter the war, but if it did he urged that every citizen would stand by flag and country. In December 1916, however, while the nation was still at peace, he also held a memorial mass for the recently diseased Catholic Kaiser Franz Joseph, the Emperor of Austria, an ally of Germany. The archbishop did not perceive such a requiem as wrong and repeated the mass in the six languages of that empire also represented in St. Louis: German, Hungarian, Bohemian, Slovakian, Croatian, and Ruthenian.[66]

After Germany announced its resumption of unrestricted submarine warfare, St. Louisans began to unite in their support for Wilson and his decision to sever diplomatic relations with Germany and to arm merchant ships.[67] Most St. Louisans, including German-Americans, remained hopeful that Wilson would fulfill his campaign promise to keep the nation out of war, even after the release of the Zimmermann Telegram, a German proposal of war between Mexico and the United States. Regretting Germany's actions, the *Amerika* advocated for calmness and agitated for peace by all means necessary. The Improvement Association of the Tenth Ward (one of the German wards) sent a petition to Missouri's congressmen and the president imploring them not to listen to speculators and munitions manufacturers who tried to pull the nation into war for their personal benefit. Over one thousand members of the North St. Louis Businessmen's Association and other organizations signed a petition to the president urging him to avoid war with Germany by all honorable means possible.[68] Few of the signatories could have predicted that signing these petitions could have repercussions just one year later.

The Central Trades and Labor Union in St. Louis also took a firm stance against American involvement in the European conflict. In February 1917 it adopted an antiwar resolution which included outright opposition to conscription and an accusation that capitalists and commercial interests were pushing the United States into war for personal benefit. In March the CTLU in a 67–39 vote declined the motion that it provide space in its publications free of charge to the government during the war. These decisions were contrary to Samuel Gompers's announcements on behalf of the American Federation of Labor, calling for the National Council of Defense to effectively prepare the nation for the coming war and promising that all trade unions would support the government as long as it recognized their contributions to war and the economy.[69] In other words, the St. Louis CTLU, a German-American and Socialist-led association of trade unions broke with the nationally recognized leader of all trade unions. Such action did not ingratiate the CTLU and its leaders to St. Louisans.

Many German St. Louisans were not deterred from supporting the old home country by the growing inevitability of war. The St. Louis War Relief Bazaar Association sent $2,500 to the Relief Fund for German and Austrian Prisoners in Siberia. Prominent German-Americans, including Dr. Carl Barck and Dr. George Gellhorn, created the American Physicians' Expedition Committee to send several American doctors and nurses to Germany, just as similar American organizations had sent medical teams to England and France. Although Gellhorn abandoned the expedition once it appeared that the United States would enter the conflict, St. Louisans questioned his and his wife's loyalty during the war because of these actions.[70] The German Society of St. Louis continued to sponsor speakers to educate the general public about the truth of the war and to expose the untruths that the partisan press printed. For example, Mrs. Edgar Hanfstängel, a "born American but patriotic German," gave three well-attended speeches about the heroism of German women on the German home front. The *Westliche Post* congratulated the society on its growing success and noted approvingly the resulting growth in Germanness in the city.[71] In fact, the editor of the *Westliche Post* created suspicion as well by continuing to report the war from a pro-German perspective. Even after Germany had resumed unrestricted submarine warfare, the paper continued to excuse the tactic as a reaction to British practices and praised its "glorious results." Although disappointed that Germany would use such an "unfortunate choice of means" as the Zimmermann Telegram, the editor also interpreted the delay of its release to the public as another chess move by the Allies and war hawks intent on pulling the United States into the war.[72]

Despite this sense of ethnic unity, the split within the German-American community in St. Louis also widened during the growing war crisis. For example, seven hundred members of the German Theater Club protested that the German-American Alliance continued to send money to the German-Austrian Red Cross instead of donating it to the American Red Cross, now that it appeared that the United States would enter the conflict.[73]

As the diplomatic crisis worsened, St. Louisans not only read and heard about German sabotage activities elsewhere in the United States, but, more important, they also discovered that the enemy resided in the city. Erich Ralph von Gersdorff, a mining engineer and lieutenant in the German reserves, was arrested at the Brevoort Hotel for espionage. He had registered under an assumed name and had in his possession two telegrams warning a friend not to travel on the *Lusitania* because it had two heavy guns on board. Joseph Daucher, the blacksmith in Battery A, First Regiment, Missouri National Guard, was arrested on March 29 for suspected sabotage activity. He allegedly intended to poison military horses and mules and then leave for Mexico. These arrests certainly raised the bar of fear, and St. Louisans became very suspicious of all things German, or as the *Westliche Post* asserted began to "see ghosts everywhere."[74]

At the same time, St. Louisans read in newspapers that Congress considered legislation that would toughen punishment for espionage and sedition. Aliens who lived in St. Louis also learned that the Justice Department would watch out for spies and saboteurs among the foreign-born population. And the *Republic* warned German-Americans in St. Louis that if their "devotion to the German cause" would lead them "to abuse the hospitality of the United States, internment will be the likely outcome."[75] Possibly in anticipation or reaction to these warnings, three sisters, who had come to St. Louis over twenty-five years previously but had been unable to find husbands, decided that now was the best time to apply for citizenship. Residents from several European countries followed their example, and the naturalization bureau experienced a sudden flurry of activity.[76]

Military mobilization also began in St. Louis well before Congress considered a declaration of war. The First Regiment of the Missouri National Guard stationed in St. Louis mobilized in March for the purpose of protecting bridges, waterworks, and the armory from possible attack. In addition, the guard, several secret service agents, and private detectives watched laboratories at universities and munitions factories in St. Louis. Army recruiters used any means possible to attract volunteers, and by the end of March had to work overtime to evaluate enlistees. German-American men, whether inspired by true patriotism or by the perceived pressure to demonstrate their loyalty, volunteered in great numbers, representing an estimated 28 percent of all volunteers, according to the *Republic,* despite the possibility of fighting relatives.[77] As a result, many residents of St. Louis knew about and felt the war before it officially began. This, too, raised the bar of fear as well as expectations of patriotism.

On March 28, St. Louisans decorated most public and private buildings with American flags and banners in response to a call by the St. Louis chapter of the National Security League not to lag behind other major cities such as Kansas City in their proclamation of patriotism. St. Louis club women volunteered their services to the United States, and newspapers began to print a replica of the flag on their front pages.[78]

In April, St. Louis held its mayoral election, and in this time of heightened fear and patriotic display, loyalty became a major political issue during the campaign. Mayor Henry Kiel, the son of German immigrants, ran for reelection on the Republican ticket. Democrats not only called Kiel a "machine politician" but also used the rising suspicion of the foreign element to discredit him. They argued that Kiel and the Republicans assaulted Americanism and were under the spell of Henry Kersting, former president of the alliance and "one of the leading German propagandists of St. Louis."[79] Republicans, in return, proclaimed that the mayor's loyalty was beyond reproach due to his father's selfless service in the Civil War and Kiel's dedication to St. Louis, Missouri, and America. Kiel indeed asserted that he was an American and that America would always come first for him.[80]

The *Westliche Post* enthusiastically endorsed Kiel and expressed disappointment that German-American leaders, such as Isaac Lionberger, would use this election campaign to denounce a fellow American of German descent for political gain. More important, the *Westliche Post* interpreted these accusations of disloyalty as the seeds of fear and mistrust, watered and fertilized by partisanship and misinformation, and bearing fruit. During these sad times there should be no doubt about the citizens of German ancestry, the editor argued. They knew true Americanism. They had always been true to this country and had done their duty as American citizens, often more than old-stock Americans, in the Civil War, Indian Wars, and Spanish-American War. The editor was confident they would do so again now.[81]

Despite the accusations of disloyalty, Mayor Kiel carried all but the fourth and fifth wards and defeated his opponent by an overwhelming majority of 70,193 to 46,792 votes, because St. Louisans liked his personality and his progressive reforms, including zoning changes and city beautification.[82] One of his first acts in his second term would be a proclamation pledging the loyalty of St. Louis to the nation as the United States entered World War I.

THREE

"No Time for Slackers"

The Missouri Council of Defense and Governor Gardner's
Approach to Fighting the Kaiser at Home

> There can be no half-hearted allegiance. . . .
> Those who are against us are pro-German.
>
> *Frederick D. Gardner, April 8, 1918*

ON APRIL 5, 1917, one day before Congress declared war on Germany, Missouri Governor Frederick D. Gardner announced that "this is no time for slackers, copperheads, or soft pedalists. If there are any such among us, it is our duty to drive them out and brand them as traitors." One year later, during a Third Liberty Loan campaign speech on April 8, 1918, he asserted that all pro-Germans were German spies and threatened to declare martial law in Missouri if "at any time I become convinced that there is in any community in this state an organized movement of these traitorous wretches." If found and convicted, these enemies of the nation should "face a firing squad and thus suffer that fate which traitors so richly deserve." Yet only three years earlier he had praised the Germans and their intellectual, economic, and industrial progress.[1] Gardner's transformation from pro- to anti-German sentiment within such a brief time symbolized the growing resentment of anything German in the state and the nation during the First World War.

Indeed, public opinion in Missouri underwent a transformation during the early months of 1917. Some, although disappointed with the events that pushed the United States into the European conflict, continued to rationalize German submarine warfare as a legitimate tactic, denounced Great Britain and capitalists for pulling the nation into war, and reminded Wilson that he had been reelected for his ability to keep the country out of war.[2] The majority, however, realized that American involvement was inevitable. The Missouri General Assembly through a joint resolution announced the state's willingness to follow Wilson's leadership and protect American rights "regardless of cost or of sacrifices." Governor Gardner, although regretting that the relationship between the United States and Germany had deteriorated beyond compromise, called upon Missourians to support their president and government. English- and German-speakers alike began to unite behind the president, denounced Germany for its unwillingness to recognize American rights, and asserted their loyalty to the United States.[3]

The nation's financial and industrial commitment to the Allies, Germany's resumption of unrestricted submarine warfare in January, the infamous Zimmermann Telegram in February 1917, and nearing bankruptcy of Great Britain convinced President Woodrow Wilson to ask Congress to declare war against Germany, and Congress obliged on April 6, 1917. Wilson's progressive ideology transformed this military engagement into a crusade against militarism and to make the world "safe for democracy." As the president asked for the mobilization of every available resource to wage this righteous war, he could not be sure that the American public would support this war because he had been elected on the mandate to keep the country out of war. Furthermore, the nation would fight a global military conflict with a country that had sent one of the largest immigrant groups to the United States. Thus, in order to unite the American public in support of a war against Germany, Wilson established the Committee on Public Information (CPI) by executive order on April 14, 1917.[4]

George Creel, a "prominent muckraker" and reform-minded newspaperman from Kansas City, Missouri, who headed this government agency, believed that the government should educate the public about the unavoidable yet moral obligation for the United States to enter the conflict, explain the government war programs, and define patriotism in order to create a "white-hot mass instinct" for war. Loyalty in this context meant that every American should purchase Liberty Bonds and War Savings Stamps to finance the war. Ideally, men would answer the call to the Selective Service and, when drafted, enter the military willingly and joyfully without asking for exemptions. Women ought to become the soldiers of the home front, knit sweaters, conserve foodstuff, and volunteer for the Red Cross. Children should write patriotic essays in school, cultivate victory gardens, invest in Baby Bonds, and buy Thrift Stamps. In accordance with Woodrow Wilson's definition of Americanism, any expression of dissatisfaction, disagreement, or outright unwillingness to do any of the above would be interpreted as supporting the enemy.[5]

Members of the CPI distributed this government definition of patriotism to the American people through virtually every existing communication channel, including the press, motion pictures, cartoons, billboards, pamphlets, and public speakers. However, the theme of liberating humankind also constructed the enemy as a murderous aggressor and obstacle to everything America represented. The CPI thus blatantly appealed to existing stereotypes, emotions, and fears of everything "foreign" and rallied public opinion to unite behind a war of good versus evil in a life-and-death struggle between democracy and autocracy. Officially approved advertisements and speeches not only created a willingness to sacrifice life and money for a noble cause abroad but also encouraged intolerance of anything pro-German and thus un-American at home.[6]

Such measures seemed unnecessary, at first sight, because a majority of Americans and Missourians supported the president's request for mobilization. Even proponents of strict neutrality, such as Senator William J. Stone and Representative Dorsey Shackleford, both from Missouri, who voted against the declaration of war, supported the president and urged Missourians to do likewise.[7] The declaration of war also produced several spontaneous demonstrations of patriotism throughout the state. Boonville businesses closed shops on the afternoon of April 6 and participated in an impromptu "support-the-war rally." Residents of Malta Bend, a town in Saline County, hoisted a huge American flag on a flagpole, decorated business windows with the Stars and Stripes, and pinned miniature versions of the flag on their lapels. And in several communities citizens and veterans in uniforms filled the streets, marched to music, waved flags, and sang patriotic songs.[8]

Many German-Americans also expressed their patriotism within hours of President Wilson's address to Congress or the official declaration of war. Some argued that it was not necessary for them to demonstrate their loyalty through public exhibition because their record of patriotism during the Civil War, Indian Wars, and Spanish-American War spoke for itself. Others, including members of the St. Joseph's Turnverein in Concordia, removed all German flags and portraits of notable Germans from homes and society halls and replaced them with the American flag and pictures of American statesmen.[9] German-American laborers who represented the leadership in the Missouri State Federation of Labor followed the example of American Federation of Labor president Samuel Gompers by expressing support for the war effort as long as they did not lose any labor concessions gained in the recent past and were protected against the abuses by big business in the rush to produce war material.[10]

During these initial demonstrations of patriotism Missourians learned how to publicly express their loyalty. Displaying the flag or its replica in the window, on the lapel, or on the front page of a newspaper served as an obvious sign of patriotism and as a convenient way to express love of county. Participation in public mass meetings, regardless of personal convictions, and deference to the flag also offered ways to deflect accusations of disloyalty. However, leaders in several communities throughout Missouri also believed that saluting the flag and military service were not enough. They called for "real and unalloyed Americanism" and urged all citizens to do their utmost to "meet the exigencies of a war thrust upon the nation."[11]

Indeed, the initial demonstrations of patriotism and assurances that German-speakers were loyal were not enough to ease the fears of the enemy within at the national level. United States Attorney General Thomas Gregory quickly issued a warning to all German-born aliens to abide by the law and to remain quiet. As long as German immigrants followed these guidelines they had nothing to worry about from the government.[12] In other words, passivity and doing the minimum necessary was acceptable. In order to stymie opposition and to catch spies, traitors, and saboteurs the U.S. Congress passed increasingly restrictive federal legislation, including the Espionage Act in June 1917, the Trading-with-the-Enemy Act in October 1917, and the Sedition Act in May 1918. Government officials, such as Postmaster General Albert S. Burleson, gained the authority to control dissent and to repress radicals, pacifists, and all the enemies who attempted to stop America's quest to build a new world order.[13]

Numerous private and semi-official organizations supplemented official authority in the search for the enemy within and abridged individual rights in the process. The largest of these groups was the American Protective League (APL), an auxiliary organization of volunteer detectives connected to the Justice Department. The APL, according to its historian, believed that it had to defend the nation against an army of over 250,000 "highly trained" German spies living in the United States. These amateur sleuths investigated passport and naturalization applicants, federal employees, civilians who applied for overseas duty, and any rumors of disloyalty and spy activity.[14]

Historians have argued that Allied propaganda depicting Germans as barbarians, combined with CPI publicity hoping to produce eager support for the war, and legislation aiming to catch German spies and traitors, created a climate of suspicion and distrust of anything associated with Germany. Zealots demanded that every American show his true colors and prove his loyalty to the United States. They also interpreted the official rhetoric of unity as permission to force their opinion on others, to hunt so-called disloyal individuals as criminals, and to oppress their civil rights. Superpatriots arrested draft dodgers without warrants, tarred and feathered outspoken opponents, and forced slackers to kneel and kiss the flag. As the war progressed it became increasingly unpopular to say anything because the prowar forces could no longer distinguish between the real threats to the country's security and those who simply criticized American war policies, opposed war on principle, or advocated peace.[15]

German-Americans seemed to bear the brunt of the hysteria because nationalists believed that German spies lurked around every corner and aimed to destroy the American way of life. Hostility toward Germany as a nation extended itself to hostility to all things German in the United States. German-Americans who expressed the slightest pacifist inclination or disagreement with the government could expect humiliating flag kissing or tar and feather ceremonies, public whippings, and other acts of physical abuse and violence.[16] A vacationer with a German name who reacted to a cold snap in Florida with the expression, "Damn such a country as this," was arrested for defaming the nation and violating the Espionage Act. In Connecticut, a group of men surrounded the house of Maximilian von Hoegen, dragged him away from his protesting family to a nearby square, administered a public beating, and forced him to kiss the flag and sing "The Star Spangled Banner" because he had written *Deutschland über alles* (Germany above everything) and other pro-German sentiments on his draft questionnaire. Historians have called this hysteria "an American Reign of Terror" conducted under the guise of patriotism.[17] These superpatriotic activities and witch-hunts, according to many historians, eventually culminated and climaxed in the mob lynching of Robert Prager on April 5, 1918, in Collinsville, Illinois. Prager, a German-born coal miner, allegedly made disrespectful remarks about President Wilson. Patriotic miners, encouraged by alcohol, decided that he should publicly declare his loyalty in a flag-kissing ceremony. The local police rescued Prager, but the mob regained custody of him. Incensed by the delay and the mayor's order to close all taverns for the night, the crowd decided to conduct a tar and feather ceremony. Unable to find sufficient tar, the "more vicious" members of the crowd determined that he should hang. None of the vigilantes was convicted of murder.[18]

Contrary to accepted wisdom, Carl Weinberg points out in his regional study of coal miners in southwest Illinois that Prager's death did not simply represent anti-German sentiment run amok. Instead, the presence of Joseph Riegel, the leader of the lynch mob who was also a German-American who could still read German and was under suspicion for disloyal behavior, demonstrates that class conflict and the complex struggle for laborers between fighting "for their collective needs as workers" while also remaining patriotic Americans explain the events of that fateful day.[19] Germans and non-Germans in Missouri fought similar personal battles and, consequently, their experience during the Great War was more complex than earlier historians have represented.

Missouri participated to some degree in the madness that spread through the United States during World War I. Map 3.1 outlines the type and location of reported events in Missouri directed at opponents of war, including accusations of disloyalty, job loss due to perceived unpatriotic behavior, prosecution under the Espionage Act, and mob incidents.[20] St. Louis contained the largest concentration of suspected disloyal behavior, but Missourians anywhere

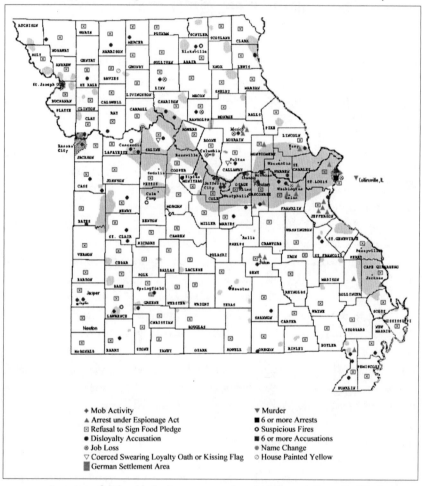

◆ Mob Activity
▲ Arrest under Espionage Act
☒ Refusal to Sign Food Pledge
● Disloyalty Accusation
⊗ Job Loss
▽ Coerced Swearing Loyalty Oath or Kissing Flag
▮ German Settlement Area

▼ Murder
■ 6 or more Arrests
○ Suspicious Fires
■ 6 or more Accusations
● Name Change
⊘ House Painted Yellow

MAP 3.1. Location of disloyal behavior, as reported to the Missouri Council of Defense, published in newspapers, and noted in records of the United States District Court, Eastern District of Missouri. Map background reprinted from Russel L. Gerlach, *Settlement Patterns in Missouri: A Study of Population Origins,* by permission of University of Missouri Press. Copyright © 1986 by the Curators of the University of Missouri.

did not hesitate to accuse their neighbors of traitorous remarks or behaving in a disloyal manner. Allegedly, John Adcock of Portageville in New Madrid County in southeast Missouri, criticized the war effort, and David Cook of Amity in DeKalb County in northwest Missouri was accused of disloyal behavior because he fed wheat to his chickens.[21]

If enough evidence existed, individuals were arrested, charged, and convicted under the Espionage Act. E. J. Deane from Mexico in Audrain County, for example, was charged with obstructing recruitment and enlistment services. He received a two-year sentence at Fort Leavenworth for offering a drug to draft registrants that would affect their eyes and allow them to fail the physical examination.[22] Others, including Ernest Scheunemann, a teacher in Moberly, and George Russell, a rural mail carrier in Benton City, who were arrested for accusing President Wilson and "Wall Street plutocrats" of causing the war, lost their jobs for expressing a perceived un-American opinion. A physics professor at the University of Missouri in Columbia resigned after secret service agents intercepted his letters to a brother in Austria boasting how cleverly he spread pro-German propaganda in the classroom.[23] Missourians also attributed several suspicious occurrences to German agents, including the burning of Science Hall at the Normal School in Kirksville where the Student Army Training Corps had drilled and a failed attempt to dynamite the "Frisco railroad bridge" in Lawrence County. Residents in Brunswick attributed tainted water and subsequent sickness to German sympathizers, and Governor Gardner called out the Home Guard to protect the city's water supply.[24]

Rarely, however, did Missourians resort to violence to coerce conformity or teach perceived un-Americans a lesson in patriotism. In Daviess County patriots painted a slacker's house yellow to encourage him to do his part in the war effort.[25] The arrival of the Home Guard unit from Marshall avoided a mob lynching in Saline City of four "pro-Germans accused of disloyalty." In Jefferson City, Fritz Monat was publicly whipped and forced to kiss the flag for his pro-German remarks. In Osage County, Erwin Walz had to kiss the flag for defaming the local Home Guard. During the Lead Belt Riot in St. Francois County, a mob nearly lynched an Austrian laborer.[26] However, as map 3.1 demonstrates, these incidents represent the exception, not the norm, in Missouri during the war.

Anti-German sentiment existed; however, the low number of violent events and their late occurrence also suggest absence of hysteria and widespread fear of the enemy, especially when compared to the events depicted in the literature discussing the war's impact in South Dakota, Ohio, Wisconsin, Minnesota, and Iowa.[27] Although it is possible that some events were not reported, the basically peaceful approach to dealing with disloyals reveals that Missourians abided by and enforced the law, showed restraint, and limited vigilante justice.

One factor in the lack of violence is the possible existence of a general sentiment of opposition to government interference in daily life as a result of war. In contrast to many midwesterners who held a more favorable view of government in general, rural southerners held a generally negative perception of the war effort. Despite a public perception of virulent southern support for war, southern populists, rural Democrats, and Socialists had opposed preparedness for war during the neutrality period, disapproved the apparent inequalities in exemptions from military service which seemed to benefit the elite and wealthy, and rejected the financial profit northern industrialists and financiers reaped from a war in which poor people fought.[28] A similar mind-set existed in the border state of Missouri where many residents had maintained a southern identity based on heritage and proximity. Public perception as expressed through impromptu war rallies and speeches was one of widespread support for going to war. However, Christopher Gibbs's in-depth study of draft exemptions, liberty loan contributions, food conservation pledges, and labor unrest suggests that when it came to expressing patriotism in kind, many Missourians were less than enthusiastic about the war effort.[29] Such reluctance also shaped perceptions of ethnic groups, including the Irish- and German-Americans, who may have been passive rather than enthusiastic about the war. As long as a person did not overtly express pro-German thoughts and brought attention to an area, Missourians regardless of ethnic background initially left each other alone.

In this context the relative absence of anti-German propaganda in Missouri acquires significance. Government information in the form of emotionally loaded posters and advertisements did not reach Missouri until the fall of 1917. According to William Saunders, the secretary of the Missouri Council of Defense, government leaders in Missouri were interested "in arousing patriotic enthusiasm and loyalty" in the state. But the absence of government publicity and instructions often led to confusion and misinformation at the local level. Throughout 1917, volunteers for the war effort mentioned in their reports to Jefferson City and Washington, D.C., that more information was absolutely necessary to bring about more support for the war. They urgently requested that the Council of National Defense send "visible material evidence of war," such as veterans and war machinery, to the state so that they could stimulate the sense of urgency, because "we are so far away from the seat of government that it is difficult for our people to realize that we are engaged in a serious war." Mrs. Walter McNab Miller, the state chairman for the campaign to register housewives who would pledge to conserve food, noted in a letter to Herbert Hoover that during the campaign people had come to her "in tears, saying that the government was going to take them out of their homes and send them to France . . . as soon as they could get their names." This fear, in her opinion, was most widespread in the rural areas, and she urged better publicity and education in those areas.[30]

During the early months of American involvement in the war, newspapers were more likely to print local and state news that affected them directly than the national news about a war far away that concerned them little and that very rarely had a direct impact on them. Missourians, therefore, did not always read or hear about the anti-German propaganda disseminated by the Committee on Public Information and other patriotic organizations unless they had access to metropolitan publications such as the *Kansas City Star,* the *St. Louis Republic,* or the *New York Times.*[31] Instead, Missourians were more likely to hear and read about the speeches that local politicians gave than about the laws on the national level. As a result they did not immediately harbor a well-defined hatred of everything German.

In this context, the Missouri Council of Defense acquires significance because it directed the flow of information and the war effort at the state and county level. Secretary of War and chairman of the Council of National Defense Newton D. Baker requested on April 9, 1917, that all state governors create state councils of defense "as the official war emergency organization of the states . . . charged with conducting all of the war activity of the states not directly within the fields of the established executive departments."[32] Within three days Governor Frederick D. Gardner responded and called for a state-wide conference to establish the Missouri Council of Defense. The conference assembled on April 23, 1917, at the new capitol building in Jefferson City, and Gardner appointed Frederick B. Mumford, the dean of the Missouri College of Agriculture, as the council's chairman. National Defense Council instructions required that Missouri establish a state council and county councils, but delegates to the conference decided to create additional councils at the township and school district level. The governor and state council appointed seven men to each county council, who then appointed seven men to each township and school district council. Members were usually local leaders, including mayors, county clerks, bankers, doctors, merchants, and wealthy farmers. German-Americans who had achieved social and political success also served on these councils. Eventually 11,487 members and patriotic citizens "worked at every level of government from township to state" to carry out the state council's mission. Missouri's detailed system of subcouncils set a precedent and served as an example for several states.[33]

The duties of the state council included the mobilization of all state resources and cooperation with the National Council of Defense, the secretary of agriculture, the federal trade commission and the war and navy departments. Additional tasks ranged from reducing unnecessary consumption to increasing farm production and encouraging "municipal and community gardening." The Missouri Council of Defense thus became the sole coordinating body between the national government, state departments, and citizens of Missouri during the war. However, the Missouri Council of Defense, unlike councils in other states, did not have legislative powers, because the General Assembly was not in session during America's participation in the Great War. The council thus could use only such powers as delegated by the Council of National Defense, a congressionally approved agency, and the governor, and had to rely on private donations to cover operating costs. This fit well into the state's political culture that emphasized "individualism" and "traditionalism," or a minimalistic government and preservation of the traditional social and political order.[34]

The lack of authority and appropriation, however, did not prevent the council from persuading Missourians to support the nation's war effort. It kept the state in line with national loyalty and mobilization guidelines by advocating volunteerism and appealing to the patriotism of all its citizens, and especially to the sense of duty of the state's foreign-born residents. But unlike Wisconsin, which gained a reputation as a "Fortress of Opposition" because Germans and Socialists controlled its Council of Defense, Missouri did not have to clean up an image of disloyalty. The council, instead, had to simply preserve the image of patriotism established in the early days of the war and maintain law and order.[35]

During the early months of the war in 1917, the council's primary function was to increase food production and reduce food consumption in conjunction with the Food Administration. The state council, working with the College of Agriculture and the University of Missouri's extension center, created essays and ads explaining how to grow more and improved wheat and corn, how to increase egg production, and how to use barnyard manure wisely, and sent agricultural agents to farms teaching new methods and distributing informative pamphlets (see figure 3.1). This education campaign, combined with higher prices, was quite successful, because Missouri farmers increased acreage, production, and overall value of crops despite a drought in 1917.[36] During the fall of 1917 and winter of 1918, the council also distributed pre-set type plates from the United States Food Administration to newspapers, featuring concise essays about food conservation and articles such as "Are You Doing Your Share?" which repeated the government's themes of service and sacrifice and explained that conservation would win the war. Most newspapers simply

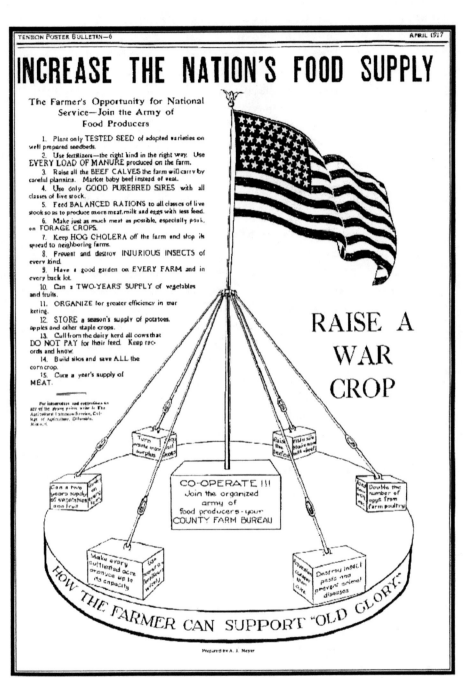

FIGURE 3.1. Appeal to farmers to "Raise a War Crop"

included these pre-set articles and cartoons, possibly under local pressure and to look patriotic, but saw no need to elaborate.[37]

Council officials recognized that one essential component in mobilizing the state would be the aid women could contribute to the war effort. Nearly 120,000 women responded to the governor's call for volunteers on July 28, 1917; they included suffragists, reformers, and social workers who applied their experience in the club movement to the organization of the war effort. The Missouri Woman's Committee of the Council of Defense organized chapters in 113 counties, 237 townships, and 137 school districts. In September 1917, Governor Gardner appointed the state, county, and township chairwomen as members of the corresponding councils of defense. These women served the war effort by demonstrating food conservation in homes and at club meetings and walking from house to house to encourage Missourians to sign the Hoover Food Pledge and agree to reduce waste so that America might feed its soldiers and the Allies. Women also distributed travel kits, gave speeches, held Americanization classes, trained as nurses and stenographers, wrote articles for newspapers, and helped raise money for the Red Cross, YMCA, and Liberty Loans.[38]

The Missouri Council of Defense, similar to the CPI, also concerned itself with creating positive public opinion. For that purpose it published *Missouri on Guard* monthly between June 1917 and December 1918 and distributed it to county councils, state officials, and public libraries free of charge. Articles carried the messages of the governor and state council to readers and recounted the activities of county and township councils in the war effort. To reach an even broader audience the council also created its own Patriotic Speakers' Bureau in August 1917. The bureau, in cooperation with the CPI's Speaking Division, organized mass meetings and speaking campaigns throughout the state to "mobilize public opinion and stimulate patriotic service" and to spread the government's patriotic message. The council estimated that over the lifetime of the bureau hundreds of speakers, or "Tongues of Fire," war veterans, and Four-Minute-Men, who addressed audiences in movie theaters during the four-minute reel change, "performed an indispensable task" of educating Missourians as to why the United States was at war, explaining how every individual "could best serve and contribute to the winning of the final victory," and preaching Americanism to about one million people at county fairs, movie theaters, clubs, churches, schools, and fraternal associations.[39]

The council, following Council of National Defense suggestions and in order to more effectively reach and gain the support of the large German-American population in Missouri, also experimented with a German-speaking division in the state's Patriotic Speakers' Bureau. Although not unique in its inception, this plan reflected the progressive nature of several council members as well as Missouri's relative tolerance toward German-speakers. Under the leadership of Max F. Meyer, professor of psychology at the University of Missouri in Columbia, the division organized "mass meetings in German districts" and sent individuals "of German origin but unquestionable loyalty," who could address these meetings in the German language, arouse public opinion in favor of the war, and thus guard against the infiltration of German propaganda. Initially the division had good success and much support. Among its sixteen speakers were the Reverend Joseph Frenz from Festus, whose effective speeches on behalf of the Red Cross and the YMCA resulted in improved contributions, and the Reverend Walner from Jarvis, whose passionate oratory in German communities resulted in more food pledges than any other speaker could inspire. George E. Cansler, treasurer of Maries County and the chairman of the county's council, thought this an excellent approach because it would "point" especially the wealthier German farmers of his county "in the right direction."[40] Elliott Dunlap Smith, member of the State Councils Section in the Council of National Defense was very impressed by this "friendly" method to turn reluctant German-speakers into enthusiastic war supporters. Although he realized that it was "perfectly natural and right" to "feel some resentment against the use of the German language for official purposes," the sympathetic approach through speakers who were and knew German was more effective than a "more militant attack," and he encouraged its continuation.[41]

The appeals to patriotism and self-sacrifice through publications and speeches defined what it meant to be patriotic in Missouri and produced the desired results. Service to country exhibited the highest degree of patriotism, but not all Missourians, whether of German or American birth, could follow the patriotic example of Fred Bierig, a naturalized German-born retired baker, who had five sons serving in the military.[42] Nevertheless, more than 3,700 Missourians volunteered for the federalized National Guard and the United States Army and Navy. During the first registration for the draft in June 1917 nearly 300,000 men registered in Missouri. Although slightly more than 50 percent of registrants filed for allowable exemptions, that was lower than the 60 to 70 percent nationwide, and few resisted conscription outright.[43] Those who were too old for the draft or disabled but still wished to join the war effort in a military capacity could join the Home Guard. More than seven thousand Home Guard volunteers received military training and took over the duties of the Missouri National Guard after its induction into federal service in August 1917.[44]

Voluntarily conserving food, purchasing Liberty Bonds, and supporting the Red Cross served as obvious means for civilians to demonstrate their patriotism.

In November 1917 more than one million Missourians signed the Hoover Food Pledge, and Missouri ranked first among all the states with pledges in proportion to its population and second in the total number of signers, according to the United States Food Administration and the Missouri Council of Defense. Missourians also oversubscribed the state quota in each of the five Liberty Loan drives.[45] The Red Cross, more than any other organization or campaign, received the most widespread and voluntary support. Counties and townships throughout the state organized chapters and conducted elaborate fund-raisers. Women knitted sweaters and rolled bandages. Both English- and German-language newspapers carried Red Cross advertisements by the fall of 1917. It was easy to support a well-known and respected relief organization that represented the concept of universal humanitarian aid. Indeed, the Red Cross was an organization anyone—patriotic American, zealous pro-German, or someone in-between—could support. And, naturally, it looked patriotic.[46] The Missouri Council of Defense thus could proudly claim that it was successful in "securing civic cooperation" for the war. The transformation of Missouri's motto from "Show Us" to "Show You" probably had an impact and encouraged Missourians to demonstrate their loyalty to country.[47]

Nevertheless, the council also had to deal with opposition to the war and suspected disloyal activity. As early as September 1917, members of the council indicated that some Missourians were hesitant in supporting the war effort and, as Mrs. McNab Miller noted, that it would be "increasingly hard to get money for anything but the Red Cross." Although nearly one million Missourians signed the Hoover Pledge, most counties also sent to the state council lists of nonsigners.[48] To gauge the level of opposition and maintain law and order, the state council requested that county council chairmen inform William Saunders, the secretary of the council, of any substantiated disloyal activity within their communities, and the council would "send out investigators" to examine the situation.[49] Such action intended to weed out frivolous accusations and aimed to take care of any emerging problems before they could attract national attention.

Local councils followed these guidelines and reported anything they interpreted as suspicious or disloyal to the state council. Residents of Belle in Maries County complained that the local movie theater showed the film *The German Side of the War*. The title suggested to many that the movie contained pro-German propaganda. Further investigation, however, revealed that Edwin Weigle, staff photographer of the *Chicago Tribune,* a newspaper with a known antiwar stance, had produced a harmless film about the war in France in 1915 that was "truthful in content and rather entertaining," but it would "certainly disappoint any German propagandist." Concerned citizens in St. Clair County, worried about rumors of "anti-draft talk," asked the state council for assistance and a possible "secret service" investigation.[50] Throughout the summer and fall of 1917 county councils of defense reported additional cases of suspected disloyalty to the state council, including unwillingness to register for the draft, refusal to sign the Hoover Food Pledges, hoarding of wheat, not purchasing enough Liberty Bonds, and refusing to contribute to the Red Cross.

In reaction to this evidence of opposition to the war, and in order to preserve the image of Missouri as a patriotic state, council officials advocated the prosecution of those who violated the Espionage Act and encouraged persuasion, friendly coercion, intimidation, and "ostracism" as the most effective measures to bring slackers into line.[51] For example, the state council officially endorsed a color-coded card warning system that Henry County developed to deal with opponents to war and draft dodgers. A white card warned a slacker to mend his ways; if complaints continued after one week he could receive a blue card, and finally a red card indicating that the Secret Service would investigate any further accusations.[52]

County councils took the endorsement seriously and used coercion to keep perceived opponents of war in line. Cole and Daviess Counties created a card index of suspected disloyals and persons who did not participate in government programs. St. Clair County council officials successfully dealt with an antidraft organization and outspoken critics of the war by giving each individual "a good lecture" about the consequences if they did not conform. The Franklin County council used more extreme coercion and openly stated in the newspaper that it compiled a "secret list" of persons who refused to sign the Hoover Food Pledge, would pass this information to the Secret Service for investigation, and observed those who did sign it to assure that they would indeed "keep their word."[53]

The Missouri Council's recommendation of intimidation contributed to the preservation of law and order in the state throughout 1917 and diverted control over loyalty issues to the local level. This fit well with national guidelines of decentralization and Governor Gardner's instruction that county councils were "the supreme local authority in all matter relating to the mobilization of the resources of the counties and cities."[54] Placing the responsibility of assuring support for the war into the hands of county officials also encouraged superpatriots to investigate the private affairs of their neighbors and to coerce loyal behavior. This intimidation at the community level, although violating constitutional rights and protections, created the public image of relative calm and patriotism in Missouri.

Initially this approach seemed to work well. Citizens maintained restraint, limited themselves to accusations, and turned over suspected slackers to the legitimate local authorities. Accusers directed their allegations against persons of all ethnic and economic backgrounds and did not single out German-Americans. By the winter and spring of 1918, however, the number of accusations grew dramatically as the nation and state prepared for the Third Liberty Loan Campaign. By now the war had also changed as American soldiers participated and died in battles in the Saint Mihiel salient and the Ansauville sector. The war now directly affected Americans; it was no longer distant or someone else's fight.[55] Furthermore, the labor militancy, brewing since 1916, now exploded. Kansas City came to a virtual standstill for six days in March 1918 when brewery workers, building trades unionists, hotel and restaurant employees, cooks, motion-picture operators, stagehands, and bakers joined laundry workers in a general strike. A wave of strikes also hit St. Louis in February and March, and newspaper editors began to wonder whether the labor trouble in nearby Stanton, Illinois, would spill over into Missouri.[56]

At the same time, the Committee on Public Information had also reached the central part of the country, especially rural areas, with its emotionally laden publicity campaign. Publishers of English- and German-language newspapers increased the number of CPI articles and pre-set type columns because they were available and because editors believed that it was in their best interest to include such material and appear patriotic. In addition, the Trading-with-the-Enemy Act had required since October that German-language newspapers file translations of articles with sensitive information about the war with local postmasters. And the government ordered that enemy aliens, particularly men born in Germany and Austria, register with the local postmaster.[57] The arrival of CPI information also allowed newspapers to become more outspoken in their attitude toward Missourians and German-Americans who opposed the war. For example, the *Sedalia Democrat* until the winter of 1918 had confined war reports to pages 2 and 3 without headlines. However, by March 1918 front-page editorials advocated that Americans strike out against "ENEMY AGENTS" and German propagandists who were gloating about recent German battlefield successes and "TURN 'EM IN."[58]

Thus more Missourians read about the war, became more aware of and learned to fear the perceived enemy within, increased the surveillance of their neighbors, and sent lengthy lists of accused disloyals and their allegedly un-American expressions to the Missouri Council of Defense. Consequently, the content of accusations and accused also changed. During 1917, most reports interpreted opposition to the war as "slacking." Now, concerned citizens specifically accused residents "who were of German birth or descent" of disloyalty and construed any criticism of the draft, government, war, and food conservation or the refusal to support the war financially as proof of pro-German sympathies.[59]

Overwhelmed by the increase in requests for investigations, council officials, now perceiving the presence of real disloyalty, suggested that counties establish their own chapters of the American Protective League. Local operatives could then determine whether accusations deserved further scrutiny for accuracy and whether they warranted action under the Espionage Act. Saunders hoped that the "mere process of investigation by the [APL] representative cures the evil" and that those investigated became "passively or actively loyal."[60] Interestingly, Emerson Hough, the historian of the APL, indicated that there might have been little disloyal activity to report in Missouri. He noted that whereas states such as Wisconsin and Ohio had chapters in virtually every county and community, Missouri had few amateur sleuths who concentrated their work on catching draft dodgers in St. Louis and Kansas City, and that it was "All Quiet Along the Missouri." However, Saunders, himself a private investigator in the St. Louis chapter, estimated that over thirty counties either had their own APL chapter or shared one with a neighboring county.[61]

As more and more Missourians watched each other and interpreted anything associated with Germanness as disloyal behavior, members of the Missouri Council of Defense also became targets. E. M. Grossman, the state chairman of the Missouri chapter of the Four-Minute-Men, learned that defending an accused disloyal person with a German name could have unforeseen consequences. Members of the Missouri state council argued that, through his insistence to excuse Frederick C. Schrader's alleged seditious utterances as personal disagreement and Republican criticism of a Democrat, Grossman had lost his "usefulness" as chairman of the Four-Minute Men. Grossman, believing that it was his "duty as a loyal American to step aside for the good of the nation," resigned his prestigious position on April 2, 1918, a mere fourteen days after he decided to assist Schrader.[62]

In this context of growing suspicions, Governor Gardener's widely reported Third Liberty Loan address on April 8, 1918, acquires great significance. Three days after the Prager lynching in Illinois and the Monat whipping in Jefferson City, he proclaimed: "There can be no half-hearted allegiance at a time like this. . . . A pro German is no better than a spy. . . . If . . . necessary I shall . . . declare martial law . . . suspend the right of habeas corpus and order all enemies of the republic tried by court martial, and, if they be found guilty, . . . they would face a firing squad and thus suffer the fate which traitors so richly deserve. Missouri is no place for traitors while I am Governor!"[63] It was no coincidence that Gardner chose the beginning of the Third Liberty Loan campaign as the occasion to make this speech. As governor he read the major newspapers and received regular reports from the Council of Defense about its efforts to keep the state in line with national guidelines and expectations. Gardner had already expressed his opinion about patriotic enthusiasm on April 5, 1917, well before any government effort to create united public opinion began. Now, one year later, the state, which had received accolades for its patriotic efforts in 1917, was acquiring an image of less-than-perfect patriotism, owing to increasing reports of disloyal activities. Because of the growing paranoia in the United States, it is understandable that the governor moved into a heightened sense of zealous patriotism and believed that it was necessary to speak out forcefully against the perceived enemy within. Possibly Gardner believed he had to appear tough and to distance himself from his past expressions regarding Germany because the council had announced at the Missouri War Conference in January 1918 that it was "imperative to measure every public servant and every political candidate by the standards of unquestioned patriotism and loyalty to the nation." Considering that he had actively courted the German-American vote in 1916 and had future political aspirations, Gardner may have used this speech to demonstrate his personal loyalty to state and nation.[64]

Gardner nevertheless contributed to the growing paranoia as his outspoken anti-German sentiment made the war real and immediate. Several newspapers interpreted his speech as a warning to pro-Germans that they would be treated as spies and placed before firing squads "at sunrise."[65] Missourians immediately responded to Gardner's speech and within a few days flooded the state council with letters reporting disloyal utterances and activities. For example, L. Gibson Adams accused Fritz Schlomann, a wealthy German-American businessman in Hoberg, Lawrence County, of making disloyal utterances, expressing pro-German sympathies, spreading German propaganda, and purchasing only $100 in liberty bonds, although his bank account supposedly had a balance of $2,583.[66]

The Missouri Council of Defense also became more outspoken in April 1918. Articles in *Missouri On Guard* informed readers that "Disloyalty must be stamped out" and that the "suppression of disloyal activities" had become the council's "foremost" task. It warned that every county now had a "committee on disloyalty," whose members kept an "unremitting lookout" for enemy activity. Although officials had not uncovered any "organized enemy movement," they had jailed or interned several individuals who opposed government war activities.[67]

County councils continued to apply their own solutions to dealing with disloyalty cases despite such oversight and William Saunders's attempts to persuade county chairmen to utilize the Sedition Act and the authority of the courts.[68] The Fulton Township Council of Defense and the Callaway County Council, for example, decided to hold a joint meeting to hear the accusations against and the defense of John R. Ebersole. The German-American allegedly stated that money donated to the Red Cross would never reach the soldiers and that the government was "nothing but a set of cut throats [*sic*]." The council decided that signing and publishing a solemn oath of loyalty would publicly humiliate and reform Ebersole. The mail carrier indeed apologized and signed an "Oath of Allegiance" promising to support the United States government and the Constitution, purchase Liberty Bonds according to his ability, subscribe to the Red Cross and the YMCA, and display an American flag in front of his home.[69]

The Audrain County Council of Defense established a "vigilance committee" that visited wealthy residents of the county who had not contributed to the Red Cross and Liberty Loan campaigns according to their financial ability and quickly "secured satisfying results."[70] In Saline County, council members called on the Home Guard Company from Marshall to arrest Ed Leimkuehler, Ed Fischer, Charles Jaeger, and Frank Rose in Saline City for allegedly making pro-German statements. After the foursome swore allegiance to the United States and publicly kissed the American flag, officials released all but Rose, who had failed to register for the draft. He was immediately drafted and assigned to the local quota of troops slated to leave for military training on April 26. The editor of the *Weekly Democrat-News* approvingly argued that "a few more raids . . . no doubt will serve to put a complete end of pro-German talk. . . . [D]isloyal talk of any character will not be tolerated."[71]

As these examples demonstrate, local community leaders became judge and jury and used coercive persuasion and publicity to create a "salutary effect on others of like feeling."[72] German-Americans in particular now experienced increasing pressure to demonstrate their loyalty to country. In reaction, German-American leaders in several communities, including Circuit Court Justice Kelln from Jackson, urged all German-Americans to develop unity in favor of the war and dispel any misunderstandings about loyalty. They also used the local media to encourage patriotism and silence. The editor of the *Sweet Springs Herald* used a subtle approach and reprinted Hermann Hagedorn's article "Where Do You Stand?" without editorial comment. The prominent German-American poet argued that support for America would result in respect; however, opposition to the war would garner bitterness. The *Missouri*

Volksfreund in Jefferson City announced to its readers that under the present circumstances *Schweigen ist Gold* (silence is golden); the newspaper cautioned that people should keep their thoughts to themselves even in the company of closest friends and relatives.[73]

In addition to local and state council scrutiny, Missouri German-Americans also had to worry about national legislation, particularly the Trading-with-the-Enemy Act. Under this act, A. Mitchell Palmer, the alien property custodian, had the authority to confiscate property and securities that belonged to the enemy, that is, any citizen of Germany or person residing in Germany. The custodian eventually confiscated 17,339 properties in the United States, including 648 properties owned by American-born persons living in Germany.[74] In May 1918, the alien property custodian and Council of National Defense requested that state councils help locate enemy-owned property in the United States, even if through "unverified" information.[75] Members of the Missouri council were initially hesitant to use such means, but once Missouri Attorney General Frank W. McAllister declared that the state could legally take land owned by an enemy alien, the council sent Instructional Letter No. 52 to all county councils of defense asked chairmen to survey their counties for property owned by enemy aliens.[76] Although the state council's final report did not state how much property it found, the alien property custodian seized several businesses in St. Louis and took over 23 percent of the Regnier and Shoup Mercantile Company in St. Joseph and 36 percent of the M. Wallstein Mercantile Company in Kansas City.[77] It is unclear what happened to these properties after the war. If owners could prove their American citizenship and loyalty, they could—after a lengthy legal battle—regain full ownership. Property of German nationals remained U.S. property, and the custodian could oversee operation of such property or liquidate it. After amendments to the Trading-with-the-Enemy Act in 1923, German nationals could file claims for up to $10,000 against property the custodian still held in trust or had sold.[78]

Although the alien property custodian did not hesitate to confiscate the property of suspected enemies, only a few county chairmen actually carried out the state council's guidelines. J. Frank Mermoud, chairman of the Barry County Council, aimed to wait until all Women Enemy Aliens had registered on June 20, 1918. This would give him the opportunity to get "all the names of the men as well as the women who are enemy aliens," and he would then be in a "better position to find out and get a record of [their] property."[79] Joe Kirby, the Randolph County Council chairman, despite reminders, had not followed the instructions as late as November 1918 and by then the war was almost over.[80] The Franklin County Council could not send information about enemy-owned property to Jefferson City because several postmasters in the county refused to release the list of registered aliens, arguing that only postal officials had access to such sensitive information.[81] The search for alien-owned property again demonstrates that Missourians did not always follow national or state instructions but maintained control over mobilization and coercion at the local level.

Within this heightened climate of suspicion of anything German, several county council representatives and prominent Missourians agitated for an end to the use of the German language. They argued that the German tongue jarred "the sensitive ears of true Americans," that those using the language might not be loyal Americans and could not be trusted, and that the German language represented a propaganda tool for the enemy because few could understand it. German-Americans might look loyal, but the average American could not distinguish them from German spies planning to sabotage the war effort. In the agitators' opinion, speaking German gave aid and comfort to the enemy.[82] The idea made sense to people during this national emergency. At the same time, removing the most obvious reminder of the enemy offered German-Americans an opportunity to demonstrate loyalty.

German-language newspapers became the obvious targets for the elimination of the enemy tongue. The federal government already scrutinized their content for un-American expressions under the Trading-with-the Enemy Act.[83] By contrast, the state council did not perceive the state's German-language press as a threat but initially hoped to use it to mold public opinion. On the suggestion of the National Council of Defense, and despite "influential men" accusing the council of "coquetting with the German newspapers," the state held a special conference for editors of foreign-language newspapers in St. Louis on June 26, 1918. All but four of Missouri's German-American editors attended and discussed how they could best support the war effort. Robert Glenn, the editor of *Missouri on Guard* and chairman of the conference, suggested that they form a "small sub-committee of loyal German-language editors" to "receive, read and study . . . daily and weekly German-language newspapers . . . with a view to passing on their subject matter." In other words, censor each other. The idea seemed very intriguing to the council but obviously not to the editors. They refused the suggestion without exception because they thought they were already demonstrating their loyalty by printing war-related articles according to government guidelines and did not need censorship of any kind.[84]

The German-language press adopted several strategies that resulted in a balance between ignoring the pressure to conform to public demands and publishing the minimum necessary to demonstrate patriotism, keep censorship at bay, and maintain subscription levels. Daily German-language newspapers in larger cities, such as the *Westliche Post* in St. Louis and the *Missouri Volksfreund* in Jefferson City, competed with daily English-language papers and more often came under the scrutiny of the public eye. They quickly adopted the national war rhetoric, filing translations, passing increasing costs on to their subscribers, and donating certain percentages of space to the Council of Defense, Food Administration, and CPI.[85] It is debatable whether editors cheerfully adopted these measures because they truly supported the war, gave in to readers who threatened to end subscriptions if the paper did not appear more loyal, or aimed to divert the attention of government officials.

Indeed, editors quickly realized that criticism of the government and opposition to the war during the neutrality period and the early days of the war led to reduction in subscription and advertisement rates, the crucial elements for the survival of foreign-language papers, as for any newspaper. The *Sedalia Journal,* which had criticized Wilson's pro-British bias, experienced drastically declining readership owing to its outspokenness, and stopped publication in May 1917.[86] The *Missouri Staats Zeitung* in Kansas City, also outspoken in its criticism of the government during the early days of the war, could possibly have survived the war because of its sizable readership. But the prosecution and conviction under the Espionage Act of its publisher and editor Carl C. Gleeser for arguing that the Selective Service Act was unconstitutional, forced its merger with the competing German-language paper, the *Kansas City Presse.*[87] Although newspapers had to deal with advertiser and readership pressure, there is no evidence in Missouri that German-language newspapers disappeared during transportation or that newspaper boys refused to deliver them or that critics of German-language papers painted publication houses yellow, as happened in Ohio.[88]

Rural newspapers, further removed from the government's influence, adopted publishing strategies that fit their local needs and circumstances. Those who could not afford the costs of translations began to reduce coverage of the war. The *Warrenton Volksfreund* temporarily suspended war coverage until December 1917 to avoid the expenses and inconveniences associated with translating articles and to eliminate possible criticism of supporting one side in the conflict over the other.[89] Others showed only the minimum patriotism necessary to survive without attracting attention and used their privilege not to publish government propaganda. Several papers, including the *Deutsche Volksfreund* and *Missouri Thalbote,* began to print in two languages. Articles of general interest, such as the local and county news, would still appear in the German language, but war-related articles were printed in English.[90] Although several patriotic papers, such as the *Thalbote* in Higginsville and the

Volksfreund in Warrenton, fell to economic pressures, including increasing costs for paper and ink owing to war shortages, ten German-language papers survived despite the war. Interestingly, the few English-language newspapers that reported the end of German papers did so primarily in a matter-of-fact fashion, occasionally expressing regret, but not cheering their demise.[91]

Missourians concerned about the use of the German language also pushed to end its use in public conversations and on the telephone. Sedalia citizens petitioned their city council to pass an ordinance banning the use of German on the streets. Barry County officials debated whether they should pass an ordinance "whereby the German language would not be spoken on the streets of Monett." Cass and Linn county councils responded to public demands and successfully "asked the telephone companies to prohibit the speaking of German over telephones." The Franklin County Council of Defense resolved that conversing in any foreign language in public would be "unwise and un-patriotic" and asked citizens to "speak the American language."[92]

On June 2, 1918, the board of aldermen in Tipton, Moniteau County, passed a resolution to "earnestly request that any and all persons please refrain from conversing in any language except the American language in any public place" within the city limits.[93] The wording of this particular resolution would lead one to believe that this did not mean prohibition of German. Two well-known German citizens of the town found out otherwise. Charles Steinkraus and Fred Dahl, who had been out of town during the aldermen session, unknowingly violated this ordinance and were arrested. Their attorney, S. C. Gill of California, Missouri, who was also the prosecuting attorney of Moniteau County, consulted the state attorney general's office whether the city of Tipton had the authority to pass such an "ordinance." Attorney General McAllister thought the ordinance "a little drastic" but did not "care to attempt to pass upon [its] validity." He admitted, however, that "the German who violates it is in a very poor position to complain" because "the patriotic citizens in a community are not in a frame of mind to tolerate a few Germans 'bowing their necks' over a matter of this kind." He suggested that the accused "plead guilty, pay a nomi-nal fine and hereafter obey the ordinance."[94] During Steinkraus's trial before Mayor F. W. Patterson, the city attorney, J. B. Gallagher, insisted on a one hundred dollar fine. The mayor, however, determined to handle the case as any first offense and fined the defendant twenty-five dollars.[95]

Although the fine may have represented a week's pay for the defendant, the case demonstrates the problems associated with decentralization during the war.[96] Countless individuals questioned the authority of local governments to establish such drastic measures and flooded the Missouri Council of Defense with letters requesting clearly stated guidelines. Members of the state council indeed hesitated to take such drastic steps as prohibiting the speaking of German in public. They instead argued that prominent German-American leaders should lead by example, avoid speaking German in public, and pour their hearts and souls "into the patriotic work against [America's] enemies." "Public sentiment," usually "stronger than law," would persuade others to avoid using the obviously offensive language.[97]

Ironically, the state council had to abandon its German speaker division for that same reason. Persons who could speak German were too few in number, and organizing meetings for "German speaking and German thinking people to be addressed by patriotic Germans" proved very unpopular in a climate of rapidly growing public opposition to the use of German. Max Meyer and the council therefore declared the project "futile" and "a failure" by late June 1918.[98]

Missourians concerned about the use of German also thought that officials should drop German-sounding names from all public accommodations, streets, towns, and schools. Several companies and organizations, hoping to continue their businesses indeed changed their names or dropped the offensive "German" from their title. For example, the board of directors of the German Hospital of Kansas City, well known for its groundbreaking research in medicine, decided to rename it Research Hospital and thus rid the institution of anything that "tends to connect it with Germany" and to show their American patriotism.[99] Initially, the Missouri Council of Defense did not publicly endorse such name-changing efforts because it believed that these were local matters and that municipal authorities were most qualified to deal with them. In September 1918, however, the council reacted to requests for more centralized leadership and announced that "citizens of all towns and communities in the state named for German functionaries or towns be requested to change [their] names."[100] But Missouri did not go as far as Wisconsin, where the state legislature allowed even underage children to change their German-sounding names without the consent of parents.[101]

To many English-speaking Missourians it also made sense to remove German from religious services and parochial schools because German churches had been quite successful in maintaining German education, tradition, and language. This perceived maintenance of a separate identity created suspicion among Americans. Missourians, like many Americans, associated German Catholics with the Pope and feared his potential influence. They were particularly suspicious of Lutherans whom they directly associated with Germany and whose pastors refused to endorse war bonds and did not offer church property for war rallies because such actions violated liturgical propriety and the separation of church and state. Registration of enemy aliens in February 1918 had also revealed that 70 percent of all Lutheran pastors living in the United States were born in Germany. Yet German-American Catholics, Lutherans, and Jews did not experience the destruction of property and physical beatings that, for example, the Hutterites in South Dakota did.[102]

Missourians, instead, used "public sentiment" or "friendly persuasion" to achieve results. The Zion Evangelical Church in St. Joseph discontinued its German services and dropped the word "German" from its name in late April 1918. The congregational meeting of St. John's Lutheran Church in Hannibal voted to eliminate the two remaining German services it offered every month because it was "practically an English congregation" and dispensed with German classes at its parochial school as well. The Evangelical Reformed Church of Zoar in Bates County had persisted in conducting all of its services in German until the spring of 1918, but this led to "much local friction in that community," and so the congregation "resolved to use the English language exclusively."[103]

The majority of the clerics, however, resisted the demands to abandon German church services entirely. Indeed, many pastors in German churches in Missouri already conducted services in English and German, divided as morning and evening services or held on alternate Sundays. Allen Greebuer, pastor of Salisbury, and Charles Bunger, pastor of Cole Camp, however, reasoned that dropping German altogether would be a great injustice to the older church members. Surely, no one would want to deprive loyal Americans the right to hear "the Gospel in the language they understand." A. W. Mueller, the Lutheran pastor of Forest Green, had a problem many German pastors shared. He would be willing to preach in English if he could speak the language well enough. The congregation promptly appointed Reverend A. Graegner from Salisbury as his assistant to conduct one monthly sermon in English.[104]

The leaders of the Lutheran Church–Missouri Synod left the decision of transition to English to ministers based on local need. They did not agree, however, on how to react to the demands of demonstrating patriotism. For example, by December 1917, Theodore Graebner, a professor at Concordia Seminary in St. Louis and the son of August L. Graebner, who had agitated for transition to English in the synod in the 1890s, became a strong advocate for cooperation with the government. As the editor of the *Lutheran Witness,* Graebner aimed to convince everyone that Lutherans were patriotic Americans, that the use of German did not evidence German sympathies or support of the kaiser's government; he maintained that being a patriotic American also meant having the right to criticize. He published reports of Lutheran parochial schools displaying the American flag, school children listening to

speakers, teachers selling War Savings Stamps in their classes, and congregations resolving to buy Liberty Bonds. His editorials in the *Witness* also argued
that the national government had the right to enlist churches to communi-
cate important messages during a national emergency, implored his readers to
avoid criticism of the war, and predicted trouble if the synod did not demonstrate its loyalty.[105] In contrast, ultraconservative leaders and the editor of *Der
Lutheraner* remained silent until April 1918 when growing anti-German sentiment finally convinced them to endorse the Food Administration and the Red
Cross. According to one historian of the synod, the Treasury Department's request for Liberty Bond purchase reports convinced synod president Frederick
Pfotenhauer to overcome aversion to political involvement, endorse pastors
as patriotic speakers, and cooperate with the war effort. He, however, insisted
that individual pastors should make decisions based on local circumstances.
In June 1918 the synod also established the War-Time Bureau to oversee distribution of government information as well as to advise congregations and
pastors accused of disloyalty and to represent them before state officials.[106]

The Missouri Council of Defense entered the debate as well and used the approach of persuasion and sympathy to maintain peace and order. The council,
for example, established an honor roll of churches and parochial schools that
adopted the English language as their official language. Secretary Saunders also
preferred peer pressure as a powerful force to persuade preachers to change their
habits. For example, he wrote to the Reverend William A. Richter, pastor of the
German Lutheran Church in Jefferson City, and asked him to use his influence
on the Reverend Paul M. Breitag, pastor of the German Lutheran Church in
Creighton, Missouri, because Breitag "was not showing the proper attitude" toward the English language.[107] Council officials were also very sympathetic to the
spiritual needs of older church members as well as the Amish who spoke only
in German. They suggested that pastors continue "the use of German where it
would be more or less necessary," such as priests hearing confessions or performing religious rites primarily for "the older German people" while also opening
church buildings for patriotic meetings.[108] The Council of National Defense
strongly endorsed this "tactful" and "statesman-like method" of dealing with
the sensitive subject of religious freedom during a national emergency.[109]

Although most of the clergy were willing to implement this agreeable compromise, by July council members had nevertheless become disappointed that
not all churches were accommodating, and they saw this as inviting disorder.
They now interpreted the argument that adoption of English did not prove
loyalty as stubbornness and defiance. To coerce compliance William Saunders
implied that the legislature would "undoubtedly" pass legislation targeted at

churches that still used the German language during its upcoming session in January 1919.[110]

Several concerned Missourians hoped to wipe the German language from the curriculum in parochial and public schools. Many believed as did W. S. Dearmont, the president of the Missouri State Normal School in Cape Girardeau, that religious freedom did not include the teaching of the enemy's tongue in parochial school. He argued that teaching of German was one of the "greatest hindrances to the proper education of children," resulting in thousands of German-Americans dropping out of school because they never learned to properly speak or read English. This, he believed, also had a negative impact on the state's economy.[111]

The battle against the German language in the public schools was more successful than its removal from churches because in this case centralized authority and clearly stated power existed at the national, state, and local level. The U.S. commissioner of education, P. P. Claxton, objected to eliminating German as a subject from the high school and university curricula but opposed the teaching of German in elementary grades and insisted that English be the language of instruction in all public, private, and parochial schools.[112] Missouri Superintendent of Schools Uel W. Lamkin did not "entirely" object to teaching foreign languages in high school and universities but believed that knowledge of the English language was absolutely necessary for life in America and argued that English should be the language of instruction even in communities where foreign-born citizens controlled the school board. He also believed that the state legislature "should lose no time in passing a law requiring all instruction in all elementary schools . . . in the English language only."[113] By state law, Lamkin had the authority to instruct superintendents to investigate the qualifications of teachers and to update curriculum. Lamkin, upon the state council's decision, used this power to revoke J. W. Lind's teaching certificate because his refusal to teach his pupils how to salute the flag allegedly made him unfit as a teacher.[114]

Lamkin also pointed out that "local school boards," under Missouri statute, had "final authority" to control the curriculum taught at a school.[115] The board of directors of the School District of St. Joseph, for example, believed that the language of the "degenerate" Prussian regime had to be destroyed to make the world "safe for democracy." The board, therefore, resolved to abolish "the study of the German language in the public schools of St. Joseph" as a step toward "obliterating Prussian influence and power forever from the face of the earth." In Kirksville, the school board removed German from the high school curriculum because it thought that a teacher "could not conscientiously teach German anymore."[116] In heavily German-American populated areas, such as Westphalia in Osage County, the opposite could be true. There, board members determined to keep German not only as a teachable subject but also as the language of instruction. But the mounting internal and external pressure to stop the use of German had an impact even in Hermann, Missouri's most German city. The school board decided during the summer of 1918 to cease instruction in German and to suspend the teaching of the language for the duration of the war.[117] Colleges and universities also gave in to the pressures to discontinue the study of German, at least for the duration of the war. William Woods College barred German from its curriculum to evade "German ruthlessness" and its source for propaganda.[118]

The nationwide antipathy toward anything German grew so strong by July 1918 that the Missouri Council of Defense finally decided to take an official stand on the subject. It abandoned its German-speaking section of the speakers' bureau because a speaker who aimed to address an audience in German would "quite likely be ordered to stop his address . . . by the local authorities."[119] On July 12, 1918, the council also released an official proclamation opposing "the use of the German language in the schools, churches, and lodges and in public meetings of every character." It considered the adoption of English "a national duty," as "essential to the development of a true patriotic sentiment among all the people," and "as the clearest evidence of loyalty." The state superintendent of schools reinforced the council's announcement with a public statement that elementary and high schools as well as the state's normal schools could no longer teach the "Hun language."[120]

The council, however, quickly learned that the resolution did not clear up confusion over legal authority and enforcement powers. Numerous churches and German organizations never stopped the use of German, or they suspended its use only temporarily. The Lawrence County Council of Defense was unable to convince the pastor of the Lutheran Church, teachers in its Sunday school, and congregation members to abandon the use of German. In Franklin County, German-American preachers refused to abide by the state council's proclamation because it was not an "order abolishing the use of [German]."[121] Indeed, enforcement of any language resolution remained a major problem throughout the war and county council chairmen, such as Franklin H. Kean from St. Louis County, were surprised to hear that persuasion and coercion were the only tools available to them.[122]

Why was that the case? Missouri's General Assembly was not in session between April 1917 and January 1919. This is one important factor that sets Missouri apart from its midwestern neighbors. The Missouri Council of Defense, unlike councils in other states, did not have legislative approval, and thus they had limited enforcement powers. The council could use only such powers as the Council of National Defense and the governor delegated. It is unclear why Governor Gardner did not call the General Assembly into special session and secure more power for the state council, but he may have believed it was not necessary. After all, the Council of National Defense declared state councils as the "official organization to correlate and centralize all voluntary activity relating to the war" and also as "otherwise independent state bodies" that could "adapt national programs to local conditions."[123] Missouri council leaders simply followed these instructions, acted as the central organizing and supervising agency in prosecuting the war effort, established county councils, and delegated most responsibilities for fund-raising and volunteer work to them. Zealous county council members interpreted this empowerment to mean they could control the behavior of suspected pro-Germans and limit the use of the German language. That did not mean that the Missouri Council of Defense lost control to local authorities, as one historian argued happened in several midwestern states.[124] Instead, leaders such as Chairman Mumford and Secretary Saunders believed that enforcement of national guidelines was the responsibility of local entities. As long as Missouri maintained its label as a patriotic state the state council did not interfere in the activities of county councils.

Missouri government leaders also were more tolerant and tried to preserve law and order through persuasion and lessen the intensity of any anti-German frenzy by arguing that "Loyal and Zealous Americans should refrain from violence and disorder" and under no circumstances oppress or physically harm "any class of our citizens." They, however, supported verbal coercion that curtailed the freedom of speech and religion as a necessity of war and to maintain Missouri's image as a loyal state. The Americanization Committee of the state council also resolved to petition the General Assembly in its 1919 session "to pass a law prohibiting the teaching of any language except English language in all public and parochial schools in Missouri."[125] But during the war, no state law existed forbidding the use of German. Indeed, Saunders suggested that county councils print a statement to that effect in the newspapers—simply advising, not threatening, against the use of German.[126] Although such published advisement may have encouraged further intimidation where it already existed, the statement would have also empowered German-speakers to more comfortably continue using the language where there was no serious pressure to give it up. An in-depth study of the experience in St. Louis as well as Gasconade and Osage County will reveal the circumstances that contributed to coercion or the absence thereof in these areas.

FOUR

From the "Most American City" to Seeing German Ghosts Everywhere

St. Louis during the Great War

German Propaganda Is Busy in St. Louis

—St. Louis Globe-Democrat

Newspaper headlines such as "The Alien Enemy Problem," "Plot to Invade U.S. Is Bared," and "U.S. Discovers Spies Work in St. Louis Cafes" taught St. Louisans to fear the German enemy as early as March 1917. As a major metropolitan area in the Midwest, St. Louis possessed the necessary transportation and communication links to larger eastern centers and thus had ready access to government information on the war effort. During the neutrality period, residents of St. Louis learned more about the war and suspected German sabotage activities than rural areas. At the same time, the city's large labor and mixed ethnic population did not hesitate to express varied opinions about the war, and the activism of a number of organizations contributed to growing mistrust and the potential for unrest. Once the United States prepared for and entered the war, government regulations also affected St. Louisans more directly than most Missourians. More important, newspaper reports revealing the number of voting enemy aliens in St. Louis, who according to state law had the right to vote and thus influence municipal elections and rumors that the Busch family had funneled millions of dollars into German propaganda confirmed that the enemy also lurked within.[1] As a result, St. Louisans defined the enemy much sooner and in ethnic terms, were more easily frightened, and more likely to spy on each other, accuse neighbors of disloyal behavior, turn them over to the authorities, and use intimidation and violence to deal with perceived disloyal behavior.

After the discovery of spies in St. Louis and a mayoral campaign that included the loyalty issue, it is not surprising that St. Louisans believed they had to express their allegiance to the nation on the eve of war. On April 3, 1917, several German-American leaders, as would their counterparts in Chicago, Cincinnati, and Milwaukee a few days later, declared their fidelity to the United States and their support for the president after his speech to Congress. On the evening before Congress declared war, St. Louis also held a loyalty rally at the Coliseum and Governor Fredrick D. Gardner read a proclamation from St. Louis citizens declaring that they stood behind President Wilson and would aid him in securing a "lasting world peace."[2]

St. Louis, in fact, quickly organized for the war effort in response to Wilson's call for service and conservation. Before Governor Gardner could establish the Council of Defense, the St. Louis Chamber of Commerce created the Federated Committee on Food Conservation for Missouri and the Women's Central Committee on Food Conservation, later renamed the St. Louis Food Administration chapter and the Woman's Committee of the Missouri Council of Defense.[3] Indeed, middle-class women from the more affluent western wards were among the first volunteers, reflecting their tradition of club and social activism in the city. The suffrage thrift league of St. Louis and the Catholic Women's League organized local gardening and canning clubs. Members of the Woman's Committee gave speeches urging food conservation, held regular canning classes, and opened several demonstration kitchens, including one at the Famous Barr Dry Goods Company. More than one hundred St. Louis women volunteered for Americanization work, taught French to soldiers, and filled positions men had left when they were drafted. During the Hoover Registration in July, Zitella Bass and Carrie Nugent broke records for organizing "a ward and precinct machine" of over 35,000 women in less than two weeks' time. They advertised this registration of housewives "into a national thrift army" as a way to support the war in home and kitchen and as an important opportunity for women to demonstrate their social and professional worth to society. When compared to Chicago's 10,000 and Pittsburgh's 23,000 signatures, reflecting less than 1 percent and 7.8 percent of their respective total female populations, St. Louis could proudly boast an 8.9 success rate, which in their opinion demonstrated a high degree of patriotism. This activism and extensive organization of women in St. Louis also received the approval of Herbert Hoover and served as a model for food conservation and female patriotism in other cities.[4]

In April, the Chamber of Commerce also organized an Americanization committee, chaired by James R. Dunn, chief of U. S. Immigration Service in St. Louis, and encouraged immigrants to become naturalized citizens through programs in schools, churches, and worker unions and advertisements in foreign-language newspapers. The war seemed to justify such intense assimilation efforts. By May 1917, in time for the First Liberty Loan Campaign, St. Louis already had Four-Minute Men addressing movie theater audiences during reel changes about the reasons for the war and the necessity to purchase war bonds. And by June 1917, the St. Louis Council of Defense was fully established and oversaw the war effort in the city, much sooner than in the majority of rural counties.[5]

Although such early activism demonstrated the loyalty of St. Louis in general, the fear of the enemy also remained real because St. Louisans continued to read and hear about German sabotage and spy activities elsewhere in the United States.[6] More important, the arrest of thirty-five Germans for disloyal remarks or actions in May demonstrated that the enemy also lurked in St. Louis. The increase in Justice Department surveillance, for example, discovered that several cooks and waiters from St. Louis were part of a nationwide spy ring. Newspapers fanned the flames of fear by arguing that "there is nothing Germany is not capable of if she thinks it will serve her ends" and that Americans had to guard themselves and their nation at all times.[7]

President Wilson's request for security zones near major transportation hubs and military installations resulted in the division of St. Louis into restricted zones that stretched from the Mississippi River in the east to 15th Street in the west and from Chouteau Avenue in the south to Brooklyn Avenue in the north. This engulfed the greater downtown area and included several theaters, city hall, the post office, municipal court buildings, Wagner Electric Company and Curtis Company, as well as the *Westliche Post* and *Amerika* (see figure 4.1). Alien enemies, that is, individuals born in Germany or the Austrian Empire and not citizens of the United States, had to move out of the restricted zone, request passes to work there by July 1, 1917, and obtain character references from employers and American citizens. The *Westliche Post* urged Germans to follow the law to eliminate suspicion and possible internment for the duration of the war.[8] These government regulations that restricted the movement of alien enemies and required them to turn in their firearms now clearly identified Germans as the enemy to America. Subsequent arrest and internment of 154 "alien enemies" for living in the restricted zones or for working there without passes demonstrated to many St. Louisans that they could not be trusted.[9]

St. Louisans thus knew the enemy during the early months of the war and the consequences if they behaved in an un-American or pro-German manner.

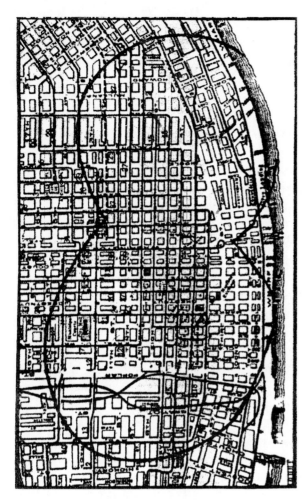

FIGURE 4.1. Restricted zones. "Die Sperrzonen der unteren Stadt," *Westliche Post*, May 21, 1917.

As a result, loyalty and patriotism were clearly defined as being either American or not by the summer of 1917, much sooner than in most of Missouri, especially the rural areas. St. Louisans were confident that nearly all German-speakers were peaceful and "anxious to get along with their American neighbors," however, some including the editor of the *St. Louis Republic* predicted trouble.[10]

Indeed, those who publicly expressed pro-German sentiment quickly learned the consequences. On the day that the United States officially entered the conflict, St. Louisans had to deal with "a gang of pro Germans" who tore American flags from homes in a four-block area of Page Boulevard, ripped them into shreds and trampled on them. Women in the neighborhood quickly organized "Home Flag Guards" to prevent desecration of new flags and promised to shoot anyone who might try to destroy any flags.[11] The wealthy and famous were not immune from suspicion. Several female members of Liederkranz's mixed chorus, later identified as a "clique of irreconcilable pro-Germans," created an incident at the Odeon when they refused to sing the "Star-Spangled Banner." After the vigorous remonstration of spectators, conductor Ernst Prang Schramm resolved the embarrassing predicament by striking the opening bars of the anthem thus forcing the chorus to sing along with the audience.[12] Edna Gellhorn, a well-known suffragist in Missouri, daughter of Dr. Washington E. Fischel and wife of Dr. George Gellhorn, was unable to chair the Woman's Central Committee on Food Conservation because concerned citizens thought that she, her husband, and family held pro-German views, owing to the arrest of Dr. Gellhorn's brother in Scotland in 1916 for allegedly spying.[13]

Expression of anti-American or pro-German sentiment could also result in altercations as early as May 1917. John H. Zimmer, a naturalized citizen, appeared to threaten Navy recruiter Elmer E. Steele when in response to the latter's "fiery, patriotic speech" he rose from his seat, shook his fist in the air, and allegedly cursed Steele. Members of the audience, enraged, rose and shouted, "Get that fellow! . . . Hit him!" Steele ordered his squad to rescue Zimmer from the mob to avoid a riot. With their pistols drawn, six sailors rushed the crowd, compelled it to step back, and led Zimmer from the Kings Theater to the nearest police station where he was arrested for disturbing the peace.[14]

In reaction to such events, many St. Louisans quickly eliminated anything that could identify them with the enemy. Several officials, such as former judge Wilbur F. Boyle and former police chief Matthew Kiely, threw away awards they had received in 1902 during Prince Henry's visit to the city.[15] Because newspaper editors also associated socialism with Germanism, especially after the Socialist Party had proclaimed its opposition to the war on April 7, 1917, through its "St. Louis Proclamation," several German-Americans withdrew their membership thus further weakening the St. Louis chapter of the party. Members of the Central Trades and Labor Union also hoped to eliminate any possible pro-German accusations by electing a "safe" candidate, P. J. Grimes, as president over Peter Beisel, a known Socialist, German-American, and outspoken opponent of the war.[16]

German immigrants and their descendants living in St. Louis now had to decide where they stood in this conflict because they could no longer be something in between American and German. Most probably continued to support Germany in private; publicly, however, they abandoned overt association with the old fatherland and followed the suggestion of the *Westliche Post* that in order to eliminate mistrust and suspicion it was best to keep critical thoughts to themselves and to do their duty quietly. They proclaimed heartfelt loyalty to America and did what was necessary to divert attention and eliminate the possibility of disloyalty charges. Those who were not yet citizens applied for naturalization papers; so many did that the naturalization office ran out of applications by May.[17] August A. Busch ordered the removal of portraits of German notables, which had originally been part of the 1904 World's Fair, from the Anheuser-Busch Brewery in order to avoid scuffles between workers and the perception that the company held pro-German views. The central verein resolved that love for mankind surpassed any love for former country and advocated that every member of the Catholic faith knowing this duty do his utmost to follow the law and the government guidelines during the war. Members of the German-American Alliance, still under suspicion and, in reaction to President Kurt von Reppert's comparing Wilson to an "ape," attempted to dissociate themselves from its pro-German reputation through the forced resignation of officers and public condemnation of the kaiser.[18] By early September 1917, even the CTLU and associated unions dominated by German-Americans decided to end their antiwar stance and turn Labor Day into a patriotic celebration.[19]

Dissociating oneself from articles or persons that could be interpreted as pro-German and proclaiming one's loyalty were initially quite successful. In August 1917 the *Republic* conducted an in-depth study in St. Louis of the attitudes regarding war of immigrants from twenty-nine nations. It concluded that the approximately 150,000 foreign-born living in St. Louis in 1917, including Germans, were loyal to the United States.[20]

St. Louisans had ample opportunity to demonstrate that loyalty to the United States. For men the easiest way to do that was to volunteer for military service. However, St. Louis men did not sign up for the guard, army, and especially the navy in the numbers that the War Department expected. The city quickly fell behind Des Moines, Indianapolis, and Omaha in its recruitment efforts and, according to the *Republic,* acquired a "stigma of shame" and the label of "slacker city."[21] The solutions to the problem were appeals to patriotism, constant reminders of slacker status, and a special patriotic rally. These efforts resulted in Washington University's organizing a complete ambulance corps and the 21st Hospital Unit and 967 men volunteering within a record fourteen days for the Fifth Regiment of the Missouri National Guard, an entirely new infantry regiment. St. Louis soon ranked in second place among Midwest recruiting stations for the army and marines. A "monster military review" at Forest Park in May and a military parade at Jefferson Barracks in August celebrated this success and evidence of patriotism in St. Louis.[22]

The passage of the Selective Service Act on May 18, 1917, brought the draft to St. Louis. A *St. Louis Republic* survey of theatergoers found that they

supported universal military service. The *Westliche Post* reflected that conscription was fair. Although eligible men had to abide by the law and register,
they also had the right to use exemptions as long as the reasons were honest.
Yet the editor strongly and somewhat sarcastically urged German-Americans
to abide by the act because the "Eye of the Law is obviously watching us with
particular love and attentiveness."[23] The majority of St. Louis men indeed
followed the law, and 76,511 eligible men registered with Selective Service on
June 5, including 5,828 noncitizens and 503 individuals born in Germany or
the Austrian Empire.[24]

During the subsequent examinations in August and September for the
first draft or call-up, local boards quickly realized that nearly 62 percent of
registrants used all the legal exemptions available to them to stay out of the
military and war. Although St. Louis did not differ from the national average,
examination boards, like so many across the United States, had greatly under-
estimated the number of exemptions and physical disabilities. Board members had to call additional registrants for examination to meet their quota
of 5,430 men and reexamined the physically disqualified, especially those ex-
cused for "trivial physical defects." Realizing that the majority of exemption
requests came from the upscale western wards, boards shamed wealthy men
who claimed that they were the sole support for the family into taking back
their exemption claims.[25]

Those who did not register or did not show up for examination quickly
learned the legal repercussions if they were discovered. Police canvassed the
city to find draft dodgers. Although the *St. Louis Republic* estimated that 1,000
men were arrested, the federal grand jury indicted only forty-eight of them for
failure to register under Section 5 of the Selective Service Act. Arno B. Pallme,
who did not register in the Eleventh Ward, pled guilty, explaining that as a
Socialist he opposed the war. Eastern District Court Judge David P. Dyer sentenced him to ten weeks in the city jail, released him for time already served
and ordered him to register with the local board. In March 1918, Pallme was
inducted into the military, and he served as a medic overseas between June
1918 and July 1919.[26]

Although Pallme had German-born parents, census records for the remaining
defendants indicate that the prosecution of draft dodgers did not disproportionately target German-Americans. Nor did Pallme, as a German-American,
receive harsher punishment. Sentences for the eighty-eight draft dodgers convicted in St. Louis District Court between 1917 and 1920 ranged from $10
to $100 fines or one day to six months in the St. Louis City Jail. Most were
released immediately for time already served and followed Judge Dyer's order

to register with the local board. In accordance with the rules of the District Appeals Board that all convicted slackers were automatically drafted, the majority of those convicted before November 1918 were subsequently inducted into service, and one volunteered for the navy.[27]

Men who were not eligible for service in the army, navy, or National Guard could still serve their country in a military capacity by joining the Home Guards, which had been created to take over the duties of the National Guard after President Wilson ordered it into federal service. Home Guard recruiting parades and the slogan "Protect Your Homes" resulted in over 1,500 men, including a seventy-four-year-old veteran, volunteering and several individuals and companies donating over $67,000 for uniforms and supplies. By August 1917, St. Louis had completed the recruitment for the First Regiment, and companies were already drilling each day. So many men volunteered that the adjutant general authorized the creation of the Second Regiment of Home Guards. Entrusted by the governor with the duty of protecting the city and instilling patriotism, the Home Guard drum corps and drill unit also participated in many events, including the rally for the Christmas Red Cross Campaign at the Coliseum in December 1917 and the unveiling of the Liberty Statue on April 11, 1918. Governor Gardner and Mayor Kiel interpreted such eagerness to serve as clear evidence of patriotism in St. Louis.[28]

In addition to the military, entire families could also serve their country and proclaim their patriotism through the signing of the Family Hoover Pledge, supporting the Red Cross and purchasing War Savings Stamps. In November 1917, police deputies participated in the Hoover Pledge campaign, going house to house, and within three days had raised the number of pledge signatures from 125,000 to 267,927. Seeing a policeman at the door asking for a signature possibly coerced many to sign the pledge. Consequently, despite pockets of "bitter opposition," more than one third of the St. Louis population or 322,061 persons signed the pledge to conserve food.[29] St. Louis oversubscribed its Red Cross fund-raising quota in June 1917 and May 1918, and an estimated 500,000 St. Louisans became members during the Christmas campaign, thus demonstrating "true and fervent patriotism."[30] War Savings Stamps were popular means to express one's support for the war; the "princely sum" of twenty-five cents for a savings stamp offered even the poor and children the opportunity to invest some money in the future. Postmaster Colin M. Selph established a unique approach to demonstrate patriotism. St. Louis women earned the privilege to kiss a sailor for every $5 War Savings Stamp they purchased.[31]

Investment in the four Liberty Loans, however, became the most effective method to prove one's loyalty. Contributions to the First Liberty Loan

Campaign were slow at first because the Committee on Public Information had not yet inundated the country with advertising material, and the Liberty Loan committee had to resort to the publication of contributor lists to shame the wealthy into subscribing according to their income. Locally produced movies, posters, and slogans, such as "A Liberty Bond in Every Home," subsequently adopted and distributed by the CPI, demonstrated St. Louis's patriotism (see figure 4.2). Individuals could also publicly display their loyalty because they received a Liberty Button for every Liberty Bond they bought. Through these efforts, St. Louis eventually oversubscribed its $25 million quota by $17 million and an estimated 50,000 households owned a bond, a good start to fulfill the slogan.[32]

The Second Liberty Loan Campaign in October 1917 began slowly, and St. Louis acquired the label of "slacker city." However, the arrival of CPI-produced advertisements and bond posters explaining the reasons for the war and the necessity to purchase bonds throughout St. Louis and in English- and German-language newspapers, a special "Liberty Loan Drive," and huge individual and business investments in bonds eventually brought the city over its $68 million quota.[33]

By April 1918, and in time for the Third Liberty Loan Campaign, the CPI and Liberty Loan committee had become fully organized and experienced in transmitting information throughout the United States. Nevertheless, purchase of bonds was slow, and St. Louis again acquired the "slacker" label. Secretary of the Treasury William McAdoo cancelled his trip to St. Louis because he was disappointed with the city's contributions. Consequently, the loan committee adopted more coercive measures. Published contributor lists no longer aimed to shame but promised secret service investigations for those who did not invest in the war. Now, appeals targeted German-Americans in particular and asserted bonds were not just good investments but evidence of loyalty that would assure their recognition as true Americans. The previously antiwar CTLU now voted to use $500 of its $587.74 in available funds to purchase Liberty Bonds. Intimidation, in-depth organization, intense advertisement, and huge mass meetings finally brought about the desired result when during the last day of the campaign St. Louis surpassed its quota.[34]

In September 1918 the Fourth Liberty Loan campaign began with much enthusiasm and support; newspapers encouraged Americans to dig deep into their pockets one more time for the final push toward victory. The loan committee again maintained lists of contributors, ascribed a per capita quota of $50, and bond salesmen received the authority to use all measures necessary, including American Protective League (APL) investigations, to increase the

FIGURE 4.2. First Liberty Loan poster. During the First Liberty Loan Campaign the majority of posters used in St. Louis were produced locally. The Committee on Public Information eventually used the slogan "A Liberty Bond in Every Home," initiated in St. Louis, throughout the United States. *St. Louis Republic*, May 24, 1917.

sale of bonds. Despite the increased concern about the influenza epidemic, St. Louis again oversubscribed its quota with an average subscription of $115.[35]

These contributions and compliance with government guidelines represented obvious evidence of patriotism. St. Louis's diverse ethnic groups, especially Poles and Italians, reinforced this notion with several loyalty rallies and parades. On President Wilson's urging, the city celebrated the contributions and patriotism of residents from twenty nations during the Fourth of July festivities, dedicated to loyal immigrants. The Chamber of Commerce must have been correct when it claimed after a detailed study that St. Louis was the "most American city" because Red Cross contributions and Liberty Bond sales were much higher than those in cities such as Boston, Chicago, and Milwaukee.[36]

St. Louisans, however, remained uneasy. The simmering anti-German sentiment in St. Louis began to boil over in December 1917 after St. Louis Secret Service Chief Steve Connell and U.S. District Attorney Arthur L. Oliver announced a new approach to dealing with slackers in the city. They promised that draft evaders, enemies, traitors, and every disloyal man and woman, regardless of social position, would be arrested and prosecuted to the fullest extent of the law.[37] From that point on, life in St. Louis changed. Newspaper reports and CPI information in 1918 constantly reminded the population of alleged spy activities in the nation and in St. Louis, and that the persistent presence of pro-Germanism marked the city as disloyal. St. Louisans now became even more watchful and aware of persons who might oppose the war or aid the enemy. The editor of the *St. Louis Republic,* for example, announced that the paper would publicly denounce any current officeholder and future candidate for office, regardless of political affiliation, if such person expressed "lukewarm patriotism," made pro-German comments, and placated Germans in the United States.[38]

Federal legislation intended to limit the activities of the German enemy also contributed to the heightened awareness of his presence. Alien enemy men had to register at police stations in February 1918 and female alien enemies had to register in June 1918. The registration of over 5,000 German-born men and 2,684 women who had not yet become U. S. citizens demonstrated how many alien enemies actually lived in the city. These included several American-born women who had married German nationals because, according to the 1907 Naturalization Law, a husband bequeathed his citizenship to his wife upon their marriage, even if she was born in the United States.[39]

The Trading-with-the-Enemy Act also illustrated to unsuspecting St. Louisans how widespread German influence had been. Under this act, A. Mitchell Palmer, the alien property custodian, had the authority to confiscate property and securities in the United States that belonged to the enemy, including any citizen of Germany, person residing in Germany, or corporation conducting business in any of the Central Power nations. The property custodian placed into trust enemy interests in a number of St. Louis–based firms: Finck Estate, Griesedieck Real Estate Company, Northern Fur Company, Szilassy Investment Company, and William B. Tamm Investment Company. St. Louis police also discovered that the alien property custodian would take possession of a stolen car because the insurance company that had already paid the owner for his loss belonged to a German corporation.[40]

The Busch family experienced that the act did not exempt U.S. citizens from losing property. Clara von Gontard and Wilhelmine Scharrer, the American-born daughters of Adolphus Busch, had married German citizens, lived in Germany, and technically were German citizens through marriage. Palmer confiscated both their inheritances, which amounted to two-eighths of the entire Busch estate. Eliza "Lilly" Busch, the widow of Adolphus Busch and a U.S. citizen through her father and husband, had visited her daughters in 1914 and decided to remain there in case one of her daughters should become a widow. Consequently, she lost her inherited estate, consisting of one-eighth stock ownership of the Anheuser-Busch Brewery and property in California worth millions of dollars. Mrs. Busch, after hearing about the loss, immediately left Germany and upon her return from a harrowing journey filed the necessary forms to reclaim her property, but the news remained gloomy.[41] Palmer refused to release her property even after the signing of the Armistice, arguing that Mrs. Busch was born in Germany, had become a naturalized citizen only through her father, that her daughters were married to influential German nationals, and she had lived for over nine months in Germany after the United States declared war. Her activities in Germany, such as contributing millions of dollars to hospitals and turning her home into a rehabilitation center for German soldiers, fit the interpretation of aiding and abetting the enemy, and she had returned to America only to regain her property. The family's attorneys and political influence that reached all the way to the White House finally broke the impasse and she regained her property in December 1918. Ironically, Mrs. Busch also learned that the German government had seized her small estate in that country as alien property shortly after her departure.[42]

The city became a center of name changes, job losses, violence, and legal action in Missouri. The *St. Louis Republic* was instrumental in a widespread name-changing campaign. Initially, the paper did not support the efforts that cities, such as Chicago, undertook to change the German names of towns or streets, because Americans should acknowledge the contributions of German people such as Steuben and Schurz. However, by April 1918 the editor had changed his opinion and initiated a citywide campaign changing street names from offensive-sounding German to acceptable American names in order to "Make St. Louis 100 percent American."[43] This resulted in the renaming of Berlin Avenue to Pershing Avenue, Kaiser Street to Gresham Street, Von Versen Avenue to Enright Street, and Knapstein Place to Providence Place. When compared to Chicago (where municipal government changed 76 of 115 German-sounding street names), Cincinnati (changed 20 of 102 names), and Milwaukee (changed 4 of 41 names), St. Louis fared quite well with 4 of 124 German-sounding street names changed.[44] Several companies, such as the German Mutual Life Insurance Company, also decided to drop the word German from their title to express their Americanism and to survive as businesses. The German-American Bank changed its name to United States Bank of St. Louis; the German Savings Bank became the Liberty Bank of St. Louis; and the German Theater changed its name to Victoria Theater.[45]

Several German-Americans lost their employment because of their real or alleged pro-German sentiments. The Champion Shoe Machinery Company dismissed Oscar Seifert after he allegedly stated that Wilson ought to be lynched. Brown Shoe Company fired Cuenda Westphalen after eighty-five of her co-workers threatened to go on strike to demand her dismissal because she had not purchased any bonds. The "highly patriotic" Mary Institute, the girls' preparatory school for Washington University, dismissed Auguste Harkort, a naturalized citizen born in Austria, who had been the French teacher for twelve years, because she had expressed pro-German views in 1914. The St. Louis Musicians Union dismissed nine members because they were enemy aliens and suspended eleven for one week until they had filed their second and final citizenship application papers.[46]

Everything German became suspect. The St. Louis Symphony excluded the music of German composers from its concert season. Libraries removed German books from shelves. City police denied Fritz Kreisler, a renowned violin virtuoso, entry into St. Louis because he was an Austrian citizen, thus an enemy alien, and the Odeon Theater where he had an engagement was located inside the forbidden zone. Patriotic Missourians attributed suspicious vandalism and fires to Germans. German sympathizers allegedly wrecked the Hammett Place Christian Church in St. Louis, tore an American flag and a service flag to shreds, and wrote "Kaiser Bill" on the church blackboard. Editorials called the event a "Flagrant Case of Disloyalty" and stated that even "American hoodlums" would not commit such an outrageous act.[47]

Even the Anheuser-Busch brewing firm could no longer escape accusations of disloyalty although the company had associated itself with Americanism and patriotism from the day the war began in Europe in 1914 and had promptly cooperated with every government agency and liberally assisted the United States after the nation's entry into the global conflict. The company's subscription to Liberty Loans ran in the millions, its Red Cross contributions were the highest in St. Louis, and its service flag contained 150 stars, representing the number of employees who served on the front.[48] Prominence, nevertheless, made the business and its owners easy targets. One rumor alleged that the Budweiser label carried the German emblem, because there was a Russian eagle in one corner and an American eagle in the other corner of the label. To quiet the gossip that had benefited the competition and to remove the stigma of disloyalty from the company, Anheuser-Busch changed the Budweiser label so that two American eagles appeared on it. Newspapers reported that Busch family members supported the German government. Kurt Reisinger, the grandson of Adolphus Busch, allegedly assisted Dr. Edward A. Rumley in the purchase of the *Evening Mail* for the purpose of turning the New York–based paper into a German propaganda organ. During the investigation, deputy New York state attorney general Alfred L. Becker found a list of notable German-Americans who had purchased German war loan bonds before the United States entered the war. Among the names were "Adolphus Busch of St. Louis, who bought $400,000 worth; A. A. Busch, his son, who took $100,000 worth; and Mrs. Lillie [*sic*] Busch, who bought $400,000 worth." August Busch did not deny the purchases but explained that many Americans legally bought German war bonds before the United States entered the war because ads appeared in respectable newspapers.[49] These explanations and protestations had little effect on the growing perception that St. Louis's most prominent family held pro-German views.

The APL was also quite busy in St. Louis. Between April 1917 and November 1918, 3,000 volunteer and 50 full-time operatives investigated 1,142 alleged violations of the Espionage Act, 1,741 instances of alleged pro-German propaganda, 11 sabotage acts, 48 pacifist or IWW incidents, 7,075 draft evasion cases, 589 character and loyalty inquiries, and 225 cases of alleged alien enemy activities in St. Louis. With the assistance of local police, they arrested many suspects including 50 men at Union Station who did not carry registration cards. During the required registration of noncitizens born in Germany, members of the APL were in the police stations, observed the registrants, and took notes in order to "assist the government." The operatives discovered that Eleanor von Boehmer, a nurse, was an alien enemy and allegedly had "been actively spreading pro-German propaganda." She became the first woman from Missouri to be interned for the remainder of the war.[50]

In addition to the APL, St. Louis also established a chapter of the "Anti-Yellow Dog Club," one of several national so-called patriotic organizations. Approximately 10,000 young boys served as private detectives to "stamp out German propaganda" in the city. Articles in local newspapers, such as the *St. Louis Republic,* appear to have approved of citizens becoming "volunteer sleuths" to ferret "out persons suspected of disloyal actions or utterances."[51]

APL investigations of German-Americans at times revealed what old-stock Americans thought surprising situations. Henry Froos had been voting in municipal elections since 1893 because filing his first papers, or intent to become a citizen, had given him that right. Henry L. Weeke, Republican central committeeman in the Eighteenth Ward and commissioner of weights and measures, had to resign from these lucrative positions because he too was an alien enemy.[52] To St. Louisans, such discoveries clearly indicated that investigations were necessary, that only loyal Americans should have such rights and hold such positions, and that no one could trust Germans.

What made the situation in St. Louis worse was a wave of strikes that hit the city in February and March 1918 and placed it into the undesirable category of being second only to New York City in the number of strikes.[53] Union membership had continued to grow as a result of prewar activism as well as due to wartime legislation that created the National War Labor Board, Shipbuilding Labor Adjustment Board, and Emergency Construction Wage Commission, which appeared to support unionization, establish living wages, and call for government mediation in disputes between labor and management.[54] The problem in St. Louis was not lack of jobs. Instead, employers often did not recognize new unions and did not always implement government contract stipulations such as the eight-hour day, overtime compensation, and equal pay for women. Furthermore, new production and wage standards required that workers produce more in less time, and war-related inflation had reduced their standard of living.[55]

The labor unrest began in February 1918 when streetcar workers went on strike against United Railway Company for not recognizing their union. The *Westliche Post* opposed this strike because of the animosity and violence it might cause. The German and Socialist-led CTLU, however, donated $500 to the workers. Through National War Labor Board mediation the strike ended when the company recognized the union, but this did not end the union activism.[56] In March women at Ligett & Meyers Tobacco went on strike when the company denied them the opportunity to unionize. Male and female clerks at downtown retail stores aimed to unionize as well, and on March 8, "hundreds of grocery . . . and hardware clerks . . . joined them." Soon workers in several war plants were on strike, including at Wagner Electric, St. Louis's largest munitions manufacturer,

Monsanto and Mallinckrodt, the city's two largest chemical producers with war contracts, and Plum Tools, which produced bayonets. Employees on strike in ten garment factories caused "a severe slowdown in the manufacture of uniforms." Even bakers, elevator operators, and janitors were striking.[57] Again the CTLU came to the assistance of many of these strikers. For example, it helped grocery and retail clerks publicize their grievances in its two publications and collected nearly $4,000 in donations for them during the strike.[58]

These strikes certainly contributed to accusations of disloyalty. Management in general interpreted unionization and strikes during the war as either outright disloyal behavior or evidence of German propagandists instigating workers to interrupt the war effort. Workers and their union representatives, in contrast, accused employers of disloyal behavior when they maintained unfair business practices despite the stipulations in their government contracts. National War Labor Board representatives, often sympathetic to the workers, seemed to agree, and, for example, suggested that "Wagner Electric management" orchestrated a "conspiracy . . . to prevent the . . . Board from functioning." These mediators, however, also encouraged workers to demonstrate their patriotism by returning to work and relying on arbitration to effect redress of grievances.[59] In order to maintain the image of patriotic workers, laborers censored each other. For example, workers at the Heine Safety Boiler Works forced co-workers Theodore Oesterlei and Andrew Petersdorf, two American citizens of German-born parents, to kiss the United States flag and to shout "'Hurrah for Wilson, to Hell With the Kaiser'" because they had expressed support for Germany and lamented that higher wages as a result of war production did not offer them any gains because they had to purchase Liberty Bonds.[60] Although reports about a "Loyalty and Americanization Movement" in nearby Stanton, Illinois, may have contributed to the incident, the context of the strikes and necessity to appear patriotic in contrast to management also required that German-Americans control fellow German-Americans.

Federal mediators from the Labor Board reduced the number of strikes by April 1918 through concessions for union recognition, increases in wages, and promises to investigate poor working conditions. Labor relations, however, remained tense. St. Louisans remained suspicious of the local Socialist Party chapter since it had proclaimed opposition to the war in 1917 despite its declining influence in the city. Although strikes declined in number, St. Louis slipped only into fourth place in the number of strikes for the remainder of the war, behind New York City, Chicago, and Philadelphia.[61]

Most St. Louisans, nevertheless, did not resort to violence when punishing those who behaved in a disloyal manner. Instead, most concerned citizens took advantage of existing legislation, in particular the Espionage and Sedition Act, the presence of the federal grand jury and the U.S. District Court, Eastern District of Missouri, in the Gateway City, and reported their neighbors and co-workers to local authorities for disloyal speech and activity. Before the passage of the Espionage Act, the federal grand jury in St. Louis indicted seven in disloyalty cases under a law Congress passed on February 14, 1917, also known as the Threat Statute, that dealt with persons who threatened President Wilson's life. For example, Edward Pardick, a salesman, allegedly stated that he "would like to put a bomb under Woodrow Wilson and blow him to hell." Pardick pleaded guilty, and Eastern District Court Judge David P. Dyer fined him $100 because he had a good character and cared for his elderly mother.[62]

After Congress passage the Espionage Act in June 1917, U.S. Attorney Arthur Oliver prosecuted those charged with disloyal expressions and actions as violations of Section 5 of the act, or trying to interfere with military recruitment or the mission of winning the war and creating disloyalty in the military forces.[63] Out of the seventy-four Espionage Act indictments brought before the Eastern District Court, forty-nine originated in St. Louis, and sixty-three of the eighty-three defendants lived in the city.

Thomas Carnell became the first person indicted, prosecuted, and convicted under the Espionage Act in St. Louis. He was a Socialist who gave a speech on August 23, 1917, on the steps of the Rose Fanning School, arguing that any man who went into the army was a fool because this was a war of the rich, and a poor or working man had no business in it. The federal grand jury indicted Carnell for "knowingly, willfully and feloniously" obstructing "the recruiting and enlistment service of the United States." A jury found him guilty, and Judge Dyer sentenced him to two years at Fort Leavenworth. Carnell could have received a sentence of up to twenty years in the penitentiary, but his punishment proved to be the exception rather than the norm in Judge Dyer's court. President Wilson commuted Carnell's sentence to one year and one day in April 1919.[64]

Only two other defendants from St. Louis, August Scheuring and William Schubert, received such lengthy prison terms at Leavenworth. Scheuring, the only German-born in the group, allegedly stated in a streetcar in front of uniformed soldiers that Germany's "twenty million soldiers . . . will lick every man in the world"; said, referring to the president, that "the son-of-a-bitch ought to be killed"; and asserted that "the Kaiser will win the war anyway." The president also commuted Scheuring's sentence to one year and one day in April 1919.[65] Schubert, however, was lucky when Judge Dyer changed his penitentiary sentence to a fine. Sixty-three St. Louisans signed and sent to the judge a petition that requested leniency explaining that as "a loyal and law-abiding citizen" Schubert had organized a service at the Nazareth Evangelical Church for the sole benefit of the Red Cross and had bought bonds during the first and second Liberty Loan campaigns. Furthermore, his family had a long tradition of loyalty because his German-born father and father-in-law had fought on the side of the Union in the Civil War. Dyer took the argument under advisement, set aside the prison sentence, and fined Schubert $250.[66]

Charges under the Espionage Act did not necessarily result in convictions. Indeed, only nineteen of the cases led to convictions, and only ten defendants received jail sentences. For example, Emil Albrecht, who stated that the "Kaiser will lick them all and come over here in submarines and blow you all to hell," received one year in the city jail for trying to "cause disloyalty in the military."[67] Four defendants received fines. William Frederick Wehmeyer, indicted on twenty-seven counts, received the highest monetary punishment. He allegedly "hoorayed" for the kaiser and stated in a public place that "the President is like an old woman; he is like all other politicians, like prostitutes, they all have their price; if they can't get that, they will take less." The jury found him guilty, and Judge Dyer fined him $1,000 for his outspokenness. By contrast, William Stephenson, who asserted that "the head of our Army of France, Pershing, is a traitor, and the man over him, Wilson, is also a traitor," had to pay only a $250 fine.[68]

In an interview with the *St. Louis Post-Dispatch* District Attorney Oliver indicated that Judge Dyer would "levy no severer penalty than a fine" when it came to Espionage Act cases. Although Dyer denied that this was his set policy, comparison with how many convicted defendants received punishments of one to twenty years in Ohio, Wisconsin, and Illinois demonstrates that he was more lenient than judges in those states.[69] Judge Dyer expected certain behavior from Americans and immigrants alike, including a given level of patriotism and support of country during a national crisis. For example, he stated during the Schubert sentencing that "no man should make such remarks [as Schubert had made] whether he lived here or in any other country. If he does live here and was born here the offense is worse." During August Scheuring's sentencing Dyer dismissed the defense attorney's plea for leniency due to drunkenness with, "I don't care whether this man was drunk or sober. It is such men as these who come from other countries and make what they can out of being here performing no duties as citizens, and when the country is involved in war they do what they can to cause disloyalty in our military forces." Consequently, when the evidence indicated that the accused behaved contrary to Dyer's concepts of patriotism, a jail sentence or serious fine was justifiable. If the district attorney and defendant worked out a plea agreement, then Judge Dyer was inclined to apply briefer jail sentences and lighter fines. But if clear evidence of interference with the military existed, if the defendant was a Socialist, and if a jury convicted the defendant, then a prison sentence was more appropriate. It therefore appears that Judge Dyer already realized in early 1918, as would members of the Justice Department by October 1918, that the majority of accusations under the Espionage Act were frivolous charges.[70]

Indeed, accusations and grand-jury indictments did not always result in conviction or punishment. Only five cases resulted in a trial, and of those three ended in a guilty verdict and two in acquittals. In addition to Carnell and Wehmeyer, only Frank Strnad received a guilty verdict. He allegedly stated that he would shoot Ignace Kosarican if he enlisted in the army. During the subsequent trial, Judge Pollock, who assisted Dyer with the workload, instructed the jury that it could convict only if the prosecution had delivered clear evidence of interrupted military service. The jury found Strnad guilty although Kosarican had enlisted and served in the army. Although the judge could not change the jury verdict, he could apply a lenient sentence, and he fined Strnad only $50.[71] In contrast, the jury acquitted Henry C. Koenig, who refused to support the Red Cross because he believed they were "a bunch of crooks and thieves," and Harry Turner, who allegedly tried to use the postal service to convey false information and interfere with the success of the American military, for lack of evidence.[72]

Judge Dyer dismissed or struck from the docket several grand jury indictments for lack of evidence or inability to locate the defendant.[73] The remaining twenty-two cases were continued beyond the end of the war and resulted in *nolle prosequi* or the U.S. attorney's decision to no longer prosecute. Several of the defendants were wealthy enough to hire experienced attorneys for an extended period. These cases demonstrated the primary weakness in the Espionage Act. It infringed on freedom of expression and encouraged local intimidation, but once someone was charged, it was not easy to convict unless the prosecutor could prove that the expressions "knowingly, unlawfully and feloniously" attempted to interfere with registration, limited the success of the military, and caused disloyalty or insubordination in the military.

One additional and important factor that contributed to the lack of convictions was the caseload. The district court docket filled up so quickly with indictments under the Espionage Act that U.S. Attorney General Thomas Gregory had to appoint Charles P. Williams, former counselor for St. Louis, as special prosecutor to expedite proceedings. Several justices, including Judge Page Morris from St. Paul, were also reassigned to St. Louis for brief periods to assist Judge Dyer.[74] Due to the increase in the workload, cases were easily continued beyond the end of the war and then no longer prosecuted.

Analyzing the background of the sixty-three defendants demonstrates that in St. Louis as in other states most were either Socialists or German-Americans. Twenty-seven of the defendants were confessed Socialists and twenty-two were either born in Germany or had German parents.[75] Passionate pro-German exclamations made them easy targets. Nevertheless, names such as Boyce and Sikic also indicate that St. Louisans did not hesitate to accuse anyone who publicly expressed opposition to the war and to report them to the authorities. Newspaper coverage, however, centered on the German-American defendants. For example, the *Westliche Post* pointed out to its readers that John Ungerer's father was born in Germany and had deserted from the German army. Thus, the son, who allegedly said "this country is not worth a damn. . . . I am a German and proud of it," was no better than the father, because he, like his father, was not loyal to his birth country. The *Post-Dispatch* informed its readers that August Weiler, a naturalized citizen, not only attempted to cause disloyalty and refusal of duty in the military, but he also tried to bribe witnesses.[76]

The most famous and headline-grabbing trial in St. Louis of a German-American for disloyalty involved Dr. Charles H. Weinsberg, the president of the Missouri chapter of the National German-American Alliance. As a result of its political activism, the National Alliance was scrutinized during hearings before Congress in early 1918 and dissolved in April 1918. In St. Louis, city police raided the offices of the local alliance chapter several times, suspecting it of selling alcohol on Sundays. Interestingly, before the war, police had not conducted such investigations. In the context of the war, however, the enforcement of Sunday liquor laws became a convenient way to keep an eye on an organization that had expressed pro-German sentiments during the neutrality period. During an interview with a *Post-Dispatch* reporter on April 12, 1918, that addressed these issues, Weinsberg had not only attested to the loyalty of alliance members but also predicted that the war would end in six months and that Germany would either have won it or be suing for peace. Reaction to the article was instant. Within hours of its publication, the U.S. attorney's office in St. Louis was flooded with demands for action. United States marshals arrested Weinsberg that same evening on a warrant that charged him with trying to cause mutiny in the military forces. The trial began on July 2, but before the case could go to the jury on July 5, Judge Page Morris acquitted Weinsberg, arguing that the government failed to show intent on Weinsberg's part to cause insubordination in the military. The judge suggested that the defendant should have been more "prudent" with his expressions but should not be punished for carelessness. The publicity surrounding the case eliminated the little respect the alliance and its members had and resulted in the chapter's dissolution.[77]

Two Germans from St. Louis had unique experiences in the district court. On October 28, 1917, Wilhelm Stremmel allegedly stated in reaction to a train wreck that he wished that it "was a soldier train" and that it had killed "every one of the damned Americans on it." The case was dismissed in May 1918 because his expressions did not interfere with the Selective Service. However, the prosecutor discovered during the investigation that Stremmel was an alien enemy and ordered him detained for the remainder of the war. Fritz Schmook pleaded guilty to a three-count indictment for interfering with the success of the American military because he had stated that President Wilson ought to be hanged, that the kaiser should rule the world, and that "the Kaiser has more brains than the son-of-a-bitch Wilson." Schmook was immediately interned at Jefferson Barracks because he was an enemy alien and was later sent to an internment camp for the duration of the war. He was one of fifty-nine German-born men from Missouri interned as enemy aliens at camps such as Fort Oglethorpe, Georgia.[78]

The first indictments under the Sedition Act appeared before Judge Dyer in November 1918. Charges, including attempts to incite insubordination and disloyalty in the military, were similar to the previous indictments under the Espionage Act. Now, prosecutors no longer had to provide evidence of impact, because under the Sedition Act the mere expression of intent was illegal. The five-count indictment against August Weist, the deputy collector for St. Louis, alleged that he stated, "Our boys have no damned business being over there. . . . To hell with Wilson. . . . The Government has no damned business conscripting our boys over here. . . . That damned gang in Washington fired on the flag in 1861, and the Germans defended it and saved the country." Weist's case moved surprisingly quickly through the court. At the end of a brief trial on November 1, 1918, the jury returned a guilty verdict on the second count, obstructing recruitment, but cleared him of all other charges. Judge Dyer deferred sentence until Chester Krum, the defendant's attorney, could file a motion to arrest judgment. This motion argued that the Espionage and Sedition Act "violated the First Amendment to the Constitution and abridged the freedom of speech." Again Dyer was lenient and fined Weist $200.[79]

Henry Dickhoener's five-count indictment alleged that he "did . . . orally utter certain language intended to incite, provoke and encourage resistance to the United States." Judge Dyer sustained several but not all his demurrers that argued that he had expressed a personal opinion and did not intend to obstruct the work of the government. The case was set for trial in January

1919, but since the war had ended, the district attorney no longer desired to prosecute.[80] Clearly, in St. Louis, cases under the Sedition Act were just as unlikely to result in convictions as indictments under the Espionage Act.

The brevity of American involvement in the Great War and the clogging of the court assured that few of those who were indicted during 1918 were punished for their disloyal remarks. One can make the argument that knowledge of relatively lenient punishment did not deter the serious opponent. At the same time, the Espionage and Sedition Acts limited freedom of speech, and knowledge that St. Louisans would not hesitate to accuse friends and neighbors of disloyal expression caused many to keep quiet.

The combination of coercive, violent, and legal measures adopted to deal with the disloyal element in St. Louis had an impact on the behavior of German-Americans. They knew they were under constant surveillance, and several organizations canceled dances or festivals due to "the current situation." Anti-German sentiment, however, did not intimidate Prince Karneval of the Olympic Turnverein, and, despite encouragement to adjust to "the new times," the Turnverein held its *Narrenkünste* (folly) as planned on February 2, 1918. Indeed, the social season of dances and masquerade balls during the 1918 winter continued as in the years prior to the war.[81] German organizations, however, increasingly used these festivals and other gatherings to demonstrate loyalty through the playing of the "Star-Spangled Banner" or other patriotic songs instead of or in addition to traditional German folk songs. For example, youth members of several Turnvereine decided to create a human American flag during the sports festival held at the Coliseum on March 2, 1918. The Liederkranz appeared to be the most active in correcting past misinterpretations and portraying a picture of loyalty as it bought $500,000 in Liberty Bonds, held benefits for soldiers, and, although it usually gave only private concerts, presented a public singing program for the benefit of the Red Cross. Such displays of loyalty worked because public proclamation from officials such as Postmaster Colin M. Selph stressed that loyal German-born citizens deserved the utmost respect from Americans.[82]

Nevertheless, widespread anti-German sentiment in St. Louis grew because throughout 1917 and early 1918 several German organizations had continued to celebrate the German culture and insisted on the use of the German language. For example, the Bavarian Society, although recognizing the "serious times," held its annual picnic as a true German festival, including the traditional Schuhplattler dance and sauerkraut, and added patriotic music. The singing society Vorwärts sang *"An des Rheines grünen Ufern"* (On the Green Shores of the Rhine) and other traditional German songs during its twenty-ninth annual festival. German Methodists asserted during their yearly conference that Martin Luther would have certainly continued to speak in German under similar circumstances. The Ancient Order of United Workmen, after heated debate, decided to retain the German language for recording and publication purposes. Fifty-six new German books also arrived at the Central Library in May 1918.[83]

It is thus not surprising that during a war with Germany many St. Louisans called for the end to the primary evidence of enemy presence, the German language. German-language newspapers became the initial targets. Editors already knew that the federal government scrutinized them for expressing opposition to the allies, the U.S. government, or the war in general. G. A. Buder, the owner and editor of the *Westliche Post,* had continued to criticize the government on occasion during 1917 because he believed that internal dissent was necessary and healthy for a democracy.[84] The passage of the Trading-with-the-Enemy Act in late September 1917 requiring that German-language newspapers file translations of war-related articles with the postmaster or print them in English pleased many St. Louisans because it would silence editors such as Buder. Indeed, although expressing disappointment over the shameful mistrust this legislation expressed, Buder promised to abide by the law, offered the pages of his paper to the government, and adopted the motto, "A Newspaper Standing for American Ideals and Principles" on its front page. The paper also published several government announcements in English, and members of the staff invested heavily in Liberty Bonds and volunteered for the Red Cross. As a result, the *Post* became one of only two German-language papers in Missouri that received the official stamp of loyalty from the national government and by December 1917 no longer had to file translations.[85]

Whereas the Missouri Council of Defense was content using loyal German-language publications for the dissemination of the government's messages, St. Louisans wanted to eliminate any evidence of the enemy. The editor of the *Republic* agitated for an end to the German-language press, arguing that Germans remained ignorant of American culture and institutions because they received misinformation and "dangerous doctrine" (see figure 4.3). The St. Louis branch of the National Security League aimed to eliminate German-language papers by persuading advertisers no longer to conduct business with these papers and encouraging newsstands no longer to sell them. P. B. Conner tore up and burned a copy of *Amerika* on the floor of the St. Louis Exchange because he believed that all German-language papers should be suppressed during the war.[86]

The board of aldermen also decided to cease the publication of city council minutes and public notices in German in the *Westliche Post* because such

FIGURE 4.3. "Step On It!" Cartoons such as this in the *St. Louis Republic* aimed to convince readers that the German-language press in the United States did not provide an educational service but instead served as a tool for German propagandists. *St. Louis Republic*, June 5, 1918, folder 92, WWI, Newspaper Clippings, Western Historical Manuscript Collection, University of Missouri–Columbia.

practice was "un-American" and cost the city $25,900 per year. During the heated discussions that led to the passage of the Haller-Udell Bill, establishing an independent city journal, St. Louisans interpreted Mayor Kiel's suggestion that the city create its own magazine and eliminate publication of city business from all newspapers in the context of the heightened sense of patriotism as evidence of his disloyalty.[87]

The push to end the use of German was not limited to newspapers. A committee of concerned citizens began to agitate for the end of the German classes that the German School Society had provided on Saturdays in public schools. The school board, although it could not find evidence of German propaganda, decided to deny the society access to public school buildings. Consequently, the *heimatlose* (homeless) society decided to cancel the classes.[88] The St. Louis Chamber of Commerce also called for the elimination of German in elementary schools but agreed that high school students should learn it as a modern language. The school board gave in to the demands and resolved to let German fade gradually from the curriculum.[89]

Due to this pressure, several German-American organizations in St. Louis began to conduct their meetings and keep their minutes in English. The St. Louis Turnbezirk, consisting of fifteen Turnvereine in and around St. Louis, for the first time held its annual meeting in English in 1918. The Deutsche Kellnerverein (German Waiters' Association), upon the complaint from the national waiters' union that the St. Louis chapter used only the German language, decided to dissolve and donate any remaining funds to the Red Cross.[90]

To many English-speaking St. Louisans it also made sense to reform German churches. After all, as the *Westliche Post* had admitted, German churches served as the preservers of culture for Germans in the United States and had been quite successful in maintaining German education, tradition, and language.[91] German Catholics, their associations, and publications became targets early on for disloyalty accusations. The daily *Amerika* had to file translations of articles pertaining to the conflict with the postmaster for the duration of the war. The Deutsche römisch-katholische central Verein experienced government investigation because its weekly publication the *Herold des Glaubens* had published outspoken anti-British editorials. The anti-Catholic *Menace,* published in Aurora, Missouri, used the war hysteria to define the verein as an "Incubator of Sedition" and to attack its members as a "bunch of traitors and henchmen of the Pope," who deserved deportation to Germany. The director of the verein, Frederick P. Kenkel, received a threatening letter from a writer who identified himself as "one who knows," but who apparently did not know that Kenkel had two sons serving in the military.[92] Several St. Louisans questioned the loyalty of even Archbishop John J. Glennon, who oversaw a diocese of many immigrants with numerous languages and sympathies. He supported President Wilson's Fourteen Points for world peace and encouraged all residents in the diocese to support the war effort. He also argued, however, that "we are not making war on languages" but fought for principles of justice and right, and he insisted that a person could express sentiments of disloyalty and loyalty in any language. Consequently, he allowed priests and parishioners to use the German language, despite the anti-German frenzy, for such tasks as confessions.[93]

The majority of German Protestant churches in St. Louis already offered German and English services, but only one, Bethel Evangelical, conducted all its services in English. Although several of the Evangelical and Lutheran parochial schools continued their practice of teaching subjects in both German and English, schoolchildren now also learned about loyalty, held patriotic festivals, and learned about the atrocities Germans committed in Belgium. Pastors proclaimed their congregations' patriotism during Sunday services and strongly encouraged parishioners to purchase Liberty Bonds to the fullest extent of their ability and to join the Red Cross. However, anniversary celebrations that advertised optional English services in the evening or English speeches in addition to German sermons must have looked as if participants still celebrated German traits.[94]

In response to the local demand as well as to pressures from within congregations, pastors in Lutheran and Evangelical churches and Archbishop Glennon took the language issue under advisement. Indeed, several Lutheran and Evangelical churches, including Trinity Evangelical Lutheran Church, decided to end the use of German in parochial schools and to offer more English services. Finally, non-German St. Louisans approved when they read that the Missouri Council of Defense supported the movement to abolish the use of the German language in the entire state.[95]

In contrast to German Catholics and German Protestants, German Jews in St. Louis did not experience such pressures. Although they experienced some anti-Semitism, it was neither widespread nor a major problem. Despite speaking Yiddish, a mix of High German, Hebrew, and Slavic terms, and although many were members of secular German associations, German Jews considered themselves American Jews, not German-Americans. Indeed, World War I, according to Walter Ehrlich, served as a unifier between the older, more secular German Jewish community and the recently arrived orthodox Jewish population, because "common loyalties to the United States transcended any religious differences." Both supported humanitarian organizations and relief efforts in European areas torn apart by Germany before, during, and after American participation in the war. Like Jews throughout America, the St. Louis Jewish population also heeded the call to do what the federal and state governments asked them to do, including fight, buy bonds, conserve food, and work in the war industry because such efforts helped free old homelands from German occupation. According to the historian of St. Louis Jews, none were accused of disloyalty.[96]

Local relationships in St. Louis were such that residents were more aware of the war than smaller towns in rural areas. National policies, such as the creation of restricted zones and required registration of enemy aliens, also clearly identified to everyone who was American and who was not. Labor was well organized and active through strikes. Although the local chapter of the Socialist Party was not as radical as elsewhere in the Midwest, proximity to militant unionism in the nearby coal mines of southwestern Illinois contributed to fear. Not only did St. Louisans have to worry about the enemy nearby, but the presence of pro-Germanism within also marked the city as disloyal. Consequently, St. Louisans were more watchful of the person who might represent pro-Germanism or give aid to the enemy. St. Louis thus experienced what Luebke called an "oppressive climate of coercive patriotism" much sooner, for a longer period, and to a much stronger degree than the rest of the state.[97]

Although internal division existed within the ethnic group and cultural identity had waned, the actions of leaders and organizations presented a public image of unity and ethnic pride. Those who spoke out loudly against the war and insisted on the preservation of culture stood out and attracted the attention of the rising conformist movement. Consequently, nativists, who had been primed with hateful propaganda, vented their anti-German sentiment on individuals whom they perceived as a threat. Although legal measures such as prosecution under the Espionage Act were preferred, a few also experienced job loss and violence. St. Louisans were fairly successful in their efforts to eliminate the German culture and language. That raises the question whether German-Americans who lived in the so-called German counties in rural Missouri experienced similar pressures and what impact the war had on their lives.

FIVE

Resisting Interference in Daily Life

Gasconade County during World War I

> Mrs. E. F. Rippstein . . . is a courageous,
> determined, patriotic woman [who] has
> made herself very unpopular with . . . the
> Gasconade County Council of Defense.
>
> —*William Saunders to Frederick
> Mumford, February 1918*

ROSE SOPHIA Rippstein was what the leaders of the Missouri Council of Defense defined as the embodiment of the patriotic spirit during the Great War. She tirelessly traveled throughout Gasconade County to teach women how to conserve food, assisted her husband in his function as county chairman of the Liberty Loan in 1917 by selling war bonds, volunteered for the Red Cross, and kept Jefferson City updated about the county's war effort. In the process she also created many enemies because she considered the county council of defense ineffective.[1] As the sister of George Klenk, a successful businessman and the mayor of Hermann, and as the wife of Eugene F. Rippstein, director and cashier of Hermann Savings Bank, trying to inspire farmers and the wealthy in the county to support the war effort, she also represented local class tensions. She believed that those not supporting the war either did not have enough information and thus needed education or were more concerned with local political interests than the success of the war. Although the granddaughter of German immigrants and the wife of an American born to Swiss immigrants, she defined hesitance, slacking, and less than enthusiastic support for the war effort in ethnic terms and reported this ethnic interpretation to officials of the Missouri Council of Defense in Jefferson City.[2] These outsiders then investigated the county and confirmed the suspicions of disloyalty. Several residents of the county indeed opposed the war. Most, however, did not eagerly support the war effort because they objected to the intrusions the war brought into their daily lives. They did what was necessary to keep accusations of disloyalty to a minimum and expected the wealthier segment of society to do its fair share in the war.

When war broke out on the European continent, the large German-American population in Gasconade County did not celebrate. Instead, they reacted in an almost matter-of-fact fashion to a conflict that they could not shape. Gasconade County's German-language newspaper, the *Hermanner Volksblatt,* and its English counterpart, the *Advertiser-Courier,* regularly published *Nachrichten vom Kriegsschauplatze* (news from the theater of war) or the "Weekly War News Digest" and printed the facts national news services provided to these rural papers; but only on occasion did the editor embellish articles or pictures with personal opinions.[3] Nevertheless, residents living in Hermann learned about the war more from a German than British or Allied perspective. Although not supporting the kaiser or his regime, the *Volksblatt* recognized and made public the German-American sympathy problem through poems, such as Friedrich Fiedel's *Hast du's gewußt?* (Did You Know It?), that discussed the aching heart the German-American felt for his old fatherland and the disgust he held for England. The few editorials Theodore Graf, the editor of these two papers, wrote also expressed opposition to Great Britain, especially its practice of confiscating American ships and its censorship of information and mail across the Atlantic, and at times criticized Wilson's lack of true neutrality. Both papers supported German relief agencies, including the German Red Cross and the Hilfsverein Deutscher Frauen (German Women's Aid Society). The *Volksblatt* also regularly printed eyewitness accounts and letters about daily life in Germany during the war and the *Advertiser-Courier* defended German military tactics.[4] The Hermann papers, and their readers, were not alone in this mind-set. The English-language *Bland Courier* in southwestern Gasconade County also printed letters from Germany that described the situation in Europe and urged President Wilson to keep the United States neutral and out of the war. John D. Seba, the editor of the *Bland Courier,* opposed the preparedness movement because it would not preserve peace but would necessarily lead to war.[5]

By contrast, the *Gasconade County Republican,* published in Owensville, provided a pro-Allied and pro-American view of the war. But this English-language newspaper also catered to German-American readers in southern Gasconade County and on occasion offered a two-column report in German titled *Vom Schauplatze des europäischen Völkerkrieges* (From the European Theater of the World War). At the same time, it did not hesitate to criticize the American yellow press for its sensationalistic reporting.[6]

The papers of Gasconade County, however, agreed on the subject of submarine warfare, if they discussed it. The *Republican* took up the subject only once, during the *Lusitania* crisis. The editor W. O. Boyd argued that his readers had to recognize that during a war international laws would be broken, that the British blockade justified submarine warfare, and that those who had been warned yet traveled on the liner could expect to be hurt. The *Advertiser-Courier* echoed this sentiment when it quoted Senator Stone's declaration that passengers had been warned.[7]

Unlike St. Louis and other places with large German populations, German-Americans in Gasconade County did not experience pressure to Americanize; they maintained their German traditions uninhibited throughout the neutrality period. In 1914, the county held its German Day celebration in Morrison and on September 24, 1916, more than ten thousand people celebrated German Day in Hermann. On the following day, Hermannites welcomed the Missouri chapter of the German-American Alliance to the shores of the Missouri River for its annual meeting. The alliance had chosen Hermann because it resembled the German towns along the Rhine River, and people were still proud of their German descent; they maintained German customs and freely talked in German, and the city council still kept its minutes in the German language.[8] Movies, such as *Germany's Fighting Forces* shown at the Concert Hall in April 1916, also celebrated the German military and its successes (see figure 5.1).

Germany's Fighting Forces

General Staff
Motion Pictures

Positively the only real German Pictures to reach this country. Taken by enlisted camera men for the National Archives of the Imperial German Government

AUTHENTIC --- OFFICIAL --- EXCLUSIVE

SEE --- the devastated cities left in the wake of Germany's great drive into Poland.

SEE --- the bombardment of Liege by the famous big Berthas.

In the trenches and on the march with the German Army from
BAGDAG TO WARSAW

CONCERT HALL

One Night Only—FRIDAY, APRIL 7th

Admission 10 and 15c. Positively the same pictures that recently showed at the Garrick theatre at St. Louis at 50c.

FIGURE 5.1. Movie advertisement. Evidence of pro-German sentiment during the neutrality period emerged in Gasconade County through the advertisements of movies such as this one for *Germany's Fighting Forces. Hermann Advertiser-Courier*, April 5, 1916.

The 1916 election in Gasconade County, in contrast to St. Louis, was relatively quiet. In a strongly Republican county it is not surprising that all four Republican papers supported or endorsed Hughes for president. They dissociated Hughes from the loud "anti-hyphen" voices within the party and argued that Hughes recognized German-Americans as "hardworking and loyal citizens." The county's Republican Party committee praised Wilson's moral character but denounced his policies that supported England and most likely would lead to war with Mexico. Letters to the editor, nevertheless, argued that Germans in Gasconade County should not automatically vote for Republicans; instead they should investigate a candidate's true character and consider his position on the war in Europe and American neutrality.[9] The *Bland Courier*, a newspaper with progressive views, added the perspective of rural versus urban German-Americans during the presidential campaign. Editorials, for example, argued that the German-American Alliance in St. Louis was wrong in publicly endorsing candidates for office. The editor viewed the alliance as the voice for big-city brewery interests and feared that its political activism would lead to a break in the Republican Party and thus contribute to a Democratic victory in the November election.[10]

In a Republican county it is no surprise that Hughes defeated Wilson with a comfortable majority in each of its eighteen precincts by a total vote of 2,513 to 510. Senator James A. Reed also lost Gasconade County to his Republican opponent Walter S. Dickey by almost 2,000 votes. Results for the gubernatorial candidate Frederick Gardner were virtually the same, despite his pro-farmer land-bank platform based on German ideals. Although statewide prohibition received little coverage in local newspapers, voters in this wine-making county overwhelmingly defeated Amendment No. 6 by 2,469 to 464 votes.[11]

After the election the war scare escalated for the United States through Germany's resumption of unrestricted submarine warfare. The *Volksblatt* in an editorial differentiated Gasconade County from the eastern war hawks by arguing that people in the county had not benefited from the prosperity of neutrality, nor would unrestricted submarine warfare worsen their situation. Unlike the pro-war, jingoistic press in the East, they defined patriotism as preserving peace and preventing war. But if called upon, they said they would be the first to volunteer and would not enrich themselves from the tragedy of war. Consequently, German-Americans, although most were Republicans, saluted Democratic Senator Stone for his opposition to the war. They also continued to criticize Wilson for his clear partiality toward England instead of addressing the problem of growing inflation at home. Yet, by the end of March, Gasconade countians became resigned to the inevitability of war. Although they regretted the circumstances that had brought about the "unfriendly relations" between Germany and the United States, they nevertheless promised to do anything to defend the honor of America as long as their sacrifices would not "uphold England's dictatorship."[12]

The arrival of war for the United States did not receive headline coverage.[13] Although Gasconade County did not hold an immediate war rally, its people, like so many Missourians, proudly displayed their patriotism by flying the American flag in front of their homes or businesses. The *Advertiser-Courier* taught its readers how to properly display and handle the flag, and the *Volksblatt* began to publish poems that celebrated the flag and the American Pledge of Allegiance. These newspapers in Hermann also quickly stopped any criticism of the administration and provided space for announcements from the county and state councils of defense, the Red Cross, and later from the Committee on Public Information. However, they also continued to criticize England and published reports from Germany that asserted that it would not be defeated.[14] At the same time, they also encouraged German-Americans in the county through poems such as *Sag' nichts den Leuten* (Don't Tell Anyone Anything) to keep quiet, no matter how dedicated one was to Germany.[15]

By contrast, the *Gasconade County Republican* in Owensville, the more American section of Gasconade County, immediately defined Americanism to its readers as civilians, soldiers, and sailors walking in step with each other for the common good of the United States. Although displaying one's flag indicated patriotism, that was not enough. Instead, only "undivided support to the government" could demonstrate true loyalty.[16] Unlike the remaining three papers in the county, the *Republican* by May began to regularly publish news from Washington, D.C., papers, including cartoons that defined slacking, wastefulness, and patriotism. When the Missouri Council of Defense was established in July 1917, the paper also printed announcements from the state and county councils of defense; the national, state, and county food administrators; and the Red Cross. In addition, the *Republican* printed occasional reports about the enemy's atrocities overseas, subversive activities in the United States, and disloyal behavior in Missouri.[17] Thus the *Republican* appeared more supportive of the war effort than the other three papers during the early months of the war.

Interestingly, the *Republican* was the only paper to discuss the necessity of curtailing freedom of speech during a national emergency through such legislation as the Espionage Act. The editor, W. O. Boyd, nevertheless reserved the right to criticize the government. For example, he asserted that taxes for the war placed a heavier burden on the "little guy" than on the wealthy.[18] Boyd also argued that Americans of German birth or heritage were no different from those who fought alongside Franz Sigel during the Civil War and called the movement to rename streets or towns "childish" and a "silly fad" because none of "these harmless German names could conjure up submarines or Zeppelins." He also asserted that the establishment of daylight saving time was "one of the colossal acts of foolishness" Congress passed because it distracted from the task of "whipping the Kaiser's legions."[19]

By the fall of 1917, the *Advertiser-Courier* and *Volksblatt* had caught up with the *Republican* and contributed at least one column per page and often entire pages to the war effort. Thus any advantage in regard to knowledge about the war effort for the people living in and around Owensville quickly disappeared. The government guidelines and cartoons printed in the local papers defined patriotism as raising victory gardens, maintaining meatless and wheatless days, purchasing War Savings Stamps, becoming members of the Red Cross, and proving 100 percent Americanism by buying a Liberty Bond. The *Volksblatt* and *Republican* echoed this mind-set when they defined the meaning of true patriotism as the sum of a number of acts. The closer these acts resembled sacrifice, the truer one's patriotism. In the editors' opinions, the person who sacrificed financially to the limit of his ability was a greater patriot than he who merely waved the flag.[20] Therefore, residents of Gasconade County believed that as long as they followed these guidelines they would demonstrate patriotism and prove their loyalty to country.

Despite obvious loyalty, the *Volksblatt,* as required through the Trading-with-the-Enemy Act, had to abide by the law and file translations with the postmaster at Hermann for any and all German-language articles that pertained to the war effort. In order to save money and maintain its patriotic image, the publisher of the *Volksblatt* limited war news to announcements from local organizations, such as the exemption board, and to pre-set type plates in German or English from the government. The paper, for example, simply tabulated the ten reasons why Americans should sign the Hoover Food Pledge in a one-column-wide seventeen-line insert in November. The *Republican,* by contrast, explained each one of these ten points in detail and used eighty-two lines that spread over two columns.[21] Contrary to those in St. Louis, however, all papers of Gasconade County lacked the emotional representation of the war as a fight between good and evil.

Although newspapers could reflect public opinion and patriotic sentiment, state and national guidelines required more. Following Missouri Council of Defense instructions, the Gasconade County Council of Defense organized during the summer of 1917. Members adopted as their slogan "Keep your mouth shut and keep busy." For the council members, the majority of whom were German-American, this meant to do as much as possible or necessary and not complain.[22] Gasconade County residents followed that recommendation.

For German immigrants the easiest way to express loyalty was to become a citizen of the United States, and by February 1918 five residents had filed their first papers and several, including Hermann Stritzel, had become citizens.[23] German-born men and women also abided by the law and, if not yet citizens, registered as "alien enemies" as required by federal law. Nineteen men registered in Hermann, eighteen in Owensville, three in Potsdam, and four in Bay. Eighteen women, including five American-born women, registered as enemy aliens in Hermann.[24] More important, as the *Republican* suggested, German immigrants and their American-born descendants could demonstrate their patriotism by once and for all declaring verbally whether they were Germans or Americans; they could not be both. Indeed, as Germans they ought to fight in Germany, live in an internment camp, or "bear watching."[25]

The most obvious way for men to demonstrate their loyalty was to enlist in the military forces and to abide by the Selective Service Act. Unlike men in St. Louis, very few men from Gasconade County volunteered for the military. Only nine enlisted in the army and marines, and six volunteered for the navy. The Bland community called itself the most patriotic area in the county because it held a loyalty day in May 1917, and six men volunteered for the military. There is also no evidence that Gasconade County intended to establish a Home Guard unit. The first indication of interest emerged in Morrison in August 1918, in reaction to the regular Chamois Home Guard drills many people from Gasconade County observed in neighboring Osage County.[26]

Nevertheless, all eligible men abided by the Selective Service Act and registered for the draft on June 5, 1917. Extensive articles about the federal guidelines in all local newspapers let registrants know what they could expect during the examination process, including the several categories of acceptable deferments. Of the 990 registered men, 336, or 34 percent, did not claim any exemptions. However, 533 claimed exemptions due to dependent relatives, 87 for physical ailments, and 43 requested exemptions for other reasons. These numbers fit well within the 60 to 70 percent range of filed exemptions nationwide.[27]

As long as these exemptions were legitimate, the local board of exemptions and the county council quickly approved them. During the initial call-up in August 1917, the local board immediately exempted fifty-five registrants for physical reasons, including temporary ailments, and approved thirty of fifty exemptions based on marital status, even if the nuptials occurred after the United States entered the war. The county council of defense went so far as to publicly express opposition to the decision by the district board at Poplar Bluff to deny "the exemption claims of young men who are indispensable on our farms." The county exemption board continued to allow deferments for young farmers and farm laborers despite assured denial at the district board level even after General Enoch Crowder, the head of the Selective Service, changed the classification system in December 1917.[28] In other words, although local officials did not oppose the draft and the war itself, they nevertheless believed that registrants should receive exemptions if they met the guidelines and that the draft should not interfere with the livelihood of the county.

Eventually, 318 men from Gasconade County were drafted and departed to training camps in Kansas, Iowa, and Texas with heartfelt good wishes during patriotic send-off ceremonies. The majority came from the two largest communities in the county: 112 from Hermann and 55 from Owensville. Most remained in the United States, but 99 served in France. Of those, 27 were wounded or gassed and 10 were killed in action. An additional 10 men from Gasconade County died in training camps in the United States through accidents or the Spanish Influenza.[29] Despite the patriotism and loyalty that the men demonstrated through their service to country, the Missouri Council of Defense believed that Gasconade County was a "weak" and possibly disloyal county.[30] Analysis of the actions publicly defined to represent patriotism illustrates that residents of the county could have done more but were not necessarily disloyal.

The men and women of Gasconade County who did not join the military aided the war effort through food conservation to feed the soldiers and Allies overseas. However, during the August 1917 Hoover Women Registration Campaign, the county council collected only fifty-one signatures.[31] Whereas women in St. Louis were at the forefront of the volunteer effort during the war, most Gasconade County women, whether German or American, were wives of farmers and did not come from a tradition of reform activism. German-American women, in particular, did not have the assortment of secular societies that their counterparts in St. Louis had and interacted with each other primarily through church societies such as the Frauen Verein (Women's Association). As the wives of farmers, they also had less time than urban middle-class women to dedicate to volunteer work.[32] Consequently, women from the larger communities such as Hermann and Owensville, and usually the spouses of businessmen, served on the county's woman's committee and believed that they carried the load of the entire county on their shoulders. For example, Claudia Hatton, the food demonstrator for Owensville, also served the Drake and Hermann communities and coordinated several canning classes in neighboring Osage County. Rose Sophia Rippstein gave speeches throughout the county and in Jefferson City, organized the county for food conservation, canvassed the county to gain signatures for food conservation, aided in Red Cross Work and Liberty Loan sales, and worked herself to exhaustion and a nervous breakdown.[33]

Although Gasconade countians followed Herbert Hoover's call for conservation and reduced their wheat and meat consumption, they did not always do so quietly or happily. A *Volksblatt* editorial, arguing that cornbread was good, nevertheless asked why Europeans were still allowed to eat wheat bread. During the Family Enrollment Campaign in November, only 2,032 persons or 16 percent of the county's population signed pledges to conserve food, less than the 21 percent statewide. Rose Rippstein had to resort to emotional language in order to encourage reduction in food consumption, including appeals to mothers in phrases such as "the last word on a man's lips as he goes over the top is 'mother,' and 'mother' they cry when they are wounded and 'mother' . . . when they are dying."[34]

In contrast, Gasconade County wholeheartedly embraced the Red Cross because it was a universal humanitarian organization that aided anyone during a crisis. The city of Hermann led by example and established the first Red Cross chapter in the county in August 1917 with 48 members. Mr. and Mrs. Rippstein and Rose's brother, Mayor George Klenk, were among the charter members. Owensville soon followed and established the second chapter in October 1917 with 186 members. By the time the Red Cross Christmas Membership Drive began in December 1917, Bland also had a chapter, and the county could boast 630 members overall. In January 1918, the county had reached and topped its quota of 1,876 members, or 16 percent of the entire population.[35] Throughout 1918, the county's support for the organization remained quite impressive. Churches, including the Catholic St. George's Church, set up Red Cross support organizations. Young adults created Junior Red Cross Societies, or Sammy Clubs, throughout the county. Sammy girls provided entertainment and sold cookbooks, and the Hermann WCTU chapter, in cooperation with the local Red Cross chapter, sent comfort bags to soldiers. Community bake sales, pie suppers, and moving-picture shows donated their proceeds to the Red Cross. Although communities such as Morrison and Bland topped their individual quotas during the summer Red Cross fund-raising campaign, the county as a whole still needed $758 to meet its quota of $11,188 by August. Consequently, county leaders resorted to defining as slackers those who did not contribute according to their income, especially the wealthy.[36]

The Liberty Loan Campaign provided proof that the county was less than enthusiastic in its financial support for the war. Newspapers did not widely advertise the First Liberty Loan Campaign, and none printed the final numbers. The county fell short of its goal during the Second Liberty Loan campaign when the county's quota was $227,500. Despite deliberate appeals to emotions and patriotism, the subscription of 191 individuals added up to only $114,550. That amounted to an average of $600 per subscriber and 1.5 percent of the population buying bonds. That was well below the state average of 3.8 percent and defined Gasconade County as a slacker county.[37] Consequently, in April 1918, the county's Third Liberty Loan Campaign committee organized more efficiently. They held several mass meetings, exhibited war gear from the European front, reminded people that the county received the slacker label during the previous bond campaign, inundated newspapers with announcements and used CPI advertisements such as "Don't Slacken—Loosen!" The promise that everyone who bought a bond in the value of $50 or over would receive a Liberty Loan Button to display their patriotism on the lapel also convinced residents to invest in Liberty Bonds. The county oversubscribed the Third Liberty Loan by more than $100,000, and 19.2 percent of the population, or 2,377 individuals, purchased bonds with an average amount of $138, and that was much higher than the state average of 11 percent. More important, the county received sixteen honor flags for each township and incorporated town, and residents truly believed that their financial support of the war effort had finally demonstrated "patriotism, loyalty and true love of country."[38]

By contrast, the War Savings Stamp campaign was a tough campaign. Posters advertised these stamps as the poor man's Liberty Bonds. School children could not only purchase stamps for a quarter at a time, but they could also win them in poster drawings and essay writing contests. The war savings stamp committee also brought Mathilda Dallmeyer, the "Joan of Arc of Missouri" and daughter of a well-known German-born business owner from Jefferson City, to Hermann. Her captivating speech inspired excitement and patriotism and resulted in the sale of $6,500 in stamps and pledges for nearly $12,000 more. Such mass meetings and appeals to patriotism eventually resulted in twelve school districts topping their individual quotas. But the county had not yet reached its quota of $264,000, or $20 for every man, woman, and child, by the end of the war. Even the usually patriotic Owensville failed to create the necessary enthusiasm to meet its $13,700 quota.[39]

One explanation for the less than enthusiastic support for the war effort is that Gasconade County residents opposed the relentless intrusions into their daily lives. By spring of 1918 persons felt totally overwhelmed by the daily demands to buy bonds and stamps, support the YMCA, contribute to the Red Cross, produce larger harvests but make do with less wheat and sugar.[40]

According to correspondence in the Missouri Council of Defense files, German-Americans in the county criticized the food work and questioned why they should deprive themselves of food just so it could be sent to England and France. They argued that conservation and reduction of waste were not new practices to German farmers. Furthermore, the war also demanded that they suddenly change traditional farming practices, and they were unable or un-willing to do that.[41]

Throughout 1917 patriotic volunteers also mentioned in their reports to Jefferson City and Washington, D.C., that more information was absolutely essential to bring about more local support for the war effort and eliminate confusion and misunderstanding. They believed that people living in the re-mote areas of the county did not always have access to and thus did not know the requirements of the war effort. For example, Mrs. Walter McNab Miller, the chairman of the Missouri Hoover Registration, explained that residents from Gasconade County had come up to her during a mass meeting there in August 1917 informing her that they had changed their opinions about the war because they finally had received useful information. Rose Rippstein expressed similar thoughts and lamented on several occasions that the public, the county council, and the Red Cross lacked information about the war effort. She was surprised about "the foolish questions" her neighbors in Her-mann asked, and in her opinion the "people around here don't understand and don't realize the seriousness of the Hoover Plan and Red Cross." Clarence Baxter, the county chairman of the Hoover Family Enrollment Campaign, echoed these thoughts in November 1917 when he explained that the col-lection of 1,000 signatures in the southern half of the county was "an up-hill business" because the people did not "understand the significance of the cam-paign."[42] The numbers, especially the success of the Third Liberty Loan cam-paign, indeed indicate that once national information about the war arrived in the county, people became more enthusiastic.

Rippstein, however, also interpreted the perceived unwillingness by of local newspapers to print her articles about food conservation and the duties and expectations of the county council as evidence of disloyalty and limited en-thusiasm. In her opinion the "editors don't seem to be in the right spirit" and are "very much like some of the Council . . . afraid to do a thing too much."[43] Yet, it is understandable that newspapers might not want to publish the article of an individual when state officials already urged editors to print information from the official council of defense and food administration.

Nevertheless, August Mann, the secretary of the county council, an-nounced in October 1917 that "all people of the county are loyal and busily engaged in their usual and regular occupations, trying to conserve and produce all in their power in the line of food and . . . as is necessary for the defense and welfare of our citizens and our country."[44] In other words, they followed the county council motto of keeping busy. Publication of new members for the Red Cross and the list of contributors to the liberty loans, while serving as instruments of pride and as evidence of patriotism, probably also encouraged some to contribute as well.[45] This approach paid off. A newspaper article in May 1918 told readers that Robert Glenn, a representative from the state council of defense, had declared the county loyal as well.[46]

Yet despite their best efforts the Missouri Council of Defense still looked on Gasconade County as one of the worst counties in the state. Additional factors must have influenced the creation of such a negative perception. Indeed, evidence of actual disloyal behavior had already emerged during the early weeks of the war. A Bland resident, August Heidbreder, one of the richest farmers in the county, was arrested in June 1917 for having threatened President Wilson's life. Heidbreder, a sixty-two-year-old naturalized citizen of German birth, allegedly stated that Wilson should be stuffed into a cannon and shot out to sea. Eastern U.S. District Court Judge David P. Dyer fined Heidbreder $100 for his outspokenness.[47]

The incident did not appear to harm the family's reputation because his son, County Assessor Henry Heidbreder, served on the Third Creek Township Council of Defense. There is also no reason to suspect that this single incident prejudiced leaders in Jefferson City against Gasconade County. Since the entire case went through the proper legal channels, it served to alleviate perceptions of disloyalty, and, as the *Gasconade County Republican* suspected, the case served as an example to stop all "treasonable utterances" in the county.[48]

Edward A. Ahrens, however, did not keep quiet. During a sermon in October 1917 he allegedly remarked that he would not "pray for the victory of the United States in this war" and asserted that the money used to purchase Liberty Bonds "was blood money." The federal grand jury, upon the eyewitness accounts of Herman Weise and Jackson Smith, indicted Ahrens on three counts of violating the Espionage Act. The Ahrens case did not receive coverage in the local newspapers and thus did not attract widespread attention. Possibly Ahrens fled, or residents in the county encouraged him to leave the area, because court officials could not find him in the eastern district, and court records indicated that he might have moved to Iowa. The 1920 census confirmed that Ahrens lived in Diagonal Town, in Washington Township, Iowa, and continued his work as a minister.[49] In short, his removal from the area resolved the problem.

Others, however, continued to express pro-German sentiment, although they must have known the consequences. For example, Charles Egley, a Swiss-born schoolteacher from Hermann, and Louis Blomberg, a farmer and son of German immigrants from Owensville, allegedly made such strong pro-German remarks that officials in Jefferson City believed they should be charged for violating the Espionage Act. Since no charges were brought against the two and the incidents did not appear in the newspapers, it is likely that local leaders quietly enforced the county council's motto to keep quiet. The majority of these accusations originated in the southern, slightly more American part of Gasconade County. It is likely that residents there paid more attention to the expressions their neighbors made, because, as noted earlier, they had competed with German-Americans for land and jobs and had more information about the war through the *Republican*. Consequently, assertions of disloyalty did not necessarily damage the reputations of the accused, especially if they lived in the northern, more German, areas. Egley, for instance, worked as a realtor and served as the census enumerator for Hermann in 1920.[50]

One controversy that arose during December 1917, nevertheless, did receive attention from council officials in Jefferson City. A. B. Walker, a member of the county council, stood accused of having discouraged support for the Red Cross and the purchase of Liberty Bonds. However, William Saunders, the secretary of the Missouri Council of Defense, could not find evidence to support the accusation. Furthermore, officials feared that a formal inquest into Walker's alleged disloyalty would turn people who had been willing to invest in bonds away because Walker, as a banker and brother of the former county prosecutor, had a better reputation and more local influence than those accusing him of disloyalty.[51]

These examples illustrated the presence of possible disloyal thought and behavior in the county as well as class animosity. The lack of effective leadership in the county council of defense and its perceived unwillingness to do the work necessary to fight the war, or slacking, also increasingly annoyed local volunteers, such as Rose Rippstein. For example, she somewhat sarcastically called the members of the county council "hard workers" because "they meet and pass resolutions" but never accomplished anything.[52]

Rose Rippstein, like so many middle-class women during the war, was eager to get involved in the war effort and became one of the most devoted volunteers in the county. She served as the county's chairman of the Woman's Committee and the Women's Food Conservation Committee and the Missouri Council of Defense appointed her as a member of the Gasconade County Council in September 1917. In this capacity she organized the few women who volunteered their services, went house to house to collect signatures for the Hoover Pledge, organized several send-off festivities for men departing to training camps, solicited contributions to the Red Cross, and organized speaking arrangements for war veterans. Yet, she quickly realized that a dozen women could not organize the entire county. She was also frustrated that her work was not taken seriously by the men in the community or by newspapers outside the county. At times she also felt overwhelmed by the many state council and federal government guidelines because they limited her flexibility in encouraging volunteerism in a rural county.[53]

Despite the challenging work, Rose Rippstein became the virtual eyes and ears of the state council, and she took the requirement that counties report regularly to Jefferson City very seriously. But she reported primarily on the lack of enthusiasm in the county. Her negative perceptions predisposed Missouri Council officials to view Gasconade County in a less than positive light. Mrs. Rippstein then affirmed the assessment of slacking when she reported that the council leadership refused to follow the council's guidelines.[54]

William Saunders believed that part of the problem lay with Gasconade County's council secretary August Mann, the county superintendent of schools and third generation German-American, who was, "not disloyal enough to be got at through the agencies of the Department of Justice" but "disloyal enough to throttle all the work of the Council of Defense."[55] When Judge Frank Oncken resigned in October 1917 as chairman of the county council, the appointment of Edward A. Meyer as the new chairman did not improve the situation. Mrs. Rippstein was suspicious of Meyer's motivations for holding this office, and evidence of disorganization under his leadership only added to the perception that Gasconade County did not intend to fully support the war effort. Indeed, within five months of taking office, the Missouri Council of Defense rated Meyer's competency as E, or ineffective.[56]

Further debate arose in early 1918 when the county council, dominated by leaders from northern Gasconade County, refused to recognize Clarence Baxter, an attorney from Owensville, as a member of the council. His membership should have been automatic because Mumford had appointed him as county food administrator in November 1917. Baxter, whom Saunders deemed "an excellent man, . . . loyal, of good standing, and deeply interested in his work," also served as the county chief of the American Protective League. County council members, therefore, objected to his membership on the council because he was a non-German and, more important, because he could spy on them.[57]

More controversy arose after Edward Meyer announced his candidacy for county collector in January 1918. William Saunders noted Meyer's political aspirations in a February letter to Mumford, the state council chairman.[58]

Then in March 1918, during its monthly meeting in Kansas City, the Missouri Council of Defense decided that chairmen could not be candidates for public office to assure fairness and to protect "the best interests of the defense work."[59] In the context of the war, Meyer's political aspirations now became an excuse to push for the removal of a county council chairman who was perceived to be inactive. Saunders informed Meyer of the new regulation and requested that he resign. Meyer did so, and the county council promptly elected Frank Gaebler to replace Meyer as chairman. However, in doing so, the county again did not abide by state council guidelines, which stated that only the state chairman could appoint county council chairmen. Saunders interpreted the county's action as defying state guidelines, as pro-German, and suggested that the state council "take a firm stand on this matter."[60]

Worse yet, Gaebler's reputation was not the best. Most considered him "in general a good citizen" because he had taught school in the county, owned a large store, and served as postmaster in the town of Swiss, and two of his sons served in the army. But people, including Rose Rippstein, questioned Gaebler's loyalty because he had supported Germany and had been outspoken against England during the neutrality period. Nevertheless, Mumford approved Gaebler's appointment because he was "very influential among the Germans" and therefore "might be the right man for the place."[61]

Once in office, the new chairman quickly gained a reputation as being not as enthusiastic and effective as he could be despite the persistent pressures to hold mass meetings, utilize the state council's excellent speakers, acknowledge every communication and instruction letter he received from Jefferson City, work closely with Rose Rippstein and Clarence Baxter, and improve Gasconade County's defense work. Gaebler, however, added stipulations. While approving the general idea of holding mass meetings, he did not think such gatherings should be held during the planting season. Furthermore, the Missouri Council should be careful in the selection of speakers because the wrong man "may do more harm than good." For example, a speaker should not talk about the atrocities committed by Germans because "these people have brothers and cousins and nephews fighting in the German armies and they know those stories are untrue." Instead, he insisted that speakers should appeal to their pride in and love for this country. Furthermore, upon the suggestion to establish a speakers' bureau for the county so that the Committee on Public Information (CPI) could better direct its information to the people, Gaebler replied that "for the present I have no time to organize a Speakers Bureau." Although he attributed the lack of time to sickness in the family, the refusal further tarnished his and the county council's reputation.[62]

Robert A. Glenn, sent as a special agent to investigate Gasconade County, believed that most of the problems in the county were due to a "split into factions political, social and moral."[63] Indeed, further investigation supports the notion that preexisting geographic divisions and economic competition could have limited the effectiveness of the council. The majority of members hailed from the northern, more German region of the county while Baxter lived in Owensville. Eugene Rippstein (Rose's husband), A. B. Walker, Edward Meyer, and Frank Gaebler also held interests in four competing banks in the county. They not only competed for account holders and depositors, but since banks were the primary sellers of Liberty Bonds, they also competed for the prestige of selling the most bonds.[64]

Political disagreements existed as well. Frank Gaebler may have been less effective in the county because he was not only a Democrat in a primarily Republican county but he was also "an intense prohibitionist" in a wine-making county.[65] Rose Rippstein associated Edward Meyer's inactivity with his candidacy for office, because he did not wish to upset any of the German voters in the county. In addition Rose Rippstein's brother George Klenk had defeated A. B. Walker during the 1916 and 1918 mayoral elections in Hermann. In what the *Volksblatt* called an "especially exciting" mayoral campaign in 1918, Walker, who had been accused of not supporting the Red Cross and of hindering the sale of bonds in 1917, accused Klenk of mishandling the administration of the town, Klenk also served as a Four-Minute Man, addressing audiences in movie theaters during reel changes, and on the festival committee of the Gasconade County chapter of the National German-American Alliance.[66] Those who had access to St. Louis newspapers would have known about the declining prestige of that organization and therefore resented anyone associated with it. It is thus likely that, as historian Stephen Gross has argued for farmers and merchants in general, the working-class segment of Hermann and farmers throughout Gasconade County disliked the middle-class interference into daily lives through socially and politically influential volunteers such as Mrs. Rippstein and Mayor Klenk.[67]

In reaction to these internal problems and the perception that Gasconade County was less than loyal, supporters of the war became, in Robert Glenn's words, even more "intensely and aggressively patriotic." He believed that the only reason the county oversubscribed the Third Liberty Loan was due to Mayor Klenk, Mrs. Rippstein, and other "loyal Americans" getting into automobiles and canvassing the entire county. More than that, "they used the methods of the Big Stick, mincing no words but calling the wealthy Germans who refused to subscribe 'slackers' and 'yellow.' . . . This got the money, but caused a lot of resentment."[68]

This resentment had consequences. As William Saunders, the secretary of the state council, recognized, Mrs. Rippstein, a "courageous, determined, patriotic woman" through her undying devotion to duty, "made herself very unpopular with the members of the county council by trying to push them to do the work." According to Saunders, she and her husband "deserve a good deal of credit because they face with perfect understanding the loss of a great deal of banking business by pressing our patriotic plans." Indeed, Eugene Rippstein decided in March not to serve as the chairman of the Third Liberty Loan Campaign in Gasconade County, and in June had to deal with "unjust accusations" asserting that he privately sold Liberty Bonds through the bank.[69]

Thus it appears that by May 1918 the barometer of patriotism and suspicion had risen dramatically in Gasconade County. The numbers indicated that the county followed its motto to keep busy and did what was necessary to demonstrate patriotism. Still, state officials and neighboring counties viewed Gasconade County as less than loyal because relentless complaints painted a picture of slacking. By now, superpatriots also used ethnicity to explain this persistent disloyalty of the majority of the county's inhabitants. Rose Rippstein, for example, viewed the county as "all German" and thus automatically concluded that the majority of the population held pro-German views on the war. She may have used this argument to appear more American and dissociate herself from the German label because in 1915 she had participated as an actress, alongside her husband and stepson, in the German comedy *Der Zugvogel* (The Drifter), which the German Dramatic Society had presented at the Concert Hall in Hermann.[70]

State council members also associated perceived disloyalty with German ethnicity. Mrs. Gus V. R. Mechin, the chairman of the Speakers' and Organization Committee of the Woman's Committee believed that "the most serious situation that exists in Gasconade County is pro-Germanism." She thought that Morrison, Hermann, and Potsdam had a particularly "strong element of pro-German origin."[71] William Saunders, after a personal visit to Hermann in February 1918, argued that the Gasconade County Council was in "bad shape" and mired deep in "pro-German mud" because Germans had controlled it "from the beginning."[72]

Within this climate of growing suspicion, the continued use of the German language in public schools and churches in the county became a mark of disloyalty. The state council became especially concerned when a Jefferson City paper asserted that Gasconade County was one of only 3 of the state's 114 counties that refused to follow State Superintendent Uel Lamkin's suggestion to stop teaching the "enemy's tongue" in schools. Indeed, the article asserted that Gasconade County "seems most disinclined to drop the teaching of the Hun language." Thus Gasconade County appeared to distinguish itself as the lone resister to state and national guidelines to curtail the use of German.[73] Consequently, giving up the old language became an additional requirement for Germans in Gasconade County to demonstrate their loyalty.

The inability or unwillingness to immediately give in to these pressures only confirmed the perception that German-Americans in Gasconade County were not patriotic. What most non-Germans did not realize was that German-Americans did not see maintenance of the German language as resistance. Instead they dealt with the real life issue of generational conflict, the natural process of acculturation, and the inability to suddenly change and abandon traditions. Gaebler, for example, believed that council members did not "fully understand" the language issue in the county. He noted as an example that the younger element demanded English in churches but the older generation could understand only German. In addition, few ministers could preach in both languages and were willing to administer to the poorer rural congregations. In his opinion, time would solve the problem. Furthermore, he suggested that "if we want no foreign language used in the church" then why "discriminate against the German" and not "take action against the Bohemian and Italian churches and bar the use of Latin in the Catholic Church."[74] Although state council officials could understand the church issue, they nevertheless strongly agitated for the elimination of German from school.[75]

Undeniably, the mounting internal and external pressure to stop the use and teaching of German had an impact. German pioneers in Hermann had established the German School to turn the town into a truly bilingual community. However, by 1918, being bilingual was no longer an asset but a mark of disloyalty. Consequently, the Hermann school board and teachers decided to end the teaching of German in grade school for the duration of the war. The city council had printed its protocol and proceedings in both the German and English language for years. However, due to the war, the council decided to suspend the German version "temporarily" for the duration of the conflict. The Elks lodge, as well, announced that it would no longer use the enemy alien language.[76]

By contrast, the push to end the use of German in churches had only limited results in Gasconade County. St. Paul's Church in Hermann had introduced one English service on Sundays in 1910 and did not increase that number; but Reverend R. H. Kasmann did discuss "inviolable patriotism" and similar subjects during Sunday sermons. The St. Johannes Church in Gasconade due to the mounting pressure began to experiment with an English Sunday evening service.[77] Although the pressure to stop speaking in German had some immediate impact, in the long term any serious language changes would not begin until the late 1920s.

Thus, by the summer of 1918, the barometer of intolerance of less than patriotic behavior in Gasconade County was rising quite high. Then events in a small town located on the western bank of the Gasconade River in northwest Gasconade County by the name of Potsdam affirmed the perception that the county was indeed disloyal (see figure 5.2).

Problems first began when the school board of Richland Township suddenly decided to "shut off the privilege of using the Potsdam school building for Farm Bureau meeting purposes." A. F. Wulff, a teacher and chairman of the Gasconade County Farm Bureau Clubs, attributed this action to "anti-war sympathies."[78] Then the school board refused to open the schoolhouse for the widely advertised National War Savings Day on June 28, 1918. The closure was puzzling because on April 23, the community had held its Liberty Bond rally at the schoolhouse as part of the end of the school year celebrations, on May 17, Reverend Kassman from Hermann had given a speech explaining the purpose of the Red Cross, and three weeks later, the community had held a Flag Day ceremony at the school.[79] Although "almost all the people of the community attended the W.S.S. [War Savings Stamp] meeting" in front

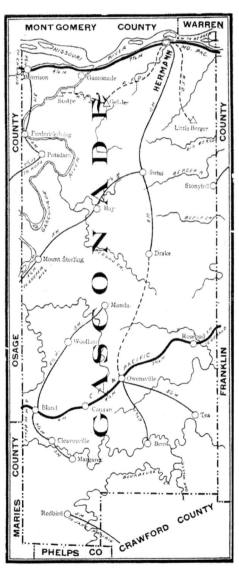

FIGURE 5.2. Postal routes in Gasconade County, 1904. Located in Vertical File, Gasconade County Historical Society.

of the school building, none could actually purchase any stamps because the president of the school board and the district clerk were absent. Missouri Council of Defense officials were truly astonished when they heard the news because they knew of no other schoolhouse in the state that refused to open its doors for patriotic gatherings.[80]

County council chairman Frank Gaebler immediately consulted with August Mann, the county superintendent of schools, who directed the school board to "at once open the schoolhouse for all patriotic meetings or for any purpose that might aid in winning the war." This attention had impact. On July 24, the Farmers Club again advertised its monthly meeting as taking place in the schoolhouse, and on August 17, county, state, and national war-savings-stamp representatives descended upon Potsdam for a special patriotic meeting held at the school. During that meeting, people from Potsdam bought $2,745 in stamps and pledged to purchase the remaining $1,435 to meet their quota within ten days. That the War Savings Stamp Committee printed the names of individuals who owned and pledged to purchase stamps also helped.[81]

Reopening the schoolhouse for public gatherings did not end the controversy because several St. Louis newspapers heard about the Potsdam incident and published scathing articles, thus bringing even further attention to the region. For example, the *St. Louis Star* asserted that the YMCA had not received any support in Potsdam and that the large subscriptions of a few people were the primary reason why Potsdam barely met its Third Liberty Loan quota. The *Star*'s placement of this article next to an essay discussing the meaning of Potsdam in Germany only added to the suspicion of pro-Germanism. C. K. Meyer, the manager of the YMCA War Work and Third Liberty Loan Campaign for the Potsdam School District, in a widely published editorial responded by providing the actual facts and figures, such as that Potsdam had oversubscribed its Third Liberty Loan quota by $2,000 and that all but three residents owned bonds. Meyer argued that he did not want to cover up disloyalty but merely intended to establish the truth and prove that Potsdam was loyal.[82] Nevertheless, Potsdam experienced pressure to demonstrate loyalty more fervently.

Inspired by all the publicity, on Sunday, July 14, 1918, a group of eleven men from neighboring Osage County drove to Potsdam and nailed an American flag to the porch of the post office. The following day this rather old and worn flag disappeared, and two new ones took its place. The Missouri Patriotic Speakers' Bureau quickly organized a truly patriotic mass meeting in Potsdam on August 25 to benefit the Red Cross despite local attempts to boycott it.[83] After all this excitement and turmoil it is not surprising that one civic-minded couple in the town, Dr. Howard and Lottie Workman, began a petition drive to change the name of the post office from Potsdam to Pershing. Although Mrs. Workman did not hold any "animosity or anti-German feelings" and was glad that she and her husband had been "very well accepted into the community," she still believed that her town should no longer hold the name of the kaiser's home but should be named after a Missouri hero. More important, such a name change would also prove the loyalty of the community and divert attention. Eventually, fifty people signed the petition, a decided minority in the community.[84]

Potsdam, a small community of 260 people, as a result of all this turmoil, attracted for a brief moment virtually the entire attention of the state council of defense. Saunders, believing that "we have dealt too gently with those people," suggested that the state council appoint a "brand new council" for the county.[85] The state council of defense also ordered an in-depth investigation and learned that Potsdam was divided over the war. Approximately one half of the population was 100 percent American and the other half hindered the establishment of a Red Cross center, did not sign food pledges, and refused to contribute to the YMCA and purchase bonds. These opponents to war allegedly had also refused the request of American citizens in the community to conduct at least one Sunday school class at the Reformed Zion German Church in English. Supposedly "the people of German lineage openly taunt and defy the Americans, calling them 'No-Accounts' and 'Swine.'"[86]

Although the United States Postal Service officially changed the name to Pershing in October 1918, the situation remained "tense and volatile" because Potsdam postmaster, constable, and member of Richland Township Council of Defense, Frank Kicker, initially refused to change the name since a second petition signed by two hundred people had been sent to Washington opposing the name change. The postal service, however, maintained the Pershing name. In opposition to the name change people attempted to boycott a Red Cross rally. Allegedly, citizens of Potsdam also "scoffed" at the state council's request to discontinue the German language in public gatherings and when conducting business. Several council officials feared that "soldiers returning from overseas service . . . might act harshly against . . . people who did not wholly support their righteous cause."[87]

Gasconade County council chairman Frank Gaebler aimed to alleviate such fears by explaining that "Potsdam had factional quarrels long before we got into the war." One of these factions included a group of "about half a dozen chronic kickers" who harassed the entire community and nagged "people on account of their German ancestry." In his opinion, the inhabitants of

Pershing "are strictly loyal," and most residents bought more bonds and war savings stamps than those who boasted about Americanism.[88]

Gaebler explained that explicit resistance to the war more often reflected the opposition to persistent and increasing government involvement in daily routines and traditions than pro-German or antiwar sentiment. He argued, for example, that the state council of defense could not interfere with the agricultural habits of farmers because that would be economically harmful and would certainly stir up resentment. Furthermore, Gaebler did not think that officials should demand that people give up their language overnight because people were naturally unable to change and abandon traditions suddenly.[89]

Nationalists such as Rose Rippstein and members of the state council in Jefferson City interpreted resistance to their leadership and guidelines as opposition to the war effort and thus as evidence of disloyalty. Some resistance to the war itself indeed existed, and those who expressed that kind of sentiment, such as Heidbreder, quickly learned the consequences. The majority of residents did not support the German imperial government. Instead, they were loyal Americans who just happened to speak German, attend German church services, and eat German foods. They followed the county council guideline to remain busy and quiet, in part to avoid attention and persecution and in part to express true loyalty to the Unites States, but they also objected to the government's intrusion into their daily lives. To borrow Gasconade County Council chairman Frank Gaebler's words, "These people are as loyal and patriotic as any in the state. They have been that in all past years in our history, and they are so now."[90] However, internal preexisting problems and the actions of a few often shaped the events and definition of loyalty at the local level. Informed by insiders that the causes for nonsupport must have come through pro-German sentiment, Missouri council leaders, who looked in from the outside, were then quick to place the ethnic label on this perceived disloyalty.

Neighboring Osage County also had a relatively high German population in Missouri and received attention for suspected disloyal behavior; however, this county would also experience true superpatriotism during World War I.

SIX

Superpatriotism in Action

Osage County during World War I

DURING THE late evening hours of July 7, 1918, several young men in Chamois, Osage County, forced Erwin Walz, the son of a German preacher, to salute and kiss the American flag because he had made derogatory remarks about the local Home Guard unit and stated "God damn the Flag, to hell with it!" The incident soon turned into a serious brawl as supporters for Walz appeared in the streets willing to defend his honor. The group of nationalistic citizens grew as well and began to force several Walz supporters to kiss the flag. Some of the pro-Germans then ran to get guns. Richard Garstang, the captain of the local Home Guard unit, received frantic phone calls urging him to step in and maintain law and order. But he could not act without the authorization of the mayor, who happened to be out of town at the time. In desperation, he gathered a few guardsmen, approached the mob in civilian clothing and persuaded the crowd to disperse, thus avoiding a serious riot.[1]

Why did this event occur in Chamois and not elsewhere in Osage County? German immigrants had established tightly knit ethnic communities in Osage County between 1830 and 1910 along the alluvial bottomlands of the Maries and Osage rivers in Jackson, Washington, and Linn townships, where they and their American-born children represented the majority of the population

133

and controlled the local economy and politics. However, by the turn of the century, the American-born children of German parents moved into northern Osage County, particularly Benton Township, including the town of Chamois, where they challenged the dominance of old-stock Americans from Tennessee, Kentucky, and Virginia. Here, competition over valuable river-bottom land, for business, and for elective office increased tensions between those of German descent and those of other heritage prior to the war. In northern Osage County the definition of patriotism during the war also took on a more dramatic meaning than in the southern parts of the county through widespread volunteerism and service to country. Here, local circumstances created a climate in which disloyal expressions contributed to mistrust and spawned animosity as well as superpatriotic activity.

The beginning of the Great War in Europe in 1914 was not a divisive issue, and residents of Osage County freely expressed their opinions. Two English-language newspapers, the *Unterrified Democrat* and the *Osage County Republican* published in Linn, the county seat, as well as the German-language newspaper, the *Osage County Volksblatt* published in Westphalia, greeted the arrival of the war without banner headlines. Although heralding Allied battle victories on occasion, these three papers in general favored the German side in the conflict. Articles argued, for example, that the kaiser's leadership and so-called German traits, such as organization and thoroughness, explained Germany's early success.[2] The *Volksblatt*, in particular, defended the Central Powers. The editor, Henry Castrop, supported the actions Austria and Germany took in response to the assassination of Archduke Franz Ferdinand as justified even though they resulted in war. Through a poem titled *Militarismus* (Militarism), the *Volksblatt* argued that Great Britain, not Germany, was the most militaristic nation in the world because it had beheaded Scotland's Mary, used force in India, and annihilated the American Indian. The paper also defended the actions of German soldiers accused of having committed atrocities in Belgium arguing that Belgians had had a secret alliance with France and, by not allowing Germany free travel through Belgium, invited some military action.[3]

These three papers also criticized Britain's control and censorship of information from Europe and its scathing anti-German propaganda. The editor of the *Volksblatt*, again, was the most outspoken. He believed that *England's Hetze* (England's smear campaign) directed against Germany had only one purpose and that was to pull the United States into the war and to again dominate America as a tyrant and to turn its citizens into vassals. As late as April 5, 1917, the day before the declaration of war, the *Volksblatt* stood steadfast in its belief that Germany had to win the war. Although resigned to the inevitability of America's entry, the editor argued that only a German victory would finally end British control over the press and loosen the grip England and the money interests had on the Wilson administration. Only then could America be truly free again.[4] Since Britain controlled and censored war news sent to the United States and thus tried to mislead the American public in favor of the Allied cause, the English- and German-language newspapers in Osage County throughout the neutrality period published letters from relatives who lived in Germany. This correspondence intended to represent the truth, discussed the limited impact the war had on Germany's civil and commercial life, and inspired hope that the war would end soon.[5] Although the publication of letters certainly added a different perspective to the war coverage, these newspapers clearly catered to the interests of German-American readers in the county.

These papers, moreover, did not hesitate to criticize President Woodrow Wilson's lack of true neutrality.[6] The *Volksblatt* was the most vocal, although not alone in this sentiment. As early as October 1914, editorials portrayed Uncle Sam as a *Heuchler* (hypocrite) who went to church to pray for peace, yet sold war materials to the Allies the very next day. In August 1916, the editor agreed with and printed the Catholic central verein's resolution that reprimanded Wilson for mistrusting German-Americans. The central verein argued that Wilson's suspicions were unfounded because German-Americans had been exceptional citizens of indisputable loyalty and patriotism since their arrival in the United States. In a subsequent editorial that reflected the same self-image as better Americans than the native-born, the editor reminded the president and the readers that Germans had fought on the side of the Union whereas Wilson's relatives had fought on the side of the Rebels.[7]

Like so many newspapers in Missouri, Osage County weeklies agreed that submarine warfare was a legitimate tactic for Germany during the war to limit the effect of Britain's blockade. Although saddened about the loss of lives, the editors could understand why German submarines had sunk the *Lusitania*; after all the ship had carried weapons. Furthermore, American newspapers had warned readers not to travel on belligerent ships. But the editors also congratulated Wilson for his "coolheadedness, farsightedness and patriotism," which kept America "at peace with the world" during this crisis. Indeed, keeping the United States out of the war was more important to the editors than empathy toward one side or the other in the European conflict. But should the unthinkable happen and America enter the war, they were confident that the entire county, including "our German-American fellow citizens[,] will be found in the forefront upholding the Stars and Stripes and the American Government as their fathers did before them."[8]

Nevertheless, the newspapers of Osage County argued that German-Americans had the right to defend their old fatherland in this global conflict, just as those from English and French backgrounds naturally sympathized with the Allies. The *Volksblatt,* in particular, encouraged its readers to remain German at heart during the conflict and to support the victims of war, including the widows and orphans of German soldiers who died at the front. During the first state-wide German Day celebration in August 1916, the editor called upon his readers, especially those *denen deutsche Wesen und deutsche Art am Herzen liegen* (who hold German customs and manners dear to their hearts), to take part in this huge festival and to show the German strength in the state.[9]

In contrast to the *Volksblatt,* the *Unterrified Democrat* argued that Republican German-Americans, such as Representative Richard Bartholdt, who openly denounced Wilson for not being truly neutral, were not to be trusted. Editor Ell M. Zevely believed that "such detestable blatherskates as Bartholdt" aimed only to create sentiment against Wilson among German-American voters and thereby benefit the Republican Party. Therefore, a man like Bartholdt was "little less than a traitor to his country."[10] Such criticism indicated that Osage countians of German descent did not refrain from criticizing their own countrymen during the neutrality period. They would do so again during the war.

The prohibition issue and presidential campaign for the fall election in 1916 brought much excitement to Osage County. Prohibition had not been a divisive issue before the war, nor would it be when the movement to end the manufacture of liquor gained strength and the Missouri legislature placed the issue on the November 1916 ballot. Advertisements and editorials regarding prohibition in the two English- and one German-language newspapers revealed that the county continued to oppose prohibition because it would limit local options, reduce revenues, and harm the state's economy. The editor of the *Volksblatt* viewed prohibition in the most dramatic and ideological terms. In his opinion, prohibition represented a great danger because it limited personal freedom. The United States, as a result, would no longer be the freest nation in the world but return to the restrictive Puritan way of life.[11] The election results in November indicate that the public thought likewise. The county overwhelmingly defeated the prohibition amendment by an almost three-to-one ratio. Only four election districts supported it, and one district was tied on the issue. Although German-American communities opposed the prohibition amendment by overwhelming majorities, the American districts in Bonnots Mill, Chamois, and Freedom defeated the amendment by huge margins as well.[12] Thus, prohibition was not a divisive issue in Osage County.

In contrast, the 1916 presidential election campaign revealed political division along ethnic as well as party lines. As their names indicated, the two English language newspapers supported the candidate of the party with which they affiliated.[13] The *Unterrified Democrat* as early as February 1916 urged voters to support the Democratic Party because Republicans, while in power, had adopted a "program of carelessness and criminal indifference for the safety of the county" and had left behind a navy at one-third of its efficiency and power "and no army at all worth speaking of." The editor feared that Republicans were "secretly and seditiously plotting to destroy the neutrality of the United States and thus plunge our country into that bloody . . . foreign fury that is placing a continent in ashes and a world in mourning and tears." In the editor's opinion, only President Wilson would be able to keep the nation out of war. Although he was not perfect, Wilson's progressive principles were considered to be right for America because he had taken "plutocracy and privilege out of popular government" and preserved peace and prosperity. Consequently, the paper called on every German-American to withstand the pressure of the Republican press and to vote for Wilson.[14]

In contrast, the *Osage County Volksblatt,* despite its support for Democrats, argued that German-Americans had lost confidence in Wilson and his foreign policies. They could no longer allow him to determine the nation's destiny because that would mean that the United States would "go into the fire with Great Britain." Instead German-Americans should vote for Hughes. He might associate with nativists such as Theodore Roosevelt, but he was the lesser of two evils because Wilson supported England and opposed Catholicism.[15]

The Republican candidate Charles Evans Hughes indeed defeated the Democrat Woodrow Wilson in Osage County by a vote of 1,769 to 1,383. The election result thus continued the electoral trend in the county since 1896, with Republican presidential candidates winning by a margin of about 300 votes. Hughes received his major support from election districts in Benton Township including Chamois, as well as in Crawford, Jefferson, and Linn townships, areas settled primarily by old-stock Americans. Wilson, however, won in Westphalia, Rich Fountain, Freeburg, and Loose Creek, the largest German-American communities, because in Osage County German-Americans had a long-standing tradition of voting for Democrats.[16]

The county was thus divided geographically along ethnic and party lines on the eve of American entry into World War I. Many German-Americans moved to the northern areas of the county by 1910 and elected German-born Henry Ernstmeyer and William Pahmeier as mayors of Chamois after 1900. Thus by 1917 there were already political tensions in Republican areas, such as Benton Township.[17]

These political divisions would on occasion come to the forefront. For example, one of the most hotly debated issues during the early days of the war was the location of a bridge and new state highway (today's Highway 50) through Osage County to Jefferson City. The *Volksblatt* supported a bridge near Kliethermes Ford on the Maries River because that would have tremendously improved Westphalia's economy and the German region. The county court's decision to place the bridge near Holtermann Ford on the Osage River benefited the northern, more American region of the county. There is no evidence of physical altercations, but such hotly debated political issues added to preexisting tensions. The *Volksblatt* indeed received much criticism in the county for its activism during the bridge controversy.[18] Not only did the paper take a stand contrary to the mainstream on a local issue but it also spoke out more strongly against the Allies and the administration during the neutrality period than the remaining papers in the county. Thus it placed itself in a position that would become precarious once the United States entered the Great War.

President Wilson, while campaigning and winning reelection on the promise to keep the nation out of the war, in the end was not able to do so. Between the November election and February 1917, local newspapers rarely discussed the war. However, Germany's resumption of unlimited submarine warfare, the suspension of diplomatic relations between the United States and Germany, and the Zimmermann Telegram brought the war back into the homes of readers. Although newspapers and residents in Osage County were not happy to see the arrival of war, the *Unterrified Democrat* was glad that Wilson, "not a fire-eater," was at the helm during this crisis and was confident that Wilson would do his best to preserve "peace with honor." Once it became clear that the United States would enter the war, after all, the two English-language newspapers became very supportive of the administration and echoed President Wilson's argument that the United States did not enter the war to fight the German people but to replace the kaiser and his military autocracy with democracy in a "righteous" cause. They argued that "the time for criticism of America's Foreign Policy has about passed" and that "in this hour of stress" it was finally time to "rally round the flag" and to "uphold, support and defend" the United States.[19] Poems such as Thomas Becket's "The Red, White and Blue" aimed to inspire patriotism, and the *Osage County Republican* urged those who could not serve their country through the military to still follow Governor Gardner's call to make some sacrifices and "rally round the plow, spade and hoe."[20] Although they may have agitated for peace months earlier, the editors now recognized that their duties included the transmission of important information from state and federal authorities to the people of Osage County.[21]

The *Unterrified Democrat* and its old-stock American editor, former pro-
bate judge and county clerk Ell M. Zevely, kept the coverage of the war effort to a minimum until the establishment of the Osage County Council of
Defense in October 1917.[22] By contrast, the editor of the *Osage County Republican* began to publish local and state material regarding the war effort as
soon as it became available and thus maintained an image of patriotism much
sooner than his competitor. As a Swiss immigrant and German speaker, John
Feuers may have believed it was necessary to display that patriotism more
overtly. Nevertheless, the editor also maintained his right to criticize mobilization and Congress. For example, he opposed conscription and favored a
military based on volunteerism because that represented true American values. He sarcastically noted that Congress in reaction to the American people's
oversubscribing the First Liberty Loan could "hardly restrain itself from passing a censorship bill" and increasing taxes. The editor also questioned why
the *Missouri Volksfreund* in nearby Jefferson City, in his opinion one of the
"best all round German papers," had to file translations of war information
articles with the local postmaster. Finally, he thought it a shame that the German people living in the United States, who had proven their loyalty many
times, were perceived as disloyal owing to the acts of a few German spies and
saboteurs. There is no evidence that Feuers experienced any backlash for such
expressions, but his paper certainly presented an image of enthusiastic patriotism through the amount of space he dedicated to the war effort.[23]

Citizens of Osage County, although far removed from the federal government, thus had access to news regarding the war effort. They realized as early
as April 1917 that the war would not only affect their daily lives but would also
limit their freedom of speech. The *Unterrified Democrat,* explaining that it did
so at the request of U. S. Attorney General Francis W. Wilson, published an
official announcement from the Department of Justice declaring that German
aliens living in the United States, who had not conspired against the country,
did not have to fear the Department of Justice as long as they observed the
following warning: "Obey the Law; Keep Your Mouth Shut."[24] The *Democrat*
was the only paper in Osage County and the surrounding area to publish this
announcement, but word of mouth probably spread this warning quickly to
both Germans and Americans alike.

This warning must have encouraged pressure to conform, because within
days of the announcement the editor of the *Volksblatt* already informed his
readers about the growing push to unite public opinion and to suppress opposition to the war. He warned that unless the readers wanted to be considered
disloyal they had to *heulen mit den Wölfen* (howl with the wolves), bow to

hyperpatriotism, and wave the flag at every opportunity. Nobody would be exempt, not even the sons of *Dollar Fürsten* (moneyed aristocrats). He also predicted that the growing pressure to appear patriotic would surely break friendships and weaken neighborly relations.[25]

Indeed in May residents in Osage County learned what could happen to a person, especially a German-American, who opposed the war. The *Unterrified Democrat* explained in detail why August Heidbreder of Bland in neighboring Gasconade County had been arrested under the Espionage Act after he had remarked that President Wilson should be stuffed into a cannon and shot out to sea. The case received widespread coverage because he was rich and a well-known farmer and served as an example of what might happen to others who acted like him. Indeed, the *Democrat* warned its readers that federal authorities would be "zealous in suppressing remarks" such as Heidbreder's even if his "utterances" were "merely a species of inconsequential raving." The Heidbreder arrest suggested that during this war a person should watch what he was saying or pay the consequences.[26]

Maybe the editor of the *Osage County Volksblatt* should have taken Heidbreder's arrest for disloyal expression more seriously. After the United States entered the war, the *Volksblatt* continued to express anti-British thought and did not refrain from criticizing the war effort. The editor, Henry Castrop argued, for example, that Wilson should live up to his rhetoric of self-determination and asserted that Congress was beginning to use dictatorial powers to control manufacturing as well as the sale and pricing of foodstuffs. Castrop also addressed the debate over the Selective Service Act and in a front-page editorial offered an explanation for why the nation had to resort to the draft to man the military. He explained that the numbers of volunteers were so low because few honorable men, who under normal circumstances would gladly support their country, would want to dethrone a kaiser who had never hurt them, or sacrifice limb and life for England or millionaires.[27]

It is thus not surprising that the *Volksblatt* published its final issue and closed its doors on July 19, 1917. Henry Castrop stated in his farewell address that rising prices for paper and material and fewer paying subscribers forced him to "turn out the lights." He attributed this decline to Germans who abandoned their mother tongue and chose stimulation through pulp fiction and trashy reporting. Circulation numbers, however, indicate that the *Volksblatt* had enjoyed a steady readership with 600 subscribers in 1900, 584 in 1910, and 591 in 1915. The circulation numbers for 1916 and 1917 are not available and could certainly have declined dramatically as the war approached. Nevertheless, survey of the paper during the neutrality period and early 1917 indicated that the number and type of advertisements had changed very little during the war.[28] Therefore, additional reasons for closure must have been present.

One explanation was Castrop's recent increase in work because he had been appointed as State Senator Sam B. Cook's clerk, and he had already warned his readers that during the legislative session he might not always be able to print the weekly paper. The editor also recognized in his final issue that the pressure to appear patriotic by speaking and reading only English might have reduced readership.[29] Indeed, the more likely reason for ceasing publication was the editor's sense of duty to stand up for and defend the German people who had been insulted, disdained and portrayed as "uncivilized barbarians."[30] This made him, the paper, and its readership appear pro-German and un-American. It is likely that the leadership of Westphalia, the place of publication as well as the largest German settlement in Osage County, pressured him into either ending his criticism or closing his paper. One can hypothesize that the paper might have survived had it published pro-American material. However, a paper with a history of un-American expression would have brought attention to the area, especially once the Missouri Council of Defense required that township councils send in newspaper clippings from patriotic papers.[31] Therefore, the absence of this particular German-language newspaper made it less likely for government officials to know the attitudes of German-Americans in Osage County and to interpret them as un-American.

The demise of the *Volksblatt* is the only evidence for southwestern Osage County that the growing anti-German sentiment during the Great War limited freedom of speech or resulted in the closure of a business. German-Americans already knew the punishments that awaited them should they express opposition to the war. In response they adopted a strategy for the duration of the war that assured their survival. Most were indeed loyal to the United States, but they also complied with the official definition of loyalty at the level that was absolutely necessary to avoid persecution.

Flag Day, June 14, 1917, became the first opportunity for the German-Americans of Osage County to show their loyalty publicly. This celebration took place on the grounds of St. George's Catholic School in Linn, and the "large crowd" enjoyed a program of patriotic music and speeches that demonstrated respect and affection for the American flag.[32] These festivities acquire significance when one considers that Father Muckermann, who initiated and directed the entire ceremony, was a German-born priest who still presented sermons in German, and that students who sang patriotic tunes still learned German at the parochial school. In other words, this flag ceremony demonstrated the patriotism not only of the entire county but also of the German-speaking population in particular.

A front-page article in the *Unterrified Democrat* in July 1917 confirmed this definition of loyalty. Hugh McGuire, the author, explained that patriotism included daily acts that demonstrated a person's love for nation, country, flag, and home. This love or patriotism should be part of daily life and should be cultivated and taught to children.[33] German-Americans and the rest of the county took these suggestions to heart and proved their loyalty to the country throughout the war. Osage County men demonstrated their patriotism by enthusiastically following the call to duty. Shortly after the United States entered the Great War, several young men enlisted in the military services, including William L. Zevely, the son of the owner and editor of the *Unterrified Democrat* Ell Zevely. By the end of the war, thirty-five additional men from Osage County had enlisted in the army or navy.[34]

Patriotism also became evident with the passage and implementation of the Selective Service Act in June 1917. All men between the age of twenty-one and thirty-five who had not volunteered had to register for the draft on June 5, 1917. County newspapers fully informed the men about the registration procedures, including detailed explanations of forms, exemption guidelines, what they could expect during the examination process, and who served on the local exemption board.[35] Analysis of the Selective Service registration cards, especially the answers to question 12 that asked whether registrants wanted to claim an exemption and for what reason, demonstrates that Osage County men were patriotic. Of the 1,054 men who registered in the county, only 366 men requested an exemption. They included 279 men who claimed dependent family members, 75 who asked for physical disqualification, and 12 who claimed religion or essential work. This is much below the nation's average of about 60 percent.[36]

Analysis of individual towns indicates that neither geography nor ethnicity was a factor in asking for exemptions. All towns, whether located in the German or the American areas, had few requests for exemptions. Westphalia and Chamois, however, stand out with proportionately few exemption requests: 14 percent and 21 percent, respectively.[37] It is possible that young men of German descent in Westphalia believed they had to demonstrate a higher sense of patriotism than others in the county in order to avert attention and accusations of disloyalty. In Chamois, as subsequent pages will illustrate, the sense of patriotism was high in general and thus increased the pressure for any man in the community to appear loyal. Nevertheless, the low rate of exemption requests for the entire county indicates loyalty and a high level of patriotism for the men of Osage County.

During the first call-up or draft in August 1917 the proportions of exemptions granted did rise somewhat. The board examined 138 registrants, passed 45 as "qualified for service," disqualified 41 as physically unfit, and temporarily granted deferment to 40 for having dependent children, siblings, or parents. Interestingly, only 61 had asked for specific exemptions such as family or employment. Nine of the 138 registrants left question 12 blank although they were married on June 5, and it is unclear whether they meant to serve in the military or whether they expected board members to automatically grant exemptions for marriage. The latter may have been true because the board granted deferment for the 9 registrants and only denied 2 requests for marriage exemptions because registrants married after June 5. Although deferment based on dependent family was temporary until the district board issued its final classification, the local board assured men that it had been "very careful and judicious in all its proceedings" and that those who received temporary deferments would probably receive exemptions from the district board as well.[38] In other words, if justified and legitimate, men who received their exemptions were still patriotic.

Despite this evidence of patriotism, editorials in local newspapers indicate that several citizens were concerned about conscientious objectors and slackers. Ell M. Zevely, whose son volunteered during the early days of the war, for example, believed that requests for exemption consisted largely of two elements—treason and cowardice. As a member of the Linn registration precinct, he knew about the types of exemptions requested and worried that, in addition to legitimate exemptions, seemingly frivolous requests such as "head hurts," "fondness of food," and "weak minded" would tarnish the county's reputation of patriotism. He also could not imagine why a conscientious objector would claim that the taking of a human life, even during war, was unjustifiable while "their fellow citizens" fought, bled, and died "so that the blessings of liberty may be theirs." In his view, therefore, neither the conscientious objector nor the person requesting exemptions for other reasons deserved any consideration from the government or citizens.[39]

In addition to young men serving in the military, men and women also demonstrated their patriotism as public speakers, including several highly respected members from the German communities. For example, W. A. Willibrand from Freeburg gave an address at the courthouse in Linn on July 28, 1917, on the subject of why the nation was at war. He repeated the government line and argued that pan-Germanism and military autocracy were threatening democracy and democratic institutions. The *Unterrified Democrat* applauded Willibrand's stand on the war issue in an editorial and compared his reputation with such notable Germans as Carl Schurz and Dr. Pretorious.[40]

Women demonstrated their patriotism through commitment to food conservation and volunteering for the Food Administration. However, the August registration campaign for women revealed the first signs of suspected disloyal behavior. Ida Zouck, the county's chairperson for the woman's committee, was very disappointed in the low number of pledges because she wanted her county to make a good showing. She blamed the Germans of the county, because "it is very hard to make their women folk understand just what we mean by food conservation, when they have spent their lives in saving." Files of the Missouri Council of Defense reveal that indeed only twenty-one women signed the food conservation pledge in Osage County; of those, twelve were from Chamois and six from Linn, none came from the German towns of Freeburg or Rich Fountain.[41]

By contrast, most residents of Osage County supported the Red Cross. High school students in Linn signed up members during the Christmas membership drive. Junior Red Cross members cultivated thrift gardens, knitted sweaters and socks, and invested in war savings stamps. During the May fundraising campaign, the county quickly oversubscribed its quota by $6,360.[42]

People in Osage County also proved their loyalty through subscriptions to the four Liberty Loans. The First Liberty Loan received scant coverage in local papers, and it is unclear whether the county met its quota because papers did not publish the results. Newspapers contributed more space to the Second Liberty Loan, and a well-organized telephone campaign urged citizens to get involved. But, again, the results were not published, and it is likely that the county did not reach its quota.[43]

As in neighboring Gasconade County and throughout Missouri, in-depth organization and widespread advertisement had an impact during the Third Liberty Loan campaign. The liberty loan committee appointed postmasters, ministers, and priests as associate publicity directors to spread the government's message throughout the county. Intimidation, such as defining those who did not purchase bonds as "slackers" who were "not fit to associate with real Americans," also encouraged subscriptions. Although six school districts did not meet their quota, the county oversubscribed its quota of $142,000 by over $71,000 after 1,919 subscribers bought an average of $111.27 in bonds. Bonnots Mill received the county's Honor Flag for oversubscribing by the largest margin. Chamois subscribed $21,750, the largest amount in the county. The major German school districts all surpassed their quotas and Rich Fountain claimed the highest per person subscription, $319.23.[44]

Osage County also very quickly topped its quota during the Fourth Liberty Loan campaign in the fall of 1918. Yet, despite the growing influenza scare and the success of the campaign, the loan committee urged the school districts that had not met their share in the previous three drives and again in the fourth to finally prove their loyalty. Newspapers published the membership list of the "Thousand Dollar Club" to shame the wealthy in the county to contribute according to their ability. Campaign officials also announced that they kept an accurate list of those who had not purchased bonds and promised to turn this list over to the secret service for investigation after the end of the campaign. They would also show a copy to returning soldiers. R. V. Cramer, the chairman of the campaign, asserted that "if there is no law to reach bond slackers, public opinion," especially that of returning soldiers, would "show the slacker the road to travel."[45]

In addition to these efforts to demonstrate patriotism and loyalty, local papers occasionally reminded readers to remain vigilant in their lookout for the enemy and what could happen to him if found out. The *Unterrified Democrat*, for example, printed a warning from Herbert Hoover that stated that German spies might cause irreparable damage to the 1917 wheat harvest. The paper intensified the urgency of this warning by reporting that "a few days ago . . . wheat fields in Kansas had been fired by supposed German agents." Although the paper was "not inclined" to believe such reports, "we have learned by experience there is nothing Germany is not capable of, if she thinks it will serve her ends."[46] The *Unterrified Democrat* also published a warning to readers who might not be entirely loyal. It had learned that the Missouri Council of Defense intended to "stamp out seditious talk and treasonable acts" through a color-coded card warning system. The editor, while believing this system to be a good idea in general, nevertheless realized the possible abuses of it and insisted that the cards only be used for legitimate reasons and that they should be signed.[47]

The definition of loyalty for Osage County during the first year of the war was such that willingness to personally sacrifice through enlistment in the military service, following the draft guidelines, food conservation, and bond purchase were enough evidence to demonstrate patriotism. And, according to this definition of loyalty, neither the county nor its German areas could be deemed overtly disloyal.

Northern Osage County, however, raised the stakes because loyalty there took on a much more complex meaning. Here, one town demonstrated a particularly strong sense of patriotism that would raise expectations for others. The city of Chamois stood out in the county and surrounding area for its volunteer spirit through the creation of the Second Missouri Field Hospital, a new and entirely volunteer National Guard company, on June 21, 1917. Later renamed the 138th Field Hospital, 110th Sanitary Train, 35th Division, the unit served in France from June 1, 1918, through April 5, 1919, and saw action in the Gerardmer Sector of the Vosges Mountains during the St. Mihiel Offensive and in the Meuse-Argonne Offensive in September 1918. Fifty-eight members of the unit were wounded, and six were killed.[48] The majority of the troops came from Chamois and northern Osage County, and included seven men whose parents or grandparents had been born in Germany. Their volunteerism distinguished this particular geographic area for its powerful sense of service to country, and Sergeant Ben Meyer, former staff member of the *Unterrified Democrat,* regularly updated the newspaper and its readers about training, promotions, and sickness.[49] In this context of public spirit any disloyal remarks would have been interpreted as disrespectful to the sacrifices of these young men.

In addition to this intense patriotism, Chamois was also the only town in Osage County to organize a Home Guard unit, Company M of the 5th Regular Missouri Home Guards. The guard unit was fully established by August 11, 1917, and members had elected their officers. J. Richard Garstang, city attorney and co-founder of the 2nd Field Hospital, served as captain, D. A. Gibbs as first lieutenant, and Joseph Miller as second lieutenant.[50] The Home Guard, with its low physical qualification requirements, offered many aged war veterans, those physically disqualified from active service, and retired guardsmen the opportunity to serve.

Home Guard members did not just protect local bridges from saboteurs but also had the duty to stimulate interest in all war activities, to keep alive the spirit of patriotism, and to stamp out disloyalty. If the adjutant general's assessment of the average attendance and holding of drills held true for the unit in Chamois, 80–90 percent of members would have attended three drills per week. These drills, often accompanied by the town band were advertised in Jefferson City as well. On Labor Day 1918 the Chamois unit also conducted a "Sham Battle" with the Jefferson City unit; the outcome, however, is unknown.[51] In Chamois, a town of 649 residents, the Home Guard through its drills and participation in parades became the visual representative of the war effort. Any verbal attack upon it would raise the anger of guard members and would certainly result in some form of discipline.

Chamois also established the first Red Cross chapter in the county. Several residents of Chamois, such as Charley Marquand, the cashier at the Bank of Chamois, and Henry Steinmann, the county surveyor, served in leadership positions for Red Cross, Liberty Loan, and War Savings Stamp campaigns. The village and Benton Township subscribed in proportionately larger numbers to the Liberty Loan and donated more money to the Red Cross than most communities and townships in the county, possibly owing to enthusiasm for the men serving in the military.[52] Such activism must have raised the level of expectations for the rest of the population, and anything less would reveal slacking or aiding the enemy.

Osage County, as a result of this service to country, certainly looked as if it were patriotic. Nevertheless, it appears that the county as a whole was not living up to expectations, because the Missouri Council of Defense classified Osage County as "C" or "Medium" in activity and effectiveness in April 1918 and ordered an official investigation. It is unclear just what caused this order, with the exception of the questionable support of the first two Liberty Loan campaigns, because there is no evidence of slacking or outright disloyal behavior or remarks in the correspondence with the Missouri Council of Defense prior to March 1918. The investigation, as well, did not uncover evidence of slacking or aiding the enemy. Consequently, Robert Glenn, the investigator, defined the county as loyal.[53] However, as in the case of Gasconade County, the correspondence of one dedicated and patriotic person continued to paint a picture of less than 100 percent loyalty.

Former prosecuting attorney J. Richard Garstang exemplified patriotism. He co-organized the hospital unit, served as captain of the Home Guard, set up a letter-writing campaign that sent 10,600 letters to American soldiers stationed overseas, and as an attorney, he provided free legal services to soldiers and their families. In his correspondence with the Missouri Council of Defense, he indicated that several citizens of Chamois still did not trust some of their German neighbors who initially had supported Germany's side in the war. He noted, for example, that the mayor, Dr. Otto J. Keuper, appeared to be only a "lukewarm patriot" because he was afraid to offend the German members of the town board. Garstang also believed that the Benton Township Council of Defense seemed "cold-footed" and pro-German because members were afraid to lose business. Interestingly, only two members, Chairman Fred Stonner and Walter Lagemann, had parents born in Germany.[54]

The highly successful Third Liberty Loan campaign seemed temporarily to ease the tensions; but that too was not enough. Possibly inspired by Governor Gardner's warning that "there can be no half-hearted allegiance. . . . Those who are against us are pro-German," local newspapers reminded residents that they were behind in their purchase of War Savings Stamps, that the county "occupies a status of a slacker," and that this was "an intolerable condition."[55] Within this environment of heightened pressure to appear loyal, anything that would have blemished the area's reputation even further would have to be dealt with quickly.

The opportunity presented itself on May 27, 1918, when the county held a Red Cross rally at St. George's Hall in Linn. The main speaker was Clara Steichen, the wife of a U.S. Army captain, who told about her experiences in France when the war began, including atrocities committed by German soldiers. Although this "did not please the German sympathizers" in the county, the meeting nevertheless resulted in "quick and generous" contributions that allowed the county to go over its quota for the second Red Cross campaign.[56] Newspapers reported this positive outcome but omitted the disloyal remarks Paul Paulsmeyer, son of a German immigrant, had made at the meeting. Paulsmeyer allegedly called Mrs. Steichen a "damned old whore," because, according to Garstang's report, he believed that all female Red Cross volunteers were prostitutes.[57]

Although the event occurred in Linn, the accusers as well as the accused lived in Chamois. They not only lived in the same community, but accuser Hugo Lecuru was also the bugler for the 2nd Field Hospital in 1917 and Joseph Miller served as second lieutenant of the Chamois Home Guard unit from August 1917 through May 1918. Moreover, this appeared to be just the latest evidence of Paulsmeyer's suspected disloyalty. He allegedly had tried to evade the draft and had "sneeringly refused to join the Home Guard or any other institution standing out openly for Americanism." Patriots of Chamois now feared that without further action, "we are likely to have a tar & feather party" because feelings of animosity were "running pretty high."[58]

The Missouri Council of Defense referred the matter to the Secret Service in Kansas City for further investigation, but there is no evidence that a government agent actually came to Chamois. Instead, community leaders solved the matter locally, quietly, and to everyone's satisfaction. In order to give Paulsmeyer the opportunity to demonstrate his loyalty, the local draft board canceled his exemption for physical disability, and on June 25, 1918, he left for Camp Pike, Arkansas, for military training. Paulsmeyer remained a private during his service at a medical infirmary and was honorably discharged at demobilization. The incident did not hurt Paulsmeyer's future because after the war he returned to Chamois and his position as the assistant cashier at the People's Bank of Chamois.[59]

Newspapers did not address the Paulsmeyer incident, and it is unclear to what extent the public knew about it.[60] However, Erwin Walz, who replaced Paulsmeyer as assistant cashier at the People's Bank during the latter's military service, must have known that any opposition to the war effort would have serious consequences because his father, Reverend Walz, officiated at Paulsmeyer's wedding on June 20, 1918.[61]

On July 3, Frank Oidtmann, a private in the local home guard unit, met Walz at the local barber shop and asked him whether he knew why his supervisor, cashier Joseph Kuster, had not reported for drill duty. Walz allegedly responded, "Oh, to hell with the Home Guards!" On the following day, as participants for the Fourth of July parade lined up, Home Guard members realized that Erwin Walz would be the marshal of the parade on behalf of the Boy Scouts of Chamois. The Home Guard unit stepped out of the lineup and refused to march in the same parade as Walz. To avoid a Home Guard "mutiny on Main Street," Second Lieutenant Harry Steinmann, the officer in charge, approached Walz and requested that he not participate in the parade. Walz initially refused, believing the grievance was based on a personal matter, but left after the manager of the parade urged him to do so.[62] Later that evening, Steinmann and Walz met again and during the heated argument regarding the events of that morning, Walz allegedly stated angrily that no "self-dubbed Captain or self-dubbed Lieutenant" had any authority over him, thus again denigrating the Home Guard. The following day Walz lost his position at the bank and faced charges under the Espionage Act.[63]

During the investigation of Walz's "disloyal and reprehensible conduct" it became apparent that he had made insulting remarks about the Home Guard, the flag, and the war effort at previous times. For example, Walz on several occasions allegedly refused to salute the American flag and allegedly said "to hell with the flag." Such expressions indicated to the investigators "an evil intention and unfriendly feeling toward American military organizations."[64] But no one had bothered to report him, and it appeared that he was not the only person to make such disloyal remarks. Officers and members of the Home Guard had been the subject of "constant and repeated insult and ridicule" and high tensions had "been brewing for some time."[65] And when it became clear that Walz's remarks would not be prosecuted under the Espionage or Sedition Act, after all, patriotic citizens took the law into their own hands and forced Walz to kiss the flag.[66]

Several reasons or possibilities explain why Walz received this public rebuke. Walz obviously expressed thoughts that were contrary to the definition of loyalty in Chamois. He was also a German-American and an outsider. His father, Reverend Hermann Walz, was a German immigrant who had been a prominent preacher in St. Louis as well as a member of the German-American Alliance. The family had moved to northern Osage County in October 1917 to take over the German congregations in Chamois and Deer.[67] Not only was he an outsider, but as a person from a major city and the son of a well-known preacher, he might have appeared to be arrogant and conceited. His becoming the assistant cashier immediately after Paulsmeyer left for the military must have indicated to many in Chamois that he had good connections within the German community. This "connection" may have been one reason why his alleged behavior and remarks were not punished sooner, thus leading to resentment among Americans and Germans alike.

Indeed, several members in the Home Guard were German-Americans, and his alleged insults also outraged them. For example, Second Lieutenant Harry Edward Steinmann was the grandson of German immigrants on his father's side, and Private Frank Oidtmann's grandparents had been born in Germany.[68] Thus Walz's remarks raised tensions among individual members of the German-American community. Furthermore, his remarks about the flag and Home Guard would eventually bring more attention to the German-American community as a whole if he were to proceed unhindered. If those whom he denigrated, including German-Americans, did not punish him, then it would be possible for people to think that German-Americans were not loyal but only conformed outwardly while inwardly believing as Walz did. Tensions had "been brewing for some time" and could easily result in trouble because "seditious utterances go unpunished, and the people simply will not stand for such execrations upon the American flag when they have boys over there giving their lives to uphold that same flag."[69] Even Reverend Walz, the father of Erwin, in an open letter in the *Chamois Enterprise,* recognized that the situation in Chamois had deteriorated to the point that "it might take only a spark to kindle a fire of unjustice [sic] and hatred and lawlessness." Ironically, Reverend Walz had also argued during a German-American Alliance meeting in St. Louis in 1917 that, although freedom of speech was protected, one should express criticism of the government in private not public, in order to avoid misunderstandings.[70] In this environment, Erwin Walz's behavior and expressions had crossed the invisible line of tolerance within the American as well as the German-American community, and punishment would have to be swift and decisive to send a message to *all* to conform.

With the exception of eleven men from Chamois and Linn driving to Potsdam in neighboring Gasconade County and nailing an American flag to the porch of the post office an July 14, 1918, there is no further evidence of violence or mob activity in Osage County. Erwin Walz returned to St. Louis, and it is possible that the Walz incident did defuse some of the tensions in the Chamois area.[71] However, resentment toward nonconformists remained elevated because the event also coincided with the statewide push to banish the use of the German language in public places.

The Osage County Council of Defense adopted a resolution during its July 6, 1918 meeting that called on all citizens to "refrain from teaching the

German language in any school or talking it over the telephone, or in any public place during the continuation of the war." According to Chairman R. H. Bryan, the council opposed the use of German in schools, lodges, and in public because it was the enemy's language, served as a venue for harmful German propaganda, was offensive to the ears of patriots, and hindered the assimilation process. Furthermore, speaking English assured recognition as a true American and would reduce bitterness and the possibility of rioting in the county.[72] The resolution persuaded several pastors to set aside the German language for the duration of the war, especially after the Missouri Council of Defense also encouraged the abandonment of German through its resolution in July. But most remained defiant despite being fully aware that the singling out of this one language and ethnic group would result in what Reverend Walz called a "mob-spirit . . . against everything what is not of American blood."[73]

Discussion over the language issue continued for several weeks into August 1918, and since neither the county nor the Missouri Council of Defense had enforcement powers in this regard, the impact of the resolution on the use of the German language was limited.[74] To make matters worse, Benton Township Council Chairman Fred Stonner gave Walz's congregation, the German Evangelical Church of Chamois, special permission to continue services in German. The county council, as well, endorsed a lenient interpretation of the resolution in regard to the use of German in churches and allowed pastors to adjust its use gradually according to the needs and circumstances of individual congregations. This outraged loyal leaders because granting special privileges to one church further demonstrated that the council did not act in the best interest of the country but that members aimed to protect their own business or political interests.[75] Thus, the language resolution and enforcement problems kept tensions at an elevated level for several weeks.

Reports of disloyal behavior and speech also continued to arrive at Secretary William Saunders's desk. For example, M. J. Murphy, a speaker from Springfield, Missouri, and member of the second division district draft board for the western district of Missouri, whom William Saunders thought was a patriotic Catholic, allegedly criticized the Missouri Council of Defense during his speech at the dedication of a service flag in Linn on July 28, 1918, saying that the council had "no business to meddle" with the German language and that the "Kaiser was not whipped yet 'by a long shot.'"[76] Since evidence of disloyal behavior continued to arrive in Jefferson City in October, Robert Glenn suggested an investigation through the American Protective League. However, there is no evidence that such an investigation actually took place.[77]

Coercive pressures through the CPI and Missouri Council of Defense to demonstrate one's patriotism cannot and should not be ignored in the discussion of the reasons for the injustice directed toward German-Americans during World War I. However, as this example demonstrates, local relationships and circumstances were often more important in creating the climate that spawned violence. Although the case of Osage County is by no means unique in Missouri, it nevertheless demonstrates that the definition of patriotism at the local level shaped the treatment of opponents to the Great War. In the German townships of southwestern Osage County, the meaning of loyalty was such that keeping quiet and supporting the war at the required level were enough to keep outside pressures to Americanize at bay. Silencing opposition to the war from within during the early days of the conflict assured that the area would not receive the "slacker" or "disloyalty" label. The strategy of publicly demonstrating loyalty, getting rid of a possibly un-American newspaper, and the fact that German-Americans made up the majority of the population in southwest Osage County allowed them to continue to speak German and maintain their German traditions throughout World War I. For example, Martin Schulte, who was a child during the war, responded to the question whether anyone had told him or his parents to stop speaking German with: "Hell No! This is a free country."[78]

By contrast, in northern Osage County local circumstances had created an environment that raised tensions. Here, the meaning of loyalty was more complicated because both American and German-American volunteers had created the hospital unit and a Home Guard company, and the sense of service to country by local leaders raised the expectations for all. At the same time, the area appeared divided into an extremely loyal and a less than patriotic segment. In such an environment of heightened tensions and suspicions any opinion other than the mainstream opinion could smudge the image of superpatriotism. Legal measures, such as reversal of exemptions, were preferred, but, if necessary, vigilante justice could be used to punish disloyal behavior.

Becoming Americans of German Heritage on Their Own Terms

The Impact of World War I on German Culture in Missouri

THIS EXAMINATION of the roots of aggression and the meaning of loyalty during the First World War in Missouri addresses three main themes. The first aims to understand the German-American experience during the war and whether it was uniform. The second takes the German-American perspective and evaluates the reaction of German-Americans to the calls for patriotism. The third, addressed in this final chapter, focuses on the long-term impact of the war and whether German-Americans gave up their cultural identity. Contrary to accepted wisdom, many German-Americans in Missouri retained the ability to acculturate according to their own circumstances despite the war.

Historians such as Frederick Luebke and John Higham have argued that German-Americans in the United States experienced widespread harassment, physical abuse, and hatred during World War I. The obvious reasons for this anti-German sentiment were a nativist mind-set that had grown in the previous two decades as millions of immigrants entered the country, the fear of the enemy lurking around every corner aiming to destroy everything America represented, and the reckless expressions "cultural chauvinists" or "club Germans" made during the neutrality and war period.[1] Mobilization of men and material during the war demanded total loyalty to nation; patriotism became a duty;

and individuals had to subordinate personal convictions to the survival of the country. The slightest opposition hampered the war effort and supported the enemy. To fight a victorious war, the nation's molders of public opinion consolidated everything German into one category, that is, the enemy. Consequently, Americans demanded an end to divided loyalties, or the hyphen, and believed they had to stamp out the last remnants of German culture. They insisted on suppression of German-language newspapers and called for the elimination of German from the public school curriculum because the offensive tongue could spread un-American ideas. Persons who conformed could expect little harassment, but those who continued to express their opposition experienced the full brunt of the struggle to create harmony and unity. Native and foreign-born Americans could expect flag-kissing ceremonies if their actions seemed un-American and, hence, pro-German. The urge to unify the country in support of the war grew to include sporadic violent acts such as public floggings and tar-and-feather parties and culminated in the mob lynching of Robert Prager in Collinsville, Illinois. Historians have argued that most German cultural institutions did not survive this attack on everything German.[2]

German-Americans were sensitive to and aware of the demands to conform. They had been able to preserve much of their culture and language for generations while adopting many American customs. They quickly accepted the ideal of participatory government but also used their ethnic organizations, especially the German-American Alliance, to influence local, state, and national legislation. However, the alliance's efforts to stop prohibition seemed to serve only special interests, and nativists interpreted such ethnically oriented politics as un-American behavior. This antagonism between nativists and German-Americans over political activism carried over into World War I. The alliance, like so many German-American organizations, advocated strict neutrality but, at the same time, collected money for German war relief. Nationalistic Americans interpreted this dichotomy as supporting the enemy. Once the United States entered the conflict, members of the alliance were the first to experience the anti-German animosity. This argument is valid for Missouri as well. Secret Service officials investigated Kurt von Reppert, a St. Louis lawyer and alliance member, after he had called President Wilson an "ape" at the organization's monthly meeting in April 1917, Dr. Charles Weinsberg, president of the alliance's Missouri chapter, was charged with trying to interfere with the military but acquitted during the trial, and a jury convicted Carl C. Gleeser, the secretary of the Kansas City Alliance chapter, for violating the Espionage Act.[3] The alliance, consequently, lost most of its respectability, even among German-Americans, and dissolved in 1918.

In contrast to the experience of German-speakers in Nebraska, South Dakota, Minnesota, and Iowa, few German-Americans in Missouri encountered the violent aspects of what Luebke called the "fierce hatred of everything German" during World War I.[4] Missourians may have harassed German-Americans to a lesser degree than citizens of other states because they actually believed that German-Americans were loyal. They, too, had pledged their allegiance to the United States in impromptu gatherings and Americanization meetings, purchased Liberty Bonds, supported the Red Cross, and sent their sons to the front. Missourians, thus, did not necessarily think of their German-speaking neighbors as spies and traitors but instead resented their determination to preserve a heritage that was no longer necessary in the new homeland. German-Americans in Missouri were respectable and hard-working citizens. They had become acculturated quite well, and the only obstacle to their becoming true Americans was the language. Nativists thought they could easily eliminate that last remnant of German culture through persuasion or legislative measures. Furthermore, during the war, the definition of loyalty in most areas of Missouri was different from that in Minnesota, for example, where the council of defense, renamed the Commission of Public Safety, defined loyalty as subordinating everything to the support of the war. Within that context, even passivity acquired suspicion.[5] In Missouri, by contrast, remaining quiet and meeting expected quotas was enough to demonstrate one's patriotism. Physical violence, therefore, was not used unless someone committed an obvious act of disloyalty.

One additional reason for the relative absence of violence is that the government-produced anti-German propaganda transmitted through the Committee on Public Information reached urban areas like St. Louis early in the war, but did not fully gear up to inundate most rural areas until late fall of 1917, and several editors saw no need to publish it until the following spring. Instead, advertisements from the state council exhorted Missourians to be patriotic, support the Red Cross, and conserve food. Thus, outside attempts to compel Missourians to hate everything German had limited results and did not immediately foster or nurture widespread suspicions of the enemy. Indeed, as this study of St. Louis, Gasconade and Osage Counties, and Missouri in general demonstrates, the German-American experience was not universal but varied across the state and occurred in the context of local relationships.

At the state level, the Missouri Council of Defense, the organization in charge of the war effort, followed federal instructions to bring about increased farm production, food conservation, financial support, and patriotism. Council members, in accordance with government guidelines, advocated decentralization, volunteerism, and persuasion. They delegated much of that responsibility to county and township councils of defense. The state council also appealed to the state's sizable German-American element through the German division in its Speakers' Bureau and by working with German-language papers. But if necessary, council members could also advocate the use of intimidation and coercion in order to bring suspected disloyals into line.

This approach to carrying out the war effort was different from that of several midwestern states. Legislatures in Illinois, Michigan, Minnesota, South Dakota, and Wisconsin gave their state councils broad legislative powers that allowed for statewide enforcement of restrictive and oppressive resolutions, including laws that specifically targeted German-Americans and ended the use of German in public, in schools, and in churches.[6] The Missouri Council of Defense did not have these powers because the Assembly did not meet between April 1917 and January 1919, nor did council members believe they needed or should hold such authority.

Missouri's political culture was what Daniel Elazar called an "individualistic" and "traditionalistic" one based on the ideology of minimal government interference in life and economy and the preservation of the "existing social and political order."[7] Consequently, leaders at the local level dealt with the suspected or overtly disloyal element in the best way possible so as not to attract outside attention. When too much internal division existed within the county or perceived troublemakers did not receive the specified punishment based on local definitions of loyalty, then nationalistic individuals requested assistance from the state council. In addition to giving advice or assuring backup through national organizations such as the APL, the council through resolutions, including its decision in 1918 to advocate changing German-sounding place-names to other names, usually reinforced local efforts to control behavior.

At the same time, the council did not have to become an oppressive organization because it merely had to preserve an image of patriotism, not create one. Impromptu loyalty demonstrations and strong organization contributed to the immediate image that Missouri was a patriotic state and earned praise from the Council of National Defense and Food Administration chairman Herbert Hoover. Council members thus had to maintain that patriotic image through unity and continued evidence of support for the war effort. The actions of a few disloyal persons, if controlled immediately, quietly, and to the satisfaction of many, would not tarnish the state's patriotic image. Council members urged calm and restraint, placed most responsibility for assuring patriotism in the hands of county councils of defense, advocated investigations into allegations of disloyalty (although sometimes under questionable circumstances), and adhered to the letter of the law. Such leadership required fewer resources, lowered the flames of mistrust, and avoided widespread hysteria and mob action in the state.

In St. Louis the situation was complex. The press kept the population more effectively informed about the war than the press in rural areas, and as a result readers in St. Louis knew sooner than their counterparts in rural areas how to define the enemy. St. Louis, being a center of production, including important war-related manufacturing, was also more likely to attract potential spies and saboteurs. Labor was well organized and active. The Socialist Party, although not a serious political threat in the city, nevertheless expressed its opposition to the war with its "St. Louis Proclamation" on April 7, 1917. A wave of strikes in 1918 also threatened stability and became the focus of disloyalty accusations. As the establishment of the restricted zones demonstrated, government regulations or restrictions of freedom also appeared sooner in the cities than in the rural areas. Consequently, St. Louisans were more aware of potential dangers, more watchful of each other, and more likely to point out suspected threats.

Furthermore, several immigrant groups and native-born Americans and their diverse organizations competed with each other for space and jobs in the city. During the neutrality period, Americans of German, Irish, Italian, and French descent living in St. Louis contributed to a number of different war relief organizations and proudly printed the results of such fund-raisers in the city's newspapers. Obviously, reading members of the community knew where ethnic groups stood in the European conflict. Such perceived allegiance further accentuated the differences among ethnic groups in St. Louis and convinced nativists to urge assimilation. Once the United States entered the war the calls for unity were much stronger and came much earlier than in the rural areas where few differed from the norm. French, Italian, and even Irish immigrants could easily express loyalty to both their birthplace and the United States without consequences because these countries were allies in the war. German-Americans, however, represented the enemy. In St. Louis they became easy targets because their activities had contributed to a perceived image of Germanism and unity although class, religious, and regional differences had weakened the ethnic community, and German identity was realistically based on shared customs of *Gemütlichkeit,* or sociability. The lack of group cohesion or protection, in turn, made it easier for zealous St. Louisans to vent their anti-German sentiment on individuals whom they perceived as a threat.[8]

However, when compared to the German-American experience in Chicago, for example, where conflict with other ethnic groups resulted in fistfights and a quite extensive as well as successful renaming campaign, German-Americans in St. Louis fared much better. Although some conflict occurred, several businesses changed their names, and churches learned to adjust to the English language, German-Americans also dominated the labor unions, believed in cooperation rather than violent confrontation, and controlled the behavior of fellow German-Americans who threatened to unbalance a basically patriotic image, that is, a patriotic image defined according to local circumstances.

In rural areas, such as Gasconade and Osage Counties, Missourians were less likely to condemn German-Americans because in an agricultural society people depended on others, regardless of ethnic background, and knew each other well. Rural towns were more homogeneous and most inhabitants hailed from similar ethnic or religious backgrounds.[9] Where Germans constituted a majority of the foreign-born population and a sizable proportion of the total population, they also participated in local government, serving on county or township councils and on fund-raising committees during the war. Thus, they could influence the interpretation of disloyalty and prevent the passage of anti-German ordinances. At the same time, the closely knit society also made it easier for community leaders, including those of German descent, to control dissent from within and through their influence over the local press, as in the case of the *Osage County Volksblatt,* contain the spread of news. As the Paulsmeyer and Walz episodes in Osage County illustrated, expressions of disloyal thoughts would have brought shame on an otherwise patriotic town. Therefore, community leaders dealt with the perpetrators quickly and without attracting much regional or national attention.

In Gasconade County local leaders, primarily German-Americans, including members of the county council of defense and draft examination board, also represented Missouri's political culture, or "Show Me" attitude, of individualism and decentralized government. These German-Americans did not object to the draft, the necessity to conserve food, and the requirement to purchase war bonds, as long as the war effort did not upset the traditional social and economic order. In this context, Rose Rippstein's actions, especially her reports to Jefferson City, threatened to destabilize that order by inviting further government intrusion into daily life. Outsiders, in this case members of the Missouri Council of Defense, concerned that the state might lose its patriotic image through the actions of perceived pro-Germans, came to Gasconade County to investigate ethnically defined accusations of disloyalty and to encourage more cooperation with government guidelines for the war effort.

German-Americans in Missouri were aware of the growing anti-German hysteria elsewhere, knew the problems and punishments that might await them, and chose a strategy that would assure their survival. Most were indeed patriotic and proclaimed that they had been loyal to the United States for generations, because of their ancestors' pro-Union stance in the Civil War. They also adapted to the prescribed public opinion and complied with official definitions of patriotism at the minimum that was absolutely necessary to avoid attention. They knew they had to look patriotic. German-American men, for example, proved their loyalty by signing up for the Selective Service. But they also tried to stay alive by using every legal exemption available to them, often with the support of local draft boards, as the example of Gasconade County demonstrated. Although some would interpret such action as evidence of opposition to the government war effort, one can also see this as a natural instinct of self-preservation.[10]

Like most Missourians, German-Americans followed the guidelines of the U.S. Food Administration and produced more crops. It is an undisputed fact that Missouri rose from the fourteenth position in the nation in grain production to the fifth. Whether that measured loyalty and patriotism or reflected the inner drive to make a profit whenever possible can be debated.[11] Gasconade County chairman Frank Gaebler's explanation that farmers could not easily adjust their agricultural habits indicated that, when the Food Administration required farmers to change their crops and increase yields, German-Americans believed that this intruded into their daily routines as farmers. Articles such as "Let the Farmer Alone," reprinted in the *Osage County Volksblatt,* which complained that the mass of instructions was overwhelming and contrary to the American way of life and the nation's democratic principles, further suggested that not all farmers appreciated these centralized guidelines emanating from the Food Administration.[12]

German-speaking as well as English-speaking Missourians, although not necessarily opposing the war itself, nevertheless resisted the procedures that community leaders used to sign up men, women, and children during the Hoover Food Pledge drive. Volunteers, including Rose Rippstein, relentlessly knocked on doors, day and night, until they finally reached the inhabitants. They told housewives how to conserve more food, sign a pledge card, and display that card in a prominent window to prove to the neighborhood that they supported the government's conservation efforts. In St. Louis, police deputies quickly gathered signatures by walking house to house. Missouri Council of Defense files, including correspondence from Gasconade County, indicate that German- and English-speaking Missourians had one prevalent complaint about such intimidation: farmers already knew how to do with less; why should city folk and community leaders tell them how to conserve even more? Reflecting class conflict within the ethnic group, they argued that the wealthy should carry a heavier burden of the war effort.[13] State council members recognized this problem. Robert A. Glenn, who was in charge of publicity for the state council, found that so-called patriots in Gasconade County used "the methods of the Big Stick." Threats that a person would be called a "slacker" or "yellow" usually resulted in sizable donations, but Glenn lamented that such tactics also developed resentment toward authority.[14]

German-Americans supported the Liberty Loan drives according to the circumstances that controlled their lives at the time of the fund-raisers. Some, as most Americans, were caught up in the initial euphoria of fighting, expected the war to be over in just a few months because the United States had entered the conflict, and enthusiastically donated to the first Liberty Loan drive in May 1917. Others were saddened that the president had not kept his promise to keep the nation out of the war and were not yet willing to support the war effort. Although the state as a whole met its quota, the lack of reports on the results suggests that Gasconade and Osage Counties did not meet their assigned fund-raising goals. Support for the Second Liberty Loan in October 1917 diminished because farmers were busy with the harvest and had to contend with financial losses after a drought. The Third Liberty Loan drive in April 1918 was much more successful because soldiers were actually in the battlefield and advertisements asking donors to "Keep the Home Fires Burning" made sense to them.[15] This drive also coincided with the arrival of emotionally laden posters from the CPI and, as the example of Osage County demonstrated, an increase in accusations of slacking and the introduction of coercive measures. But, as the case of St. Louis illustrated, such efforts did not necessarily result in higher donations. Secretary of the Treasury William G. McAdoo canceled his visit to St. Louis on April 28, 1918, because he was dissatisfied with the city's showing in the Third Liberty Loan drive. This time even the rich inhabitants of St. Louis were not willing to part with their money for a good cause. By the time the fourth bond drive arrived in the fall of 1918, an Allied victory seemed assured, and people were becoming more concerned about the influenza epidemic. Consequently, several counties again did not meet their quotas.

This comparative community study has made clear that in the specific case of Missouri most German immigrants and their descendants, especially those living in rural areas, were not the subject of widespread hate crimes and ethnically targeted legislation during World War I. Although Missouri Germans did not entirely escape charges of disloyalty, they did not experience the rampant destruction of religious or personal property as did their counterparts in

South Dakota, Iowa, and Ohio. Instead, hostility was neither universal nor widespread but varied by location. Existing economic, political, religious, and cultural tensions combined with a heightened push for conformity during 1918 to create a climate that could but did not necessarily result in accusations of disloyalty or aggression toward opponents to war. As the case of Gasconade County demonstrated, in some places animosity cloaked in loyalty rhetoric originated within the German community itself.

German-Americans controlled, adjusted, or conformed to official guidelines according to the local circumstances. Consequently, and unlike the argument set forth by Milton Gordon, Erik Kirschbaum, and Carl Wittke, the German-American community in Missouri did recover from attempts to eliminate the last remnants of German culture in the state.[16]

Although one can debate whether voting behavior is part of one's culture, this study demonstrated that German-Americans in Missouri voted based on local interests. Historians, nevertheless, still debate whether the war had an impact on German-American voter behavior and whether they deserted Democrats, who had limited their freedoms during the war, to overwhelmingly support Republicans in the 1920 election. Burchell notes that "local conditions" rather than national events were usually responsible for any changes in political behavior.[17] Evaluation of electoral behavior at the community level in Missouri reveals that German-Americans in St. Louis and Gasconade County already voted for Republicans.[18] However, German-Americans in Osage County, who had previously voted Democratic, supported Republican presidential candidates in 1920 and 1924. The first signs of the temporary switch in party affiliation began during the 1918 congressional election. Voters in the German precincts of Westphalia, Koeltztown, and Linn, as well as an overwhelming number of voters in Chamois, a city with a growing German-American population, voted for Republican Seldon Spencer and against Democrat Joseph Folk in the senatorial race. Folk's support for prohibition probably was the deciding factor, because German-Americans voted for Democratic candidates in the remaining races. Interestingly, Republican J. Richard Garstang lost the race for prosecuting attorney to Democrat Ell M. Zevely by a margin of over six hundred votes, and he carried Chamois, his hometown, by only four votes. Voters in all the German precincts voted overwhelmingly for Zevely. Possibly, Garstang's reports to the Missouri Council of Defense, while invaluable to the historian today, created animosity.[19]

The attempt to eliminate the use of the German language at the community and state level had an impact, albeit a limited one. As in several midwestern states, numerous newspapers in Missouri succumbed to public pressure: five

German-language newspapers ceased to exist; but ten survived.[20] Papers such as the *Sedalia Journal,* which expressed opposition to the war effort, closed shop because readership and advertising revenues dramatically declined. Patriotic yet already financially strapped papers, such as the *Volksfreund* in Warrenton, could not adjust to war-related paper shortages and expenses associated with required translations. Daily and weekly papers, such as the rural *Hermanner Volksblatt* and the urban *Westliche Post,* continued to publish in German and survived because of a reliable number of subscriptions and advertisements; but they had also adjusted to the demands of their readers and government regulations. The German-language press, nevertheless, had to deal with the natural phenomenon of the decline in the use of the language, and even the papers that did survive the war eventually closed their doors.[21]

In regard to language ordinances at the state or community level, German-Americans knew that there was no statute that *banned* the use of German and that the Missouri council, and county councils did not have any authority to enforce resolutions that *requested* an end to the use of the German language, at least not for churches and private clubs. When the state council, on growing demand at the local level, resolved to end the use of German in public and in schools and churches in July 1918, several churches complied. Such conformity, however, did not last very long. Once the armistice ended the fighting on November 11, 1918, many German-Americans began to "drift back into their old ways of using German in business, religious services and in parochial and Sunday schools."[22] Consequently, English replaced German in several churches and clubs as a result of the war, but not in all.

At the state level, the most drastic and long-lasting impact of the moves against the use of the German language came in public schools, because superintendents and school boards yielded to public pressure and removed German from the curriculum at the beginning of the 1918/1919 academic year. After the Armistice, the Missouri legislature also briefly participated in the widespread effort to "purge alien influences from education" by attempting to outlaw the teaching of all foreign languages, especially German, in the schools. Nineteen states enacted laws during the spring of 1919 that restricted the teaching of foreign languages, including limiting foreign language instruction to one hour per day in all schools in Wisconsin and Minnesota, mandating English as the language of instruction for all subjects in most states, explicitly prohibiting the teaching of foreign languages in public schools but not parochial schools in Iowa for freedom of religion reasons, specifically outlawing the teaching of German in Indiana and Ohio public schools, and prohibiting the teaching of any foreign language in all public, private, and parochial schools through eighth grade in Alabama, Colorado, Delaware, Nebraska, North Dakota, Oklahoma, and South Dakota. Legal challenges to the Nebraska statute led to the *Meyer v. Nebraska* decision in 1923 in which the United States Supreme Court declared such laws unconstitutional because they violated the due process of privileges and immunities guaranteed by the Fourteenth Amendment.[23]

At the beginning of Missouri's Fiftieth General Assembly session in January 1919 several state senators and assemblymen introduced bills to ban German from parochial and public schools and to prohibit the employment of foreign-born teachers. A few of the bills survived committee readings, but the Missouri House, after brief discussion, defeated the final bill, which would have outlawed the teaching of any foreign language in all public, private, and parochial schools, by a vote of 59–46, with 36 members absent. Assemblymen who vigorously attacked the German language in January had changed their minds by the end of the session in April, in part owing to German-American political activism.[24]

Theodore C. Graebner, a Lutheran clergyman, professor at the Concordia Seminary in St. Louis, and coeditor of the Missouri Synod's *Lutheran Witness,* helped coordinate opposition to these attempts to impede parochial education. Lutheran pastors, for example, met with O. S. Harrison, the chairman of the state senate's committee on education, to persuade him and other legislators to not adopt any proposed law that would interfere with religious instruction. According to the *St. Louis Republic* (the only paper in St. Louis to publicly express this opinion), the "powerful influence of German organizations" caused Republicans of the Missouri House to unite against the bill and convinced enough Democrats to be absent at the time of the vote that the measure failed.[25] Thus, it is clear that although Missouri's German-American population was large enough to have attracted attention for their German or perceived un-American cultural traits during the war, it was also still large enough and politically powerful enough to limit any long-term efforts to assimilate them on nativist terms.

Indeed, as sentiments to banish the use of German quickly faded away statewide after the end of World War I, German-Americans could continue to evaluate their language and cultural needs on their own terms and based on local circumstances. Missouri followed the national trend of German falling behind Spanish and French as a desirable language taught and learned in public schools by 1927 because demand declined. Serious language changes in the private setting through natural assimilation and more widespread adoption of English was more complex. The spread of mass media, the automobile boom, and the expansion of the road network by the late 1920s increasingly connected once-isolated towns, such as Westphalia and Rich Fountain, with American communities and encouraged more frequent interaction between German and English speakers.[26] Communities or families that developed a different ethnic consciousness apart from religion also adopted English more quickly in the 1920s. For example, the Vatican's order in 1921 to eliminate ethnic considerations when establishing parishes contributed to further integration in American society for German Catholics living and worshipping in cities such as St. Louis.[27] Thus the German language disappeared even faster in St. Louis, where German-Americans had been more American than German before the war.

By contrast, it survived the longest in so-called language islands in rural areas where adults and children used German on a daily basis and the community was large and cohesive enough to resist acculturation pressures. Here, residents placed high importance upon ethnicity because religion and ethnic identity were closely associated and they wished to express it linguistically. In Concordia, the Hanoverian Low German dialect survived well into the 1930s. Many second-, third-, and at times fourth-generation German-Americans used English only when talking with English speakers or when conducting trade. Children by the 1930s learned English in both public and parochial schools and at times children, more than adults, would intersperse English and German words in their conversations.[28] The Evangelical St. Paul Congregation in Hermann celebrated its sixtieth anniversary in 1919 and printed the *Festprogramm* (celebration program) entirely in German. Herman K. Helmich kept the Sunday School Book in German throughout the 1920s, though the congregation adopted English for its treasury report in 1929. Reverend Kasmann added one English service per month on Sunday mornings in 1925, gradually increasing the number of English services so that by 1942, he offered three English services and one German service per month; in 1947 he began holding all services in English.[29] Pastors conducted all church services at the Zion-St. Peter's United Church of Christ in Pershing in German until 1935 when the congregation decided to introduce English services. The Notre Dame Sisters stopped teaching in German at the St. Joseph's parochial school in Westphalia in 1928.[30] St. Paul's Lutheran Church of Concordia did not introduce an optional English service until 1920, and in 1932 the minister still confirmed twenty-five students in the German language. The transition to English in the Bethany German Evangelical Church congregation in Big Berger in Gasconade County began with the arrival of Reverend Herbert Kuhn in 1939.[31] Language preservation was stronger if the church maintained a connection to the mother church in the homeland by hiring only German-trained and -educated priests. For example, the Rich Fountain community did not introduce English in its church services until the arrival of Father Christian Winkelmann in 1922. He was the first native-born pastor; all his predecessors had come from German states.[32]

Yet, as Doris Dippold has so skillfully demonstrated, and the above examples reflect as well, the diversity of religion among the German immigrants in Missouri also resulted in various speeds of acculturation. Most German Methodists had adopted English as the main language of their congregations by 1910. German Catholics began to seriously change to English under hierarchical pressure from within the church during and right after World War I. However, the more conservative Lutheran congregations, especially those that belonged to the Missouri Synod, had the strongest tendency to preserve the German language at times beyond World War II.[33] As the *Lutheran Witness,* addressing the language transition issue, argued in 1918, "English needs no pushing; it will take care of itself," however "local conditions in every case must be the deciding factor." Indeed, it would take until after 1930 that subscriptions to the *Lutheran Witness* outnumbered those to the *Lutheraner,* and as late as 1946, 15 percent of congregations in the Lutheran Church–Missouri Synod still offered German services; the majority of them were in rural areas.[34]

In many communities, World War I was only one but not the primary reason to accelerate the adoption of English. Lack of new immigration, which resulted in a lack of reinforcement of language traditions, certainly was one important factor. Internal pressure from the younger generation requesting English services was equally if not more important because they challenged leadership and their ideology and threatened survival of the congregation through their leaving. Thus, it becomes clear that the adoption of English was neither linear nor easily predictable but differed across time and space.

The same was true for the everyday use of German in public and private conversations. The 1941 edition of the *WPA Guide to Missouri* described Washington, in Franklin County, as "a tranquil German community on the Missouri River with a distinct Old-World flavor," saying that "German is often spoken on the streets."[35] As late as the 1970s, adults who were forty years or older and had grown up in the language islands could still converse in German. Professor Schroeder cited the example of men who came to the Hilkemeyer store in Westphalia during the 1970s and told anecdotes and jokes in German, insisting that the punch line did not have the same effect in English.[36]

Aspects of cultural practices from the old homeland persisted alongside the adaptations to the new country beyond the war, as well. The factors that shape the survival of ethnic traits differed across time and space because people alter their identities as they adjust to new social, political, and economic circumstances. The majority of German-Americans in Missouri during the 1920s certainly could no longer claim their entire original identity. Some more than others had adopted aspects of American culture, retained aspects of their original regional culture, and probably invented new traditions. For example, the "shooting in the New Year" and traditional charivari ceremonies during weddings or during the honeymoon survived into the 1930s in Concordia. Some would continue to call themselves "full-blooded American" and speak German and read German-language newspapers as late as 1935. But others began to formulate a new identity.[37] Indeed, once the German language was no longer part of daily conversation, the thought process, or the language of business, the German-American identity began to transform into a new one. The German-American identity of preserving certain German traits while adopting particular American customs developed into an identity of Americans celebrating their German heritage.[38]

Foods such as the *Fastnachts Küchelche* and *Schmier Käse* have survived and have become delicatessen or special treats that even Americans enjoy. Whereas some traditions, such as *St. Nickolaus Tag* (Saint Nicholas Day) melded with American customs, yearly festivals such as the traditional *Erntefest* (harvest festival) in Freistatt and the *Oktoberfest* in Hermann have become part of Missouri culture, and people no longer consider German heritage or birth as an inferior status in society.[39] In fact, today the descendants of Germans in Gasconade and Osage Counties, as well as several communities throughout Missouri, preserve a few traces of German customs, such as food, clothing, and alcoholic beverages. Hermann is unique in that it defines itself as an ethnic community and survives in part owing to the tourism generated through that ethnic identity. The town consciously preserves architecture and maintains German festivals such as the Wurstfest and Maifest.[40]

One event that historians argue influenced the lives and culture of German-Americans in Missouri immediately followed World War I. Congress's passage of the Volstead Act and the ratification of the Eighteenth Amendment in 1919 ended the production, distribution, and sale of alcohol. Hermann's wine industry, a major factor in the city's economy, experienced a devastating blow. Wine producers converted their cellars to mushroom production and the presence of a shoe factory allowed Hermann to survive prohibition.[41] In St. Louis, breweries either shut down or as in the case of Anheuser-Busch converted production to soft drinks or nonalcoholic malts.[42] Allegedly, because German-Americans could no longer consume beer during gatherings,

Gemütlichkeit, or sociability, one of the defining characteristics of the German culture and identity, diminished.

Quite to the contrary, neither the adjustment to the English language nor prohibition could end the German tradition of *Vereinswesen,* or sociability through societies and associations. Indeed, forty-eight German societies of St. Louis proudly celebrated and advertised the *deutsche Vereinswesen* (German club life) in the city through a special anniversary edition of the *Westliche Post* in 1920. Articles outlined the long history of these societies and their impact on the city of St. Louis. The German Theater resumed its program on the 161st birthday of Friedrich von Schiller, and German societies continued to play an important role in the city's social season. German societies also began again to support the old fatherland through fund-raisers.[43] German-American business and academic leaders founded the Germanistic Society in 1929 to encourage more interaction between American and German scholars. The opening of the German House in September of 1929 illustrated that the German spirit and culture would remain alive in St. Louis for years to come, albeit adjusted to societal and local trends.[44]

Future research in the form of community studies in several midwestern states may add further nuances to the argument that various circumstances shaped the German-American experience during the war. As this study has demonstrated, local relationships informed definitions of loyalty, shaped prejudices and maltreatment during the war, and influenced the degree of acculturation after the war. Unlike Luebke's argument that "their associational structures were dismantled," German-Americans in Missouri, especially those in the rural areas, maintained German associations, even the German language, well beyond the war.[45] This raises the question whether community studies and the search for the origin of aggression and the meaning of loyalty in other states may not also find that the impact of World War I on German-Americans there was less devastating than previously thought.

NOTES

Introduction

1. Newspapers did not publish the names of committee members. "Mob Flays Pro-German; Forces Him to Kiss Flag in the Jefferson Theater," *Daily Capital News* (Jefferson City), April 6, 1918; "Monat Held Pending Action of Officials," *Daily Post* (Jefferson City), April 6, 1918; "Whipped a Disloyalist," *Kansas City Times,* April 6, 1918; "Kohlengräber der Unloyalität beschuldigt, muß Fahne küssen," *Westliche Post* (St. Louis), April 6, 1918; "Kriegsneuigkeiten," *Missouri Volksfreund* (Jefferson City), April 6, 1918.

2. "Kriegsnachrichten und Sachen welche sich auf denselben beziehen," *Missouri Volksfreund,* April 11, 1918. "The Land of the Free and the Home of the Brave," *Tipton Times,* April 12, 1918.

3. Frederick C. Luebke, *Bonds of Loyalty: German-Americans and World War I* (DeKalb: Northern Illinois University Press, 1974), xiii.

4. Leslie Tischauser, *The Burden of Ethnicity: The German Question in Chicago, 1914–1941* (New York: Garland, 1990), 36; H. C. Peterson and Gilbert C. Fite, *Opponents of War, 1917–1918* (Madison: University of Wisconsin Press, 1957), 195–97; Carl Wittke, *German-Americans and the World War: With Special Emphasis on Ohio's German-Language Press* (Columbus: Ohio State Archaeological and Historical Society, 1936), 144–45, 155–56, 163, 186.

5. Milton M. Gordon, *Assimilation in American Life: The Role of Race, Religion, and National Origins* (New York: Oxford University Press, 1964), 135; John A. Hawgood, *The Tragedy of German America* (New York: Arno Press, 1970); John Higham, *Strangers in the Land: Patterns of American Nativism, 1860–1925,* 2nd ed. (New Brunswick, NJ: Rutgers University Press, 1988), 207–9; Erik Kirschbaum, *The Eradication of German Culture in the United States, 1917–1918* (Stuttgart, Germany: Akademischer Verlag, 1986), 13–15; Wittke, *German-Americans and the World War,* 3, 196; Luebke, *Bonds of Loyalty,* 311; Frank Trommler and Elliott Shore, eds., *The German-American Encounter: Conflict and Cooperation between Two Cultures, 1800–2000* (New York: Berghahn Books, 2001), xiii. Karen De Bres asserts in her community study of Hermann, Washington, and Union, Missouri, that Anglo-Americans suddenly and overtly destroyed the German-American culture during World War I. Karen Jean De Bres, "From Germans to Americans: The Creation and Destruction of Three Ethnic Communities" (PhD diss., Columbia University, 1986), 10. For arguments that World War I extinguished German culture in St. Louis see David W. Detjen, *The Germans in Missouri, 1900–1918: Prohibition, Neutrality, and Assimilation* (Columbia: University of Missouri Press, 1985), 186.

6. I use the term German-American in the generally defined way as German immigrants residing in the United States and their American-born children and grandchildren. By contrast, Missourian, or American, means non-German. That is, neither they, nor their parents, nor grandparents were born in Germany. This can include old-stock Americans who have been natural-born citizens for at least three generations and other ethnic groups, unless otherwise identified. The terms "German-speakers" or "German-speaking" includes those born in Germany, Austria, Switzerland, and other German-speaking areas of Europe, as well as their American-born children and grandchildren who still spoke German at home. I did not distinguish whether they were German-speaking Protestants, Catholics, or Jews unless necessary.

7. Luebke, *Bonds of Loyalty,* 237–43, 245–59; Peterson and Fite, *Opponents of War,* 14, 79, 146, 148–50, 168, 194, 197, 199, 280; Wittke, *German-Americans and the World War,* 157–59, 163; Sister John Christine Wolkerstorfer, "Nativism in Minnesota in World War I: A Comparative Study of Brown, Ramsey, and Stearns Counties, 1914–18" (PhD diss., University of Minnesota, 1973), 28–34, 69; LaVern J. Rippley, *The Immigrant Experience in Wisconsin* (Boston: G. K. Hall, 1985), 94–115.

8. Richard J. Hardy, Richard R. Dohm, and David A. Leuthold, *Missouri Government and Politics,* rev. ed. (Columbia: University of Missouri Press, 1995), 25, 36.

9. Matthew D. Tippens, *Turning Germans into Texans: World War I and the Assimilation and Survival of German Culture in Texas, 1900–1930* (Lexington, KY: Kleingarten Press, 2010), 5–8; Benjamin Paul Hegi, "'Old Time Good Germans': German Americans in Cooke County, Texas, during World War I," *Southwestern Historical Quarterly* 109 (April 2006): 235–58. See also Robert Paul McCaffery, *Islands of Deutschtum: German-Americans in Manchester, New Hampshire, and Lawrence, Massachusetts, 1870–1942* (New York: Peter Lang, 1996), 3, 7.

10. Katja Wüstenbecker, *Deutsch-Amerikaner in Ersten Weltkrieg: US-Politik und Nationale Identitäten im Mittleren Westen* (Stuttgart, Germany: Franz Steiner Verlag, 2007).

11. David Laskin, *The Long Way Home: An American Journey from Ellis Island to the Great War* (New York: Harper Collins, 2010); Nancy Gentile Ford, *The Great War and America: Civil-Military Relations during World War I* (Westport, CT: Praeger Security International, 2008); Christopher M. Sterba, *Good Americans: Italian and Jewish Immigrants during the First World War* (New York: Oxford University Press, 2003).

12. For recent studies on ethnic nationalism see, Jeffrey Kaplan, "Islamophobia in America?: September 11 and Islamophobic Hate Crime," *Terrorism & Political Violence* 18 (Spring 2006): 1–33; and Jerry Z. Muller, "Us and Them," *Foreign Affairs* 87 (March/April 2008): 18–35.

13. Higham, *Strangers in the Land,* 152–62; Leonard Dinnerstein, Roger L. Nichols, and David M. Reimers, *Natives and Strangers: A Multicultural History of Americans* (New York: Oxford University Press, 1996), 125; Dale T. Knobel, *"America for the Americans": The Nativist Movement in the United States* (New York: Twayne, 1996), 203–34; and Robert F. Zeidel, *Immigrants, Progressives, and Exclusion Politics: The Dillingham Commission, 1900–1927* (DeKalb: Northern Illinois University Press, 2004), 54.

14. Dinnerstein, *Natives and Strangers,* 182; Higham, *Strangers in the Land,* 175–80; Zeidel, *Immigrants, Progressives,* 119; and Cecilia Elizabeth O'Leary, *To Die For: The Paradox of American Patriotism* (Princeton: Princeton University Press, 1999), 220.

15. Dinnerstein, *Natives and Strangers,* 135; O'Leary, *To Die For,* 221.

16. Higham, *Strangers in the Land,* 196.

17. As quoted in Christopher C. Gibbs, *The Great Silent Majority: Missouri's Resistance to World War I* (Columbia: University of Missouri Press, 1988), 52–53.

18. Lawrence O. Christensen, "Popular Reaction to World War I in Missouri," *Missouri Historical Review* 86 (July 1992): 386–95.

19. Gibbs, *Great Silent Majority,* 60.

20. According to the 1910 Census, 505 persons born in Germany, Austria, and Switzerland resided in Jefferson City. *Thirteenth Census of the United States, 1910: Abstract of the Census with Supplement for Missouri* (Washington, DC: Government Printing Office, 1913), 1124.

21. "Loyalitäts Bewegung auf Mount Olive ausgedehnt," *Westliche Post,* February 16, 1918; "Mussten Flagge Küssen," *Westliche Post,* February 28, 1918.

22. David DeChenne, "Recipe for Violence: War Attitudes, the Black Hundred Riot, and Superpatriotism in an Illinois Coalfield, 1917–1918," *Illinois Historical Journal* 85 (Winter 1992): 227–31. Carl R. Weinberg, *Labor, Loyalty, & Rebellion: Southwestern Illinois Coal Miners & World War I* (Carbondale: Southern Illinois University Press, 2005), 103–11.

23. "I.W.W. Agitator Saved from Angry Crowd Last Night by City Police," *Daily Capital News,* February 23, 1918; "Disloyal Agitator Demented, Is Belief," *Daily Post,* February 23, 1918.

24. "Kriegsneuigkeiten," *Missouri Volksfreund,* April 11, 1918.

Chapter 1: American yet German

1. Carl Schurz, "Sales of Arms to French Agents," Speech, February 26, 1872, *Congressional Globe,* 42d Cong., 2d sess., 1872, 106, Appendix: 111.

2. Hans L. Trefousse, *Carl Schurz: A Biography* (New York: Fordham University Press, 1998), 162, 170–74, 235–52.

3. Kathleen Neils Conzen, "Germans," in *Harvard Encyclopedia of American Ethnic Groups,* ed. Stephan Thernstrom, Ann Orlov, and Oscar Handlin (Cambridge: Harvard University Press, 1980), 409–10.

4. Wolfgang von Hippel, *Auswanderung aus Südwestdeutschland: Studien zur Württembergischen Auswanderung und Auswanderungspolitik im 18. und 19. Jahrhundert* (Stuttgart, Germany: Klett-Cotta, 1984), 206, 210, 250–70; Mack Walker, *Germany and the Emigration, 1816–1885* (Cambridge: Harvard University Press, 1964), 66–67; Walter D. Kamphoefner, *The Westfalians: From Germany to Missouri* (Princeton: Princeton University Press, 1987), 12–39. Louis Burkel's father left Germany to evade conscription into the Franco-Prussian War. Louis A. Burkel, interview by Dr. Adolf Schroeder, February 4, 1978, Box 6, Adolf Schroeder Papers, Western Historical Manuscript Collection, University of Missouri–Columbia (hereinafter cited as Schroeder Papers, WHMC).

5. Gottfried Duden, *Report on a Journey to the Western States of North America and a Stay of Several Years on the Missouri during the Years 1824, '25, '26, and 1827,* ed. James W. Goodrich (Columbia: University of Missouri Press, 1980), 67, 69–72, 83, 93, 102,

138–9. Historians generally agree that Duden was not the primary but an influential factor to shape immigration decisions to America because it stirred enthusiasm, and it "fit well with additional romantic depictions of America." Walker, *Germany and the Emigration*, 60–61. Siegmar Muehl, "Shock of the New: Advising Mid-Nineteenth-Century German Immigrants to Missouri," *Yearbook of German-American Studies* 33 (1998): 85–101.

6. Walker, *Germany and the Emigration*, 159.

7. Walter D. Kamphoefner, Wolfgang Helbich, and Ulrike Sommer, eds., *News from the Land of Freedom: German Immigrants Write Home* (Ithaca, NY: Cornell University Press, 1991), 27–35, 496–97.

8. Kamphoefner, *Westfalians*, 40. Fred Gustorf and Gisela Gustorf, eds., *The Uncorrupted Heart: Journal and Letters of Frederick Julius Gustorf, 1800–1845* (Columbia: University of Missouri Press, 1969), 137. William G. Bek, "The Followers of Duden," *Missouri Historical Review* 14 (October 1919–July 1920): 29.

9. George Helmuth Kellner, "The German Element on the Urban Frontier: St. Louis, 1830–1860" (PhD diss., University of Missouri, 1973), 48–49. William G. Bek, "Nicholas Hesse, German Visitor to Missouri, 1835–1837," *Missouri Historical Review* 41 (October 1946): 19–44. Walker, *Germany and the Emigration*, 64–65.

10. William G. Bek, "The Followers of Duden: Fifteenth Article," "Sixteenth Article," "Seventeenth Article," and "Eighteenth Article," *Missouri Historical Review* 18 (April 1924): 415–37; 18 (July 1924): 562–84; 19 (October 1924): 114–29; 19 (January 1925): 338–52. Kellner, "German Element on the Urban Frontier," 87–88; Audrey L. Olson, "St. Louis Germans, 1850–1920: The Nature of an Immigrant Community and Its Relations to the Assimilation Process" (PhD diss., University of Kansas, 1970), 6–8; James Neal Primm, *Lion of the Valley: St. Louis, Missouri, 1764–1989,* 3rd ed. (St. Louis: Missouri Historical Society Press, 1998), 149.

11. William G. Bek, *The German Settlement Society of Philadelphia and Its Colony, Hermann, Missouri,* ed. Dorothy Heckmann Shrader (Hermann, MO: American Press, 1984), 2, 5, 75, 139, 176–77, 203, 288–89; Arthur William Apprill, "The Culture of a German Community in Missouri" (master's thesis, University of Missouri, 1935), 20.

12. Walter O. Forster, *Zion on the Mississippi: The Settlement of the Saxon Lutherans in Missouri, 1839–1841* (St. Louis: Concordia, 1953); Paul E. Kretzmann, "The Saxon Immigration to Missouri, 1838–1839," *Missouri Historical Review* 33 (January 1939): 157–70; Walter A. Baepler, *A Century of Grace: A History of the Missouri Synod, 1847–1947* (St. Louis: Concordia, 1947), 37, 97, 118.

13. Thomas Everett Churchwell, "The Founding, Growth, and Decline of the German Religious Colony at Bethel, Missouri" (master's thesis: Northeast Missouri State University, 1959); H. Roger Grant, "The Society of Bethel: A Visitor's Account," *Missouri Historical Review* 68 (January 1974): 223–31. Robert W. Frizzell, "The Low German Settlements of Western Missouri: Examples of Ethnic Cocoons," *Yearbook of German-American Studies* 33 (1998): 103–25; and Robert W. Frizzell, *Independent Immigrants: A Settlement of Hanoverian Germans in Western Missouri* (Columbia: University of Missouri Press, 2007).

14. Russel L. Gerlach, *Immigrants in the Ozarks: A Study in Ethnic Geography* (Columbia: University of Missouri Press, 1976), 40. *History of Cole, Moniteau, Benton,*

Miller, Maries and Osage Counties, Missouri (Chicago: Goodspeed, 1889; repr., Easely, SC: Southern Historical Press, 1978), 688–89; Joe Welschmeyer, *Sacred Heart Sesquicentennial, 1838–1988* (Linn, MO: Unterrified Democrat, 1988), 3–4; and John Rothensteiner, *History of the Archdiocese of St. Louis: In Its Various Stages of Development from AD 1673 to AD 1928* (St. Louis: Blackwell Wielandy, 1928), 2:357, 365–74.

15. U.S. Bureau of the Census, *Population of the United States in 1860, Compiled from the Original Returns of the Eighth Census* (Washington, DC: Government Printing Office, 1864), xxx–xxxi; Von Hippel, *Auswanderung aus Südwestdeutschland*, 180–201. Bruce Levine, *The Spirit of 1848: German Immigrants, Labor Conflict, and the Coming of the Civil War* (Urbana: University of Illinois Press, 1992), 6–8; Carl Wittke, *Refugees of Revolution: The German Forty-Eighters in America* (Philadelphia: University of Pennsylvania Press, 1920); A. E. Zucker, ed., *The Forty-Eighters: Political Refugees of the German Revolution* (New York: Columbia University Press, 1950).

16. U.S. Bureau of the Census, *Ninth Census*, vol. 1, *The Statistics of the Population of the United States, 1870* (Washington, DC: Government Printing Office, 1872), 338–39; *Report on the Population of the United States at the Tenth Census, 1880* (Washington, DC: Government Printing Office, 1883), 484–85, 493, 548–49, 832; United States Commission on Immigration, *Reports of the Immigration Commission*, vol. 3, *Statistical Review of Immigration, 1820–1910, Distribution of Immigrants, 1850–1900* (Washington, DC: Government Printing Office, 1911), 34–44. For similar national trends see also Walker, *Germany and the Emigration*, 180, 184, 186; Klaus J. Bade, "German Emigration to the United States and Continental Immigration to Germany in the Late Nineteenth and Early Twentieth Centuries," in *Labor Migration in the Atlantic Economies: The European and North American Working Classes during the Period of Industrialization*, ed. Dirk Hoerder (Westport, CT: Greenwood Press, 1985), 122; and Suzanne Sinke, "The International Marriage Market and the Sphere of Social Reproduction: A German Case Study," in *Seeking Common Ground: Multidisciplinary Studies of Immigrant Women in the United States*, ed. Donna Gabaccia (Westport, CT: Greenwood Press, 1992), 67–83.

17. David Khoudour-Castéras, "Welfare State and Labor Mobility: The Impact of Bismarck's Social Legislation on German Emigration before World War I," *Journal of Economic History* 68 (March 2008): 211–43. Ludwig Dilger to Wilhelm Dilger, August 25, 1891, and February 25, 1892, in *News from the Land of Freedom*, 496–97; Kamphoefner, *Westfalians*, 188.

18. The 1910 Census reveals that of nearly 92,000,000 American residents, 8,282,618 listed Germany as country of origin. Of those, approximately 2,500,000 had actually been born in Germany, and either one or both of the parents of 5,500,000 had been born in Germany. In Missouri, 88,224 Missourians had been born in Germany, and 279,287 residents, or 8.5 percent of Missouri's almost 3.3 million inhabitants, were native Americans whose father or mother or both had been born in Germany. U.S. Bureau of Census, *Thirteenth Census of the United States, 1910*, vol. 2, *Population: Alabama–Montana* (Washington, DC: Government Printing Office, 1913), 597, 601–28.

19. Germans or Americans with both parents born in Germany accounted for 44.4 percent of Milwaukee's population, 24.3 percent of Cincinnati's population, and 19.5 percent of Chicago's population. Katja Wüstenbecker, *Deutsch-Amerikaner im Ersten*

Weltkrieg: US-Politik und Nationale Identitäten im Mittleren Westen (Stuttgart, Germany: Franz Steiner Verlag, 2007), 28, 305.

20. For tables and statistical analysis of occupation information from the U.S. Census see Petra DeWitt, "Searching for the Roots of Harassment and the Meaning of Loyalty: A Study of the German-American Experience in Missouri during World War I" (PhD diss., University of Missouri, 2005), 40–42. See also Kamphoefner, *News from the Land of Freedom*, 500; and Olson, "St. Louis Germans," 30, 32, 34.

21. E. D. Kargau, *St. Louis in Former Years: A Commemorative Book for the German Element* (St. Louis: By the author, 1893), 253–55, Western Historical Manuscript Collection, University of Missouri–Columbia. "Dritter Quartal Bericht der Deutschen Gesellschaft in St. Louis," *Tägliche Deutsche Tribüne* (St. Louis), December 5, 1850; "The German Society of St. Louis," *Western Journal* 5 (March 1851): 343–44; "Deutscher Unterstützungs Band Distrikt 249," *Westliche Post*, January 2, 1917; "Die Deutsche Gesellschaft von St. Louis," *Westliche Post*, January 23, 1917.

22. Walter D. Kamphoefner, "Paths of Urbanization: St. Louis in 1860," in *Emigration and Settlement Patterns of German Communities in North America*, ed. Eberhard Reichmann, LaVern J. Rippley, and Jörg Nagler (Indianapolis: Indiana University Press, 1995), 258–72; Kellner, "German Element on the Urban Frontier," 145; Olson, "St. Louis Germans," 29; "Census der Stadt St. Louis," *Wöchentlicher Anzeiger des Westens*, October 24, 1858.

23. For tables and analysis of census statistics, see DeWitt, "Searching for the Roots of Harassment," 43–53. Giovanni Schiavo, *The Italians in Missouri* (New York: Italian American, 1929), 58; Gary Ross Mormino, *Immigrants on the Hill: Italian-Americans in St. Louis, 1882–1982* (Urbana: University of Illinois Press, 1986), 20; Olson, "St. Louis Germans," 27, 49–52, 62–63, 85–86; Primm, *Lion of the Valley*, 153. See also LaVern J. Rippley, *The Immigrant Experience in Wisconsin* (Boston: G. K. Hall, 1985), 25. Wüstenbecker, *Deutsch-Amerikaner*, 30, 33–34, 306.

24. Gerlach, *Immigrants in the Ozarks*, 59; Helmut Rüdiger, "Die Geographische Bedingtheit der Besiedlung Missouris" (master's thesis, University of Missouri, 1946), 39–40; Carl O. Sauer, *The Geography of the Ozark Highland of Missouri* (Chicago: University of Chicago Press, 1971), 165–70.

25. Kamphoefner, *Westfalians*, 40, 151–54; Timothy Gene Anderson, "Immigrants in the World System: Domestic Industry and Industrialization in Northwest Germany and the Migration to Osage County, Missouri, 1835–1900" (PhD diss., Texas A&M University, 1994), 227–32; Walter D. Kamphoefner, "'Entwurzelt' oder 'verpflanzt?' Zur Bedeutung der Kettenwanderung für die Einwandererakkulturation in Amerika," in *Auswanderer—Wanderarbeiter—Gastarbeiter: Bevölkerung, Arbeitsmarkt und Wanderung in Deutschland seit der Mitte des 19. Jahrhunderts*, ed. Klaus J. Bade (Ostfildern, Germany: Scripta Mercaturae Verlag, 1984), 329, 332–33.

26. Kamphoefner, *Westfalians*, 85. U.S. Bureau of the Census, *Thirteenth Census of the United States, 1910: Abstract of the Census with Supplement for Missouri* (Washington, DC: Government Printing Office, 1913), 628–32; DeWitt, "Searching for the Roots of Harassment," 88.

27. Frizzell, "Low German Settlements of Western Missouri," 103–25; *Cole Camp, Missouri: Area History, 1839–1976* (Cole Camp: Cole Camp Area Historical Society,

1986), 7; Jessie C. Miller, ed., *Lawrence County, Missouri, History* (Mt. Vernon, MO: Lawrence County Historical Society, 1974), 147–49.

28. *History of Franklin, Jefferson, Washington, Crawford, and Gasconade Counties, Missouri* (Chicago: Goodspeed, 1888; reprint, Cape Girardeau, MO: Ramfre Press, 1958), 229, 304; William G. Bek, "Survivals of Old Marriage Customs among the Low Germans of West Missouri," *Journal of American Folklore* 21 (January–March 1908): 60; Kamphoefner, *Westfalians,* 88–89.

29. For tables and statistical analysis of the 1850, 1860, 1880, 1900 and 1910 United States Census for Gasconade County see DeWitt, "Searching for the Roots of Harassment," 89–101. Arthur B. Cozzens, "Conservation in German Settlements of the Missouri Ozarks," *Geographical Review* 33 (April 1943): 286–98.

30. DeWitt, "Searching for the Roots of Harassment," 103–33. Sister John Christine Wolkerstorfer, "Nativism in Minnesota in World War I: A Comparative Study of Brown, Ramsey, and Stearns Counties, 1914–18" (PhD diss., University of Minnesota, 1973), 220–21.

31. He indicated that Germans would have German neighbors. "Farms for Sale," *Osage County Volksblatt* (Westphalia), October 15, 1914; and Anderson, "Immigrants in the World System," 167.

32. For tables and analysis of the population schedules for the United States Census from 1850, 1860, 1880, 1900 and 1910 for Osage County see DeWitt, "Searching for the Roots of Harassment," 111–23.

33. Walter D. Kamphoefner, "The German Agricultural Frontier: Crucible or Cocoon," *Ethnic Forum* 4, no. 1/2 (1984): 21–35; Rippley, *Immigrant Experience,* 71–93.

34. Kamphoefner, *Westfalians,* 4, 88; Frizzell, "Low German Settlements of Western Missouri," 103–25; Kamphoefner, "'Entwurzelt' oder 'verpflanzt,'" 335; and Conzen, "Germans," in *Harvard Encyclopedia of American Ethnic Groups,* ed. Thernstrom et al., 415.

35. William Wilke, "Remembrances of a Franklin County Farmer" (1935), 6–7, 9, Western Historical Manuscript Collection, University of Missouri–Columbia; Oscar Cornelius Nussmann, "The Town of Concordia, Missouri: A Study in Cultural Conflict" (master's thesis, University of Missouri, 1933), 8–10; Gerlach, *Immigrants in the Ozarks,* 60. See also Jon Gjerde, *The Minds of the West: Ethnocultural Evolution in the Rural Middle West, 1830–1917* (Chapel Hill: University of North Carolina Press, 1997), 206–7.

36. Conzen, "Germans," in *Harvard Encyclopedia of American Ethnic Groups,* ed. Thernstrom et al., 418; Kamphoefner, "German Agricultural Frontier," 25–26; Frederick C. Luebke, *Bonds of Loyalty: German-Americans and World War I* (DeKalb: Northern Illinois University Press, 1974), 39. See also Walter A. Schroeder, "Rural Settlement Patterns of the German-Missourian Cultural Landscape," in *The German-American Experience in Missouri: Essays in Commemoration of the Tricentennial of German Immigration to America, 1683–1983,* ed. Howard Wight Marshall and James W. Goodrich (Columbia: University of Missouri, 1986), 37.

37. Mary Beth Marquard, "Americanization in Dispersed and Clustered German Settlements in Osage County, Missouri: 1860 to 1910" (master's thesis: University of Missouri, 1997), 66. *History of Cole . . . and Osage Counties,* 682; Rothensteiner, *History of the Archdiocese,* 365–74; Welschmeyer, *Sacred Heart,* 3–4; Joe Welschmeyer,

"The Bavarians: Their Settlements and Descendants," *Unterrified Democrat,* July 21, 1982.

38. "Fronleichnam," *Osage County Volksblatt,* June 3, 1915; Welschmeyer, *Sacred Heart,* 71; Marquard, "Americanization," 70; Ralph Sellenschutter, to Petra DeWitt, July 9, 2003, in possession of author; "The One-Hundredth Anniversary of St. Paul Evangelical and Reformed Church," pamphlet, author unknown (Hermann, 1944); and Apprill, "Culture of a German Community," 37, 41. See also Linda Schelbitzki Pickle, *Contented among Strangers: Rural German-Speaking Women and Their Families in the Nineteenth-Century Midwest* (Urbana: University of Illinois Press, 1996), 84–85.

39. Kamphoefner, *Westfalians,* 134; and "'Entwurzelt' oder 'verpflanzt,'" 347. Luebke, *Bonds of Loyalty,* 35–39. Between 1860 and 1910 only 7 percent of residents in Westphalia and only 9 percent of residents in Rich Fountain married outside their ethnic group. Marquard, "Americanization," 61–63.

40. W. Schroeder, "Rural Settlement Patterns," 25–43; Kamphoefner, "'Entwurzelt' oder 'verpflanzt,'" 348–49; and Kathleen Neils Conzen, David A. Gerber, Ewa Morawska, George E. Pozzetta, and Rudolph J. Vecoli, "The Invention of Ethnicity: A Perspective from the U.S.A." *Journal of American Ethnic History* 12 (Fall 1992): 14.

41. John Bodnar, *The Transplanted: A History of Immigrants in Urban America* (Bloomington: Indiana University Press, 1985); Milton M. Gordon, *Assimilation in American Life: The Role of Race, Religion, and National Origins* (New York: Oxford University Press, 1964), 60–83; Kathleen Neils Conzen, *Immigrant Milwaukee, 1836–1860: Accommodation and Community in a Frontier City* (Cambridge: Cambridge University Press, 1976); Kathleen Neils Conzen, "The Paradox of German-American Assimilation," *Yearbook of German-American Studies* 1 (1982): 153–60; James R. Barrett, "Americanization from the Bottom Up: Immigration and the Remaking of the Working Class in the United States, 1880–1930," *Journal of American History* 79 (December 1992): 996–1020; Russell A. Kazal, "Revisiting Assimilation: The Rise, Fall, and Reappraisal of a Concept in American Ethnic History," *American Historical Review* 100 (April 1995): 438–39; Susan Jean Kuyper, "The Americanization of German Immigrants: Language, Religion, and Schools in Nineteenth-Century Rural Wisconsin" (PhD diss., University of Wisconsin–Madison, 1980); John Rex, "The Fundamentals of the Theory of Ethnicity," in *Making Sense of Collectivity: Ethnicity, Nationalism, and Globalization,* ed. Siniša Malešević and Mark Haugaard (Sterling, VA: Pluto Press, 2002), 94, 100, 109; and J. Milton Yinger, *Ethnicity: Source of Strength? Source of Conflict?* (New York: State University of New York Press, 1994), 40, 43.

42. Kamphoefner, *Westfalians,* 70–105. "Der Gräberschmückungs Tag," *Hermanner Volksblatt,* May 26, 1905. "Zum 4ten Juli!" *Hermanner Volksblatt,* June 30, 1905. Louis Brunner, interviewed by Adolph Schroeder, April 11, 1975, in Hermann, Missouri, Cassette Tape, Box 6, Schroeder Papers, WHMC; Werner Mezger, *Das große Buch der schwäbisch-alemannischen Fasnet: Ursprünge, Entwicklungen und Erscheinungsformen organisierter Narretei in Südwestdeutschland* (Stuttgart, Germany: Theiss Verlag, 1999), 8–9. The tradition of "shooting in the New Year" involved German-American men walking through village streets or from farmhouse to farmhouse discharging rifles into the air and requesting refreshments. Kasper Buersmeyer, interviewed by Adolph

Schroeder, May 24, 1974, at St. Joseph's Home for the Aged, Jefferson City, Transcripts of interviews, Box 7, Schroeder Papers, WHMC; Wilke, "Remembrances," 19–20; Georg Buschan, *Das deutsche Volk in Sitte und Brauch* (Stuttgart, Germany: Union Deutscher Verlagsgesellschaft, 1922), 22–23, 49, 66, 72.

43. Editorial, *Osage County Volksblatt,* February 4, 1915; Adolf E. Schroeder, "The Persistence of Ethnic Identity in Missouri German Communities," in *Germanica-Americana: Symposium on German-American Literature and Culture,* ed. Erich A. Albrecht and J. Anthony Burzle (Lawrence: University of Kansas, 1976), 37; and Nussmann, "Town of Concordia," 147–48.

44. Apprill, "Culture of a German Community," 52. The *Schützenfest,* comparable to a fair with shooting competitions, includes the crowning of a *Schützenkönig,* or champion marksman. Adolf E. Schroeder, "The Contexts of Continuity: Germanic Folklore in Missouri," *Kansas Quarterly* 13 (Spring 1981): 94, 96.

45. Martin Schulte, interviewed by Petra DeWitt and John Viessman, July 2, 2003, Victory Gardens, Vienna, Missouri, audio- and videotape deposited at Department of Natural Resources, Capitol Museum, Jefferson Landing, Jefferson City, Missouri. Wilke, "Remembrances," 19.

46. Bek, *German Settlement Society,* 211; Martin Schulte interview; Pickle, *Contented among Strangers,* 85–86, 141; and Adolf E. Schroeder and Carla Schulz-Geisberg, eds., *Hold Dear as Always: Jette, a German Immigrant Life in Letters* (Columbia: University of Missouri Press, 1988), 76–77.

47. Marquard, "Americanization," 42; Gerlach, *Immigrants in the Ozarks,* 1; W. Schroeder, "Rural Settlement Patterns," 37, 41; Nussmann, "Town of Concordia," 34.

48. Conzen, *Immigrant Milwaukee,* 225–28.

49. Bek, *German Settlement Society,* 245–46; and Floyd C. Shoemaker, "Hermann: A Bit of the Old World in the Heart of the New," *Missouri Historical Review* 51 (April 1957): 241.

50. Marquard, "Americanization," 58; Nussmann, "Town of Concordia," 55. Karen Jean De Bres, "From Germans to Americans: The Creation and Destruction of Three Ethnic Communities" (PhD diss., Columbia University, 1986), 7.

51. W. A. Willibrand, "When German Was King: The FLES Program around 1900," *German Quarterly* 30 (November 1957): 254; Welschmeyer, *Sacred Heart,* 71; Marquard, "Americanization," 54–56; Bek, *German Settlement Society,* 215–21.

52. Anderson, "Immigrants in the World-System," 169–72, 236, 242, 245; Gerlach, *Immigrants in the Ozarks,* 102–3, 106–7; Sauer, *Geography of the Ozark Highland,* 168; Rüdiger, "Geographische Bedingtheit," 40–41; "Cultivation of Grapes in Missouri," *Western Journal* 2 (February 1849): 127–31; Wilke, "Remembrances," 12; Cozzens, "Conservation in German Settlements," 286–98; and Adolf E. Schroeder, "To Missouri, Where the Sun of Freedom Shines: Dream and Reality on the Western Frontier," in *The German-American Experience in Missouri: Essays in Commemoration of the Tricentennial of German Immigration to America, 1683–1983,* ed. Howard Wight Marshall and James W. Goodrich (Columbia: University of Missouri Press, 1986), 1–24. See also Wilbur Zelinsky, *The Cultural Geography of the United States* (Englewood Cliffs, NJ: Prentice Hall, 1992), 29; Gjerde, *Minds of the West,* 62–63, 159; Kamphoefner, *Westfalians,* 133, 189–200.

53. Cozzens, "Conservation," 292–94. Rüdiger, "Geographische Bedingtheit," 41. Sauer, *Geography of the Ozark Highland,* 169.

54. Kellner, "German Element on the Urban Frontier," 289. Dirk Hoerder, ed., *Labor Migration in the Atlantic Economies: The European and North American Working Classes during the Period of Industrialization* (Westport, CT: Greenwood Press, 1985), 8–9. Susan Olzak, *The Dynamics of Ethnic Competition and Conflict* (Stanford: Stanford University Press, 1992), 18. Walter Ehrlich, *Zion in the Valley: The Jewish Community of St. Louis* (Columbia: University of Missouri Press, 2002), 2:2–3, 223. The archdiocese had to keep up with this movement and created new parishes such as the ethnically diverse Corpus Christi Parish in the northwestern corner of St. Louis, the all-German parish of Our Lady of the Presentation near St. Charles, and the all-German parish of Our Lady of Sorrows in the city. Rothensteiner, *History of the Archdiocese,* 693, 698–700.

55. "Ludwig Dilger," in *News from Land of Freedom,* ed. Kamphoefner et al., 486–522. "Table showing vote of Election, Tuesday November 3, 1908," *Advertiser-Courier* (Hermann), November 4, 1908; "Political Complexion of Townships," *Osage County Enterprise* (Chamois), November 13, 1902. Olson, "St. Louis Germans," 124–25. For similar trends in the Midwest see Rippley, *Immigrant Experience,* 90–91; Kuyper, "Americanization of German Immigrants," 65–77; Wolkerstorfer, "Minnesota in World War I," 19–20. Robert Lewis Mikkelsen, "Immigrants in Politics: Poles, Germans, and the Social Democratic Party of Milwaukee," in *Labor Migration in the Atlantic Economies: The European and North American Working Classes during the Period of Industrialization,* ed. Dirk Hoerder (Westport, CT: Greenwood Press, 1985), 278.

56. "Die Deutschen in Missouri," *Wöchentlicher Anzeiger des Westens,* November 12, 1860; Frederick C. Luebke, *Ethnic Voters and the Election of Lincoln* (Lincoln: University of Nebraska Press, 1971), xi, xviii–xxx; Walter D. Kamphoefner, "German-Americans and Civil War Politics: A Reconsideration of the Ethnocultural Thesis," *Civil War History* 37 (September 1991): 238, 240; and Primm, *Lion of the Valley,* 350–53.

57. "Das Wahlresultat nach Wards," *Amerika,* November 5, 1908; and Olson, "St. Louis Germans," 129. See also Ruth Warner Towne, *Senator William J. Stone and the Politics of Compromise* (Port Washington, NY: Kennikat Press, 1979), 81; and Steven L. Piott, *Joseph W. Folk and the Missouri Idea* (Columbia: University of Missouri Press, 1997), 144.

58. "Ausländische Nachrichten," *Hermanner Volksblatt,* March 30, 1883; "Aus der alten Heimath," *Hermanner Volksblatt,* October 9, 1908; "Deutsche Lokalnachrichten," *Deutscher Volksfreund,* August 28, 1914; "Aus der alten Heimath," *Amerika,* January 18, 1903; and "Aus der alten Heimath," *Amerika,* May 3, 1914. See also Kuyper, "Americanization of German Immigrants," 64; and Robert E. Park, *The Immigrant Press and Its Control* (New York: Harper & Brothers, 1922; reprint, St. Clair Shores, MI: Scholarly Press, 1970), 135.

59. Karl J. R. Arndt and Mary E. Olson, eds., *German-American Newspapers and Periodicals, 1732–1955: History and Bibliography* (Heidelberg, Germany: Quelle & Meyer Verlag, 1961; reprint, New York: Johnson Reprinting, 1965), 247–76.

60. German-born Socialist Gottlieb Höhn edited both newspapers from 1898 to 1928. Circulation for the *Arbeiter-Zeitung* was 3,000 in 1914 and 2,400 in 1924. It lasted through 1927. Arndt and Olson, *German-American Newspapers,* 252.

61. Hartmut Keil, "A Profile of Editors of the German-American Radical Press," in *The German-American Radical Press: The Shaping of a Left Political Culture, 1850–1940,* ed. Elliott Shore, Ken Fones-Wolf, and James P. Danky (Urbana: University of Illinois Press, 1992), 15–28.

62. "Gibt es eine Westphalien Zeitung?" *Osage County Volksblatt,* December 15, 1910; "Westphalia Official Directory," *Osage County Volksblatt,* March 23, 1916. Marc Shell, "Hyphens: Between Deitsch and American," in *Multilingual America: Transnationalism, Ethnicity, and Languages of American Literature,* ed. Werner Sollors (New York: New York University Press, 1998), 258.

63. Arndt and Olson, *German-American Newspapers,* 241. "Wie werde ich Bürger?" *Westliche Post,* July 9, 1914.

64. Park, *Immigrant Press,* 68–72, 117; Arndt and Olson, *German-American Newspapers,* 237–80; Kuyper, "Americanization of German Immigrants," 30.

65. Baepler, *Century of Grace,* 149–51, 209; Everette Meier and Herbert T. Mayer, "The Process of Americanization," in *Moving Frontiers: Readings in the History of the Lutheran Church–Missouri Synod,* ed. Carl S. Meyer (St. Louis: Concordia, 1964), 345–47.

66. LaVern J. Rippley, *The German-Americans* (Boston: G. K. Hall, 1976), 99, 127; Doris Dippold, "'It Just Doesn't Sound Right': Spracherhalt und Sprachwechsel bei Deutschen Kirchengemeinden in Cole County, Missouri" (master's thesis, University of Kansas, 2002), 30–31; Kamphoefner, "German Agricultural Frontier," 26–27, 31–33; and Kuyper, "Americanization of German Immigrants," 120.

67. Frederick C. Luebke, "The Immigrant Condition as a Factor Contributing to the Conservatism of the Lutheran Church–Missouri Synod," in *Germans in the New World: Essays in the History of Immigration* (Urbana: University of Illinois Press 1990), 6–7, 10; Baepler, *Century of Grace,* 11; and James S. Olson, *Catholic Immigrants in America* (Chicago: Nelson-Hall, 1987), 56.

68. Evelyn Graue, *A History of St. Paul's Church, Hermann, Missouri, 1844–1994* (Hermann, MO: St. Paul's United Church of Christ, 1994), 12, 16; Dippold, "Spracherhalt und Sprachwechsel," 78; Welschmeyer, *Sacred Heart,* 55; Byron Northwick, "The Development of the Missouri Synod: The Role of Education in the Preservation and Promotion of Lutheran Orthodoxy, 1839–1872" (PhD diss., Kansas State University, 1987); Baepler, *Century of Grace,* 118; William G. Ross, *Forging New Freedoms: Nativism, Education, and the Constitution, 1917–1927* (Lincoln: University of Nebraska Press, 1994), 8–9, 14–17; and LaVern J. Rippley, "The German-American Normal Schools," in *Germanica-Americana: Symposium on German-American Literature and Culture,* ed. Erich A. Albrecht and J. Anthony Burzle (Lawrence: University of Kansas, 1976), 66.

69. Olson, "St. Louis Germans," 110–11; Margaret LoPiccolo Sullivan, *Hyphenism in St. Louis, 1900–1921: A View from the Outside* (New York: Garland, 1990), 38; *One-Hundredth Anniversary: St. Paul Evangelical Church,* 8; Rothensteiner, *History of the Archdiocese,* 365–74; Dippold, "Spracherhalt und Sprachwechsel," 41–42.

70. Baepler, *Century of Grace,* 190–96, 209–10; Alan Niehaus Graebner, "The Acculturation of an Immigration Lutheran Church: The Lutheran Church–Missouri Synod, 1917–1929" (PhD diss., Columbia University, 1965), 95–98, 100.

71. Ross, *Forging New Freedoms,* 10, 39, 48–49; and Luebke, *Bonds of Loyalty,* 38–39.

72. Ross, *Forging New Freedoms,* 10, 20, 22, 25; Baepler, *Century of Grace,* 207–9.

73. David Thelen, *Paths of Resistance: Tradition and Democracy in Industrializing Missouri* (Columbia: University of Missouri Press, 1986), 113–15.

74. Walter D. Kamphoefner, "Learning from the 'Majority-Minority' City: Immigration in Nineteenth-Century St. Louis," in *St. Louis in the Century of Henry Shaw: A View beyond the Garden Wall*, ed. Eric Sandweiss (Columbia: University of Missouri Press, 2003), 95–96. Selwyn K. Troen, *The Public and the Schools: Shaping the St. Louis System, 1838–1920* (Columbia: University of Missouri Press, 1975), 73. David W. Detjen, *The Germans in Missouri, 1900–1918: Prohibition, Neutrality, and Assimilation* (Columbia: University of Missouri Press, 1985), 25. Olson did not give much credit to German-language consciousness in St. Louis. Olson, "St. Louis Germans," 98–107.

75. Olson, "St. Louis Germans," 109; Sullivan, *Hyphenism in St. Louis,* 41–42; "Interesse für deutschen Unterricht wächst," *Westliche Post,* July 7, 1914; "Die Deutschen Samstagsschulen," *Westliche Post,* October 23, 1914; "Deutsche Samstagsschulen," *Westliche Post,* November 5, 1915.

76. Henry W. Kiel's father, Henry F. Kiel, arrived in Missouri as a toddler with his parents (the mayor's grandparents) in 1849. U.S. Bureau of the Census, Twelfth Census, 1900, Population Schedule, City of St. Louis, 13th Ward, 275 A; "Henry W. Kiel," U.S. Passport Applications, M1490, January 2, 1906–March 31, 1925, Roll 2496, 1924, Certificate 405387, General Records of the Department of State, Record Group 59, National Archives, Washington, DC. Sullivan, *Hyphenism in St. Louis,* 77.

77. Detjen, *Germans in Missouri,* 15; Olson, "St. Louis Germans," 135–36, Primm, *Lion of the Valley,* 433; Sullivan, *Hyphenism in St. Louis,* 6. Rex, "Fundamentals of the Theory of Ethnicity," 109.

78. Kathleen Neils Conzen, "Ethnicity as Festive Culture: Nineteenth-Century German America on Parade," in *The Invention of Ethnicity,* ed. Werner Sollors (New York: Oxford University Press, 1989), 48–51; Rippley, *Immigrant Experience,* 46. "Der deutsche Tag," *Hermanner Volksblatt,* August 13, 1890; and "Der deutsche Ehrentag," *Hermanner Volksblatt,* October 10, 1890.

79. John Philip Gleason, "The Central Verein, 1900–1917: A Chapter in the History of the German-American Catholics" (PhD diss., University of Notre Dame, 1960), 8, 86, 102, 250–53. Clifton James Child, *The German-Americans in Politics, 1914–1917* (Madison: University of Wisconsin Press, 1939), 3, 5; and Detjen, *Germans in Missouri,* 80.

80. Walker, *Germany and the Emigration,* 52; Luebke, *Bonds of Loyalty,* 33–34; Rippley, *Immigrant Experience,* 51, 90; Wolkerstorfer, "Minnesota in World War I," 20; John D. Balgenorth, "A History of Vincennes, Indiana, during World War I: With Special Emphasis on the German-American Population" (master's thesis, Eastern Illinois University, 1967), 26; Olson, *Catholic Immigrants,* 1, 53. Kamphoefner, "German Agricultural Frontier," 26. Sullivan, *Hyphenism in St. Louis,* 37–38; and Kamphoefner, "Paths of Urbanization," 258–72.

81. "Gemütlichkeiten in der amerikanischen Staatenfamilie," *Anzeiger des Westens,* May 1, 1852; "Schwäbischer Sängerbund," *Westliche Post,* July 19, 1916; "Deutscher Damenchor," *Westliche Post,* September 5, 1916; "Große Abendunterhaltung des Bayerischen Männerchors," *Westliche Post,* October 28, 1916; Irene E. Cortinovis, "The Golden Age of German Song," *Missouri Historical Review* 68 (July 1974):

440–41; Kargau, *St. Louis in Former Years,* 239–58; Kellner, "German Element on the Urban Frontier," 52–53; Olson, "St. Louis Germans," 116–18; and Primm, *Lion of the Valley,* 432.

82. Gary M. Fink, *Labor's Search for Political Order: The Political Behavior of the Missouri Labor Movement, 1890–1940* (Columbia: University of Missouri Press, 1973), 1; Sally M. Miller, "Germans on the Mississippi: The Socialist Party of St. Louis," in *Race, Ethnicity, and Gender in Early Twentieth-Century American Socialism* (New York: Garland, 1996), 75, 77; Rosemary Feurer, *Radical Unionism in the Midwest, 1900–1950* (Urbana: University of Illinois Press, 2006), 4; Edwin James Forsythe, "The St. Louis Central Trades and Labor Union, 1887–1945" (PhD diss., University of Missouri, 1956), 16–19.

83. Dirk Hoerder, "The German-American Labor Press and Its Views of the Institutions in the United States," in *The German-American Radical Press: The Shaping of a Left Political Culture, 1850–1940,* ed. Elliott Shore, Ken Fones-Wolf, and James P. Danky (Urbana: University of Illinois Press, 1992), 191. Fink, *Labor's Search for Political Order,* 4, 24. Wüstenbecker, *Deutsch-Amerikaner,* 63.

84. Forsythe, "Central Trades and Labor Union," 51, 69, 74–76; Fink, *Labor's Search for Political Order,* 29–32, 34; Feurer, *Radical Unionism,* 5; Miller, "Germans on the Mississippi," 73.

85. Gleason, "Central Verein," 134, 137, 139, 148, 164, 202, 233, 247–49, 253. Kenkel was the son of German-born parents. Fourteenth Census, 1920, Population Schedule, Missouri, St. Louis City, Enumeration District 251, Ward 13, Sheet 8A.

86. Protokoll der regelmäßigen Versammlung vom 28 März 1898, Brewers, Maltsters, and General Labor Departments, Local Union No. 6, Reel 1, Collection 584, Western Historical Manuscript Collection, University of Missouri–Columbia.

87. Ernest Kirschten, *Catfish and Crystal* (New York: Doubleday, 1965), 245–47; Kellner, "German Element on the Urban Frontier," 170; Olson, "St. Louis Germans," 122–24. De Bres, "From Germans to Americans," 52–144; Welshmeyer, *Sacred Heart,* 2–4.

88. "Zum nationalen Geburtstag," *Missouri Volksfreund,* July 8, 1915. Alison Clark Efford, "Race Should Be as Unimportant as Ancestry: German Radicals and African American Citizenship in the Missouri Constitution of 1865," *Missouri Historical Review* 104 (April 2010): 138–58. Conzen, "Invention of Ethnicity," 10–11.

89. "Liederkranz Ball," *St. Louis Globe-Democrat,* February 2, 1902. "Der deutsche Ehrentag," *Hermanner Volksblatt,* October 10, 1890.

90. "West St. Louis Turnverein Masquerade," *St. Louis Globe-Democrat,* February 2, 1902; "Turnverein Gives Mask Ball," *St. Louis Globe-Democrat,* January 31, 1904. German-Americans in Philadelphia used blackface minstrels to define themselves as "old-stock" and American, or at least three generations of natural-born white American citizens, and thus distinguished from southern European immigrants and blacks. Russell A. Kazal, *Becoming Old Stock: The Paradox of German-American Identity* (Princeton: Princeton University Press, 2004), 114. Irish-Americans used blackface performances to demonstrate that they were white, free, and symbolically united with all white Americans and entitled to political rights and decent jobs. David R. Roediger, *The Wages of Whiteness: Race and the Making of the American Working Class,* rev. ed. (New York: Verso, 1999), 115–27. European immigrants through their insistence on being white or

caucasion were able to achieve the benefits that whiteness granted, namely acceptance as citizens. Matthew Frye Jacobson, *Whiteness of a Different Color: European Immigrants and the Alchemy of Race* (Cambridge: Harvard University Press, 1998), 91–135.

91. "Ethnic Influence in the United States," *St. Louis Times,* August 13, 1909; "Three German-Americans," *St. Louis Globe-Democrat,* May 25, 1914; "'Naked Truth' Memorial to Be Unveiled Today," *St. Louis Post-Dispatch,* May 24, 1914; and "Monument to Three German Editors to Be Unveiled This Afternoon," *St. Louis Republic,* May 24, 1914. "The One-Language System," *Missouri Republican,* November 1, 1887; and "Liederkranz Hop," *Missouri Republican,* November 7, 1887. Sullivan, *Hyphenism in St. Louis,* 7, 30. Olson, "St. Louis Germans," 215.

92. Andreas Daum, "Celebrating Humanism in St. Louis: The Origins of the Humboldt Statue in Tower Grove Park, 1859–1878," *Gateway Heritage* 15 (Fall 1994): 48–58. "Zum Deutschen Tag in Hermann," *Hermanner Volksblatt,* August 18, 1916; "Eleven Days More," *Missouri Republican,* October 11, 1887; "Hermann and the Battle in Teuteborg Forest," *St. Louis Globe-Democrat,* August 15, 1909, magazine section; "Das große Volksfest in Normandy Grove," *Amerika,* August 16, 1909; and Olson, "St. Louis Germans," 166.

93. Olzak, *Dynamics of Ethnic Competition and Conflict,* 40–41. Conzen, "Invention of Ethnicity," 14. Editorial, *Advertiser-Courier,* March 16, 1887; "The Spotless Town," *Osage County Volksblatt,* July 15, 1915. Gerlach, *Immigrants in the Ozarks,* 107, 109; Detjen, *Germans in Missouri,* 20–21; and A. Schroeder "Persistence of Ethnic Identity," 34. De Bres, "From Germans to Americans," 15–16. For a similar argument for Germans in Wisconsin, see Kuyper, "Americanization of German Immigrants," 63.

94. Willibrand, "When German Was King," 255. Forster, *Zion on the Mississippi,* 267–77, 349–51. Luebke, "Immigrant Condition," 9–10. George Kishmar, *History of Chamois, Missouri,* rev. ed. (Jefferson City: Jeff City, 1985), 156, 158; and Marquard, "Americanization," 50.

95. Rippley, *Immigrant Experience,* 44–53, 59–70; Balgenorth, "Vincennes," 16–17; De Bres, "From Germans to Americans," 72; and Nussmann, "Town of Concordia," 44–45. Editorial, *Hermanner Volksblatt,* August 8, 1890.

96. Kishmar, *History of Chamois,* 87, 113.

97. Kiel was one of only two mayors elected to three terms. Kirschten, *Catfish and Crystal,* 363; J. Thomas Scharf, *History of St. Louis and County* (Philadelphia: Louis H. Everts, 1883), 695, 709–13; and Primm, *Lion of the Valley,* 301, 352, 408, 422. "Mayor Kiel antwortet Demokraten," *Westliche Post,* March 22, 1917.

98. Primm, *Lion of the Valley,* 352, 354–55, 365–67.

99. Eugene V. Debs, for example, increased his vote results in St. Louis from 15,431 in 1908 to 28,466 in 1912. Miller, "Germans on the Mississippi," 85; Fink, *Labor's Search for Political Order,* 29–32; *Official Manual of the State of Missouri for the Years 1909–1910* (Jefferson City: Hugh Stephens, 1910), 733; *Official Manual of the State of Missouri for the Years 1913–1914* (Jefferson City: Hugh Stephens, 1914), 797, 851–58.

100. Primm, *Lion of the Valley,* 358–60. John Higham, *Strangers in the Land: Patterns of American Nativism, 1860–1925,* 2nd ed. (New Brunswick, NJ: Rutgers University Press, 1988), 194; Luebke, *Bonds of Loyalty,* 63; and Cecilia Elizabeth O'Leary, *To Die For: The Paradox of American Patriotism* (Princeton: Princeton University Press, 1999), 160.

101. Primm, *Lion of the Valley,* 164–73; Andreas Dorpalem, "Mühlenberg and Schurz: A Comparative Study of Two Periods of German Immigration into the United States," *American German Review* 5 (June 1939): 16; and Dale T. Knobel, *"America for the Americans": The Nativist Movement in the United States* (New York: Twayne, 1996). Sigmar Muehl, "Eduard Mühl: Hermann's Brave Fighter for Truth and Human Rights," *Der Maibaum* 11 (December 2003): 30–32. Nussmann, "Town of Concordia," 11–12, 41.

102. Bek, "Followers of Duden: Eighteenth Article," 350. Detjen, *Germans in Missouri,* 25–26; Harvey Saalberg, "The *Westliche Post* of St. Louis: A Daily Newspaper for German-Americans, 1857–1938," (PhD diss., University of Missouri, 1967), 307–8; and O'Leary, *To Die For,* 137–43, 221.

103. "Demokratische Salzbretzel," *Osage County Volksblatt,* September 20, 1900.

104. Child, *German-Americans in Politics,* 10–12; Detjen, *Germans in Missouri,* 27–8; and Rippley, *German-Americans,* 99.

105. "Dry League Is Formed," *St. Louis Republic,* October 9, 1910; "Clubs Score Prohibition," *St. Louis Republic,* October 21, 1910. "Vote Yes," *St. Louis Post-Dispatch,* November 7, 1910; "Prohibition Prohibits," *St. Louis Globe-Democrat,* October 29, 1910. "Prohibition Beaten in the State by an Estimated Majority of 150,000," *St. Louis Republic,* November 7, 1910.

106. "Das Wahlresultat in Osage County, 1910," *Osage County Volksblatt,* November 17, 1910; and "General Election Returns, Tuesday, November 8, 1910," *Unterrified Democrat,* November 17, 1910; and Kishmar, *History of Chamois,* 8, 111.

107. The *Volksblatt* cited St. Louis newspapers, including the *Westliche Post,* that printed statements from a "Methodist" eyewitness regarding this incident. "Zur Klarstellung der Sonntagsfrage in Hermann," *Hermanner Volksblatt,* June 15, 1905.

108. Lawrence O. Christensen and Gary R. Kremer, *A History of Missouri,* vol. 4: *1875 to 1919* (Columbia: University of Missouri Press, 1997), 200. Detjen, *Germans in Missouri,* 182. Primm, *Lion of the Valley,* 412–14.

109. Higham, *Strangers in the Land,* 175–93, 196; Knobel, *Nativist Movement of the United States,* xviii, 191–96, 240; Robert F. Zeidel, *Immigrants, Progressives, and Exclusion Politics: The Dillingham Commission, 1900–1927* (DeKalb: Northern Illinois University Press, 2004), 54, 86, 119.

Chapter 2: Divided Opinions and Growing Suspicions

1. "Colonel's City Club Speech," *New York Times,* June 1, 1916.

2. John Higham, *Strangers in the Land: Patterns of American Nativism, 1860–1925,* 2nd ed. (New Brunswick, NJ: Rutgers University Press, 1988), 194; David M. Kennedy, *Over Here: The First World War and American Society* (New York: Oxford University Press, 1980), 28–44; Frederick C. Luebke, *Bonds of Loyalty: German-Americans and World War I* (DeKalb: Northern Illinois University Press, 1974), 84; Stewart Halsey Ross, *Propaganda for War: How the United States Was Conditioned to Fight the Great War of 1914–1918* (Jefferson, NC: McFarland, 1996), 1.

3. Ludwig Dilger to "Dear Brother," December 6, 1914, St. Louis, in *News from the Land of Freedom: German Immigrants Write Home,* ed. Walter D. Kamphoefner, Wolfgang Heblich, and Ulrike Sommer (Ithaca, NY: Cornell University Press, 1991), 503.

4. Harold D. Laswell, *Propaganda Technique in World War I* (Cambridge, MA: MIT Press, 1971), 63, 90–101, 198–201; Ross, *Propaganda for War*, 15–16, 19, 21; Luebke, *Bonds of Loyalty*, 85–111.

5. Laswell, *Propaganda Technique*, 132–35; Ross, *Propaganda for War*, 21, 51–53. Katja Wüstenbecker, *Deutsch-Amerikaner im Ersten Weltkrieg: US-Politik und Nationale Identitäten im Mittleren Westen* (Stuttgart, Germany: Franz Steiner Verlag, 2007), 82. "Warnung," *Kansas City Presse*, February 11, 1915; "The Bryce Report," *St. Louis Republic*, May 14, 1915. "More Austrian Plots?" *Kansas City Journal*, November 15, 1915; newspaper clippings, in folder 2, Box 2, Oscar Sachs Papers, Western Historical Manuscript Collection, University of Missouri–Columbia (hereafter cited as Sachs Papers, WHMC).

6. John D. Balgenorth, "A History of Vincennes, Indiana, during World War I: With Special Emphasis on the German-American Population" (master's thesis, Eastern Illinois University, 1967), 33. "Kabel zwischen Vereinigten Staaten und Deutschland zerschnitten," *Westliche Post*, August 6, 1914; editorial, *Franklin County Tribune* (Union), September 25, 1914. "Kriegsnachrichten," *Missouri Volksfreund*, February 25, 1916; September 1 and 7, 1916; "Authentic War News," *Advertiser-Courier*, September 9, 1914. E. B. Kellogg, to Capt. L. Benecke, November 11, 1916, folder 1418, J. Benecke Papers, Western Historical Manuscript Collection, University of Missouri–Columbia (hereinafter cited as Benecke Papers, WHMC). See also Christopher C. Gibbs, *The Great Silent Majority: Missouri's Resistance to World War I* (Columbia: University of Missouri Press, 1988), 28.

7. John Clark Crighton, *Missouri and the World War, 1914–1917: A Study in Public Opinion* (Columbia: University of Missouri Press, 1947), 107; Lawrence O. Christensen, "Prelude to World War I in Missouri," *Missouri Historical Review* 89 (October 1994): 4, 10; Wüstenbecker, *Deutsch-Amerikaner*, 71.

8. "A Little Lay Sermon," *Kansas City Journal*, August 9, 1914; "Self-government is Anti-War," *Joplin News Herald*, September 25, 1914; "The Crime of the Age," *St. Joseph News-Press*, July 31, 1914; "No Disposition to Apologize," *St. Louis Republic*, April 23, 1915; "The German Empire," *Kirksville Daily Express*, September 7, 1914; "Golden Bullets," *Kansas City Journal*, September 15, 1915; "The Anglo French Loan," *St. Joseph News-Press*, October 1, 1915. See also Lawrence O. Christensen and Gary R. Kremer, *A History of Missouri*, vol. 4: *1875 to 1919* (Columbia: University of Missouri Press, 1997), 202.

9. Crighton, *Missouri and the World War*, 31, 34, 59–60, 67–70, 87, 95. "Saving Its Face on a Technicality," *St. Louis Republic*, April 10, 1915; "Facing a 'Bugaboo,'" *St. Louis Republic*, June 6, 1915; editorial, *Moberly Democrat*, September 14, 1915.

10. "Kriegsbilder in Higginsville" and "Aus Lexington," both in *Missouri Thalbote*, October 3, 1916; editorial, *Sedalia Journal*, March 2, 1916. "Diplomatische Heuchelei und Lügengewebe," *Deutscher Volksfreund*, August 21, 1914; "Die Wahrheit über den Krieg," *Deutscher Volksfreund*, November 20, 1914. "Die Deutschen gehen vorwärts," *Missouri Volksfreund*, August 20, 1914; "Über Kaiser und Deutsche," *Missouri Volksfreund*, October 8, 1914; "Kriegsnachrichten," *Missouri Volksfreund*, May 18, 1916.

11. In 1910, the *Westliche Post*, recorded thirty thousand readers in St. Louis alone; its Sunday edition, the *Mississippi Blätter*, had a circulation of sixty thousand; and

Amerika had a daily circulation of twenty-six thousand. Karl J. R. Arndt and Mary E. Olson, eds., *German-American Newspapers and Periodicals, 1732–1955: History and Bibliography* (Heidelberg, Germany: Quelle & Meyer Verlag, 1961; reprint, New York: Johnson Reprinting, 1965), 237, 274–76.

12. "Kabel zwischen Vereinigten Staaten und Deutschland zerschnitten," *Westliche Post,* August 6, 1914; "Britische Gemeinheit," *Westliche Post,* May 15, 1915; "Must Avert Inner Strife Says the Westliche Post," *St. Louis Post-Dispatch,* May 14, 1915. "Was die anglo-amerikanische Presse nicht berichtet," *Amerika,* September 4, 1914; "Was aus Deutschland eingetroffene Briefe erzählen," *Amerika,* September 27, 1914.

13. Crighton, *Missouri and the World War,* 56. Christensen, "Prelude to World War I," 4.

14. Kennedy, *Over Here,* 4–11. "The Newest German Surprise," *Amerika,* February 9, 1915; "Deutschland begründet seine Blockade Erklärung," *Deutscher Volksfreund,* February 12, 1915; "Kriegsnachrichten," *Missouri Volksfreund,* May 6, 1915; "Bernstorff warnt das reisende Publikum," *Deutscher Volksfreund,* May 7, 1915; "Eine Krise in der Beziehung zu Deutschland," *Westliche Post,* May 8, 1915; "Die englische *Lusitania* mit 1,149 Personen gesunken," *Missouri Volksfreund,* May 13, 1915. "Kriegsnachrichten," *Missouri Volksfreund,* September 21, 1916.

15. "Better Than an Embargo," *Springfield Leader,* February 27, 1915; "Saving Its Face on a Technicality," *St. Louis Republic,* April 10, 1915. "The Lusitania and International Law," *St. Louis Republic,* May 8, 1915; "The Law Still Stands," *St. Louis Republic,* May 10, 1915; "The Man at the Helm," *St. Louis Republic,* May 13, 1915; "England's Position," *St. Louis Republic,* August 5, 1915; "Strict Accountability," *St. Joseph News Press,* May 8, 1915; "The Lusitania Incident," *Columbia Daily Tribune,* May 10, 1915; "A Time for Sanity," *Kansas City Journal,* May 9, 1915; "Self-Control of a Free People," *Joplin News-Herald,* May 13, 1915; "Must Avert Inner Strife Says the Westliche Post," *St. Louis Post-Dispatch,* May 14, 1915; editorial, *Weekly Graphic* (Kirksville), May 14, 1915; editorial, *Franklin County Tribune,* May 14, 1915. See also Crighton, *Missouri and the World War,* 73–81; Christensen and Kremer, *History of Missouri,* 203.

16. Louis Benecke was the son of the famous Captain Louis Benecke from Brunswick, Missouri. Louis Benecke to "My dear Papa," May 15, 1915, folder 1402, Benecke Papers, WHMC.

17. They were Charles Nagel, former Secretary of Labor and Commerce; Edward Preetorius, editor of the *Westliche Post*; and Henry Kersting, St. Louis Alliance chapter president. "St. Louis Germans Loyal," *New York Times,* May 15, 1915. Wüstenbecker, *Deutsch-Amerikaner,* 91.

18. "Do We Want a Large Army?" *St. Joseph News Press,* September 3, 1914; "The Weakness of Our National Defense," *St. Joseph News Press,* June 5, 1915; "Facing a 'Bugaboo,'" *St. Louis Republic,* June 6, 1915; "Wanted: A Military and Naval Policy," *St. Louis Republic,* July 20, 1915; "Preparedness," *Sedalia Journal,* July 13, 1916. "Part of Mexico Where 'Punitive Expedition' Will Hunt for Villa," *Franklin County Tribune,* March 17, 1916; "Die Jagd in Mexico," *Missouri Volksfreund,* March 30, 1916; "War and the United States," *Joplin News-Herald,* April 25, 1916; "Kriegsnachrichten," *Missouri Volksfreund,* May 18, 1916. Louis Auchincloss, *Woodrow Wilson* (New York: Penguin Putnam, 2000), 57–60; Laura Garcés, "The German Challenge to the Monroe Doctrine in Mexico, 1917," in *Confrontation and Cooperation: Germany and the United*

States in the Era of World War I, 1900–1924, ed. Hans Jürgen Schröder (Providence, RI: Berg, 1993), 284. See also Crighton, *Missouri and the World War*, 117–18; Christensen, "Prelude to World War I," 5.

19. "Alpen Brau," *St. Louis Republic*, October 10, 1914; "$10,000,000 Imperial German Government," *St. Louis Republic*, April 1, 1915; "Germany Floating Big Loan," *St. Louis Republic*, April 2, 1915; "Achtung Deutsche!" *St. Louis Republic*, March 1, 1916.

20. Crighton, *Missouri and the World War*, 27. Heinrich W. von Heinrichshofen, United States Passport Applications, 1795–1925, M1490, January 2, 1906–March 31, 1925, General Records of the Department of State, Record Group 59, National Archives, Washington, DC. It is unclear what happened to him as he does not appear in the 1920 or 1930 U.S. Census.

21. Ludwig Dilger, to "My dear Albert," February 7, 1915, St. Louis, in *News from the Land of Freedom*, 503–4. Wüstenbecker, *Deutsch-Amerikaner*, 54–55; Luebke, *Bonds of Loyalty*, 118–23; Margaret LoPiccolo Sullivan, *Hyphenism in St. Louis, 1900–1921: A View from the Outside* (New York: Garland, 1990), 22, 52; Clifton James Child, *The German-Americans in Politics, 1914–1917* (Madison: University of Wisconsin Press, 1939), 42–45.

22. E. Schumann Heinzt to Professor Hermann B. Almstedt, May 13, 1915, folder 25, Hermann B. Almstedt Papers, Western Historical Manuscript Collection, University of Missouri–Columbia. Peter Hernon and Terry Ganey, *Under the Influence: The Unauthorized Story of the Anheuser-Busch Dynasty* (New York: Simon & Schuster, 1991), 79, 90.

23. "Die Kundgebung des St. Louiser Deutschthums," *Westliche Post*, August 10, 1914. "Putting on the Sewing Circle," and "Red Cross Chapter in St. Louis," *St. Louis Republic*, April 11, 1915. "Für das Rote Kreuz," *Westliche Post*, March 1, 1917.

24. W. Stenzel, to Capt. L. Benecke, November 13, 1916, folder 1418; "Zeichnungs Einladung auf die Fünfte Deutsche Kriegsanleihe," folder 2033, both in Benecke Papers, WHMC. "Aufruf an alle deutschen Stammesgenossen und deren Freunde," *Deutscher Volksfreund*, August 28, 1914; "Der große Kriegsbazar," *Westliche Post*, August 2, 1914; "Gabenliste des Central Vereins," *Amerika*, October 11, 1914; "Das Tausend endlich voll und abgeschickt," *Deutscher Volksfreund*, March 26, 1915; "Eine Bitte zur Unterstützung," *Missouri Volksfreund*, July 22, 1915; "Kehraus im Kriegs-bazar," *Westliche Post*, November 1, 1915; "Für den sibirischen Hilfsfonds," *Amerika*, September 3, 1916; "$100,000 für Kriegsnotleidende," *Westliche Post*, January 1, 1916. Child, *German-Americans in Politics*, 36–39; Audrey L. Olson, "St. Louis Germans, 1850–1920: The Nature of an Immigrant Community and Its Relation to the Assimilation Process" (PhD diss., University of Kansas, 1970), 182, 192–97. Gary Ross Mormino, "Over Here: St. Louis Italo-Americans and the First World War," *Bulletin of the Missouri Historical Society* 30 (October 1973): 44–53. For examples in the Midwest see Luebke, *Bonds of Loyalty*, 95–96; LaVern J. Rippley, *The Immigrant Experience in Wisconsin* (Boston: G. K. Hall, 1985), 96–98; and Carl Wittke, *German-Americans and the World War: With Special Emphasis on Ohio's German-Language Press* (Columbus: Ohio State Archaeological and Historical Society, 1936), 30–32, 36.

25. "Einladung zum Verbrüderungs und Wohlthätigkeits Fest," *Amerika*, October 1, 1914; "Für die Opfer des Krieges," *Amerika*, September 2, 1914. Olson, "St. Louis Germans," 262–65.

26. "Unterstützungs Beiträge," *Kansas City Presse,* November 2, 1915, folder 2, Oscar Sachs Papers, WHMC.

27. "Wer ist Amerikaner?" *Missouri Volksfreund,* September 23, 1915. "Das Deutsch-Amerikanische Picnic," *Deutscher Volksfreund,* July 16, 1915. Wüstenbecker, *Deutsch-Amerikaner,* 61.

28. In 1910, St. Louis had 47,765 immigrants from Germany, 11,171 from Austria, and 8,758 from Hungary. The number of American-born individuals in St. Louis both of whose parents had been born in Germany was 90,329; the number of those whose parents had been born in Austria was 6,574; and the number of those whose parents had been born in Hungary was 1,874. Chicago counted 182,281 immigrants from Germany, 132,050 from Austria, and 28,938 from Hungary. The number of persons in Chicago both of whose parents had been born in Germany was 244,185; the number whose parents had been born in Austria was 85,208; and the number of those whose parents had been born in Hungary was 8,288. U.S. Bureau of the Census, *Thirteenth Census of the United States, 1910: Abstract of the Census with Supplement for Missouri* (Washington, DC: Government Printing Office, 1913), 522, 1128; *Thirteenth Census of the United States, 1910: Abstract of the Census with Supplement for Illinois* (Washington, DC: Government Printing Office, 1913), 614, 636. Wüstenbecker, *Deutsch-Amerikaner,* 51.

29. Crighton, *Missouri and the World War,* 29; Gary M. Fink, *Labor's Search for Political Order: The Political Behavior of the Missouri Labor Movement, 1890–1940* (Columbia: University of Missouri Press, 1973), 61–62; Edwin James Forsythe, "The St. Louis Central Trades and Labor Union, 1887–1945" (PhD diss., University of Missouri, 1956), 126.

30. The National Security League had been active for many years prior to World War I for the purpose of debating national military preparedness. Kennedy, *Over Here,* 41. Crighton, *Missouri and the World War,* 119–27; David W. Detjen, *The Germans in Missouri, 1900–1918: Prohibition, Neutrality, and Assimilation* (Columbia: University of Missouri Press, 1985), 124; Fink, *Labor's Search for Political Order,* 61; Forsythe, "Central Trades and Labor Union," 130; James Neal Primm, *Lion of the Valley: St. Louis, Missouri, 1764–1989,* 3rd ed. (St. Louis: Missouri Historical Society Press, 1998), 434.

31. Detjen, *Germans in Missouri,* 97–101; Christensen, "Prelude to World War I," 4; Crighton, *Missouri and the World War,* 88–91, 94; Primm, *Lion of the Valley,* 434; Wüstenbecker, *Deutsch-Amerikaner,* 71–6.

32. Alan Niehaus Graebner, "The Acculturation of an Immigration Lutheran Church: The Lutheran Church–Missouri Synod, 1917–1929" (PhD diss., Columbia University, 1965), 34–37. John Philip Gleason, "The Central Verein, 1900–1917: A Chapter in the History of the German-American Catholics" (PhD diss., University of Notre Dame, 1960), 349, 355–56. "Deutsch-Amerikaner Solidarisch," *Westliche Post,* August 6, 1914; "Die Kundgebung des St. Louiser Deutschthums," *Westliche Post,* August 10, 1914.

33. "Tribut eines echten Amerikaners," *Westliche Post,* July 12, 1916; "Der Bayern Ehrentag," *Westliche Post,* September 4, 1916.

34. Child, *German-Americans in Politics,* 25–28, 53–54, 62; Detjen, *Germans in Missouri,* 96–109. Christensen and Kremer, *History of Missouri,* 201; Olson, "St. Louis Germans," 151, 176, 192; Higham, *Strangers in the Land,* 196.

35. Olson, "St. Louis Germans," 192–97; Detjen, *Germans in Missouri,* 110–14.

36. "Misrepresenting German-Americans," *St. Louis Republic,* July 26, 1915. Detjen, *Germans in Missouri,* 116.

37. "Registration beendet," *Westliche Post,* November 3, 1916.

38. Higham, *Strangers in the Land,* 200–202. Luebke, *Bonds of Loyalty,* 157–94. Sister John Christine Wolkerstorfer, "Nativism in Minnesota in World War I: A Comparative Study of Brown, Ramsey, and Stearns Counties, 1914–18" (PhD diss., University of Minnesota, 1973), 190, 208.

39. Wüstenbecker notes that the Republican Party enlisted the support of well-known Democrat Charles Boerchenstein as the head of its German-American bureau to elicit the German-American vote for Hughes. Wüstenbecker, *Deutsch-Amerikaner,* 108. See also Luebke, *Bonds of Loyalty,* 167–69, 174.

40. Wilson in a 1915 speech to naturalized citizens argued that it was "one thing to love the place where you were born" yet quite "another thing to dedicate yourself to the place to which you go." He believed that a person had to become a thorough American, but "a man who thinks of himself as belonging to a particular national group in America, has not yet become an American." Woodrow Wilson, "Americanism and the Foreign-Born," Address to Naturalized Citizens at Philadelphia, Pennsylvania, May 10, 1915, http://douglassarchives.org/wils_bo2.htm (accessed September 6, 2004). Kennedy, *Over Here,* 12; Child, *German-Americans in Politics,* 86–93, 131, 142; Higham, *Strangers in the Land,* 197–99; Luebke, *Bonds of Loyalty,* 169–83.

41. Editorial, *Franklin County Tribune,* June 16, 1916, and June 23, 1916; "No Figs From Thistles," and "Playing Both Ends Against the Middle," *Moberly Democrat,* October 27, 1916; "Wilson Had Made the U.S. Ashamed," *Kansas City Journal,* November 4, 1916; "Reasons for a Change," *Kansas City Journal,* November 5, 1916; "Duty First!" *Kansas City Star,* October 2, 1916. Detjen, *Germans in Missouri,* 121, 123.

42. "St. Louis Aroused by Col. Roosevelt," *New York Times,* June 1, 1916. Child, *German-Americans in Politics,* 146–47; and Crighton, *Missouri and the World War,* 136–39.

43. Detjen, *Germans in Missouri,* 123; Crighton, *Missouri and the World War,* 135–36; Sullivan, *Hyphenism in St. Louis,* 60; Wüstenbecker, *Deutsch-Amerikaner,* 109–11.

44. Detjen, *Germans in Missouri,* 121–24; Child, *German-Americans in Politics,* 106–8.

45. "Das Schlagwort vom Bindestrich-Amerikaner," *Westliche Post,* July 7, 1916; "Können Deutschamerikaner noch für Wilson stimmen?" *Westliche Post,* October 30, 1916.

46. Editorial, *Missouri Staatszeitung* (Kansas City), November 17, 1916. John Folz to Louis Benecke, April 28, 1916, folder 1409, Benecke Papers, WHMC.

47. "Das Schlagwort vom Bindestrich-Amerikaner," *Westliche Post,* July 7, 1916; "Charles Fairbanks gegen naturistische Hetzer," *Westliche Post,* September 2, 1916; "Richter Hughes als Kampagneredner," *Westliche Post,* September 20, 1916; "Wilson der Feindliche," *Westliche Post,* October 20, 1916; "Können Deutschamerikaner noch für Wilson stimmen?" *Westliche Post,* October 30, 1916.

48. Louis Benecke to Bion McCurry, October 6, 1916, folder 1786; and Louis Benecke, "Phantom Conspirators," newspaper clipping, name of paper unknown, November 2, 1916, folder 1418; both in Benecke Papers, WHMC. "Wilson and Decker

Landslide," clipping from *Lamar Democrat,* no page number, October 19, 1916, vol. 2, 20, Perl D. Decker Papers, Western Historical Manuscript Collection, University of Missouri–Columbia.

49. "Herr Hughes enttäuscht," *Missouri Volksfreund,* August 17, 1916; "Wie steht's Herr Hughes?" *Missouri Volksfreund,* September 7, 1916; "Was er sagte, bedeutete nichts," and "Wieder die Präsidentschaft," both in *Missouri Volksfreund,* October 5, 1916; "Preparedness," *Sedalia Journal,* July 13, 1916; "Our Stand," *Sedalia Journal,* August 24, 1916; "Der große demokratische Fest und Freudentag," *Deutscher Volksfreund,* October 6, 1916. E. B. Kellog to Cpt. L. Benecke, November 11, 1916, folder 1418, Benecke Papers, WHMC. Luebke, *Bonds of Loyalty,* 183–87.

50. "Wilson's 'Katholischer' Gegner," *Amerika,* October 17, 1912; "Die Deutsch-Amerikaner und Herr Hughes," *Amerika,* September 8, 1916; "So fortschrittlich wie neutral," *Amerika,* September 16, 1916.

51. "St. Louis for Hughes," *Westliche Post,* September 4, 1916. Crighton, *Missouri and the World War,* 142, 144–45; Christensen, "Prelude to World War I," 10.

52. "Wahlnachklänge," *Deutscher Volksfreund,* November 16, 1916; "Das Wahlresultat in Cape County," *Deutscher Volksfreund,* November 10, 1916. Christensen and Kremer, *History of Missouri,* 205–6.

53. For table and in-depth election analysis, see Petra DeWitt, "Searching for the Roots of Harassment and the Meaning of Loyalty: A Study of the German-American Experience in Missouri during World War I" (PhD diss., University of Missouri, 2005), 182. *Official Manual of the State of Missouri for the Years 1909–1910* (Jefferson City: Hugh Stephens, 1910), 675–733; *Official Manual of the State of Missouri for the Years 1913–1914* (Jefferson City: Hugh Stephens, 1914), 442–44; and *Official Manual of the State of Missouri for the Years 1917–1918* (Jefferson City: Hugh Stephens, 1918), 429–30, 457–58.

54. Hughes received 83,789 votes, and Wilson garnered 74,059 votes. *Official Manual of the State of Missouri, 1913–1914,* 797; *Official Manual of the State of Missouri, 1917–1918,* 430, 456. Since this author considers wards 1 through 3, 8 through 14, and ward 18 as the German wards, election analysis differs slightly from that of Crighton, who considered only wards 9 through 14 as German wards. DeWitt, "Searching for the Roots of Harassment," 264–66. Detjen, *Germans in Missouri,* 128–30; Olson, "St. Louis Germans," 200; Crighton, *Missouri and the World War,* 149, 153, 156. See also Edgar Eugene Robinson, *The Presidential Vote, 1896–1932* (Stanford: Stanford University Press, 1947), 255.

55. Sally M. Miller, "Germans on the Mississippi: The Socialist Party in St. Louis," in *Race, Ethnicity, and Gender in Early Twentieth-Century American Socialism* (New York: Garland, 1996), 81–90; Primm, *Lion of the Valley,* 410; Fink, *Labor's Search for Political Order,* 33.

56. "Staatsweite Prohibition," *Missouri Volksfreund,* October 9, 1916; "Staats-Prohibition und 'Single Tax,'" *Deutscher Volkfreund,* October 20, 1916; "Prohibitions Paragraphen," and "Wo euer Geld herkommt," *Deutscher Volksfreund,* October 27, 1916; "Prohibition erweist sich als großer Humbug in Kansas," *Missouri Volksfreund,* March 25, 1916.

57. Fink, *Labor's Search for Political Order,* 54

58. Detjen, *Germans in Missouri*, 31, 80, 128, 135–37. Christensen and Kremer, *History of Missouri*, 200. *Official Manual of the State of Missouri for the Years 1917–1918*, 485. "Prohibition Is Snowed Under by a Vote of 110,000 in St. Louis," *St. Louis Globe Democrat*, November 8, 1916.

59. St. Louis defeated it by a vote of 141,070 to 13,529. DeWitt, "Searching for the Roots," 183–83. Detjen, *Germans in Missouri*, 31, 135–37.

60. Gardner, born in Kentucky, came to St. Louis at age seventeen, began to work as an office boy at the St. Louis Coffin company, and by 1916 had become its president. He served as a member of the Board of Freeholders of St. Louis and in this capacity aided in the drafting of the 1914 city charter but did not hold any other public office. He worked on the personal staff of Governor Elliott Major, and in 1914 he was instrumental in persuading the Missouri legislature to adopt his land-bank plan, a low-interest loan system for farmers. William Rufus Jackson, *Missouri Democracy: A History of the Party and Its Representative Members—Past and Present*, vol. 2 (Chicago: S. J. Clarke, 1935), 130, 133; "Executive Departments," *Official Manual of the State of Missouri for the Years 1917–18*, 19; David D. March, *The History of Missouri*, vol. 2 (New York: Lewis Historical, 1967), 1256; Lawrence O. Christensen, William E. Foley, Gary R. Kremer, and Kenneth H. Winn, eds., *Dictionary of Missouri Biography* (Columbia: University of Missouri Press, 1999), 330–31.

61. "Leading Republican Paper Out for Gardner," and "Lamm Not a Businessman," *Moberly Democrat*, October 27, 1916. "Nailing a Campaign Line," *Columbia Daily Tribune*, September 20, 1916. "Col. Gardner Is a Friend of Union Labor, Says Lammert," *Columbia Daily Tribune*, November 3, 1916. Jackson, *Missouri Democracy*, 133. "Falsity of Judge Lamm's Charges Clearly Shown," *Columbia Daily Tribune*, November 3, 1916; "Gardner Again," *Weekly Republican* (Cape Girardeau), July 14, 1916; "A Political Suggestion," *Weekly Republican*, September 22, 1916; "A Chilly Reception to Candidate Gardner," *New Era* (Rolla), September 29, 1916.

62. "Col. F. D. Gardner preist Deutschland in begeisterter Rede," *Missouri Volksfreund*, June 24, 1915; "Deutsch-Amerikanische Bund feiert große Zusammenkunft," *Deutscher Volkfreund*, June 26, 1915.

63. "Trockene Bekämpfen Gardner als Gouverneur's Kandidaten," *Missouri Volksfreund*, March 18, 1916; "Gardner für Gouverneur Club," *Missouri Volksfreund*, March 25, 1916; "Warum die Deutschen in Missouri für Col. Frederick D. Gardner für Gouverneur sind," *Missouri Volksfreund*, June 15, 1916.

64. Christensen and Kremer, *History of Missouri*, 198. *Official Manual of the State of Missouri for the Years 1917–1918*, 430, 457–58.

65. Ludwig Dilger, to "My dear Albert," February 7, 1915, St. Louis, in *News from the Land of Freedom*, 503–4. Fink, *Labor's Search for Political Order*, 65–67; Rosemary Feurer, *Radical Unionism in the Midwest, 1900–1950* (Urbana: University of Illinois Press, 2006), 9–11.

66. John Rothensteiner, *History of the Archdiocese of St. Louis: In Its Various Stages of Development from AD 1673 to AD 1928*, Vol. 2 (St. Louis: Blackwell Wielandy, 1928), 711.

67. "Insurance against War," *St. Louis Republic*, March 15, 1917; and editorial, *St. Louis Republic*, March 18, 1917.

68. "Das Volk will keinen Krieg," *Westliche Post,* February 19, 1917; Sullivan, *Hyphenism in St. Louis,* 64–65; Crighton, *Missouri and the World War,* 135. "Gegen Krieg," *Westliche Post,* March 15, 1917.

69. Forsythe, "Central Trades and Labor Union," 131–32. "Arbeiterpresse nur für Arbeiterschaft," *Westliche Post,* March 14, 1917.

70. "Willkommene Gabe," *Westliche Post,* February 21, 1917; "Ärzte Expedition gesichert," *Westliche Post,* January 4, 1917; "Abreise verschoben," *Westliche Post,* February 2, 1917.

71. "Die Deutsche Frau im Weltkrieg," *Westliche Post,* January 19, 1917; "Die Deutsche Gesellschaft von St. Louis," *Westliche Post,* January 23, 1917.

72. "Deutschland beginnt heute rücksichtslose Seekriegsführung," *Westliche Post,* February 1, 1917; "Tauchbootkrieg ohne Gnade," *Westliche Post,* February 1, 1917; "Was ist der nächste Schritt," *Westliche Post,* February 2, 1917; "Unterseebootkrieg ein glänzender Erfolg," *Westliche Post,* March 21, 1917; "Die neueste Verschwörung," *Westliche Post,* March 2, 1917; "Die Zimmermannsiche Verschwörung," *Westliche Post,* March 5, 1917.

73. "An den Vorstand des Deutsch-Amerikanischen Nationalbundes," *Westliche Post,* February 16, 1917.

74. "Wilson Directs Probe of Big German Plot in Philadelphia," *St. Louis Republic,* March 12, 1917; "Spies Poison Red Cross Bandages," *St. Louis Republic,* March 29, 1917; "Wieder eine Explosion," *Westliche Post,* January 13, 1917; "Der erste deutsche Spion," *Westliche Post,* March 3, 1917; "Der Spionage verdächtigt," *Westliche Post,* March 30, 1917. "Sehen überall Gespenster," *Westliche Post,* March 15, 1917.

75. "Vorbereitung zum Krieg," *Westliche Post,* February 6, 1917; "Spionengesetz der Annahme nahe," *Westliche Post,* February 20, 1917. "Aliens in U.S. Who Obey Laws Not to Be Interned, Secretary Baker Says," *St. Louis Republic,* March 27, 1917; "The Alien Enemy Problem," *St. Louis Republic,* March 28, 1917.

76. Nearly one hundred Germans and Austrians applied for first papers in February. "Frauen lassen sich naturalisieren," *Westliche Post,* February 16, 1917; "Bürgerrechtsapplicationen vermehren sich," *Westliche Post,* February 8, 1917; "Kein Konzentrationslager," *Westliche Post,* February 13, 1917.

77. "Miliztruppen bewachen vorläufig Brücken," *Westliche Post,* March 28, 1917. "Germans in City Crowd to Enlist," *St. Louis Republic,* March 28, 1917; "Rekrutierung von Soldaten macht nur langsame Fortschritte," *Westliche Post,* March 22, 1917; "Patriotische Propaganda," *Westliche Post,* March 29, 1917.

78. "Great Kansas City Mass Meeting Backs Wilson," *St. Louis Republic,* March 25, 1917. "St. Louis Clubwomen Volunteer to Aid U.S.," *St. Louis Republic,* March 29, 1917. For example, the *Republic* began to print the American flag on its front page on April 3, 1917.

79. "Brother Albert," *St. Louis Republic,* March 23, 1917; "A Reactionary Mayor," *St. Louis Republic,* March 26, 1917; "Why Are They for Kiel?" *St. Louis Republic,* March 28, 1917; "G.O.P. Strikes Out Patriotism from Local Campaign," *St. Louis Republic,* March 29, 1917.

80. "Kiel Orators Make Attack on Wilson," *St. Louis Republic,* March 27, 1917; "Loyalitätsbeteuerung," *Westliche Post,* March 19, 1917; "Mayor Kiel antwortet Demokraten," *Westliche Post,* March 22, 1917.

81. "Loyalitätsbeteuerung," *Westliche Post,* March 19, 1917; "Wahres Amerikanertum," *Westliche Post,* March 22, 1917; "Giftsaat trägt Früchte," *Westliche Post,* March 26, 1917; "Giftmichelei der *Republic," Westliche Post,* March 28, 1917; and "Kriegszustand gegen Deutschland," *Westliche Post,* April 3, 1917.

82. "Henry W. Kiel mit gewaltiger Mehrheit wiedererwählt," *Westliche Post,* April 4, 1917; "Kiel's Plurality is 23,401," "Kiel Reelected," *St. Louis Republic,* April 4, 1917.

Chapter 3: "No Time for Slackers"

1. "Great St. Louis Meeting Proclaims Loyalty to Nation," *St. Louis Republic,* April 6, 1917. "Pro-Germans Classed as Spies by Gardner, Warned to Keep out of Missouri," reprinted from the *St. Louis Republic,* April 8, 1918, by the Missouri Council of Defense, located in folder 1702, E. Y. Mitchell Jr. Papers, Western Historical Manuscript Collection, University of Missouri–Columbia (hereinafter cited as Mitchell Papers, WHMC). "Col. F. D. Gardner preist Deutschland in begeisterter Rede," *Missouri Volksfreund,* June 24, 1915.

2. "More Frightfulness?" *Kansas City Journal,* February 2, 1917; "Wofür Deutschland kämpft," *Missouri Thalbote,* March 16, 1917; "Will It Come to War?" *Concordian* (Concordia), February 8, 1917; "Wachsames Warten Walten," *Sedalia Journal,* February 22, 1917; "Zeitgemäßiger Rath," *Sedalia Journal,* March 1, 1917; "Let Us Take It Calmly," *Weekly Graphic* (Kirksville), March 9, 1917.

3. "Eine Kolossale Dummheit," *Deutscher Volksfreund,* March 8, 1917; "Missouri Zweig der Liga zur Erzwingung des Weltfriedens," *Missouri Volksfreund,* March 1, 1917; editorial, *Sedalia Journal,* February 15, 1917; "Breaking All Ties," *Joplin News Herald,* February 1, 1917; "In Case of War," *St. Joseph News Press,* April 2, 1917.

4. Oliver Marble Gale, ed., *Americanism: Woodrow Wilson's Speeches on the War* (Chicago: Baldwin Syndicate, 1918), 43. David M. Kennedy, *Over Here: The First World War and American Society* (New York: Oxford University Press, 1980), 3–20. Stephen Vaughn, *Holding Fast the Inner Lines: Democracy, Nationalism, and the Committee on Public Information* (Chapel Hill: University of North Carolina Press, 1980), 4–5. Jörg Nagler, "Pandora's Box: Propaganda and War Hysteria in the United States during World War I," in *Great War, Total War: Combat and Mobilization on the Western Front, 1914–1918,* ed. Roger Chickering and Stig Förster (Cambridge: Cambridge University Press, 2000), 490–91.

5. Kennedy, *Over Here,* 59–61. George Creel, *How We Advertised America* (New York: Harper & Brothers, 1920; reprint, New York: Arno Press, 1972), 3–5. James R. Mock and Cedric Larson, *Words That Won the War: The Story of the Committee on Public Information* (Princeton: Princeton University Press, 1939; reprint, New York: Russell & Russell, 1968), 5–6; Vaughn, *Holding Fast the Inner Lines,* 4–5. See also H. C. Peterson and Gilbert C. Fite, *Opponents of War, 1917–1918* (Madison: University of Wisconsin Press, 1957), 14.

6. Roberta Strauss Feuerlicht, *America's Reign of Terror: World War I, the Red Scare, and the Palmer Raids* (New York: Random House, 1971), 17–18; Vaughn, *Holding Fast the Inner Lines,* 141; Stewart Halsey Ross, *Propaganda for War: How the United States Was Conditioned to Fight the Great War of 1914–1918* (Jefferson, NC: McFarland, 1996),

226; Nagler, "Pandora's Box," 492–96. Cecilia Elizabeth O'Leary, *To Die For: The Paradox of American Patriotism* (Princeton: Princeton University Press, 1999), 229–32.

7. "Senator Stone fordert Missouri auf, treu zur Regierung zu halten," *Missouri Volksfreund,* April 12, 1917, 1; Lawrence O. Christensen and Gary R. Kremer, *A History of Missouri,* vol. 4: *1875 to 1919* (Columbia: University of Missouri Press, 1997), 210.

8. Lawrence O. Christensen, "World War I in Missouri: Part I," *Missouri Historical Review* 90 (April 1996): 331–32. "Joplin Surcharged with Patriotic Fever When Citizens Show Loyalty," *Joplin News Herald,* April 5, 1917; "Patriotic Citizens Parade the Streets," *St. Joseph News Press,* April 6, 1917.

9. "Krieg mit Deutschland zur Thatsache geworden," *Missouri Volksfreund,* April 5, 1917; "St. Joseph Turnverein Replaces German Emblem with Stars and Stripes in their Turner Hall," *Concordian,* April 5, 1917.

10. Gary M. Fink, *Labor's Search for Political Order: The Political Behavior of the Missouri Labor Movement, 1890–1940* (Columbia: University of Missouri Press, 1973), 68.

11. "Heute Patrioten Tag!" *Sedalia Journal,* April 19, 1917. O'Leary, *To Die For,* 232–35. Editorial, *Weekly Graphic,* April 20, 1917; "Patriotic Proclamation," *Sedalia Democrat,* May 17, 1917.

12. "Gehorche dem Gesetz und verhalte Dich still!" *Missouri Volksfreund,* April 19, 1917.

13. The Espionage Act punished anyone who interfered with military operations, caused "insubordination, disloyalty, mutiny, or refusal of duty" in the military, or obstructed recruitment, with a fine up to $10,000, imprisonment up to twenty years, or both. It also gave the Postmaster General the authority to ban treasonous publications from the mails. The Sedition Amendment to the Espionage Act in May 1918 made it a crime to express any disloyal or profane language about the government, Constitution, and flag. The Trading-with-the-Enemy Act required that foreign-language newspapers file an English translation of any article discussing the military, the government, or the conduct of the war with the Postmaster General before publication. Kennedy, *Over Here,* 75–77.

14. Emerson Hough, *The Web* (Chicago: Reilly & Lee, 1919; reprint, New York: Arno Press, 1969), 62–72, 89; Joan M. Jensen, *The Price of Vigilance* (Chicago: Rand McNally, 1968), 19, 32–33, 78, 176–77.

15. O. A. Hilton, "Public Opinion and Civil Liberties in Wartime, 1917–1919," *Southwestern Social Science Quarterly* 28 (December 1947): 212–18; James R. Mock, *Censorship 1917* (Princeton: Princeton University Press, 1941), 5–6; Peterson and Fite, *Opponents of War,* 79, 146, 153; Nagler, "Pandora's Box," 496. "Disloyalist Lashed with Iron Whip," *New York Times,* March 21, 1918.

16. Peterson and Fite, *Opponents of War,* 14, 79, 146, 148–50, 168, 194, 197, 199, 280; Carl Wittke, *German-Americans and the World War: With Special Emphasis on Ohio's German-Language Press* (Columbus: Ohio State Archaeological and Historical Society, 1936), 157–59, 163; Frederick C. Luebke, *Bonds of Loyalty: German-Americans and World War I* (DeKalb: Northern Illinois University Press, 1974), 210–12, 247; Don Heinrich Tolzmann, *The German-American Experience* (New York: Humanity Books, 2000), 287.

17. Luebke, *Bonds of Loyalty,* 210–12, 244, 247, 280; Wittke, *German-Americans and the World War,* 191–92, 194–95, 197; Kennedy, *Over Here,* 67–68. Peterson and Fite, *Opponents of War,* 152–53, 168, 194, 199. Feuerlicht, *America's Reign of Terror,* 38.

18. Donald R. Hickey, "The Prager Affair: A Study of Wartime Hysteria," *Journal of the Illinois State Historical Society* 62 (1969): 117–34; E. A. Schwartz, "The Lynching of Robert Prager, the United Mine Workers, and the Problems of Patriotism in 1918," *Journal of the Illinois State Historical Society* 96 (2003): 414–37; Luebke, *Bonds of Loyalty,* 3–24.

19. Carl R. Weinberg, *Labor, Loyalty & Rebellion: Southwestern Illinois Coal Miners & World War I* (Carbondale: Southern Illinois University Press, 2005), 5, 199.

20. For table of incidents see Appendix 9 in Petra DeWitt, "Searching for the Roots of Harassment and the Meaning of Loyalty: A Study of the German-American Experience in Missouri during World War I" (PhD diss., University of Missouri, 2005), 469–75.

21. E. R. Stone to Missouri Council of Defense, August 11, 1917, folder 280; and William L. Reid to E. J. Brennan, February 25, 1918, folder 285; both in Collection 2797, Missouri Council of Defense Papers, Western Historical Manuscript Collection, University of Missouri–Columbia (hereinafter cited as MCDP, WHMC).

22. United States v. E. J. Deane, docket no. 6569, Record Group 21, Records of the U.S. District Court, Eastern District of Missouri, Criminal Cases, 1864–1966, National Archives, Central Plains Region, Kansas City, Missouri (hereinafter cited as RG 21, District Court, Criminal Cases, NA KC).

23. Scheunemann was a third-generation German-American. Twelfth Census of the United States, 1900, Population Schedule, Missouri, Randolph County, Creek Township, sheet 4 A. "High School Teacher Arrested," *Moberly Weekly Democrat,* January 23, 1918; "Happenings in Missouri," *Gasconade County Republican* (Owensville), February 1, 1918, and February 8, 1918; "News from Other Counties," *Advertiser-Courier,* December 12, 1917. "Missouri U. Teacher Nabbed by S.S. Agent," *Kirksville Daily Express,* December 6, 1917.

24. The governor established the Home Guard to take over the functions of the Missouri National Guard once the national government federalized all National Guard units in the United States and sent them to France alongside the first regular army units. "K.S.N.S. Science Hall Destroyed by Fire," *Kirksville Daily Express,* September 19, 1918; "Failed to Halt the Normal School S.A.T.C.," *Kirksville Daily Express,* September 23, 1998; "St. Louis Paper Sees Hun Plot in Fire Here," *Kirksville Daily Express,* September 25, 1918. Telegram, L. G. Adams to William Saunders, August 5, 1917, folder 280, MCDP, WHMC. "Calls Out Guard," *Gasconade County Republican,* June 28, 1918.

25. F. S. Tuggle to Wm. F. Saunders, May 25, 1918, folder 861, MCDP, WHMC.

26. "Home Guards Beat a Mob," *Kansas City Times,* April 9, 1918; "Mob Flays Pro-German; Forces Him to Kiss Flag in the Jefferson Theater," *Daily Capital News,* April 6, 1918; "Fourth of July Parade and the Irving Walz Incident," Report of H. E. Steinmann, July 5, 1918, folder 292, MCDP, WHMC. Christopher C. Gibbs, "The Lead Belt Riot and World War One," *Missouri Historical Review* 71 (July 1977): 413.

27. See, for example, Luebke, *Bonds of Loyalty,* 225–59, Wittke, *German-Americans and the World War,* 155–90; and Sister John Christine Wolkerstorfer, "Nativism in Minnesota in World War I: A Comparative Study of Brown, Ramsey, and Stearns Counties, 1914–18" (PhD diss., University of Minnesota, 1973), 28–34.

28. Jeanette Keith, *Rich Man's War, Poor Man's Fight: Race, Class, and Power in the Rural South during the First World War* (Chapel Hill: University of North Carolina Press, 2004), 2–3, 24–32, 85–86.

29. Christopher C. Gibbs, *The Great Silent Majority: Missouri's Resistance to World War I* (Columbia: University of Missouri Press, 1988), 38–49.

30. William F. Saunders to W. S. Gifford, director of Council of National Defense, July 6, 1917, folder 35, Mrs. Walter McNab Miller to Herbert Hoover, July 10, 1917, folder 408; Mrs. Walter McNab Miller to R. W. Wilbur, August 16, 1917 and September 3, 1917, folder 409; all in MCDP, WHMC. "War Conference in January," *Gasconade County Republican*, December 12, 1917.

31. For example, "Spies Poison Red Cross Bandages," *St. Louis Republic*, March 29, 1917; "May Raid I.W.W. at Will," *Kansas City Star*, June 11, 1917; "Local Slackers Will Be Picked Up by Policemen," *Kansas City Post*, June 12, 1917. In contrast, the *Franklin County Observer* printed its first spy article in September 1917. "Dastardly Work of German Spies Disclosed by Seized Documents," *Franklin County Observer*, September 28, 1917.

32. *National Council of Defense Bulletin* 8, p. 21, folder 202; "Organization and Work of Councils of Defense," folder 240, both in MCDP, WHMC.

33. *Final Report of the Missouri Council of Defense, 1917–19* (St. Louis: Con. P. Curran, 1919), 8. Lawrence O. Christensen, "Missouri's Response to World War I: The Missouri Council of Defense," *Midwest Review* 12 (1990): 35; Gibbs, *Great Silent Majority*, 52; Floyd C. Shoemaker, *Missouri and Missourians: Land of Contrast and People of Achievements* (Chicago: Lewis, 1943), 289.

34. Office of the Judge Advocate General of the Army, *Compilation of War Laws of the Various States and Insular Possessions* (Washington, DC: Government Printing Office, 1919), 11–12. Legislatures in Nebraska, Illinois, Michigan, Minnesota, South Dakota, Wisconsin, and Utah gave their state councils broad legislative powers that allowed for statewide enforcement of restrictive and oppressive resolutions, including laws that specifically ended the use of German in schools, churches, and in public. Frederick C. Luebke, "Legal Restrictions on Foreign Languages in the Great Plains States, 1917–23," in *Germans in the New World: Essays in the History of Immigration* (Urbana: University of Illinois Press, 1990), 31–50; "Iowa Proclamation," folder 373a, MCDP, WHMC. See also folder 243, MCDP, WHMC. The 50th General Assembly appropriated $74,165.80 in 1919 to meet the council's expenses and endorsed its wartime activities. Christensen and Kremer, *History of Missouri*, 218; Shoemaker, *Missouri and Missourians*, 289–90. Richard J. Hardy, Richard R. Dohm, and David A. Leuthold, *Missouri Government and Politics* (Columbia: University of Missouri Press, 1995), 25.

35. Katja Wüstenbecker, *Deutsch-Amerikaner im Ersten Weltkrieg: US-Politik und Nationale Identitäten im Mittleren Westen* (Stuttgart, Germany: Franz Steiner Verlag, 2007), 135, 141–43; LaVern J. Rippley, *The Immigrant Experience in Wisconsin* (Boston: G. K. Hall, 1985), 95.

36. *Final Report*, 19–20, 29; "Raise a War Crop," poster, folder 573, MCDP, WHMC. Christensen, "World War I in Missouri: Part I," 31–42; Floyd C. Shoemaker, "Missouri and the War: Sixth Article," *Missouri Historical Review* 13 (July 1919): 322; and Gibbs, *Great Silent Majority*, 109–12, 117–18.

37. See, for example, *Missouri Volksfreund,* April 11, 1918; Christensen and Kremer, *History of Missouri,* 227–28; and *Final Report,* 85.

38. *Final Report,* 21, 75–78; "What Missouri Women Are Doing," *St. Louis Republic,* July 7, 1917, 4. Elizabeth Cueny to F. B. Mumford, June 30, 1917, folder 1106; Lucy Holman Hinchcliffe to Mrs. Miller, July 29, 1917, folder 873; both in MCDP, WHMC. Christensen and Kremer, *History of Missouri,* 222–24; Gibbs, *Great Silent Majority,* 67, 126, 128; Shoemaker, *Missouri and Missourians,* 290.

39. "Report of Mrs. Frances S. Burkhardt, Secretary, Patriotic Speakers' Bureau, to the Missouri Council of Defense," March 20, 1918, folder 508; "'Tongues of Fire': How the Missouri Council of Defense Organizes Patriotic Mass Meetings," April 18, 1918, folder 529; both in MCDP, WHMC. *Final Report,* 65–69, 85.

40. W. F. Saunders to Max F. Meyer, January 21, 1918, folder 536; "Reaching the German-Speaking Population," January 1918, folder 239; W. F. Saunders to Dean Mumford, February 15, 1918, folder 93; W. F. Saunders to J. W. Moran, April 6,1918, folder 756; W. F. Saunders to Elliott Dunlap Smith, April 12, 1918, folder 164; and Geo. E. Cansler to W. F. Saunders, no date, folder 536; all in MCDP, WHMC.

41. J. Scott Wolff to W. F. Saunders, January 13, 1918, folder 535; W. F. Saunders to Elliott Dunlap Smith, April 12, 1918, folder 166; W. F. Saunders to Elliott D. Smith, April 12, 1918, folder 164; Council of National Defense to Wm. F. Saunders, April 17, 1918, folder 14; Council of National Defense to Wm. F. Saunders, April 30, 1918, folder 14; and W. F. Saunders to Elliott Dunlap Smith, June 20, 1918, folder 166; all in MCDP, WHMC.

42. "Joplin Man Has Five Sons to Aid in Defeat of Kaiser," *Joplin News Herald,* May 26, 1918. Twelfth Census of the United States,1900, Population Schedule, Missouri, Jasper County, sheet 15 B.

43. Gibbs, *Great Silent Majority,* 102–3. John Whiteclay Chambers, *To Raise an Army: The Draft Comes to Modern America* (New York: Free Press, 1987), 191, 197–98.

44. Office of the Adjutant General of Missouri, *Report of the Adjutant General of Missouri,* 1917–1920 (Jefferson City: Hugh Stephens, 1920), 37–38; "Proclamation," folder 239, MCDP, WHMC. Christensen and Kremer, *History of Missouri,* 235–37.

45. "700,000 Sign Food Pledge in Missouri," *Missouri on Guard* 1 (December 1917): 1–2; Kennedy, *Over Here,* 100–106; Christensen and Kremer, *History of Missouri,* 231; Floyd C. Shoemaker, "Missouri and the War: Second Article," *Missouri Historical Review* 12 (January 1918): 91; Gibbs, *Great Silent Majority,* 83–92.

46. Christensen and Kremer, *History of Missouri,* 233–34. "Für das Rote Kreuz," *Missouri Thalbote,* June 22, 1917; "Red Cross Work Started in Concordia," *Concordian,* August 9, 1917; "Red Cross Treats Enemy Wounded," *Concordian,* August 23, 1917; "Was Hat Euer Rote Kreuz Geld Getan?" *Missouri Thalbote,* May 10, 1918.

47. Charles F. Hatfield, secretary of the St. Louis Conventions and Publicity Bureau, authored an article titled "Missouri, the Show You State," which Representative L. C. Dyer from St. Louis read in the House of Representatives on April 16, 1917. Floyd C. Shoemaker, "Missouri and the War," *Missouri Historical Review* 12 (October 1917): 27.

48. Mrs. Walter McNab Miller to Mrs. Philip N. Moore, September 3, 1917, folder 1111; R. G. Russell to Wm. F. Saunders, December 17, 1917, folder 1100; both in MCDP, WHMC.

49. "To All County Council Chairmen," August 1, 1917, folder 240, MCDP, WHMC.

50. Robert A. Glenn to W. F. Saunders, October 8, 1917, folder 282; Ira F. Reed to Wm. F. Saunders, August 3, 1917, folder 27; both in MCDP, WHMC.

51. W. F. Saunders to W. G. Dillon, September 25, 1917, folder 761; W. F. Saunders to Cowgill Blair, January 4, 1918, folder 284; Wm. F. Saunders to Chairman Mumford, January 4, 1918, folder 91; all in MCDP, WHMC.

52. W. F. Saunders to Ira F. Reed, September 10, 1917, folder 281; W. F. Saunders to George F. Porter, September 12, 1917, folder 126; "Disloyal Remarks to Be Suppressed," newspaper clipping, name reduced to *Journal,* September 8, 1917, folder 278; W. F. Saunders to George F. Mathews, April 11, 1918, folder 287; W. F. Saunders to Chairman Mumford, April 22, 1918, folder 99; all in MCDP, WHMC.

53. Wm. F. Saunders to Honorable Floyd S. Tuggle, May 28, 1918, folder 861; F. S. Tuggle to W. F. Saunders, June 24, 1918, folder 861; Ira F. Reed to Robert A. Glenn, September 4, 1917, and Ira F. Reed to Wm. F. Saunders, September 8, 1917, both in folder 281; all in MCDP, WHMC. "Daviess Indexes Citizens Names," *Missouri on Guard* 2 (June 1918): 5. "1882 Signers to Food Pledge in Washington," *Franklin County Observer,* November 16, 1917.

54. Christensen and Kremer, *History of Missouri,* 218. "County Councils to Be Supreme," *Missouri on Guard* 1 (July 1917): 2.

55. "Our Losses Also Are Heavy," *New York Times,* March 2, 1918. Kennedy, *Over Here,* 190; Christopher M. Sterba, *Good Americans: Italian and Jewish Immigrants during the First World War* (New York: Oxford University Press, 2003), 177; Nancy Gentile Ford, *The Great War and America: Civil-Military Relations during World War I* (Westport, CT: Praeger Security International, 2008), 80, 83–84.

56. Gibbs, *Great Silent Majority,* 148–49; Fink, *Labor's Search for Political Order,* 71–77; "Tabak-Arbeiter Striken," *Westliche Post,* March 1, 1918.

57. "The Second Liberty Loan," *Deutscher Volksfreund,* October 18, 1917. "What You Can Do to Help Win This War," *Missouri Volksfreund,* January 3, 1918. Kennedy, *Over Here,* 77. During February 1918, 5,890 men registered as enemy aliens in Missouri. Jörg Nagler, *Nationale Minoritäten im Krieg: Feindlich Ausländer und die amerikanische Heimatfront während des Ersten Weltkriegs* (Hamburg: Hamburger Edition HIS, 2000), 262.

58. "Knock Down Pro-Germans! Seditious Utterances Frequent Now by Gloating Disloyalists Over Events on Western Front," *Sedalia Democrat,* March 26, 1918.

59. R. F. Palmblade to W. F. Saunders, December 19, 1917, folder 282; Cowgill Blair to W. F. Saunders, January 11, 1918, folder 284; P. M. Floyd to Missouri Council of Defense, date unknown, folder 286; J. L. Bagby to State Council of Defense, December 15, 1917, folder 282; L. L. Leonard to Wm. F. Saunders, March 29, 1918, folder 286; George F. Mathews to Wm F. Saunders, April 9, 1918, folder 9; all in MCDP, WHMC.

60. W. F. Saunders to H. F. Childers, February 19, 1918, folder 285; W. F. Saunders to Chairman Mumford, May 15, 1918, W. F. Saunders to F. B. Mumford, May 18, 1918, both in folder 102; all in MCDP, WHMC.

61. Hough, *Web,* 293–309, 410–12. W. F. Saunders to H. M. Briggs, December 13, 1917, folder 282; Wm. F. Saunders to Chairman Mumford, May 15, 1918, folder 102; both in MCDP, WHMC.

62. F. B. Mumford, William F. Saunders, and M. L. Wilkinson to W. McCormick Blair, March 23, 1918, folder 214; Wm. F. Saunders to M. L. Wilkinson, March 25, 1918; and "To the Members of the Missouri Council of Defense: Information Bulletin No. 27," April 9, 1918, folder 337, all in MCDP, WHMC. E. M. Grossman, "To the Four-Minute Men of Missouri," April 2, 1918, folder 1702, Mitchell Papers, WHMC.

63. "Governor Tells Pro-Germans to Stay Out of State," *St. Louis Post-Dispatch,* April 8, 1918.

64. "Americanism," *Missouri on Guard* 1 (February 1918): 3. Gibbs suggests that Gardner intended to run for the United States Senate. Gibbs, *Great Silent Majority,* 29.

65. "A Pro-German Is a Spy," *Kansas City Times,* April 8, 1918; "Pro-Germans, Classed as Spies by Gardner, Warned to Keep Out of Missouri," *St. Louis Republic,* April 8, 1918.

66. Schlomann's grandparents were born in Germany. Thirteenth Census of the United States, 1910, Population Schedule, Missouri, Lawrence County, Mt. Vernon Township, sheet 159. B. A. L. Gibson Adams to Wm. F. Saunders, April 9, 1918; F. W. Wilson to Wm F. Saunders, April 13, 1918, both in folder 287; MCDP, WHMC.

67. "Punish the Slacker and Traitor at Home," *Missouri on Guard* 1 (April 1918): 1; and "Combating German Influence," *Missouri on Guard* 2 (June 1918): 4.

68. W. F. Saunders to George F. Mathews, April 11, 1918; W. F. Saunders to L. Gibson Adams, April 11, 1918; W. F. Saunders to Roy Cox, April 15, 1918; all in folder 287, MCDP, WHMC.

69. Sworn statements signed by J. B. Gilpin, J. H. Harrison, E. T. Bybee, and L. C. Dunnavant, no dates; M. F. Bell to F. B. Mumford, May 6, 1918, both in folder 289, MCDP, WHMC. "Will Be Loyal Now," *Fulton Daily Sun,* May 2, 1918.

70. "Audrain Warns Contributors," *Missouri on Guard* 2 (June 1918): 5.

71. "Pro Germans Kiss the Flag," *Weekly Democrat-News* (Marshall), April 11, 1918; "Men Arrested in Saline City," *Weekly Saline Citizen* (Marshall), April 13, 1918. Leimkuehler was a third-generation and Jaeger a second-generation German-American. *Thirteenth Census of the United States, 1910,* Population Schedule, Missouri, Saline County, Clay Township, sheet 4 A; Fifteenth Census of the United States, 1930, Population Schedule, Missouri, Saline County, Clay Township, sheet 1A.

72. George W. Crowley to W. F. Saunders, July 22, 1918, folder 294; MCDP, WHMC.

73. "Eine wichtige Versammlung in Jackson nächsten Dienstag nachmittag," *Deutscher Volksfreund,* April 11, 1918; "War eine große Versammlung Deutschamerikaner am Dienstag," *Deutscher Volksfreund,* April 18, 1918. "Where Do You Stand?" *Sweet Springs Herald,* April 12, 1918. Phyllis Keller, *States of Belonging: German-American Intellectuals and the First World War* (Cambridge: Harvard University Press, 1979), 189–92. "Schweigen ist Gold," *Missouri Volksfreund,* April 25, 1918.

74. *Alien Property Custodian Report* (Washington, DC: Government Printing Office, 1919; reprint, New York: Arno Press, 1977), 7, 9, 23. See also Kennedy, *Over Here,* 311–13; and Luebke, *Bonds of Loyalty,* 256.

75. *Alien Property,* Council of National Defense Bulletin No. 96, May 21, 1918, folder 230; and Alien Property Custodian Circular of Information, folder 202; both in MCDP, WHMC.

76. McAllister cited Revised Statute of 1909, Chapter 5, Section 750. "Aliens Not Entitled to Own Real Estate in Missouri," folder 497; "Missouri Property of Enemy Aliens," Minutes of Meeting at Hannibal, Missouri, June 1, 1917, folders 499 and 504; all in MCDP, WHMC. "Missouri Council of Defense Begins Survey of All Alien Owned Property," *Missouri on Guard* 2 (June 1918): 1. "Survey Ordered of Alien Property Owners in State," *St. Louis Post-Dispatch,* June 2, 1918.

77. "Alien Property Survey," *Final Report,* 95. "Recovered Auto Likely to Go to Alien Custodian," *St. Louis Post-Dispatch,* April 3, 1918; "Palmer Makes Claim for German Legacies Left By Reisinger," *St. Louis Globe-Democrat,* July 3, 1918. *Alien Property Custodian Report,* 343, 361.

78. Charles Leich, naturalized citizen and resident of Evansville, Indiana, was stranded in Germany when the United States entered the war, and the Custodian confiscated his small business. The government finally abandoned its claims against Leich's small business in 1922. Darrel E. Bigham, "Charles Leich and Company of Evansville: A Note on the Dilemma of German Americans during World War I," *Indiana Magazine of History* 70 (June 1974): 95–121. Bess Glenn, "Private Records Seized by the United States in Wartime—Their Legal Status," *American Archivist* 25 (Fall 1962): 401–3.

79. Frank W. McAllister to William F. Saunders, September 17, 1918, folder 296; J. F. Mermoud to William F. Saunders, June 13, 1918, folder 208; both in MCDP, WHMC.

80. Frank M. Robinson to Joe Kirby, November 1, 1918, folder 252, MCDP, WHMC.

81. Thomas P. Diggs to W. B. Lane, July 3, 1918; and J. L. Bagby to Wm. F. Saunders, July 30, 1918; both in folder 211, MCDP, WHMC.

82. J. F. Mermoud to William F. Saunders, June 7, 1918; J. P. Kay to W. F. Saunders, June 6, 1918; A. H. Culver to W. F. Saunders, June 17, 1918; all in folder 373c, MCDP, WHMC.

83. Kennedy, *Over Here,* 75–77.

84. "Plans to Make German Papers Real Medium of U.S. Propaganda," newspaper clipping, folder 481; Council of National Defense to "The Several State Councils of Defense," June 5, 1918, folder 483; R. A. Glenn to Editor, *Missouri Volksblatt,* June 15, 1918, folder 484; W. F. Saunders to Judge A. M. Hough, no date, folder 484; W. F. Saunders to Elliott Dunlap Smith, July 6, 1918, folder 166; "German Language Newspapers in Missouri," no date, folder 481; all in MCDP, WHMC.

85. See, for example, *Hermanner Volksblatt,* November 9, 1917; *Missouri Volksfreund,* May 30, 1918. Gibbs, *Great Silent Majority,* vii–viii.

86. "Abschieds-Ankündigung!" *Sedalia Journal,* May 10, 1917.

87. Judge Arba S. Van Valkenburgh considered this argument as potentially inciting mutiny and thus punishable under the Espionage Act. "Clamp on Disloyals," *Kansas City Star,* April 30, 1918; and "Former Owner of Missouri Staats-Zeitung Gets 5 Years," *St. Louis Post-Dispatch,* April 30, 1918.

88. Wüstenbecker, *Deutsch-Amerikaner,* 186–87.

89. "Die Lage der deutschen Presse," *Warrenton Volksfreund,* November 16, 1917. "Allgemeines," and "Kriegsnachrichten," *Warrenton Volksfreund,* December 7, 1917.

90. "Der nichtenglischen Presse wird ein Maulkorb angehängt," *Deutscher Volksfreund,* October 4, 1917. The *Missouri Thalbote* printed English articles about the Red Cross and Third Liberty Loan in April 1918.

91. "Ein Wort zum Adschied!" *Warrenton Volksfreund,* April 26, 1918. "Dies ist die letzte Nummer des Thalbote!" *Missouri Thalbote,* July 19, 1918. See, for example, *Sedalia Daily Democrat,* May 11, 1917; *Kansas City Star,* May 10, 1917; *Wentzville Union,* May 3, 1918; *Lexington News,* July 25, 1918.

92. J. F. Mermoud to William F. Saunders, June 7, 1918, folder 373c; W. P. Kimberlin to W. F. Saunders, July 11, 1918, folder 373d; W. F. Saunders to Elliott Dunlap Smith, July 6, 1918, folder 373d; all in MCDP, WHMC. "News from Adjoining Counties," *Advertiser-Courier,* June 12, 1918.

93. "Passed Resolution," *Tipton Times,* June 7, 1918.

94. S. C. Gill to W. F. Saunders, June 20, 1918, folder 291; W. F. Saunders to Elliott Dunlap Smith, July 6, 1918, folder 373d; Frank W. McAllister to W. F. Saunders, June 28, 1918, folder 291; all in MCDP, WHMC.

95. "A Case of Unusual Interest," *Tipton Times,* July 5, 1918. Charles Steinkraus does not appear in the 1910 or 1920 U.S. Census.

96. The Bureau of Labor Statistics averages wages for before World War I at about $30 per week. Robert VanGiezen and Albert E. Schwenk, "Compensation from before World War I through the Great Depression," United States Department of Labor, Bureau of Statistics, http://www.bls.gov/opub/cwc/cm20030124ar03p1.htm (accessed June 18, 2010).

97. W. F. Saunders to Henry Krug, March 4, 1918, folder 373a; F. B. Mumford to W. G. Dillion, July 5, 1918, folder 762; and F. B. Mumford to W. R. Little, October 14, 1918, folder 745; all in MCDP, WHMC.

98. W. F. Saunders to E. D. Smith, April 12, 1918, folder 164; E. D. Smith to State Council of Defense, June 20, 1918, folder 166; W. F. Saunders to Elliott Dunlap Smith, July 8, 1918, folder 167; W. F. Saunders to J. J. Pettijohn, September 10, 1918, folder 566; all in MCDP, WHMC.

99. "Deutsches Hospital ändert seinen Namen!" *Kansas City Presse,* March 15, 1918, newspaper clipping, pp. 127–28, in Sachs Papers, WHMC.

100. Minutes of the Meeting of the Missouri Council of Defense Held in Kansas City, September 11, 1918, folder 499, MCDP, WHMC.

101. Wüstenbecker, *Deutsch-Amerikaner,* 192.

102. William G. Ross, *Forging New Freedoms: Nativism, Education, and the Constitution, 1917–1927* (Lincoln: University of Nebraska Press, 1994), 40. Wüstenbecker, *Deutsch-Amerikaner,* 278. David Laskin, *The Long Way Home: An American Journey from Ellis Island to the Great War* (New York: Harper Collins, 2010), 173–75, 178–84.

103. Henry Krug Jr. to W. F. Saunders, May 7, 1918, folder 373b; "Hannibal, MO., Lutheran Church Drops German," newspaper clipping dated May 9, 1918, no publication name, folder 483; "St. John's Church Eliminates German," newspaper clipping attached to H. A. Scheidker to W. F. Saunders, May 14, 1918, folder 373b; H. O. Maxey to W. F. Saunders, June 22, 1918, folder 373c; all in MCDP, WHMC.

104. F. G. Walther to Henry Rohwer, May 16, 1918; F. J. Ernst to Henry Rohwer, May 16, 1918; Allen Greebuer to Henry Rohwer, June 3, 1918; and Chr. Bunger to

Wm. F. Saunders, July 31, 1918; all in folder 373d; A. W. Mueller to Henry Rohwer, June 3, 1918, folder 373c; all in MCDP, WHMC.

105. Ross, *Forging New Freedoms,* 41. Alan Niehaus Graebner, "The Acculturation of an Immigration Lutheran Church: The Lutheran Church–Missouri Synod, 1917–1929" (PhD diss. Columbia University, 1965), 57–61. Everette Meier and Herbert T. Mayer, "The Process of Americanization," in *Moving Frontiers: Readings in the History of the Lutheran Church–Missouri Synod,* ed. Carl S. Meyer (St. Louis: Concordia, 1964), 374.

106. Meier and Mayer, "Process of Americanization," 374–55; Graebner, "Acculturation of an Immigration Lutheran Church," 68–69, 78–79.

107. E. D. Smith to W. F. Saunders, May 14, 1918, folder 15; W. F. Saunders to Arthur H. Fleming, July 25, 1918, folder 30; W. F. Saunders to Reverend Richter, no date, folder 373b; all in MCDP, WHMC.

108. W. F. Saunders to Elliott Dunlap Smith, April 12, 1918, folder 164; W. F. Saunders, to J. Frank Morris, May 10, 1918, folder 373b; both in MCDP, WHMC.

109. "Subject: German Mass Meetings," April 17, 1918, folder 14; "Subject: Use of the German Language," April 30, 1918, folder 14; W. F. Saunders to Elliott Dunlap Smith, April 20, 1918, folder 164; all in MCDP, WHMC.

110. W. F. Saunders to Arthur H. Fleming, July 25, 1918, folder 30; W. F. Saunders to W. S. Dearmont, July 30, 1918, folder 212; W. F. Saunders to J. L. Bagby, July 31, 1918, folder 876; all in MCDP, WHMC.

111. W. S. Dearmont to W. F. Saunders, July 26, 1918, folder 212, MCDP, WHMC.

112. Claxton to Elliott Dunlap Smith, April 15, 1918, folder 483, MCDP, WHMC.

113. Uel W. Lamkin, *Sixty-Ninth Report on the Public Schools of the State of Missouri,* Appendix to the House and Senate Journals of the Fiftieth General Assembly, vol. 1, serial 7 (Jefferson City: Hugh Stephens, 1919), 7–8, 18.

114. W. F. Saunders to Uel W. Lamkin, December 13, 1917, folder 50; W. F. Saunders to Uel W. Lamkin, December 17, 1918, folder 50; Legal Brief, Uel W. Lamkin, State Superintendent of Public Schools, December 28, 1917, folder 278; Uel W. Lamkin to W. F. Saunders, July 10, 1918, folder 499; all in MCDP, WHMC.

115. Lamkin, *Sixty-Ninth Report,* 6.

116. "Resolution Adopted by the Board of Directors of the School District of St. Joseph, Missouri," May 13, 1918, folder 204, MCDP, WHMC. "German Is Now Barred from the High School," *Kirksville Daily Express,* March 22, 1918.

117. Carol Piper Heming, "*Schulhaus* to Schoolhouse: The German School at Hermann, Missouri, 1839–1955," *Missouri Historical Review* 82 (April 1988): 296.

118. W. Ed. Jameson, to W. F. Saunders, May 18, 1918, folder 373b, MCDP, WHMC.

119. W. F. Saunders to J. W. Moran, April 6, 1918, folder 756; W. F. Saunders to Victor Lichtenstein, April 3, 1918, folder 756; Elliott Dunlap Smith to W. F. Saunders, April 17, 1918, folder 373a; W. F. Saunders to Elliot Dunlap Smith, July 6, 1918, folder 373d; and minutes of the Meeting of the Missouri Council of Defense Held in Cape Girardeau, Missouri, July 12, 1918, folders 499 and 502; all in MCDP, WHMC.

120. Minutes of the Meeting of the Missouri Council of Defense Held in Cape Girardeau, July 12, 1918, folder 499 and 502; MCDP, WHMC. "Abolition of German

Language Is Indorsed [*sic*]," *St. Louis Globe-Democrat,* July 14, 1918; "Lamkin Bars Hun Language from Schools," *St. Louis Republic,* July 14, 1918.

121. Minutes, Memorial Methodist Church, St. Louis, folder 14, 60–64, Western Historical Manuscript Collection, University of Missouri–Columbia. J. L. Bagby to Wm. F. Saunders, July 30, 1918, folder 211; MCDP, WHMC.

122. W. F. Saunders to Franklin H. Kean, June 25, 1918, folder 1101, MCDP, WHMC.

123. *National Council of Defense Bulletin* 8, "Organization and Work of Councils of Defense."

124. Wüstenbecker, *Deutsch-Amerikaner,* 226.

125. Saunders to J. O. Barkley, August 2, 1918, folder 373d; F. B. Mumford to W. Hahn, October 7, 1918, folder 1104; both in MCDP, WHMC. "Minutes of the Meeting," July 12, 1918, folder 499 and 502, MCDP, WHMC. *Final Report,* 96.

126. W. F. Saunders to W. J. Jackson, July 23, 1918, folder 373d, MCDP, WHMC.

Chapter 4: From the "Most American City" to Seeing German Ghosts Everywhere

1. "The Alien Enemy Problem," *St. Louis Republic,* March 28, 1917; "Sister of A. A. Busch Linked with German Wireless Mystery," *St. Louis Republic,* April 8, 1917; "U.S. Discovers Spies Work in St. Louis Cafes," *St. Louis Republic,* June 30, 1917; "Plot to Invade U.S. Is Bared," *St. Louis Republic,* August 2, 1917; "German Propaganda Is Busy in St. Louis," *St. Louis Globe-Democrat,* October 10, 1918. Aliens who had lived in the United States for at least two years and declared their intent to become citizens had the right to vote in most midwestern, southern, and western states. Alexander Keyssar, *The Right to Vote: The Contested History of Democracy in the United States* (New York: Basic Books, 2000), 32–33, 104–5, 136–38.

2. "St. Louis German Leaders Support Wilson in Crisis," *St. Louis Republic,* April 4, 1917; Katja Wüstenbecker, *Deutsch-Amerikaner im Ersten Weltkrieg: US-Politik und Nationale Identitäten im Mittleren Westen* (Stuttgart, Germany: Franz Steiner Verlag, 2007), 134–36; "St. Louis to Pledge Its Loyalty to Flag at Big Rally Today," *St. Louis Republic,* April 5, 1917; "Greatest St. Louis Meeting Proclaims Loyalty to Nation," *St. Louis Republic,* April 6, 1917; "Loyalitätsdemonstration nimmt begeisterten Verlauf," *Westliche Post,* April 6, 1917; Floyd C. Shoemaker, "Missouri and the War: Sixth Article," *Missouri Historical Review* 13 (July 1919): 320.

3. "Mrs. Gellhorn Accused as Pro-German, Won't Head War Food Body," *St. Louis Republic,* April 20, 1917.

4. "Suffragist Aid Offered to Hoover," *St. Louis Republic,* June 4, 1917; "130 Women Register to Work at Men's Posts," *St. Louis Republic,* June 28, 1917; "Frauen Kriegshilfe," *Westliche Post,* July 10, 1917; "Women's 'Draft' Machine Ready," *St. Louis Republic,* July 9, 1917; "Women to Help in Registration," *St. Louis Republic,* July 13, 1917; "Frauen agitieren für morgige Registrierung," *Westliche Post,* July 27, 1917; "35,592 St. Louiserinnen unterzeichnen Hoover-Gelübde," *Westliche Post,* August 6, 1917. "Revised List of Woman's Committee Speakers: St. Louis," and "Signatures for Hoover Pledges, St. Louis City," both in folder 1105, Collection 2797, Missouri Council of

Defense Papers, Western Historical Manuscript Collection, Columbia, Missouri (hereinafter cited as MCDP, WHMC). *Fourteenth Census of the United States Taken in the Year 1920,* vol. 3: *Population* (Washington, DC: Government Printing Office, 1923), 40, 44–45. "Hoover Told of Women's Work Here," *St. Louis Republic,* June 19, 1917; "St. Louis Women Most Patriotic," *St. Louis Republic,* August 6, 1917; "St. Louis Leads in Conservation," *St. Louis Republic,* September 28, 1917. Olive B. Sawn to W. F. Saunders, November 15, 1917, folder 117, MCDP, WHMC.

5. "Die Amerikanisierungs Kampagne," *Westliche Post,* April 16, 1917; "4-Minute Speakers on Patriotic Topics to Be on Movie Menu," *St. Louis Republic,* May 17, 1917. William F. Saunders to M. L. Wilkinson, June 17, 1917, folder 1106, MCDP, WHMC.

6. "Secret Radio Found in Riesinger Home," *St. Louis Republic,* April 8, 1917; "Die Explosion in Eddystone," *Westliche Post,* April 12, 1917; "Deutscher Geheimdienst in Vereinigten Staaten," *Westliche Post,* May 15, 1917; "3 Arrests Halt Poison Plot," *St. Louis Republic,* July 19, 1917; "Spies' Plot to Throw Funston in Revolt Bared," *St. Louis Republic,* September 28, 1917.

7. "Six St. Louis Aliens Taken as they Flee," *St. Louis Republic,* May 12, 1917; "Man Held on Girl's Tip as Alien Enemy," *St. Louis Republic,* April 19, 1917; "35 feindliche Ausländer in St. Louis in Haft," *Westliche Post,* May 16, 1917; and "Spione in St. Louis?" *Westliche Post,* July 9, 1917. "U.S. Discovers Spies Work in St. Louis Cafes," *St. Louis Republic,* June 30, 1917; "Guard the Grain Elevators," *St. Louis Republic,* July 9, 1917.

8. "Sechs Deutsche stellen Gesuche, verbotene Zonen betreten zu dürfen," *Westliche Post,* April 24, 1917; "New Restricted Zones for Alien Enemies," *St. Louis Post-Dispatch,* May 2, 1917; "Wichtig für feindliche Ausländer," *Westliche Post,* May 21, 1917. "Festgenommende Deutsche nur interniert," *Westliche Post,* April 13, 1917; "Kontrolle für feindliche Ausländer streng," *Westliche Post,* April 14, 1917.

9. "Des Presidenten Wahnung an das Volk," *Westliche Post,* April 17, 1917. "Aliens Rush to Give Guns to Police," *St. Louis Republic,* April 14, 1917; "Six St. Louis Aliens Taken as They Flee," *St. Louis Republic,* May 12, 1917; "First Papers Won't Do as Zone Passes for Alien Enemies," *St. Louis Republic,* May 19, 1917; "Pässe für die verbotenen Zonen in St. Louis," *Westliche Post,* May 24, 1917; "Als Prodeutscher verhaftet," *Westliche Post,* October 8, 1917; "War in verbotener Zone," *Westliche Post,* October 19, 1917; "35 Aliens Arrested in Five Weeks in Barred Zone Here," *St. Louis Post-Dispatch,* January 4, 1918; "Feindlicher Ausländer interniert," *Westliche Post,* February 19, 1918; "Werden interniert," *Westliche Post,* March 14, 1918.

10. "Dealing with the Aliens," *St. Louis Republic,* July 23, 1917.

11. "Flags in 4 Page [Boulevard] Blocks Torn Down; Women Arm and Watch for U.S. Foes," *St. Louis Republic,* April 7, 1917.

12. "Women Refuse to Sing U.S. Anthem," *St. Louis Post-Dispatch,* April 2, 1917.

13. Her grandparents were German immigrants and her husband was a naturalized citizen. Military officials also recalled her brother, Dr. Walter E. Fischel, from service because they feared that he would pass secrets to Germany. W. F. Saunders to F. B. Mumford, June 18, 1917, folder 72, MCDP, WHMC. "Mrs. Gellhorn Accused as Pro-German, Won't Head War Food Body," *St. Louis Republic,* April 20, 1917.

14. "US Sailors Save German in Theater," *St. Louis Republic,* May 25, 1917.

15. Prince Henry was the brother of Kaiser Wilhelm. "St. Louisans Now Displeased with Kaiser's Medals," *St. Louis Post-Dispatch,* December 23, 1917.

16. "Pro-Germans Fatten Socialists' Coffers," *St. Louis Republic,* April 30, 1917; "St. Louis Socialist Leader Brandt Protests Seizure of Anti-Draft Letters," *St. Louis Post-Dispatch,* June 24, 1917. The election results were 132–92. Gary M. Fink, *Labor's Search for Political Order: The Political Behavior of the Missouri Labor Movement, 1890–1940* (Columbia: University of Missouri Press, 1973), 134. Wüstenbecker, *Deutsch-Amerikaner,* 134.

17. "There Are No German-Americans," *St. Louis Globe-Democrat,* June 18, 1918. "Gehorche dem Gesetz und verhalt Dich still!" and "Schweigen des Bürgers erste Pflicht!" *Westliche Post,* April 10, 1917. "Ein Wort an Nichtbürger," *Westliche Post,* April 14, 1917. "Gutes Zeugnis für Deutsche," *Westliche Post,* April 9, 1917. "Naturalisations Formulare völlig aufgebraucht," *Westliche Post,* May 10, 1917.

18. "Kriegsvorbereitungen in vollem Gange," *Westliche Post,* April 10, 1917; "Bleibt unter bewährter Führung," *Westliche Post,* August 23, 1917; "Von Reppert's Talk to Be Investigated," *St. Louis Post-Dispatch,* April 28, 1917; "In Bad Company," *St. Louis Republic,* April 30, 1917; "Von Reppert Asks German-Americans to Let Him Resign," *St. Louis Republic,* May 10, 1917; "Kersting Expelled by Alliance," *St. Louis Republic,* May 26, 1917; "Kersting Flays Kaiser; Urges Help to Allies," *St. Louis Republic,* September 13, 1917.

19. Edwin James Forsythe, "The St. Louis Central Trades and Labor Union, 1887–1945" (PhD diss., University of Missouri, 1956), 135.

20. The *Republic* estimated that since the 1910 census, which counted 125,000 foreign-born in the city, the number had increased to 150,000. "Melting Pot of St. Louis Is Boiling Over with Patriotism," *St. Louis Republic,* August 26, 1917.

21. "Wake Up, St. Louis!" *St. Louis Republic,* April 18, 1917; "Enlist St. Louis," *St. Louis Republic,* April 24, 1917; "The Women Slackers," *St. Louis Republic,* April 25, 1917; "Pull St. Louis Out of Slacker Class, Kiel Appeal Urges," *St. Louis Republic,* April 27, 1917.

22. "W.U. Ambulance Section," *St. Louis Republic,* April 20, 1917; "To Form New Regiment of Guard Here," *St. Louis Republic,* April 28, 1917; "Neues Übungslager ausgesucht," *Westliche Post,* May 15, 1917; "W.U. Hospital Einheit reisefertig," *Westliche Post,* May 16, 1917; "Fifth Filled in 14 Days, New Record," *St. Louis Republic,* May 22, 1917; "3755 Rekruten in 50 Tagen," *Westliche Post,* May 22, 1917; "A Lesson in Patriotism," *St. Louis Republic,* June 22, 1917; "80,000 Attend Loyalty Meet," *St. Louis Republic,* August 13, 1917.

23. "Crowds in Theaters Favor Conscription in *Republic's* Poll," *St. Louis Republic,* April 21, 1917. "Einigung in der Armeevorlage erzielt," *Westliche Post,* May 11, 1917; "Zum Aushebungstag," *Westliche Post,* May 28, 1917; "Tut eure Pflicht und registriert," *Westliche Post,* June 4, 1917.

24. "Registrierung übertrifft Erwartungen," *Westliche Post,* June 7, 1917; "111 Claimed Exemptions as Officials," *St. Louis Republic,* June 9, 1917.

25. Nationwide, 60 to 70 percent of registered men requested exemptions. Christopher C. Gibbs, *The Great Silent Majority: Missouri's Resistance to World War I* (Columbia: University of Missouri Press, 1988), 102. David M. Kennedy, *Over Here: The*

First World War and American Society (New York: Oxford University Press, 1980), 156–57. "5,430 St. Louis Draft Quota," *St. Louis Republic,* July 12, 1917; "Viele Ansprüche auf Exemption," *Westliche Post,* August 6, 1917; "Aushebungs Resultate," *Westliche Post,* August 13, 1917; "3,857 Certified from St. Louis," *St. Louis Republic,* August 30, 1917; "Pastor and Judge Fail to Win Exemption for 'Farmer' in 28th Ward," *St. Louis Republic,* September 9, 1917; "Marriage Bars No Scion of Rich," *St. Louis Republic,* August 15, 1917; "Many Rejected, Get New Test," *St. Louis Republic,* August 26, 1917.

26. "1,000 Slackers in St. Louis Are to Be Arrested," *St. Louis Republic,* August 23, 1917. Gibbs, *Great Silent Majority,* 106. United States v. Arno B. Pallme, docket no. 6463, Record Group 21, Records of the United States District Court, Eastern District of Missouri, Criminal Cases, 1864–1966, National Archives, Central Plains Region, Kansas City, Missouri (hereinafter cited as RG 21, District Court, Criminal Cases, NA, KC). Arno B. Pallme, Military Service Record World War I, Soldiers Database: War of 1812—World War I, Missouri Archives, Online Database, http://www.sos .mo.gov/archives/soldiers/ (hereinafter cited as Military Service Record, WWI, Missouri Archives) (accessed June 6, 2005).

27. United States v. Samuel E. Moore, docket no. 6782; and United States v. Charles Tarleton, docket no. 6761; both in RG 21, District Court, Criminal Cases, NA, KC. Wüstenbecker, *Deutsch-Amerikaner,* 362–77. Kennedy, *Over Here,* 163.

28. Home Guard Files, Archives of the Missouri Military History, Jefferson City, Missouri. Office of the Adjutant General of Missouri, *Report of the Adjutant General of Missouri,* 1917–1920 (Jefferson City: Hugh Stephens, 1920), 37–38. "Proclamation," folder 239, MCDP, WHMC. "Die Organisierung der Home Guards," *Westliche Post,* July 24, 1917; "St. Louis Home Guard Honored," *St. Louis Republic,* July 25, 1917; "2,019 In Home Guard Regiment," *St. Louis Republic,* August 2, 1917; "Für das Rote Kreuz," *Westliche Post,* December 17, 1917; "Enthüllung der Freiheitsstatue an der 12. und Olive Straße," *Westliche Post,* April 10, 1918. Colonel Philip B. Fouke to Governor F. D. Gardner, August 1, 1917, folder 1098, MCDP, WHMC.

29. R. C. Russel to Wm. F. Saunders, no date, Family Food Enrollment Report, folder 1100; Telegram, William F. Saunders to Don Farnsworth, November 11, 1917, folder 27, both in MCDP, WHMC. "Das Hoover Gelübde," *Westliche Post,* November 19, 1917.

30. "Das Rote Kreuz," *Westliche Post,* June 16, 1917; "$1,907,044 is Given to Red Cross," *St. Louis Republic,* June 26, 1917; "All St. Louis Theaters to Give Red Cross Benefit Tomorrow," *St. Louis Post-Dispatch,* December 6, 1917; "Für das Rote Kreuz," *Westliche Post,* December 17, 1917; "Rote Kreuz Quota überschritten," *Westliche Post,* May 23, 1918.

31. "Kauft Sparmarken!" *Westliche Post,* December 17, 1917; "Zur Sparmarken-Kampagne," *Westliche Post,* January 7, 1918; "Ein Kuß für eine $5 Sparmarke," *Westliche Post,* July 26, 1918.

32. "Buy Liberty Loan United States Government Bonds," *St. Louis Republic,* May 17, 1917; "Liberty Bonds Verkauf in allen größeren Läden," *Westliche Post,* May 22, 1917; "Patriots of St. Louis," *St. Louis Republic,* May 24, 1917. "1,000 Actors in St. Louis Bond Film," *St. Louis Republic,* June 3, 1917; "Enemy Alien Purchaser of $1,000 Liberty Bonds," *St. Louis Republic,* June 7, 1917; "1,354 Buy $1,739,000 Liberty Bonds

Here," *St. Louis Republic,* June 10, 1917; "St. Louis Is [$]17 Million over Quota," *St. Louis Republic,* June 16, 1917.

33. "St. Louis Cheers as Thousands March in Great Liberty Parade Opening Bond Selling Campaign," *St. Louis Republic,* October 3, 1917; "Die Freiheitsbond Kampagne," *Westliche Post,* October 16, 1917; "City to Launch Greatest Liberty Loan Drive To-Day," *St. Louis Republic,* October 24, 1917; "Ely & Walker Dry Goods Company," *St. Louis Republic,* October 26, 1917; "Bondverkäufe in St. Louis tragen $73,000,000," *Westliche Post,* November 1, 1917.

34. "Zur dritten Freiheitsanleihe," *Westliche Post,* March 4, 1918; "Ein Appell an den Patriotismus von Kirchen und Vereinen," *Westliche Post,* March 18, 1918; "Ein Ehrentag für St. Louis," *Westliche Post,* April 9, 1918; "M'Adoo Cancels Visit, Dissatisfied with Loan Drive," *St. Louis Post-Dispatch,* April 28, 1918; "Die letzte Woche der Freiheitsanleihe," *Westliche Post,* April 29, 1918; "Die Freiheits Anleihe," *Westliche Post,* May 2, 1918; "St. Louis überzeichnet Quota," *Westliche Post,* May 3, 1918. Gibbs, *Great Silent Majority,* 86–87; Forsythe, "Central Trades and Labor Union," 139.

35. "Thousands View Big Military Parade in Downtown Streets," *St. Louis Post-Dispatch,* September 28, 1918; "Get It Off Your Conscience," *St. Louis Globe-Democrat,* September 30, 1918; "Salesmen Keeping Tab on People Who Fail to Buy Bonds," *St. Louis Globe-Democrat,* October 11, 1918. "3 Deaths, 30 New Cases on East Side," *St. Louis Globe-Democrat,* October 11, 1918; "Churchless Sunday Will Be Observed Because of Plague," *St. Louis Globe-Democrat,* October 12, 1918. Shoemaker, "Missouri and the War," 346.

36. Shoemaker, "Missouri and the War," 354–55. "Poles Enlist in Allied Army at Loyalty Rally," *St. Louis Republic,* May 13, 1918; "Patriotic Italians Celebrating War Anniversary with a Picturesque Parade," *St. Louis Republic,* June 29, 1918; "Scenes of People of 20 Nations Marched to Show Loyalty," *St. Louis Republic,* July 5, 1918. "St. Louis die 'Amerikanischste' Stadt," *Westliche Post,* March 8, 1918.

37. "Gegen Verräter und Drückeberger," *Westliche Post,* December 15, 1917.

38. "Woman Directed Work of German Spy in U.S.," *St. Louis Post-Dispatch,* December 26, 1917; "The German Whisper," *St. Louis Post-Dispatch,* June 2, 1918; "How German Agents Sow Seeds of Treason in Guise of Pacifism among Americans," *St. Louis Post-Dispatch,* June 16, 1918; "Coffin Is Opened to Locate German Plot," *St. Louis Globe-Democrat,* July 10, 1918; "German Propaganda Is Busy in St. Louis," *St. Louis Globe-Democrat,* October 10, 1918. "The Loyalty Test," *St. Louis Republic,* May 17, 1918.

39. "Germans in U.S Must Register Week of Feb. 4," *St. Louis Post-Dispatch,* December 31, 1917; "Zur Registrierung feindlicher Ausländer," *Westliche Post,* January 1, 1918; "Registration im Gange," *Westliche Post,* February 5, 1918; "Polizei gibt keine Auskunft mehr über registrierte feindliche Ausländer," *Westliche Post,* February 8, 1918; "Frauen Registrierung," *Westliche Post,* June 1, 1918; "German Enemy Alien Women Must Register," *St. Louis Post-Dispatch,* June 12, 1918; "2684 Frauen registriert," *Westliche Post,* June 27, 1918. Nancy F. Cott, "Marriage and Women's Citizenship in the United States, 1830–1934," *American Historical Review* 103 (December 1998): 1461–64.

40. *Alien Property Custodian Report* (Washington, D.C.: Government Printing Office, 1919; reprint, New York: Arno Press, 1977), 7, 310, 318, 336, 353; "Holders

of Alien Property Ordered to Report By Dec. 5," *St. Louis Post-Dispatch,* December 2, 1917; "Vom Hüter feindlichen Eigentums übernommen," *Westliche Post,* May 28, 1918; "Survey Ordered of Alien Property Owners in State," *St. Louis Post-Dispatch,* June 2, 1918; "Recovered Auto Likely to Go to Alien Custodian," *St. Louis Post-Dispatch,* April 3, 1918.

41. "Questions Status of German Busch Heirs," *St. Louis Post-Dispatch,* December 13, 1917; "U.S. Seizes Vast Estate of Mrs. Busch," and "U.S. Now in Control of Three-Eighths of Vast Busch Fortune," *St. Louis Globe-Democrat,* June 18, 1918; "Busch Sunken Garden Will Become Hospital," *St. Louis Globe-Democrat,* June 19, 1918; "Status of Busch Estate Unchanged, U.S. Official Declares," *St. Louis Globe-Democrat,* June 22, 1918; "Mrs. Busch Being Held Temporarily for Questioning," *St. Louis Post-Dispatch,* June 18, 1918. *Alien Property Custodian Report,* 473.

42. Lily Anheuser came to America as an infant and became a citizen when her father, Eberhard Anheuser, was naturalized in 1848. The attorneys were Charles Nagel, former Missouri representative and Secretary of Commerce and Labor in the Taft administration, and Harry B. Hawes, former president of the St. Louis Police Board and a Democratic nominee for governor. "Busch Tells of Mother's Efforts to Reach Home," *St. Louis Post- Dispatch,* June 1, 1918; "Mrs. Lily Busch and Harry B. Hawes Reach Cuba Port," *St. Louis Globe-Democrat,* June 16, 1918; "Kaiser Seizes Busch Estate in Germany," *St. Louis Globe-Democrat,* June 17, 1918. Peter Hernon and Terry Ganey, *Under the Influence: The Unauthorized Story of the Anheuser-Busch Dynasty* (New York: Simon & Schuster, 1991), 25–26, 94–95.

43. "German Names," *St. Louis Republic,* April 10, 1917. "Make St. Louis 100 Percent American," *St. Louis Republic,* April 10, 1918.

44. "Make It Pershing Avenue," *St. Louis Post-Dispatch,* April 30, 1918; "Petition zu Gunsten der Abänderung des Namens der Berlin Ave. in Pershing Ave. eingereicht," *Westliche Post,* May 3, 1918; "Die Änderungen der deutschklingenden Straßennamen," *Westliche Post,* May 24, 1918. Wüstenbecker, *Deutsch-Amerikaner,* 342–50.

45. "Wollen Namen ändern," *Westliche Post,* March 6, 1918; "Will Namen ändern," *Westliche Post,* March 14, 1918; "German-American Bank ändert Namen," *Westliche Post,* March 26, 1918. Margaret LoPiccolo Sullivan, *Hyphenism in St. Louis, 1900–1921: A View from the Outside* (New York: Garland, 1990), 75, 78.

46. "Man Held on Disloyal Charge," *St. Louis Post-Dispatch,* April 12, 1918; "Wollte keine Freiheitsbond kaufen," *Westliche Post,* April 12, 1918; "Mary Institute Drops 2 Teachers as Result of War," *St. Louis Post-Dispatch,* April 19, 1918; "Keine Ausländer erwünscht," *Westliche Post,* July 18, 1918.

47. Audrey L. Olson, "St. Louis Germans, 1850–1920: The Nature of an Immigrant Community and Its Relation to the Assimilation Process" (PhD diss., University of Kansas, 1970), 204–5. "Kreisler Rezitations Konzert verboten," *Westliche Post,* November 29, 1917; "Church Here Is Wrecked by Vandals," *St. Louis Globe-Democrat,* June 24, 1918; "A Flagrant Case of Disloyalty," *St. Louis Globe-Democrat,* June 24, 1918; "Not American Hoodlums," *St. Louis Globe-Democrat,* June 25, 1918.

48. The U.S. military allowed for the first time in World War I the display of a service flag or service banner in the windows of homes with sons, brothers, or husbands serving on the front, and in businesses with employees deployed to France. The

number of blue stars on the flag represented how many family members or employees served their country in harm's way. "Kriegsvorbereitungen in vollem Gange," *Westliche Post*, April 10, 1917; "Ein glänzendes Beispiel," *Westliche Post*, October 15, 1917; "Die Freiheitsanleihe Kampagne," *Westliche Post*, April 10, 1918; "American Flags Will Replace 'German' Storks," *St. Louis Post-Dispatch*, April 17, 1918. James Neal Primm, *Lion of the Valley: St. Louis, Missouri, 1764–1989*, 3rd ed. (St. Louis: Missouri Historical Society Press, 1998), 435.

49. "Mrs. Busch Credited with Helping Trap N.Y. Mail Owner," *St. Louis-Globe Democrat*, July 10, 1918; "$900,000 Busch Money in German War Bonds," *St. Louis Globe-Democrat*, July 11, 1918; "German Bonds Bought by Busch before the War," *St. Louis Globe-Democrat*, July 12, 1918.

50. Emerson Hough, *The Web* (Chicago: Reilly & Lee, 1919; reprint, New York: Arno Press, 1969), 293–302. "Hinter 'Drückberger' her," *Westliche Post*, April 11, 1918; "Polizei gibt keine Auskunft mehr über registrierte feindliche Ausländer," *Westliche Post*, February 8, 1918; "1,500 Suspected Slackers Have Been Arrested," *St. Louis Republic*, September 5, 1918. "Woman Nurse Is Arrested Here," *St. Louis Post-Dispatch*, June 25, 1918. Boehmer was interned at Fort Oglethorpe in Georgia. Jörg Nagler, *Nationale Minoritäten im Krieg: Feindliche Ausländer und die amerikanische Heimatfront während des Ersten Weltkriegs* (Hamburg: Hamburger Edition HIS, 2000), 595.

51. "Gegen Deutsche Propaganda," *Westliche Post*, July 26, 1918. "Each Citizen May Act as Volunteer Sleuth to Aid U.S.," *St. Louis Republic*, May 13, 1918.

52. "Enemy Alien Has Been Voting Republican Ticket since 1893," *St. Louis Post-Dispatch*, January 4, 1918; "'Hank' Weeke Must Give Up His $3,000 Job," *St. Louis Globe-Democrat*, June 26, 1918; "Henry C. Weeke registriert als feindlicher Ausländer," *Westliche Post*, June 26, 1918.

53. Gibbs, *Great Silent Majority*, 144; Fink, *Labor's Search for Political Order*, 76.

54. Kennedy, *Over Here*, 267–68; Gibbs, *Great Silent Majority*, 141.

55. Fink, *Labor's Search for Political Order*, 70–71, 77; Rosemary Feurer, *Radical Unionism in the Midwest, 1900–1950* (Urbana: University of Illinois Press, 2006), 9–11.

56. Feurer, *Radical Unionism*, 12–14; Forsythe, "Central Trades and Labor Union," 165; Gibbs, *Great Silent Majority*, 145. "Massenversammlung der Striker," and "Aufruhr an der Olive Straße," both in *Westliche Post*, February 4, 1918.

57. Gibbs, *Great Silent Majority*, 146; "Ladenclerks beschließen Streik," *Westliche Post*, February 26, 1918; "Tabak-Arbeiter Striken," *Westliche Post*, March 1, 1918; "Streiks dehnen sich aus," *Westliche Post*, March 9, 1918.

58. Fink, *Labor's Search for Political Order*, 80; Forsythe, "Central Trades and Labor Union," 166.

59. Feurer, *Radical Unionism*, 14; Fink, *Labor's Search for Political Order*, 81.

60. "Two Employees in Factory Here Made to Kiss the Flag," *St. Louis Post-Dispatch*, April 15, 1918; "Loyalitäts-Bewegung auf Mount Olive ausgedehnt," *Westliche Post*, February 16, 1918.

61. Fink, *Labor's Search for Political Order*, 76; Gibbs, *Great Silent Majority*, 147.

62. Threat Statute, *U.S. Statutes at Large* 39 (1917): 909. United States v. Edward Pardick, docket no. 6537, RG 21, District Court, Criminal Cases, NA, KC. "Salesman

Pleads Guilty to Making Disloyal Remarks," *St. Louis Post-Dispatch,* December 11, 1917; "Wird wegen Bedrohung des Präsidenten zu einer Geldstrafe con $100 verurteilt," *Westliche Post,* December 12, 1917.

63. *Espionage Act of 1917,* Public Law 65–24, *U.S. Statutes at Large* 40 (1919): 217–231.

64. United States v. Thomas Carnell, docket no. 6465, RG 21, District Court, Criminal Cases, NA, KC. "Erhält zwei Jahre Zuchthaus," *Westliche Post,* November 1, 1917; "Trial in February for Men Charged with Disloyalty," *St. Louis Post-Dispatch,* December 20, 1917. Inmate 13632, Box 573, Record Group 129, Records of the Bureau of Prisons, United States Penitentiary Leavenworth, Kansas, Federal Inmate Files, 1895–1920, National Archives, Central Plains Region, Kansas City, Missouri (hereinafter cited as RG 129, Leavenworth, Federal Inmate Files, NA, KC).

65. United States v. August Scheuring, docket no. 6661, and United States v. William Schubert, docket no. 6639, both in RG 21, District Court, Criminal Cases, NA, KC.; Inmate 12554, Box 486, RG 129, Leavenworth, Federal Inmate Files, NA, KC.

66. According to the petition Schubert was a foreman at the Christy-Laclede Clay Works. United States v. William Schubert, docket no. 6639, RG 21, District Court, Criminal Cases, NA, KC. "Judge Dyer Gives 2 Men 2 Years on Disloyalty Charge," *St. Louis Post-Dispatch,* February 26, 1918.

67. United States v. Emil Albrecht, docket no. 6611, RG 21, District Court, Criminal Cases, NA, KC. Louis Busch received sixty days in jail for stating "to hell with the United States," and Louis DeKoeningk received three months and five days for exclaiming "to hell with the United States and all Americans." United States v. Louis Busch, docket no. 6562; United States v. Louis DeKoeningk, docket no. 6760; both in RG 21, District Court, Criminal Cases, NA, KC.

68. United States v. William F. Wehmeyer, docket no. 6594, 6871, 6916; and United States v. William Stephenson, docket no. 6658, both in RG 21, District Court, Criminal Cases, NA, KC.

69. Wüstenbecker, *Deutsch-Amerikaner,* 352–60.

70. "Judge Dyer Gives 2 Men 2 Years on Disloyalty Charge," *St. Louis Post-Dispatch,* February 26, 1918. United States v. William Schubert, docket no. 6639; RG 21, District Court, Criminal Cases, NA, KC. "South Side Baker Fined $100 for Threatening the President," *St. Louis Post-Dispatch,* December 26, 1917; "Judge Dyer Gives 2 Men 2 Years on Disloyalty Charge," *St. Louis Post-Dispatch,* February 26, 1918.

71. United States v. Frank Strnad, docket no. 6573, RG 21, District Court, Criminal Cases, NA, KC. "Unter dem Espionagen Gesetz schuldig befunden," *Westliche Post,* March 7, 1918.

72. United States v. Henry C. Koenig, docket no. 6654, 6818 and 6880, RG 21, District Court, Criminal Cases, NA, KC. "H. C. Koenig Says He Only Defended the German Race," *St. Louis Post-Dispatch,* December 27, 1917. United States v. Harry Turner, docket no. 6617 and 6619, RG 21, District Court, Criminal Cases, NA, KC.

73. United States v. George P. Dueser, docket no. 6659; United States v. Fred Hoffman, docket no. 6767; United States v. Anton F. Landgraf, docket no. 6671; United States v. Herman Lembach, docket no. 6657 and 6769; United States v. Christian Lohmann, docket no. 6595; United States v. Ben Meyerson et al, docket no. 6762; United States v. Mato Sikic, docket no. 6536; United States v. Wilhelm Stremmell,

docket no. 6608; and United States v. Eva Meyers, docket no. 6674; all in RG 21, District Court, Criminal Cases, NA, KC.

74. "Judge Wade May Try Disloyalty Cases Here," *St. Louis Globe-Democrat,* September 17, 1918. "Special Officials Named to Handle Disloyalty Cases," *St. Louis Post-Dispatch,* June 22, 1918.

75. Twenty-six of the Socialists were IWW members charged with singing antiwar labor songs. According to the 1910 Census, only one of them had German-born parents. United States v. Ben Meyerson, docket no. 6762; United States v. Fred Hoffman, docket no. 6767, both in RG 21, District Court, Criminal Cases, NA, KC. *Thirteenth Census of the United States, 1910,* Population Schedule, Missouri, St. Louis. Shirley J. Burton, "The Espionage and Sedition Acts of 1917 and 1918: Sectional Interpretations in the United States District Courts of Illinois," *Illinois Historical Journal* 87 (Spring 1994): 41–50.

76. "Wirt soll sich unloyaler Äußerungen bedient haben," *Westliche Post,* February 27, 1918. "Testify of Bribe Offer in Disloyalty Case," *St. Louis Post-Dispatch,* June 8, 1918. United States v. John Ungerer, docket no. 6756; United States v. August Weiler, docket no. 6805; both in RG 21, District Court, Criminal Cases, NA, KC.

77. "Special Officials Named to Handle Disloyalty Cases," *St. Louis Post-Dispatch,* June 22, 1918; "Spezialrichter Morris im Bundesgericht," *Westliche Post,* June 27, 1918; "Demurrer in Case of Dr. Weinsberg to Be Decided Today," *St. Louis Globe-Democrat,* June 28, 1918; "Dr. Weinsberg May Go to Trial Today," *St. Louis Globe-Democrat,* July 2, 1918; "Dr. C. H. Weinsberg Cleared of Espionage by Order of Judge," *St. Louis Globe-Democrat,* July 6, 1918; "Zur Auflösung des Nationalbundes," *Westliche Post,* April 13, 1918; Wüstenbecker, *Deutsch-Amerikaner,* 191, 214–15; David W. Detjen, *The Germans in Missouri, 1900–1918: Prohibition, Neutrality, and Assimilation* (Columbia: University of Missouri Press, 1985), 144, 148–49, 155–56, 174, 177.

78. United States v. Wilhelm Stremmell, docket no. 6608; and United States v. Fritz Schmook, docket no. 6653, both in RG 21, District Court, Criminal Cases, NA, KC. Nagler, *Nationale Minoritäten,* 540.

79. United States v. August Weist, docket no. 6911, RG 21, District Court, Criminal Cases, NA, KC. "Federal Grand Jury Indicts 17 Persons on Espionage Charge," *St. Louis Globe-Democrat,* October 12, 1918.

80. United States v. Henry Dickhoener, docket no. 6874, RG 21, District Court, Criminal Cases, NA, KC.

81. "Ständige Ueberwachung von Deutschen," *Westliche Post,* November 20, 1917; "Achtung Preußen," *Westliche Post,* January 26, 1918; "Bayerischer Männerchor," *Westliche Post,* January 30, 1918; "Maskenball Olympic Turnverein," *Westliche Post,* February 1, 1918; "Preismaskenball der Schiller Turnerfrauen," *Westliche Post,* November 16, 1917; "Karneval des Deutschen Damenchors," *Westliche Post,* November 29, 1917; "Maskenball des Pfälzer Frauenvereins," *Westliche Post,* January 1, 1918; "Preis-Maskenball des St. Louis Bayernvereins in der St. Louis Turnhalle," *Westliche Post,* January 14, 1918.

82. "Sportfest der Municipal Athletic Association," *Westliche Post,* February 20, 1918. "Großes Sylvestertreiben in Vereinen und Klubs," *Westliche Post,* January 1, 1918, 5; "Zum Besten des Roten Kreuzes," *Westliche Post,* April 17, 1918; "Liederkranz Klub

bewirtet Soldaten," *Westliche Post,* April 22, 1918; "German-born Citizen Loyal to U.S. Deserves Respect, Says Selph," *St. Louis Republic,* April 25, 1918; "Liederkranz-Club bewirtet Mitglieder des Fliegercorps," *Westliche Post,* April 25, 1918.

83. "34. Große Bayernfest in Linn's Park heute und morgen," *Westliche Post,* September 1, 1917; "Ein echt deutsches Volksfest," *Westliche Post,* September 3, 1917; "29. Stiftungsfest des Arbeiter Gesangvereins 'Vorwärts,'" *Westliche Post,* October 8, 1917; "Jubiläums Feier der Methodisten," *Westliche Post,* September 7, 1917. "Deutsche Sprache wird beibehalten," *Westliche Post,* March 20, 1918; "Neue deutsche Bücher in der Zentralbibliothek," *Westliche Post,* May 21, 1918.

84. "Deutsche Zeitungen unter der Lupe," *Westliche Post,* September 6, 1917; "National Move to Suppress German Language Press," *St. Louis Post-Dispatch,* April 27, 1918; "Geheimsitzung im Senat," *Westliche Post,* May 8, 1917; "Eine dritte Freiheitsanleihe," *Westliche Post,* January 5, 1918.

85. "Feeling against German Language Papers Regretted," *St. Louis Globe-Democrat,* April 28, 1918. "Fremdsprachige Zeitungen im Kriege," *Westliche Post,* October 6, 1917; "Unseren Lesern zur Kenntnisnahme," *Westliche Post,* October 8, 1917; "Volksform der Staatsuniversität," *Westliche Post,* January 7, 1918; "American Foreign Language Publications," *Westliche Post,* April 8, 1918; "Wo die Westliche Post steht," *Westliche Post,* April 10, 1918; "Ein offener Brief an die Gegner der deutschsprachigen Presse," *Mississippi Blätter,* April 28, 1918; "Westliche Post in der Ehrenliste," *Westliche Post,* July 9, 1918.

86. "Movement Is Started in St. Louis to Suppress Hun-Language Press," *St. Louis Republic,* April 27, 1918; "Move to Keep Advertising from German Language Press," *St. Louis Post-Dispatch,* June 4, 1918; "Lies seine Wut an deutschsprachiger Zeitung aus," *Westliche Post,* March 8, 1918.

87. "German Language Printing," *St. Louis Post-Dispatch,* April 8, 1918; "Majority of Aldermen Pledge to the Republic to Put an End to the German Printing Waste," *St. Louis Republic,* April 10, 1918; "Protest by Westliche Post on German Language Bill," *St. Louis Post-Dispatch,* April 17, 1918. "Mayor Thinks 'Republic' Classed Him as Pro-German," *St. Louis Post-Dispatch,* April 25, 1918; "Kiel's Henchmen Stifle Ordinance Designed to Terminate German Graft," *St. Louis Republic,* April 26, 1918; "Bill for City Journal Passed by Aldermen," *St. Louis Post-Dispatch,* April 29, 1918.

88. "Verhör über Protest gegen deutsche Samstagschulen," *Westliche Post,* November 28, 1917; "Schulratskomitee entscheidet gegen Samstagschulen," *Westliche Post,* December 6, 1917; "Deutsche Samstagschulen heimatlos," *Westliche Post,* December 12, 1917; "Deutsche Samstagschulen geschlossen," *Westliche Post,* December 14, 1917.

89. "Patriotische Beschlusse der Handelskammer," *Westliche Post,* April 6, 1918; "Zur Abschaffung des deutschen Unterrichts," *Westliche Post,* April 29, 1918.

90. "Turnbezirk Proceedings to Be Conducted in English," *St. Louis Post-Dispatch,* April 26, 1918; "Turner beteuern aufs neue Loyalität," *Westliche Post,* April 29, 1918; "Aus Turnerkreisen," *Westliche Post,* May 2, 1918; "Deutscher Kellnerverein löst sich auf," *Westliche Post,* July 30, 1918.

91. "Der Evanglischen Synode zum Gruß," *Westliche Post,* May 4, 1917.

92. "U.S. Eyes Local German Paper," *St. Louis Republic,* July 19, 1917. John Philip Gleason, "The Central-Verein, 1900–1917: A Chapter in the History of the

German-American Catholics" (PhD diss., University of Notre Dame, 1960), 14, 230–31; William B. Faherty, *The St. Louis German Catholics* (St. Louis: Reedy Press, 2004), 72.

93. "Use of German Here in Lutheran Churches Ended: Tongue Used in 17 Catholic Churches," *St. Louis Post-Dispatch,* April 17, 1918. William B. Faherty, *Dream by the River: Two Centuries of Saint Louis Catholicism, 1766–1967* (St. Louis: Piraeus, 1973), 156; John Rothensteiner, *History of the Archdiocese of St. Louis: In Its Various Stages of Development from AD 1673 to AD 1928* (St. Louis: Blackwell Wielandy, 1928), 2:713.

94. "Patriotische Schulfeier," *Westliche Post,* April 19, 1918; "High Lutherans Disloyal to U.S., Official Charge," *St. Louis Republic,* July 12, 1917; "Tells Loyalty of Lutherans," *St. Louis Republic,* July 13, 1917. "Lutherische Festgottesdienste," "Aus Lutherischen Kreisen," both in *Westliche Post,* February 23, 1918; "Attacks Kaiser's Theology," *St. Louis Post-Dispatch,* April 19, 1918. "60 jähriges Jubiläum für Evangelische Freiheits Gemeinde," *Westliche Post,* October 17, 1917; "Drei Jubelfestgottesdienste," *Westliche Post,* November 2, 1917.

95. "Lutheran Churches Here Drop German in Schools and Plan English Services," *St. Louis Republic,* April 17, 1918; "Deutsche Sprache abgeschafft," *Westliche Post,* April 17, 1918; "Seventeen Catholic Churches May Drop German Language," *St. Louis Republic,* April 18, 1918; "Abolition of German Language Is Indorsed," *St. Louis Globe-Democrat,* July 14, 1918.

96. Walter Ehrlich, *Zion in the Valley: The Jewish Community of St. Louis* (Columbia: University of Missouri, 2002), 2:244–48; Christopher M. Sterba, *Good Americans: Italian and Jewish Immigrants during the First World War* (New York: Oxford University Press, 2003), 53–55, 153–74.

97. Luebke, *Bonds of Loyalty,* 19.

Chapter 5: Resisting Interference in Daily Life

1. William Saunders to Frederick Mumford, February 26, 1918, folder 94, C 2797, Missouri Council of Defense Papers, Western Historical Manuscript Collection, University of Missouri–Columbia (hereinafter cited as MCDP, WHMC)

2. Mrs. E. F. Rippstein to W. F. Saunders, November 28, 1917, folder 879; Mrs. Rose Rippstein to Mr. Saunders, April 7, 1918, folder 879; Mrs. E. F. Rippstein to William Saunders, May 27, 1918, folder 373b, all in MCDP, WHMC. Rose's father, George William Klenk, was the son of Mathias and Auguste Klenk, natives of Württemberg and Prussia, respectively. "Biographical Appendix," *History of Franklin, Jefferson, Washington, Crawford, and Gasconade Counties, Missouri* (Chicago: Goodspeed, 1888; reprint, Cape Girardeau, MO: Ramfre Press, 1958), 1094. Fourteenth Census of the United States, 1920, Population Schedule, Missouri, Gasconade County, Roark Township, City of Hermann, 2nd Ward, sheet 264B.

3. "Authentic War News," *Advertiser-Courier,* September 9, 1914; and "Nachrichten vom Kriegsschauplatze: Der Riesen-Dampfer Lusitania Versenkt," *Hermanner Volksblatt,* May 14, 1915.

4. "Hast du's gewußt?" *Hermanner Volksblatt,* January 21, 1916. "Amerikas Neutralität," *Hermanner Volksblatt,* September 17, 1915; "Echte Neutralität," *Hermanner Volksblatt,* February 11, 1916; "American Honor," *Advertiser-Courier,* July 19, 1916; "Es

kommt ihm doch bald zu dick," *Hermanner Volksblatt,* September 8, 1916; "Embargo und die Munitionsarbeiter," *Hermanner Volksblatt,* March 10, 1916; "Mit Herz und Hand für unser Land," *Hermanner Volksblatt,* April 7, 1916; "Habitually Wrong," *Advertiser-Courier,* July 19, 1916. "Weltkriegs-Pflichten," *Hermanner Volksblatt,* November 5, 1915. "Kriegsbild aus Deutschland," *Hermanner Volksblatt,* August 6, 1915; "Kriegsbrief aus Deutschland," *Hermanner Volksblatt,* October 1, 1915; "Kriegsbrief aus Deutschland," *Hermanner Volksblatt,* April 21, 1916; "Driven to Atrocities, German Commander Tells Correspondent," *Advertiser-Courier,* September 23, 1914.

5. "A Letter from Germany," *Bland Courier,* April 16, 1915; and "German Soldier in the European War," *Bland Courier,* June 25, 1915; "Among the Jingoes," *Bland Courier,* December 24, 1915.

6. "Vom Schauplatzes des europäischen Völkerkrieges," *Gasconade County Republican,* February 2, 1917; "Allies Repulse German Attack on Line," *Gasconade County Republican,* October 2, 1914; "Our Scrap Basket," *Gasconade County Republican,* November 6, 1914.

7. "Ocean Liner Lusitania Sunk," *Gasconade County Republican,* May 14, 1915; "Stone Declares Passengers Knew of Risk of Lusitania," *Advertiser-Courier,* May 12, 1915.

8. "German Day Celebration at Morrison," *Advertiser-Courier,* September 30, 1914; "State Organization of German-American Alliance Will Meet at Hermann Sep. 3–5," *Advertiser-Courier,* June 14, 1916; "Willkommen in Hermann," *Hermanner Volksblatt,* September 22, 1916; "Über zehntausend Menschen anwesend," *Hermanner Volksblatt,* September 29, 1916.

9. "Gasconade County Republicans Endorse Hon. Chas. E Hughes for President," *Bland Courier,* March 10, 1916; "Hughes über Deutsch-Amerikaner," *Hermanner Volksblatt,* October 27, 1916; "Speaking Dates," *Gasconade County Republican,* September 22, 1916. "Reasons Why Hughes Should Be Elected," and "Reasons Why Wilson Should Be Defeated," both in *Advertiser-Courier,* November 1, 1916. "Gewaltige Republikanische Massenversammlung in Bay," *Hermanner Volksblatt,* November 3, 1916. "Achtung! Deutsche Stammesgenossen," *Hermanner Volksblatt,* February 11, 1916, 1.

10. "German-American Alliance Enters Politics," *Bland Courier,* July 28, 1916.

11. Results for Reed were 509 to 2,521 and for Gardner 503 to 2,520. *Official Manual of the State of Missouri for the Years 1917–1918* (Jefferson City: Hugh Stephens, 1917), 438–39. "Official Vote for Gasconade County, Election Nov. 7, 1916," *Gasconade County Republican,* November 17, 1916.

12. Editorial, *Hermanner Volksblatt,* February 23, 1917; editorial, *Advertiser-Courier,* February 28, 1917. Editorial, *Advertiser-Courier,* March 7, 1917; editorial, *Advertiser-Courier,* March 14, 1917. Editorial, *Advertiser-Courier,* February 7, 1917; editorial, *Advertiser-Courier,* February 14, 1917.

13. "Congress Is Asked to Declare War," *Gasconade County Republican,* April 6, 1917; "America Formally Enters the War with Germany," *Gasconade County Republican,* April 13, 1917; and "Kriegsnachrichten," *Hermanner Volksblatt,* April 13, 1917.

14. "Local News Notes," *Advertiser-Courier,* May 30, 1917. "How Stars and Stripes Should Be Displayed," *Advertiser-Courier,* April 18, 1917; "American Flag Most

Beautiful of Banners," *Advertiser-Courier,* April 25, 1917; "Rot, Weiß und Blau," *Hermanner Volksblatt,* July 6, 1917; "Der Amerikanische Fahneneid," *Hermanner Volksblatt,* July 20, 1917. "Wie England sich die Vorzüge zu eigen machte," *Hermanner Volksblatt,* August 17, 1917; "Deutschland kann nicht durch Hunger bezwungen werden," *Hermanner Volksblatt,* June 22, 1917.

15. "Sag' nichts den Leuten," *Hermanner Volksblatt,* August 17, 1917.

16. "One Hundred Percent American," and "Our Colyum," *Gasconade County Republican,* April 27, 1917.

17. "Slackers," *Gasconade County Republican,* May 4, 1917; "Canned," *Gasconade County Republican,* May 11, 1917; "Doing His Bit," *Gasconade County Republican,* May 25, 1917; "Patriotism at the Table," *Gasconade County Republican,* June 15, 1917. "Help Defense Councils," *Gasconade County Republican,* July 6, 1917; "Patriotic Day," *Gasconade County Republican,* July 20, 1917; "Why Food Control Is Necessary," *Gasconade County Republican,* October 12, 1917; "Food Conservation," *Gasconade County Republican,* November 2, 1917. "Pledge of 'Disloyal,'" *Gasconade County Republican,* September 14, 1917; "Rooting Out the Spy System Here," *Gasconade County Republican,* October 19, 1917; "Happenings of the Week in Missouri," *Gasconade County Republican,* January 4, 1918.

18. "Our Colyum," *Gasconade County Republican,* May 25, 1917; "Our Colyum," *Gasconade County Republican,* June 15, 1917; "Our Colyum," *Gasconade County Republican,* November 2, 1917; "Our Colyum," *Gasconade County Republican,* February 8, 1918.

19. "Hark, Ye Germans!" *Gasconade County Republican,* October 12, 1917. "Our Colyum," *Gasconade County Republican,* June 29, 1917. "Our Colyum," *Gasconade County Republican,* March 22, 1918.

20. "Thrift Stamps to Show Patriotism," *Advertiser-Courier,* January 16, 1918. "Wahrer Patriotismus," *Hermanner Volksblatt,* April 5, 1918; "Our Colyum," *Gasconade County Republican,* April 12, 1918.

21. "Red Cross Seal für 1917," and "Your Country Calls," *Hermanner Volksblatt,* December 7, 1917. "Zehn Gründe zur Unterzeichnung des 'Food Pledge,' *Hermanner Volksblatt,* November 9, 1917; "Family Food Enrollment Campaign: Ten Reasons for Signing the Pledge List," *Gasconade County Republican,* November 2, 1917.

22. F. G. Gaebler to Wm. F. Saunders, May 12, 1918, folder 880; F. B. Mumford to W. F. Saunders, July 2, 1917, folders 73 and 150; William Saunders to Cleon Baxter, September 29, 1917; and Cleon Baxter to W. F. Saunders, October 1, 1917; both in folder 877, all in MCDP, WHMC.

23. "Circuit Court Proceedings," *Advertiser-Courier,* May 16, 1917; "Seit Kriegsbeginn haben fünf der Einwohner unseres counties ihre ersten Papiere ausgenommen," *Hermanner Volksblatt,* February 1, 1918; "Seek Citizenship by Petition for Naturalization," *Advertiser-Courier,* February 20, 1918; "Gasconade County Circuit Court," *Gasconade County Republican,* May 3, 1918.

24. "Registration of German Alien Enemies," *Gasconade County Republican,* January 25, 1918; "Nicht naturalisierte Deutsche müssen registrieren," *Hermanner Volksblatt,* February 1, 1918; "Registration feindlicher Ausländer," *Hermanner Volksblatt,* February 15, 1918; and "The Complete Number of Registrants," *Advertiser-Courier,* February 20, 1918. "Im Ausland geborene Frauen müssen registrieren," *Hermanner*

Volksblatt, May 31, 1918; "Alien Women Registration Same as That of Alien Men," *Gasconade County Republican,* May 31, 1918; "Registration of Female Alien Enemies Slack on First Two Days," *Advertiser-Courier,* June 19, 1918; "18 weibliche Ausländerinnen registrierten in Hermann," *Hermanner Volksblatt,* July 5, 1918.

25. "Our Colyum," *Gasconade County Republican,* April 26, 1918.

26. WWI Soldiers' Service Record, Gasconade County (1919), located at Gasconade County Historical Society, Archives, and Record Center, Hermann, Missouri. "County News in General," *Advertiser-Courier,* May 23, 1917. Wm. F. Saunders to F. Gaebler, August 26, 1918, folder 882, MCDP, WHMC. "Potsdam News," *Advertiser-Courier,* July 24, 1918.

27. "Not One 'Slacker' in County," *Advertiser-Courier,* June 20, 1917. "Claims for Exemption—Rules and Regulations in Regard to Claims for Discharge by Local Board," *Advertiser-Courier,* July 25, 1917. "Men Exempted by Local Board," *Advertiser-Courier,* August 15, 1917; "Exemptions Granted and Refused," *Gasconade County Republican,* August 24, 1917. Christopher C. Gibbs, *The Great Silent Majority: Missouri's Resistance to World War I* (Columbia: University of Missouri Press, 1988), 103.

28. "Großer Prozentsatz der für den Militärdienst gezogenen kommen um Dienstbefreiung ein," *Hermanner Volksblatt,* August 10, 1917; "Men Exempted by Local Board," *Advertiser-Courier,* August 15, 1917; "Exemptions Granted and Refused," *Gasconade County Republican,* August 24, 1917; "Local Board Exempts 31 of 90 Examined," *Gasconade County Republican,* October 12, 1917. "Protest Against Action of District Board," *Advertiser-Courier,* August 29, 1917. "New Regulations Revoke Previous Discharges and Exemptions," *Advertiser-Courier,* November 28, 1917; "District-Board Classifies," *Advertiser-Courier,* January 30, 1918. David M. Kennedy, *Over Here: The First World War and American Society* (New York: Oxford University Press, 1980), 166.

29. WWI Soldiers' Service Record, Gasconade County. "Forty Young Men Leave for Fort Riley," *Gasconade County Republican,* September 21, 1917; "Owensville Band Help to Entertain Drafted Men at Hermann," *Gasconade County Republican,* October 12, 1917.

30. W. F. Saunders to C. C. Carson, March 1, 1918, folder 330, MCDP, WHMC.

31. "Women of Missouri Asked to Register on July 28," *Advertiser-Courier,* July 18, 1917; "County News in General," *Advertiser-Courier,* August 8, 1917; "Women Register to Help Win the War," *Gasconade County Republican,* August 10, 1917. List of Women Pledges, folder 392, MCDP, WHMC.

32. Linda Schelbitzki Pickle, *Contented among Strangers: Rural German-Speaking Women and Their Families in the Nineteenth-Century Midwest* (Urbana: University of Illinois Press, 1996), 83–85. "Local News Notes," *Advertiser-Courier,* April 4, 1917.

33. "Canning Demonstrations Held at Henneke's Hall," *Gasconade County Republican,* July 13, 1917; "Committee on Food Conservation Visits Here," *Advertiser-Courier,* August 22, 1917. Sarah Pettit to Wm. F. Saunders, August 17, 1917, folder 377; Woman's Committee, Missouri Division, folder 701; Rose Rippstein to William Saunders, July 16, 1918, folder 881; all in MCDP, WHMC. Rose Rippstein, "Churches to Set Aside October 28 for Food Conservation Service," *Gasconade County Republican,* October 26, 1917.

34. "Herr Hoover und 'Mosch,'" *Hermanner Volksblatt,* September 28, 1917, 3. Numbers of Signed Pledges, no date, folder 877, MCDP, WHMC. Floyd C.

Shoemaker, "Missouri and the War: Second Article," *Missouri Historical Review* 12 (January 1918): 91. "More Stress on Food Conservation," *Advertiser-Courier,* September 12, 1917; "Mrs. Rippstein Appeals to the Mothers of Gasconade County to Conserve Food," *Gasconade County Republican,* December 14, 1917.

35. "Das Rote Kreuz," *Hermanner Volksblatt,* June 15, 1917; "Organizing Local Red Cross Chapter," *Advertiser-Courier,* July 25, 1917; "Hermann Red Cross Perfects Organization," *Advertiser-Courier,* August 22, 1917. "Red Cross Chapter Organized in Owensville," *Gasconade County Republican,* November 2, 1917. "What the Red Cross Is Doing in Gasconade County," *Advertiser-Courier,* January 30, 1918; "What the Red Cross Is Doing in Gasconade County," *Advertiser-Courier,* February 6, 1918.

36. "St. George's Kirche organisiert Rot Kreuz Hilfsverein," *Hermanner Volksblatt,* February 22, 1918; "Hermann Girls Organize Sammy Clubs," *Advertiser-Courier,* February 6, 1918; "Hilfsvereine werden im ganzen County organisiert," *Hermanner Volksblatt,* April 12, 1918; "Local Branch of the WCTU Sends Comfort Bags to the Soldiers," *Advertiser-Courier,* August 1, 1917; "Box Supper Nets Red Cross $93.60," *Advertiser-Courier,* February 27, 1918; "Words of Commendation," *Advertiser-Courier,* May 15, 1918; "Locals and Personal," *Gasconade County Republican,* May 24, 1918. "Round Two," and "Our Colyum," *Gasconade County Republican,* May 24, 1918; "Morrison überzeichnet sein Quotum für das Rote Kreuz," *Hermanner Volksblatt,* June 14, 1918; "Gasconade County fehlen nur noch $758 an der Rote Kreuz Quota," *Hermanner Volksblatt,* August 2, 1918.

37. "Liberty Loan of 1917," *Advertiser-Courier,* May 23, 1917; and "The Liberty Loan," *Advertiser-Courier,* June 20, 1917. "Are You a Patriot? Buy a Bond," *Gasconade County Republican,* October 19, 1917. *Fourteenth Census of the United States Taken in the Year 1920,* vol. 1: *Population* (Washington, DC: Government Printing Office, 1921), 492. Gibbs, *Great Silent Majority,* 90.

38. "Liberty Loan Workers," *Gasconade County Republican,* March 29, 1918; "Patriotische Versammlung," *Hermanner Volksblatt,* March 29, 1918; "Proclamation," *Advertiser-Courier,* March 27, 1918; "Die Dritte Freiheitsanleihe," *Hermanner Volksblatt,* April 5, 1918; "Our Colyum," *Gasconade County Republican,* April 5, 1918; "Liberty Loan Button," and "Buyer of Liberty Bonds Displays True Patriotism," *Advertiser-Courier,* April 10, 1918; "Eine Patriotische Mammuth Demonstration," *Hermanner Volksblatt,* April 19, 1918; "Enthusiastic Liberty Bond Meeting," *Gasconade County Republican,* April 19, 1918. "Over the Top," *Gasconade County Republican,* May 10, 1918; "Gasconade County Wins Sixteen Honor Flags," *Gasconade County Republican,* May 31, 1918. Gibbs, *Great Silent Majority,* 90.

39. "A Child's Savings May Shorten the War," *Advertiser-Courier,* April 24, 1918. "Don't Overlook This Chance to Show your Loyalty," *Gasconade County Republican,* December 7, 1917; "Eine unerfüllte Pflicht," *Hermanner Volksblatt,* May 17, 1918. "Miss Mathilda Dallmeyer a Favorite at Big Loyalty Meeting," *Advertiser-Courier,* April 10, 1918. *Twelfth Census of the United States, 1900,* Population Schedule, Missouri, Cole County, Jefferson City, sheet 30B. "W.S.S. Meetings Well Attended throughout County," *Advertiser-Courier,* July 3, 1918; "28. Juni in Gasconade County," *Hermanner Volksfreund,* July 12, 1918; "Big Attendance at W.S.S. Meeting," *Advertiser-Courier,* August 21, 1918; "Kriegssparmarken Versammlung in Hermann," *Hermanner Volksblatt,*

August 23, 1918; "Zwölf Distrikte haben ihre Quotas erreicht," *Hermanner Volksblatt,* August 30, 1918; "Urgent Appeal to Buy More War Savings Stamps," *Gasconade County Republican,* September 6, 1918.

40. "The 'Less' Days for Food," *Gasconade County Republican,* February 22, 1918; "Wie wir helfen können," *Hermanner Volksblatt,* March 22, 1918; "New Wheat Conservation Rules of the United States Food Administrator," *Gasconade County Republican,* March 29, 1918; "Save a Loaf a Week," *Advertiser-Courier,* May 8, 1918; "Die Red Cross Sammlung," *Hermanner Volksblatt,* May 31, 1918; "National War Savings Day Must Be Made Big Success," *Advertiser-Courier,* June 12, 1918.

41. W. F. Saunders to Chairman Mumford, February 26, 1918, folder 94; F. G. Gaebler to Wm. F. Saunders, May 12, 1918, folder 880; both in MCDP, WHMC. See also Arthur B. Cozzens, "Conservation in German Settlements of the Missouri Ozarks," *Geographical Review* 33 (April 1943): 286–98.

42. Mrs. Walter McNab Miller to R. W. Wilbur, August 16, 1917, folder 409; Mrs. Rippstein to Mrs. McNab Miller, September 10, 1917, folder 877; Clarence Baxter to W. F. Saunders, November 9, 1917, folder 878; all in MCDP, WHMC.

43. Mrs. E. F. Rippstein to W. F. Saunders, November 28, 1917, folder 879; Mrs. Rose Rippstein to Mr. Saunders, April 7, 1918, folder 879; both in MCDP, WHMC.

44. "E. A. Meyer Elected Chairman of County Council of Defense," *Advertiser-Courier,* October 31, 1917.

45. "What the Red Cross Is Doing in Gasconade County," *Advertiser-Courier,* January 30, 1918; "What the Red Cross Is Doing in Gasconade County," *Advertiser-Courier,* February 6, 1918.

46. "German Counties All Loyal, Says Mr. Glenn," *Advertiser-Courier,* May 15, 1918.

47. "Soll Drohung Gegen den Präsidenten Ausgesprochen Haben," *Hermanner Volksblatt,* June 1, 1917; "Man Charged With Saying Wilson Should Be Shot," *Gasconade County Republican,* June 1, 1917; "Heidbreder um $100 Bestraft," *Hermanner Volksblatt,* June 29, 1917. United States v. August Heidbreder, docket no. 6418, Record Group 21, Records of the United States District Court, Eastern District of Missouri, Criminal Cases, 1864–1966, National Archives, Central Plains Region, Kansas City, Missouri (hereinafter cited as RG 21, District Court, Criminal Cases, NA, KC).

48. "Man Charged with Saying Wilson Should Be Shot," *Gasconade County Republican,* June 1, 1917.

49. United States v. E. A. Ahrens, docket no. 6675, RG 21, District Court, Criminal Cases, NA, KC. Fourteenth Census of the United States, 1920, Population Schedule, Iowa, Ringgold County, Washington Township, Diagonal Town, sheet 266 B.

50. "Happenings of the Week in Missouri," *Gasconade County Republican,* January 4, 1918; January 11, 1918; and February 1, 1918. William F. Saunders to Lee Walker, April 10, 1918, folder 287; Clarence G. Baxter to W. F. Saunders, April 15, 1918, folder 880; W. F. Saunders to Dock Remley, April 19, 1918, folder 288; all in MCDP, WHMC. Fourteenth Census of the United States, 1920, Population Schedule, Missouri, Gasconade County, Roark Township, City of Hermann, 2nd Ward, sheet 268B; and Brush Creek Township, sheet 4B.

51. E. A. Meyer to W. F. Saunders, January 2, 1918, folder 284; W. F. Saunders to E. A. Meyer, January 24, 1918, folder 284; both in MCDP, WHMC.

52. Mrs. E. F. Rippstein to W. F. Saunders, November 28, 1917, folder 879, MCDP, WHMC.

53. Rose Rippstein to Mrs. McNab Miller, September 10, 1917, folder 877; Mrs. E. F. Rippstein to William Saunders, July 16, 1918, folder 881; William Saunders to F. Mumford, July 19, 1918, folder 106; all in MCDP, WHMC. "Family Enrollment Campaign," *Advertiser-Courier,* October 24, 1917. *Final Report of the Missouri Council of Defense, 1917–19* (St. Louis: Con. P. Curran 1919), 75. "Hermann, Mo., Holds Big Patriotic Rally," *St. Louis Globe-Democrat,* September 26, 1918.

54. Mrs. E. F. Rippstein to W. F. Saunders, November 28, 1917, folder 879; Mrs. E. F. Rippstein to William Saunders, May 27, 1918, folder 373b; both in MCDP, WHMC.

55. W. F. Saunders to F. B. Mumford, August 28, 1918, folder 882, MCDP, WHMC. *Gasconade County History,* vol. 1 (Gasconade County Historical Society: Taylor, 1979), 231. Twelfth Census of the United States, Population Schedule, Missouri, Franklin County, Lyon Township, sheet 8B. Fourteenth Census of the United States, Population Schedule, Missouri, Gasconade County, Roark Township, Hermann, 1st Ward, sheet 5A.

56. A. O. Mann to F. B. Mumford, October 27, 1917, folder 878, MCDP, WHMC. "County Council of Defense Elects Chairman," *Gasconade County Republican,* November 2, 1917. The categories were A for Excellent, B for Good, C for Medium, D for Inefficient, and E for Inaction. W. F. Saunders to Mumford, April 8, 1918, folder 154, MCDP, WHMC. Meyer's father was a German immigrant. Fifteenth Census of the United States, Population Schedule, Missouri, Gasconade County, Boulware Township, sheet 4A.

57. W. F. Saunders to A. O. Mann, March 2, 1918, folder 879; Mrs. Rose Rippstein to Mr. Saunders, April 2, 1918, folder 879; Clarence G. Baxter to Frank W. McAllister, September 7, 1918, folder 882; all in MCDP, WHMC.

58. "Announces Candidacy for Office of Gasconade County Collector," *Advertiser-Courier,* January 16, 1918; "E. A. Meyer Announces for County Collector," *Gasconade County Republican,* January 18, 1918. W. F. Saunders to Chairman Mumford, February 26, 1918, folder 94, MCDP, WMHC.

59. W. F. Saunders to E. A. Meyer, April 6, 1918, folder 879, MCDP, WHMC. "Pro-Germanism and Politics Are Ousted," *Missouri on Guard* 1 (April 1918): 1.

60. W. F. Saunders to E. A. Meyer, April 6, 1918, folder 879; Mrs. Rose Rippstein to Mr. Saunders, April 7, 1918, folder 879; A. O. Mann to F. B. Mumford, April 11, 1918, folder 98; Wm. F. Saunders to Chairman Mumford, April 12, 1918, folder 98; Wm. F. Saunders to Chairman Mumford, April 19, 1918, folder 99; W. F. Saunders to F. B. Mumford, August 28, 1918, folder 882; all in MCDP, WHMC.

61. F. G. Gaebler to Wm. F. Saunders, April 15, 1918, folder 880; Mrs. E. F. Rippstein to Wm. F. Saunders, April 16, 1918, folder 880; F. B. Mumford to Wm. F. Saunders, April 26, 1918, folder 880; all in MCDP, WHMC. *History of Franklin, Jefferson, Washington, Crawford, and Gasconade Counties,* 1084. *Standard Atlas of Gasconade County, Missouri* (Chicago: Geo. A. Ogle, 1913), 64.

62. Wm. F. Saunders to F. G. Gaebler, May 1, 1918; and F. G. Gaebler to Wm. F. Saunders, May 12, 1918, both in folder 880; Mrs. E. F. Rippstein to Mr. Saunders,

May 27, 1918, folder 373b; Frances S. Burkhardt to F. G. Gaebler, July 31, 1918; and F. G. Gaebler to F. Burkhardt, August 2, 1918, both in folder 561; all in MCDP, WHMC.

63. Robert A. Glenn to Wm. F. Saunders, May 14, 1918, folder 880, MCDP, WHMC.

64. A. B. Walker was director of the Peoples Bank of Hermann. E. F. Rippstein was a director and cashier of the Hermann Savings Bank. Edward A. Meyer was a director for the State Bank of Bay. Frank G. Gaebler was a director of the Farmers & Merchant Bank in Hermann. The Hermann Savings Bank led the competition. By 1918, the Farmers & Merchant Bank in Owensville moved up from fifth to fourth place and displaced Bland Commercial Bank. "Banken zeigen Guthaben im Betrage von über \$3,000,000," *Hermanner Volksblatt,* March 29, 1918.

65. Robert A. Glenn, "Report on Gasconade County Council of Defense," May 14, 1918, folder 880, MCDP, WHMC. "Official Election Returns of Gasconade County," *Advertiser-Courier,* November 11, 1914.

66. W. F. Saunders to Chairman Mumford, February 26, 1918, folder 94, MCDP, WHMC. "Erwählung von George H. Klenk zum Mayor von Hermann," *Hermanner Volksblatt,* April 7, 1916; "George H. Klenk wiedererwählt als Mayor von Hermann," *Hermanner Volksblatt,* April 5, 1918. "Verhandlungen des Hermanner Zweigvereins des Deutsch-Amerikanischen Nationalbundes," *Hermanner Volksblatt,* June 16, 1916.

67. Gross argues that World War I provoked conflict between the small-town middle-class merchant group and farmers, because merchants supported the war and the push to demonstrate loyalty to limit the war's impact on their business and ethnic interests. Stephen J. Gross, "Perils of Prussianism: Main Street German America, Local Autonomy, and the Great War," *Agricultural History* 78 (Winter 2004): 78–116.

68. Robert A. Glenn, "Report on Gasconade County Council of Defense," May 14, 1918, folder 880, MCDP, WHMC.

69. W. F. Saunders to Chairman Mumford, February 26, 1918, folder 94; E. F. Rippstein to Wm. F. Saunders, March 3, 1918, folder 436; W. F. Saunders to Mrs. E. F. Rippstein, June 4, 1918, folder 880; all in MCDP, WHMC.

70. Rose Rippstein to Mrs. Miller, September 10, 1917, folder 877, MCDP, WHMC. "German Theater at the Concert Hall," *Advertiser-Courier,* May 12, 1915.

71. G. V. R. Mechin to Mrs. F. S. Burkhardt, August 26, 1918, folder 1120, MCDP, WHMC.

72. Wm. F. Saunders to Chairman Mumford, February 28, 1918, folder 879; W. F. Saunders to F. B. Mumford, August 28, 1918, folder 882, MCDP, WHMC.

73. "The Enemy Tongue," *Daily Capital News,* May 22, 1918. Wm. F. Saunders to A. O. Mann, May 23, 1918, and Wm. F. Saunders to Mrs. E. F. Rippstein, May 24, 1918, both in folder 880, MCDP, WHMC.

74. F. G. Gaebler to Wm. F. Saunders, no date, folder 373b; F. G. Gaebler to Frank Robinson, November 27, 1918, folder 297, MCDP, WHMC.

75. F. M. Robinson to F. G. Gaebler, December 2, 1918, folder 297, MCDP, WHMC; "Schools of State Dropping German," *Gasconade County Republican,* May 17, 1918. Minutes of Meeting, Cape Girardeau, July 12, 1918, folder 409 and 502, MCDP, WHMC. "Stopping the Use of German," *Advertiser-Courier,* July 31, 1918.

76. Mrs. Rippstein to W. F. Saunders, July 16, 1918, folder 881, MCDP, WHMC. Carol Piper Heming, "*Schulhaus* to Schoolhouse: The German School at Hermann, Missouri, 1839–1955," *Missouri Historical Review* 82 (April 1988): 287, 289, 296. "Stadtrat entscheidet sich für temporäre suspension des deutschen Protokolls," *Hermanner Volksblatt,* May 10, 1918; "The Use of Enemy Alien Language," *Advertiser-Courier,* July 17, 1918.

77. "Kirchliches," *Hermanner Volksblatt,* January 18, 1918; Untitled Annual Report from Rev. Kasmann, *Advertiser-Courier,* January 30, 1918; "Erntedankfestgottesdienst in der St. Johannes Kirche in Gasconade," *Hermanner Volksblatt,* September 28, 1917.

78. Robert A. Glenn to W. F. Saunders, June 5, 1918, folder 880; "Memorandum to Mumford," June 6, 1918, folder 881; Telegram, W. F. Saunders to August Wohlt, June 14, 1918, folder 881; all in MCDP, WHMC.

79. "Potsdam Schools Close," *Advertiser-Courier,* May 1, 1918. "Potsdam Items," *Advertiser-Courier,* May 29, 1918; "Flag Day Exercises at Potsdam Schools," *Advertiser-Courier,* June 12, 1918; "Special Announcement for War Savings Meetings in Gasconade County on June 28th, 1918," *Hermann Advertiser-Courier,* June 19, 1918; "The War Savings Stamp Campaign," *Hermanner Volksfreund,* June 21, 1918; "Potsdam News," *Advertiser-Courier,* June 26, 1918. W. F. Saunders to F. G. Gaebler, July 1, 1918, folder 881, MCDP, WHMC.

80. "Potsdam News," *Advertiser-Courier,* July 3, 1918; "Berichte von Potsdam," *Hermanner Volksblatt,* July 5, 1918. W. F. Saunders to F. G. Gaebler, July 1, 1918, folder 881, MCDP, WHMC.

81. F. G. Gaebler to W. F. Saunders, July 2, 1918, folder 881, MCDP, WHMC. "Potsdam News," *Advertiser-Courier,* July 24, 1918; "Big Attendance at W.S.S. Meeting," *Advertiser-Courier,* August 21, 1918; "Kriegssparmarken Versammlung in Hermann," *Hermanner Volksblatt,* August 23, 1918; "Zwölf Distrikte haben ihre Quotas erreicht," *Hermanner Volksblatt,* August 30, 1918.

82. Mrs. E. F. Rippstein to Wm. F. Saunders, July 16, 1918, folder 881, MCDP, WHMC. "Potsdam, Mo., Buys Only $26 in War Stamps," *St. Louis Star,* July 9, 1918; "Potsdam—That's Where Kaiser and His Gang Plotted the War," *St. Louis Star,* July 9, 1918. "Facts and Figures," *Advertiser-Courier,* July 17, 1918; "Richland Township Proud of Liberty Loan Record," *Advertiser-Courier,* May 29, 118.

83. "Potsdam News," *Advertiser-Courier,* July 24, 1918. Francis. S. Burkhart to Mrs. G. V. R. Mechin, August 14, 1918, folder 881, MCDP, WHMC. "Potsdam News," *Advertiser-Courier,* August 28, 1918.

84. Joe Welschmeyer, "Down at Pershing," *Osage County Observer* (Linn), September 26, 1979; and Joe Welschmeyer, "From Potsdam to 'Pfoersching': Pershing's History Mirrors Germany's," *Unterrified Democrat* (Linn), September 9, 1998. Marylin Shaw Smith to Petra DeWitt, September 24, 2002, letter in possession of author.

85. W. F. Saunders to F. B. Mumford, August 28, 1918, folder 882, MCDP, WHMC.

86. Mrs. G. V. R. Mechin to Mrs. F. S. Burkhardt, August 26, 1918, folder 1120; Frank M. Robinson to F. G. Gaebler, November 13, 1918, folder 882; both in MCDP, WHMC. "Pro-Germanism Rampant in 2 Towns, is Charge," *St. Louis Republic,* September 4, 1918.

87. "Post-Office Named in Honor of Gen. Pershing," *Advertiser-Courier,* October

16, 1918. Post Office Department, Fourth Assistant Postmaster General, August 12, 1921, Roll 3, Gasconade County, Record Group 28, U.S. Post Office Geographic Site Location Reports, National Archives, located as MS292 at State Historical Society of Missouri, Columbia. Francis S. Burkhardt to G. V. R. Mechin, August 14, 1918, folder 881; Frank M. Robinson to F. G. Gaebler, November 13, 1918, folder 882; both in MCDP, WHMC.

88. Frank Gaebler to Frank Robinson, November 27, 1918, folder 297, MCDP, WHMC.

89. F. G. Gaebler to Wm. F. Saunders, May 12, 1918, folder 880; F. G. Gaebler to Wm. F. Saunders, no date, folder 373b; F. G. Gaebler to Frank Robinson, November 27, 1918, folder 297, MCDP, WHMC.

90. F. G. Gaebler to Wm. F. Saunders, May 12, 1918, folder 880, MCDP, WHMC.

Chapter 6: Superpatriotism in Action

1. J. Richard Garstang to W. F. Saunders, July 8, 1918, folder 293, Missouri Council of Defense Papers, Western Historical Manuscript Collection, University of Missouri–Columbia (hereinafter cited as MCDP, WHMC).

2. Copies of the fourth paper in the county, the *Osage County Enterprise* in Chamois, no longer exist. "Allies Repulse Fresh German Attack on Line, *Unterrified Democrat*, October 1, 1914. "Kaiser Wilhelm," *Osage County Volksblatt*, January 7, 1915; "German Thoroughness and Patience Responsible for Success," *Unterrified Democrat*, March 11, 1915; "Polite to Victims," *Osage County Republican*, May 6, 1915.

3. "Weltkrieg entbrennt," *Osage County Volksblatt*, August 27, 1914. "Militarismus," *Osage County Volksblatt*, January 28, 1915. "Belgien," *Osage County Volksblatt*, September 14, 1914. Karl J. R. Arndt and Mary E. Olson, eds., *German-American Newspapers and Periodicals, 1732–1955: History and Bibliography* (Heidelberg, Germany: Quelle & Meyer Verlag, 1961; reprint, New York: Johnson Reprint, 1965), 280.

4. "Und so weiter," *Osage County Volksblatt*, May 27, 1915; "Zum Geburtstage Washington's," *Osage County Volksblatt*, February 22, 1917. "Ein freies Amerika," *Osage County Volksblatt*, April 5, 1917.

5. "Close View of War," *Osage County Republican*, February 18, 1915; "Und so weiter," *Osage County Volksblatt*, May 27, 1915; "Erin go bragh," *Osage County Volksblatt*, June 1, 1916; "Ridiculous Stories Circulated by Allies as to Condition in Germany," *Unterrified Democrat*, June 10, 1915; "Interesting Letters from Germany," *Unterrified Democrat*, February 18, 1915; "Nicht lange mehr," *Osage County Volksblatt*, March 2, 1916; "From Germany," *Osage County Republican*, March 30, 1916.

6. Examples include "Wer kann's fassen? Das Elend oder die Gemeinheit!" *Osage County Volksblatt*, May 18, 1916; editorial, *Osage County Republican*, March 11, 1915; "Zurechtweisung für Wilson," *Osage County Volksblatt*, August 31, 1916.

7. "Von der Weltbühne," *Osage County Volksblatt*, November 19, 1914. "Zurechtweisung für Wilson," *Osage County Volksblatt*, August 31, 1916. "Lokales," *Osage County Volksblatt*, September 21, 1916.

8. "Allerlei," *Osage County Volksblatt*, May 20, 1915. "German American Loyalty," *Unterrified Democrat*, May 20, 1915; editorial, *Osage County Republican*, September 2,

1915; "Knock Out the Hyphen," *Osage County Republican,* January 27, 1916; editorial, *Osage County Republican,* March 29, 1917.

9. "Überall deutsch!" *Osage County Volksblatt,* August 26, 1914; "Für die Opfer der Krieges," *Osage County Volksblatt,* September 3, 1914; "Für das Deutsche Vaterland," *Osage County Volksblatt,* September 14, 1914. "Aufruf zur Betheiligung an der Feier des ersten Missourier Deutschen Tages," *Osage County Volksblatt,* August 17, 1916.

10. "Bryan Vindicates the President," *Unterrified Democrat,* June 24, 1915.

11. "State-wide Prohibition in Mo.," *Unterrified Democrat,* October 12, 1916; "Pro-hibitions-Paragraphen," *Osage County Volksblatt,* October 26, 1916; "Statewide Prohibition Means State Wide Ruin," *Osage County Republican,* November 2, 1916. "Die Freiheit in großer Gefahr," *Osage County Volksblatt,* July 22, 1915; "Staatliche Prohibition und 'Single Tax,'" *Osage County Volksblatt,* October 19, 1916.

12. "Official Election Returns for Osage County, November 7, 1916," *Unterrified Democrat,* November 16, 1916. *Official Manual of the State of Missouri for the Years 1917–1918* (Jefferson City: Hugh Stephens, 1918), 447–48.

13. "Republican Thrift Is Squandered under Wilson," *Osage County Republican,* September 14, 1916.

14. Editorial, *Unterrified Democrat,* February 3, 1916; "Americanism," *Unterrified Democrat,* May 11, 1916; "Wilson, the Iron Man of America," *Unterrified Democrat,* June 8, 1916. "America 'Prepares' under Wilson," *Unterrified Democrat,* April 13, 1916. Editorial, *Unterrified Democrat,* June 15, 1916; "Why Wilson Should Win," *Unterrified Democrat,* June 22, 1916.

15. "Die richtige Ansicht," *Osage County Volksblatt,* October 19, 1916; "Wilson or Hughes," and "Wilson vs. Hughes," both in *Osage County Volksblatt,* November 2, 1916.

16. The exception is the 1912 election. Edgar Eugene Robinson, *The Presidential Vote, 1896–1932* (Stanford: Stanford University Press, 1947), 253. "Official Election Returns for Osage County, November 7, 1916," *Unterrified Democrat,* November 16, 1916.

17. George Kishmar, *History of Chamois, Missouri* (Jefferson City: Jeff-City, 1975), 21–22. Thirteenth Census of the United States, 1910, Population Schedule, Missouri, Osage County, Benton Township, Chamois City, 1st Ward, sheet 8A; and Chamois City, 2nd Ward, sheet 23B.

18. "Bridge to Be Built at Holtermann Ford," *Unterrified Democrat,* February 5, 1915; "Die Bürger Westphalia's protestieren," *Osage County Volksblatt,* January 28, 1915; "Die Brücke bei Holtermann's Ford wird gebaut werden," *Osage County Volksblatt,* February 4, 1915; "Reasons Why," *Osage County Volksblatt,* June 24, 1915; "Pro and Con," *Osage County Volksblatt,* July 29, 1915. "Yet No Vindication," *Osage County Volksblatt,* July 15, 1915; "Wie die deutschen Steurzahler von einem deutschen Beamten vertreten und ihre Presse gekuebelt wird," *Osage County Volksblatt,* May 25, 1916.

19. "The Whole Country Will Support the President," *Unterrified Democrat,* February 8, 1917. Editorial, *Osage County Republican,* March 29, 1917; editorial, *Unterrified Democrat,* April 5, 1917; editorial, *Osage County Republican,* April 5, 1917; editorial, *Unterrified Democrat,* April 12, 1917.

20. "Governor's Proclamation," *Osage County Republican,* April 19, 1917; editorial, *Osage County Republican,* April 26, 1917.

21. Editorial, *Unterrified Democrat,* May 3, 1917; editorial, *Unterrified Democrat,* May 17, 1917.

22. Ell Zevely was third-generation American born. Thirteenth Census of the United States, 1910, Population Schedule, Missouri, Osage County, Crawford Township, Linn Town, sheet 2B. "Council of Defense," *Unterrified Democrat,* October 4, 1917; "Secretary M'Adoo Gives Full Explanation of Second Liberty Loan Bond Issue," *Unterrified Democrat,* October 11, 1917; "Ten Reasons for Signing the Pledge List," *Unterrified Democrat,* November 1, 1917; "Buy Red Cross Seals," *Unterrified Democrat,* December 6, 1917.

23. Editorial, *Osage County Republican,* May 31, 1917; editorial, *Osage County Republican,* July 12, 1917; editorial, *Osage County Republican,* November 1, 1917; "Brief Items of Passing Interest," *Osage County Republican,* April 4, 1918. Fourteenth Census of the United States, 1920, Population Schedule, Missouri, Osage County, Crawford Township, Linn City, sheet 176A.

24. "Statement," *Unterrified Democrat,* April 19, 1917.

25. "Heraus mit dem Banner," *Osage County Volksblatt,* April 26, 1916. "Ein Privatissmus über Patriotismus," *Osage County Volksblatt,* May 17, 1917.

26. "A Bland Man Nabbed," *Unterrified Democrat,* May 31, 1917. "Local and Personal," *Unterrified Democrat,* July 5, 1917.

27. Editorial, *Osage County Volksblatt,* June 14, 1917. "Wer den Bogen überspannt," *Osage County Volksblatt,* June 28, 1917. Editorial, *Osage County Volksblatt,* May 24, 1917.

28. "Zum Abschied," *Osage County Volksblatt,* July 19, 1917. Arndt and Olson, *German-American Newspapers and Periodicals,* 280. Issues of *Osage County Volksblatt* for June 15, 1915; November 4, 1915; September 14, 1916; March 1, 1917; and July 5, 1917 show no changes in number or type of advertisements.

29. "An die Leser," *Osage County Volksblatt,* February 1, 1917. "Zum Abschied," *Osage County Volksblatt,* July 19, 1917.

30. "Zum 20. Jahrtag," *Osage County Volksblatt,* June 24, 1915; "Zum Abschied," *Osage County Volksblatt,* July 19, 1917.

31. "Send in Clippings," *Missouri on Guard* 1, no. 6 (March 1918): 7.

32. "Flag Day in Linn," *Unterrified Democrat,* June 21, 1917; editorial, *Osage County Republican,* May 24, 1917.

33. "Patriotism," *Unterrified Democrat,* July 12, 1917.

34. "Local and Personals," *Unterrified Democrat,* May 3, 1917. C. J. Vaughan, *Osage County Directory and Statistical Compendium* (Jefferson City: Hugh Stephens, 1915), 26, 30. "Are Not Slackers," *Unterrified Democrat,* August 23, 1917; "Enlisted in the Navy," *Osage County Republican,* June 6, 1918; "Enlisted in the Navy," *Unterrified Democrat,* June 20, 1918; "Soldiers and Sailor Boys," *Unterrified Democrat,* June 27, 1918.

35. "Military Registration Day June 5," *Unterrified Democrat,* May 24, 1917; "Dienstag den 5 Juni ist allgemeiner Registrierungstag im Lande," *Osage County Volksblatt,* May 31, 1917; "Notice of Call and to Appear for Physical Examination," *Osage County Republican,* August 2, 1917; "Proceedings of Exemption Board," *Unterrified Democrat,* August 16, 1917.

36. World War I Selective Service System Draft Registration Cards, M-1509, Rolls 1751–52, Missouri, Osage County, National Archives, Central Plains Regional Center,

Kansas City, Missouri (hereinafter cited as Selective Service Registration Cards, M-1509, NARA). Christopher C. Gibbs, *The Great Silent Majority: Missouri's Resistance to World War I* (Columbia: University of Missouri Press, 1988), 102–3. For table see Petra DeWitt, "Searching for the Roots of Harassment and the Meaning of Loyalty: A Study of the German-American Experience in Missouri during World War I" (PhD diss., University of Missouri, 2005), 410.

37. Selective Service Registration Cards, M-1509, NARA.

38. Selective Service Registration Cards, M-1509, NARA; "For Physical Examination," *Unterrified Democrat,* August 2, 1917; "Proceedings of Exemption Board," *Unterrified Democrat,* August 16, 1917. "Cases to Be Appealed," *Unterrified Democrat,* August 16, 1917; "Notice of Second Call for Registered Men," *Unterrified Democrat,* August 16, 1917; "Selected by Draft," *Unterrified Democrat,* September 13, 1917; "Selected by Draft," *Unterrified Democrat,* September 20, 1917.

39. "The Conscientious Objector," *Unterrified Democrat,* September 13, 1917. Frank Linnenbrink noted "head hurts"; Martin Odaud noted "fondness of food"; and Fritz Wenger noted "weak minded" in question twelve. Selective Service Registration Cards, M-1509, NARA.

40. "An Able Address," *Unterrified Democrat,* August 2, 1917; "Korrespondenzen: Westphalia," *Missouri Volksfreund,* October 3, 1918.

41. "Women Should Register," *Osage County Republican,* July 26, 1917; "Ladies 'Do Your Bit,'" *Osage County Republican,* September 6, 1917. Ida M. Zouck to Mrs. Walter McNab Miller, August 22, 1917, folder 1042; "Hoover Cards," folder 403; both in MCDP, WHMC.

42. "Buy Red Cross Seals," *Osage County Republican,* December 6, 1917; "The Red Cross," *Osage County Republican,* December 20, 1917; "To Members of Red Cross," *Osage County Republican,* January 31, 1918; "Junior Red Cross Is Doing Splendid Work," *Osage County Republican,* April 4, 1918; "Red Cross Campaign," and "Enthusiastic Meetings," *Unterrified Democrat,* May 30, 1918; "'Over the Top' for Red Cross," *Osage County Republican,* May 30, 1918.

43. "Liberty Loan Bonds," *Osage County Republican,* May 24, 1917. "Liberty Loan Bonds: What They Are and How Obtained," *Osage County Republican,* October 18, 1917; "Telephone Campaign is Proving Big Success," *Osage County Republican,* October 25, 1917.

44. "Third Liberty Loan," and "Buyer of Liberty Bonds Displays True Patriotism," *Unterrified Democrat,* March 28, 1918; "Liberty Loan Notes," *Unterrified Democrat,* April 25, 1918. "Slacker!" *Osage County Republican,* May 2, 1918. "Liberty Loan Report," *Unterrified Democrat,* May 16, 1918; "Liberty Loan Report," *Osage County Republican,* May 16, 1918.

45. "All Osage County Bond Subscribers Should Pay at Least Ten Percent of Their Subscription by October 15th," *Unterrified Democrat,* October 10, 1918; "Local and Personal," *Unterrified Democrat,* October 3, 1918; R. V. Cramer, "Fourth Liberty Bond Slackers," *Unterrified Democrat,* October 17, 1918.

46. "Guard Grain Elevators," *Unterrified Democrat,* September 20, 1917; "Protect Stockyards," *Osage County Republican,* November 8, 1917; "Germany's Barbarous Policy Built on a Foundation of Most Vicious Philosophy," *Unterrified Democrat,* April 4, 1918.

47. Editorial, *Unterrified Democrat,* September 20, 1917.

48. "Field Hospital No. 2 Notes," *Unterrified Democrat,* September 6, 1917, and September 20, 1917. Office of the Adjutant General of Missouri, *Report of the Adjutant General of Missouri, 1917–1920* (Jefferson City: Hugh Stephens, 1919), 98.

49. "Field Hospital No. 2, N.G.M." *Unterrified Democrat,* June 28, 1917; "Hospital Co. No. 2," *Unterrified Democrat,* August 23, 1917. Fourteenth Census of the United States, 1920, Population Schedule, Missouri, Osage County.

50. J. R. Garstang to Wm. F. Saunders, August 11, 1917, folder 1042; "Proclamation," folder 239; both in MCDP, WHMC. *Report of the Adjutant General of Missouri, 1917–1920,* 37–38. "Home Guards," *Unterrified Democrat,* September 6, 1917; "Home Guards," *Unterrified Democrat,* September 27, 1917.

51. *Report of the Adjutant General of Missouri, 1917–1920,* 37–38; "Chamois Entertains," *Daily Post* (Jefferson City), July 22, 1918; "Come to Chamois Labor Day," *Daily Post,* August 31, 1918. "The Sham Battle," *Unterrified Democrat,* August 22, 1918.

52. "Brief Items of Passing Interest," *Osage County Republican,* April 19, 1917; "Council of Defense," *Osage County Republican,* October 4, 1917; "Purchase W.S. Certificates," *Unterrified Democrat,* January 10, 1918; "Red Cross Meeting," *Unterrified Democrat,* January 31, 1918; "Third Liberty Loan," *Unterrified Democrat,* March 28, 1918; "Red Cross Campaign," *Unterrified Democrat,* May 30, 1918. List of Chairmen, Third Liberty Loan, folder 436, MCDP, WHMC. "Liberty Loan Report," *Osage County Republican,* May 16, 1918; "Enthusiastic Meetings," *Unterrified Democrat,* May 30, 1918.

53. Wm. F. Saunders to Mumford, April 8, 1918, folder 154; Robert A. Glenn to Wm. F. Saunders, May 14, 1918, folder 880; both in MCDP, WHMC.

54. Henry E. Steinmann had German-born grandparents on his father's side. Fourteenth Census of the United States, 1920, Missouri, Osage County, Benton Township, Chamois City, sheet 7A. Biography of John Richard Garstang, attachment to letter, Phyllis Garstang, to Petra DeWitt, January 15, 2004; letter in possession of author. J. Richard Garstang to W. F. Saunders, July 8, 1918, folder 293, MCDP, WHMC. Dr. Otto Keuper and Fred Stonner, according to the 1920 census, were the sons of German immigrants; Lagemann's mother was born in Germany, his father was American born to German parents. Fourteenth Census of the United States, 1920, Population Schedule, Missouri, Osage County, Benton Township, sheet 7A, sheet 7B, and sheet 15A.

55. "Pro-Germans Classed as Spies by Gardner, Warned to Keep Out of Missouri," reprinted from the *St. Louis Republic,* April 8, 1918, by the Missouri Council of Defense, located in folder 1702, Mitchell Papers, WHMC. "A Pro-German Is a Spy," *Kansas City Times,* April 8, 1918. "The Next Campaign," *Unterrified Democrat,* April 25, 1918; "A Patriotic School District," *Unterrified Democrat,* February 28, 1918; "W.S.S. Campaign Report," *Unterrified Democrat,* September 5, 1918.

56. J. Richard Garstang to F. B. Mumford, June 5, 1918, folder 1044, MCDP, WHMC. "Red Cross Campaign," *Unterrified Democrat,* May 30, 1918; "Local and Personal," *Unterrified Democrat,* May 30, 1918.

57. J. Richard Garstang to F. B. Mumford, June 5, 1918, folder 1044; J. Richard Garstang to W. F. Saunders, July 8, 1918, folder 293; both in MCDP, WHMC. "Local and Personal," *Unterrified Democrat,* May 30, 1918. Fourteenth Census of the United States, 1920, Population Schedule, Missouri, Osage County, Benton Township, sheet 4A.

58. "Hospital Co. No. 2," *Unterrified Democrat,* August 23, 1917. J. Richard Garstang to Wm. F. Saunders, August 11, 1917, folder 1042; J. Richard Garstang to F. B. Mumford, June 5, 1918, folder 1044; both in MCDP, WHMC.

59. F. B. Mumford to J. Richard Garstang, June 7, 1918, folder 1044, MCDP, WHMC. "Notice of Call and to Appear for Physical Examination," *Osage County Republican,* August 2, 1917; "Proceedings of Exemption Board," *Unterrified Democrat,* August 16, 1917; "Soldiers and Sailor Boys," *Unterrified Democrat,* June 27, 1918. Paul J. Paulsmeyer, Military Service Record World War I, Soldiers Database: War of 1812–World War I, Missouri Archives, Online Database, http://www.sos.mo.gov /archives/soldiers/ (hereinafter cited as Military Service Record, WWI, Missouri Archives) (accessed June 6, 2005). Paulsmeyer worked as the assistant cashier until 1935 when the bank closed. Kishmar, *History of Chamois,* 114.

60. With the possible exception of the *Osage County Enterprise* for which I have been unable to find copies. Yet the absence of the publication of this incident in the newspapers speaks volumes in itself. Local leaders may have thought that evidence of such disloyalty would smudge the image of Chamois as a superpatriotic and loyal town.

61. "Paulsmeyer-Robinson," *Osage County Republican,* June 27, 1918.

62. Affidavit of Private Frank Oidtmann, July 5, 1918, folder 292; "Conduct of Irving Walz," J. Richard Garstang, to Adjutant General of Missouri, July 6, 1918, folder 292; Report of H. E. Steinman to CPT J. Richard Garstang, July 5, 1918, folder 292; Statement, Erwin Walz, July 8, 1918, folder 293; all in MCDP, WHMC.

63. Report of H. E. Steinman to CPT J. Richard Garstang, July 5, 1918, folder 292; "Conduct of Irving Walz," J. Richard Garstang to Adjutant General of Missouri, July 6, 1918, folder 292; Statement, Erwin Walz, July 8, 1918, folder 293; E. Walz to W. F. Saunders, July 8 1918, folder 293; J. Richard Garstang to W. F. Saunders, July 8, 1918, folder 293; all in MCDP. WHMC.

64. Adjutant General Harvey C. Clark to J. R. Garstang, July 5, 1918, folder 292; "Conduct of Irving Walz," J. Richard Garstang to Adjutant General of Missouri, July 6, 1918, folder 292; Statement, Erwin Walz, July 8, 1918, folder 293; all in MCDP, WHMC.

65. "Conduct of Irving Walz," J. Richard Garstang to Adjutant General of Missouri, July 6, 1918, folder 292; J. Richard Garstang to W. F. Saunders, July 8, 1918, folder 293; both in MCDP, WHMC.

66. On further investigation it became clear that Walz's initial expression "To Hell with the Flag" did not violate the Espionage Act and that he had made the remark before the passage of the Sedition Act, in May 1918. W. F. Saunders to Harvey C. Clark, July 8, 1918, folder 293, MCDP, WHMC.

67. "Schwaben ehren Landesmann," *Westliche Post,* October 19, 1917; "Kersting is Expelled by Alliance," *St. Louis Republic,* May 26, 1917.

68. Fourteenth Census of the United States, 1920, Population Schedule, Missouri, Osage County, Benton Township, sheet 149A; *Thirteenth Census of the United States, 1910,* Population Schedule, Missouri, Osage County, Benton Township, sheet 6A.

69. J. Richard Garstang to W. F. Saunders, July 8, 1918, folder 293, MCDP, WHMC.

70. "From Rev. Walz," newspaper clipping, date unknown, attached to J. Richard Garstang to W. F. Saunders, July 12, 1918, folder 293, MCDP, WHMC. "Kersting Is Expelled by Alliance," *St. Louis Republic,* May 26, 1917.

71. "Potsdam News," *Hermann Advertiser-Courier,* July 24, 1918. Fourteenth Census of the United States, 1920, Population Schedule, Missouri, City of St. Louis, 11th Ward, sheet 306A.

72. "Speak United States," *Osage County Republican,* July 11, 1918; "Speak United States," *Unterrified Democrat,* July 11, 1918. "German Talk Must Cease," *Osage County Enterprise* (Chamois), date unknown, newspaper clipping attached to letter, J. Richard Garstang to W. F. Saunders, July 12, 1918, folder 293, MCDP, WHMC. "Council of Defense," *Unterrified Democrat,* August 15, 1918.

73. Minutes of Meeting, Cape Girardeau, July 12, 1918, folder 409 and 502; Dr. L. E. Souders to W. F. Saunders, August 2, 1918, folder 373d; H. Walz to Wm. F. Saunders, July 25, 1918, folder 295; all in MCDP, WHMC.

74. J. Richard Garstang to W. F. Saunders, July 15, 1918, folder 294; W. F. Saunders to J. O. Barkley, August 2, 1918, folder 373d; both in MCDP, WHMC.

75. "Council of Defense," *Unterrified Democrat,* August 8, 1918. J. Richard Garstang to W. F. Saunders, July 15, 1918, folder 294, MCDP, WHMC. Fred Stonner, the son of a German-born father, was the proprietor of the meat market in Chamois and would serve as mayor of Chamois from 1927 through 1928. Kishmar, *History of Chamois,* 21, 29, 130.

76. "Flag Dedication at St. George's," *Unterrified Democrat,* August 1, 1918. Wm. F. Saunders to R. H. Bryan, August 2, 1918; M. J. Murphy to Wm. F. Saunders, August 3, 1918; William Saunders to Father Muckermann, August 3, 1918; M. J. Murphy to R. H. Bryan, September 30, 1918; and R. H. Bryna to M. J. Murphy, October 2, 1918; all in folder 1046, MCDP, WHMC.

77. R. A. Glenn to Chairman Mumford, October 14, 1918, folder 110, MCDP, WHMC.

78. Martin Schulte, interviewed by Petra DeWitt and John Viessman, tape recording, July 2, 2003, Victory Gardens, Vienna, Missouri, located at Capitol Museum, Department of Natural Resources, Jefferson City, Missouri.

Conclusion: Becoming Americans of German Heritage on Their Own Terms

1. Frederick C. Luebke, *Bonds of Loyalty: German-Americans and World War I* (DeKalb: Northern Illinois University Press, 1974), 42, 67–68, 93, 95, 100, 121, 126–27, 151, 311–17; John Higham, *Strangers in the Land: Patterns of American Nativism, 1860–1925,* 2nd ed. (New Brunswick, NJ: Rutgers University Press, 1988), 110.

2. Leonard Dinnerstein, Roger L. Nichols, and David M. Reimers, *Natives and Strangers: A Multicultural History of Americans* (New York: Oxford University Press, 1996), 135. Cecilia Elizabeth O'Leary, *To Die For: The Paradox of American Patriotism* (Princeton: Princeton University Press, 1999), 221. Luebke, *Bonds of Loyalty,* 312–15.

3. "Von Reppert's Talk to Be Investigated," *St. Louis Post-Dispatch,* April 28, 1917. David W. Detjen, *The Germans in Missouri, 1900–1918: Prohibition, Neutrality, and Assimilation* (Columbia: University of Missouri Press, 1985), 146, 166. Walter Kamphoefner, *The Westfalians: From Germany to Missouri* (Princeton: Princeton University Press, 1987), 175.

4. Minnesota, for example, threatened to use a firing squad to rid the state of the so-called disloyal element. Luebke, *Bonds of Loyalty,* 244, 268.

5. Katja Wüstenbecker, *Deutsch-Amerikaner im Ersten Weltkrieg: US-Politik und Nationale Identitäten im Mittleren Westen* (Stuttgart, Germany: Franz Steiner Verlag, 2007), 177–78.

6. Frederick C. Luebke, "Legal Restrictions on Foreign Languages in the Great Plains States, 1917–23," in Luebke, *Germans in the New World: Essays in the History of Immigration* (Urbana: University of Illinois Press, 1990), 31–50. "Iowa Proclamation," folder 373a, MCDP, WHMC.

7. Richard J. Hardy, Richard R. Dohm, and David A. Leuthold, eds., *Missouri Government and Politics,* rev. ed. (Columbia: University of Missouri Press, 1995), 25, 28.

8. Susan Olzak, *The Dynamics of Ethnic Competition and Conflict* (Stanford: Stanford University Press, 1992), 40–41.

9. Mary Neth, *Preserving the Family Farm: Women, Community, and the Foundation of Agribusiness in the Midwest, 1900–1940* (Baltimore: Johns Hopkins University Press, 1995), 40, 43. Walter D. Kamphoefner, "The German Agricultural Frontier: Crucible or Cocoon," *Ethnic Forum* 4, no. 1/2 (1984): 26

10. Christopher C. Gibbs, *The Great Silent Majority: Missouri's Resistance to World War I* (Columbia: University of Missouri Press, 1988), 101–8.

11. Lawrence O. Christensen, "World War I in Missouri: Part I," *Missouri Historical Review* 90 (April 1996): 352. David M. Kennedy, *Over Here: The First World War and American Society* (New York: Oxford University Press, 1980), 242–43.

12. F. G. Gaebler to Wm. F. Saunders, May 12, 1918, folder 880, MCDP, WHMC. "Let the Farmer Alone," reprint of article from *Glasgow Missourian* in *Osage County Volksblatt,* May 31, 1917.

13. "St. Louis County Food Pledge Report, 1917," folder 1100; Ida M. Zouk to Mrs. Walter McNab Miller, August 22, 1917, folder 1042; "Pledge for United States Food Administration," Report for Lafayette County (no date), folder 963; and Melyde Downs to John Keith, November 2, 1917, folder 965; all in MCDP, WHMC.

14. "Report on Gasconade County Council of Defense," May 17, 1918, folder 880, WHMC.

15. "Keep the Home Fires Burning," Liberty Loan advertisement, *Missouri Volksfreund,* April 4, 1918.

16. Milton M. Gordon, *Assimilation in American Life: The Role of Race, Religion, and National Origins* (New York: Oxford University Press, 1964), 135; Erik Kirschbaum, *The Eradication of German Culture in the United States, 1917–1918* (Stuttgart, Germany: Akademischer Verlag, 1986), 13–15; and Carl Wittke, *German-Americans and the World War: With Special Emphasis on Ohio's German-Language Press* (Columbus: Ohio State Archaeological and Historical Society, 1936), 3, 196.

17. Kennedy, *Over Here,* 86, 293–94. Luebke, *Bonds of Loyalty,* 322–28. LaVern J. Rippley, "Ameliorated Americanization: The Effect of World War I on German-Americans in the 1920s," in *The Relationship in the Twentieth Century,* vol. 2 of *German-Americans in the Twentieth Century,* ed. Frank Trommler and Joseph McVeigh (Philadelphia: University of Pennsylvania Press, 1985), 225. R. A. Burchell, "Did the Irish and German Voters Desert the Democrats in 1920? A Tentative Statistical Answer," *Journal of American Studies* 6 (August 1972): 158, 160.

18. "Die letzte Kampagnewoche," *Westliche Post,* October 23, 1920; "Neuen Gründe gegen Cox," *Westliche Post,* October 26, 1920; "Das Wahlergebnis in Missouri," *Westliche Post,* November 4, 1920.

19. *Official Manual of the State of Missouri for the Years 1919–1920* (Jefferson City: Hugh Stephens, 1919), 530–31. *Official Manual of the State of Missouri for the Years 1921–22* (Jefferson City: Hugh Stephens, 1922), 288. Edgar Eugene Robinson, *The Presidential Vote, 1896–1932* (Stanford: Stanford University Press, 1947), 253.

20. Karl J. R. Arndt and Mary E. Olson, eds., *German-American Newspapers and Periodicals, 1732–1955: History and Biography* (Heidelberg, Germany: Quelle & Meyer Verlag, 1961; reprint, New York: Johnson Reprinting, 1965), 237–80. Nationwide, only 234 of 554 newspapers survived. Wüstenbecker, *Deutsch-Amerikaner,* 302.

21. Leonard John Busen, "A History of the Newspapers of Gasconade County, Missouri, from 1843 to 1960" (master's thesis, University of Missouri, 1960), 29–30. Harvey Saalberg, "The *Westliche Post* of St. Louis: A Daily Newspaper for German-Americans, 1857–1938" (PhD diss., University of Missouri, 1967), 366–69, 373, 381, 402.

22. C. A. Keith to Robert A. Glenn, January 18, 1919, folder 967, MCDP, WHMC.

23. William G. Ross, *Forging New Freedoms: Nativism, Education, and the Constitution, 1917–1927* (Lincoln: University of Nebraska Press, 1994), 61–62, 94, 148. Paul J. Ramsey, "The War against German-American Culture: The Removal of German-Language Instruction from the Indianapolis Schools, 1917–1919," *Indiana Magazine of History* 98 (December 2002): 285–303.

24. *Journal of the Senate of Missouri, 50th General Assembly,* vol. 1 (Jefferson City: Hugh Stephens, 1919), 48, 65, 107, 123–24, 145, 196, 827–28, 1162, 1167–68. *Journal of the House of the State of Missouri, 50th General Assembly,* vol. 1 (Jefferson City: Hugh Stephens, 1919), 71, 97, 131, 241, 271–72, 308, 359, 388, 1353.

25. Ross, *Forging New Freedoms,* 63. "Bill Forbidding Alien Tongues in Schools Killed," *St. Louis Republic,* April 15, 1919; "Republicans in House Defeat Foreign Language Measure," *St. Louis Post-Dispatch,* April 15, 1919; "Bill to Bar German in Schools Killed," *St. Louis Globe-Democrat,* April 15, 1919; "Für Verfassung-Konvention," *Westliche Post,* April 16, 1919.

26. Wüstenbecker, *Deutsch-Amerikaner,* 250. Mary Beth Marquard, "Americanization in Dispersed and Clustered German Settlements in Osage County, Missouri: 1860 to 1910" (master's thesis, University of Missouri, 1997), 58. *Souvenir of the Diamond Jubilee of Saint Boniface Church, Koeltztown, Missouri, 1877–1952* (1952), 22, 24, located in vertical file, Osage County Historical Society, Linn, Missouri.

27. Doris Dippold, "Spracherhalt und Sprachwechsel bei Deutschen Kirchengemeinden in Cole County, Missouri" (master's thesis, University of Kansas, 2002), 24–28. See also Marion Lois Huffins, "Pennsylvania German: 'Do they love it in their hearts?'" in *Language and Ethnicity Focusschrift in Honor of Joshua A. Fishman on the Occasion of His 65th Birthday,* ed. James R. Dow (Philadelphia: John Benjamins, 1991), 11, 22; Rippley, "Ameliorated Americanization," 217–18, 220; and Wüstenbecker, *Deutsch-Amerikaner,* 274.

28. Oscar Cornelius Nussmann, "The Town of Concordia: A Study of Cultural Conflict" (master's thesis, University of Missouri, 1933), 120–21, 126.

29. *Festprogramm zum Diamanten Jubiläum der Evangelischen St. Pauls Gemeinde zu Hermann, Missouri* (Hermann: Graf, 1919); *Sonntags-Schul Lehrer Klassen Buch* [Sunday

School Book]; and "An Outline of St. Paul's History;" in "Our German Heritage" folder located in Parsonage, St. Paul United Church of Christ, Hermann, Missouri.

30. The 80th Anniversary, Zion-St. Peter's United Church of Christ, Pershing, Missouri, October 20, 1963, Microfilm, M72, State Archives of Missouri, Jefferson City, Missouri. Martina Holterman to Petra DeWitt, September 29, 2003, letter in possession of author; Wilke, "Remembrances," 2; Gary Kremer, "Persistence and Change in the German Ozarks," *Ozarks Watch* 3 (Summer 1989): 8–10.

31. Nussmann, "Town of Concordia," 122, 123–24. *125th Anniversary 1825–1977, Bethany United Church of Christ, Big Berger, Missouri* (1977), located in vertical file, Gasconade County Historical Society, Hermann, Missouri.

32. Marquard, "Americanization," 56–57.

33. Dippold, "Spracherhalt und Sprachwechsel," 47, 75, 92. Luebke argues that leaders of the Missouri Synod approached transition to English cautiously and deliberately to preserve traditional orthodoxy, "denominational self-consciousness," and membership. Luebke, *Bonds of Loyalty,* 315–26.

34. As quoted in Everette Meier and Herbert T. Mayer, "The Process of Americanization," in *Moving Frontiers: Readings in the History of the Lutheran Church–Missouri Synod,* ed. Carl S. Meyer (St. Louis: Concordia 1964), 380–81. Alan Niehaus Graebner, "The Acculturation of an Immigration Lutheran Church: The Lutheran Church–Missouri Synod, 1917–1929" (PhD diss., Columbia University, 1965), 143–47. Wüstenbecker, *Deutsch-Amerikaner,* 279–80.

35. *Missouri: The WPA Guide to the "Show Me" State* (St. Louis: Missouri Historical Society Press, 1998; reprint of 1941 edition), 392.

36. Adolf E. Schroeder, "Deutsche Sprache in Missouri," in *Deutsch als Muttersprache in den Vereinigten Staaten: Teil I, Der Mittelwesten,* ed. Leopold Auburger, Heinz Kloss, and Heinz Rupp (Wiesbaden, Germany: Franz Steiner Verlag, 1979), 139–40.

37. Nussmann, "Town of Concordia," 131, 144. Wilke, "Remembrances," 19.

38. LaVern J. Rippley, *The German-Americans* (Boston: G. K. Hall, 1976), 127. Russell A. Kazal, *Becoming Old Stock: The Paradox of German-American Identity* (Princeton: Princeton University Press, 2004), 6.

39. Nussmann, "Town of Concordia," 39–40, 148.

40. William G. Bek, *The German Settlement Society of Philadelphia and Its Colony Hermann, Missouri,* trans. Elmer Danuser, ed. Dorothy Heckmann Shrader (Hermann, MO: American Press, 1984), 300–301.

41. Bek, *German Settlement Society of Philadelphia,* 288, 297.

42. James Neal Primm, *Lion of the Valley: St. Louis, Missouri, 1764–1980* (St. Louis: Missouri Historical Society Press, 1998), 436.

43. "Das deutsche Vereinswesen in St. Louis," *Westliche Post,* July 1, 1920, 4. "Große bayerische Kirchweih bei Schuhplattler-Gesellschaft 'Almenrausch,'" *Westliche Post,* October 22, 1020, 7; "Deutsches Theater," *Westliche Post,* November 13, 1920, 3; and "Weihnachtshilfe für Mitteleuropa," *Westliche Post,* December 10, 1920, 7.

44. Gregory Kupsky, "'We, Too, Are Still Here': German Americans in St. Louis, 1919–1941," *Missouri Historical Review* 103 (July 2009): 212, 216.

45. Luebke, *Bonds of Loyalty,* 329.

BIBLIOGRAPHY

Primary Sources

Manuscript Collections

Almstedt, Hermann B. Papers. Western Historical Manuscript Collection, University of Missouri–Columbia.

Benecke, L. Papers. Western Historical Manuscript Collection, University of Missouri–Columbia.

Brewers, Maltsters, and General Labor Departments, Local Union No. 6. Minutes, 1898–1940. Western Historical Manuscript Collection, University of Missouri–Columbia.

Decker, Perl D. Papers. Collection 92. Western Historical Manuscript Collection, University of Missouri–Columbia.

Kargau, E. D. *St. Louis in Former Years: A Commemorative Book for the German Element.* St. Louis: By the author, 1893. Western Historical Manuscript Collection, University of Missouri–Columbia.

Memorial Methodist Church, St. Louis. Western Historical Manuscript Collection, University of Missouri–Columbia.

Missouri Council of Defense Papers. Collection 2797. Western Historical Manuscript Collection, University of Missouri–Columbia.

Mitchell, E. Y., Jr. Papers. Collection 1041. Western Historical Manuscript Collection, University of Missouri–Columbia.

Sachs, Oscar. Papers. Western Historical Manuscript Collection, University of Missouri–Columbia.

Schroeder, Adolf. Papers. Western Historical Manuscript Collection, University of Missouri–Columbia.

Wilke, William. "Remembrances of a Franklin County Farmer." Western Historical Manuscript Collection, University of Missouri–Columbia, 1935.

World War I, Newspaper Clippings. Western Historical Manuscript Collection, University of Missouri–Columbia.

Government Documents, Published

Alien Property Custodian Report. Washington, DC: Government Printing Office, 1919. Reprint, New York: Arno Press, 1977.

Congressional Globe. 106. Washington, DC. 1872.

Office of the Judge Advocate General of the Army. *Compilation of War Laws of the Various States and Insular Possessions.* Washington, DC: Government Printing Office, 1919.

Record Group 21, Records of the United States District Court, Eastern District of Missouri. Criminal Cases, 1864–1966. National Archives, Central Plains Region, Kansas City, Missouri.

Record Group 28, U.S. Post Office Geographic Site Location Reports, Post Office Department, Fourth Assistant Postmaster General, August 12, 1921, Roll 3, Gasconade County. National Archives. Located as MS292 at State Historical Society of Missouri, Columbia, Missouri.

Record Group 59, Records of the Department of State, U.S. Passport Applications. M 1490, January 21, 1906–March 31, 1925, Missouri. National Archives, Washington, DC.

Record Group 129, Records of the Bureau of Prisons, United States Penitentiary Leavenworth, Kansas. Federal Inmate Files, 1895–1920. National Archives, Central Plains Region, Kansas City, Missouri.

U.S. Bureau of the Census. *Population of the United States in 1860, Compiled from the Original Returns of the Eighth Census.* Washington DC: Government Printing Office, 1864.

———. *Ninth Census.* Vol. 1, *The Statistics of the Population of the United States, 1870.* Washington DC: Government Printing Office, 1872.

———. *Report on the Population of the United States at the Tenth Census, 1880.* Washington, DC: Government Printing Office, 1883.

———. *Thirteenth Census of the United States, 1910.* Vol. 2, *Population: Alabama–Montana.* Washington, DC: Government Printing Office, 1913.

———. *Thirteenth Census of the United States, 1910: Abstract of the Census with Supplement for Illinois.* Washington, DC: Government Printing Office, 1913.

———. *Thirteenth Census of the United States, 1910: Abstract of the Census with Supplement for Missouri.* Washington, DC: Government Printing Office, 1913.

———. *Fourteenth Census of the United States Taken in the Year 1920.* Vol. 1, *Population.* Washington, DC: Government Printing Office, 1921.

———. *Fourteenth Census of the United States Taken in the Year 1920.* Vol. 2, *Population.* Washington, DC: Government Printing Office, 1922.

———. *Fourteenth Census of the United States Taken in the Year 1920.* Vol. 3, *Population.* Washington, DC: Government Printing Office, 1923.

———. *Fourteenth Census of the United States, States Compendium: Missouri.* Washington, DC: Government Printing Office, 1924.

United States Commission on Immigration. *Reports of the Immigration Commission.* Vol. 3, *Statistical Review of Immigration, 1820–1910, Distribution of Immigrants, 1850–1900.* Washington, DC: Government Printing Office, 1911.

VanGiezen, Robert, and Albert E. Schwenk. "Compensation from before World War I through the Great Depression." United States Department of Labor, Bureau of Statistics. http://www.bls.gov/opub/cwc/cm20030124ar03p1.htm (accessed June 18, 2010).

Government Documents, Unpublished: Census Population Schedules

Twelfth Census of the United States, 1900. Population Schedule, Missouri. State Historical Society of Missouri, University of Missouri–Columbia.

Thirteenth Census of the United States, 1910. Population Schedule, Missouri. State
   Historical Society of Missouri, University of Missouri–Columbia.
Fourteenth Census of the United States, 1920. Population Schedule, Missouri. State
   Historical Society of Missouri, University of Missouri–Columbia.
Fifteenth Census of the United States, 1930. Population Schedule, Missouri. State
   Historical Society of Missouri, University of Missouri–Columbia.

State Government Documents

Home Guard Files. Archives of the Missouri Military History, Missouri National
   Guard Headquarters, Jefferson City, Missouri.
Journal of the House of the State of Missouri. 50th General Assembly. Vol. 1. Jefferson
   City: Hugh Stephens, 1919.
Journal of the Senate of Missouri. 50th General Assembly. Vol. 1. Jefferson City: Hugh
   Stephens, 1919.
Lamkin, Uel W. *Sixty-Ninth Report on the Public Schools of the State of Missouri.* Ap-
   pendix to the House and Senate Journals of the Fiftieth General Assembly. Vol. 1.
   Serial 7. Jefferson City: Hugh Stephens, 1919.
Military Service Records World War I. Soldiers Database: War of 1812–World War I.
   Missouri State Archives. Online Database, http://www.sos.mo.gov/archives/soldiers/
   (accessed June 6, 2005).
Missouri Council of Defense. *Final Report of the Missouri Council of Defense, 1917–
   1919.* St. Louis: Con. P. Curran, 1919.
Missouri Council of Defense. *Missouri on Guard.* University of Missouri Archives,
   Columbia, Missouri.
Office of the Adjutant General of Missouri. *Report of the Adjutant General of Missouri,
   1917–1920.* Jefferson City: Hugh Stephens, 1920.
Official Manual of the State of Missouri for the Years 1909–1910. Jefferson City: Hugh
   Stephens, 1910.
Official Manual of the State of Missouri for the Years 1913–1914. Jefferson City: Hugh
   Stephens, 1914.
Official Manual of the State of Missouri for the Years 1917–1918. Jefferson City: Hugh
   Stephens, 1918.
Official Manual of the State of Missouri for the Years 1919–1920. Jefferson City: Hugh
   Stephens, 1920.
Official Manual of the State of Missouri for the Years 1921–1922. Jefferson City: Hugh
   Stephens, 1922.

County Archives

Gasconade County Soldiers Service Record, WWI, 1919. Gasconade County Historical Society, Archives, and Records, Hermann, Missouri.

Memoirs and Edited Collections of Letters and Speeches

Creel, George. *How We Advertised America.* New York: Harper & Brothers, 1920;
   reprint, New York: Arno Press, 1972.

Duden, Gottfried. *Report on a Journey to the Western States of North America and a Stay of Several Years on the Missouri during the Years 1824, '25, '26, and 1827.* Edited by James W. Goodrich. Columbia: University of Missouri Press, 1980.

Gale, Oliver Marble, ed. *Americanism: Woodrow Wilson's Speeches on the War.* Chicago: Baldwin Syndicate, 1918.

Gustorf, Fred, and Gisela Gustorf, eds. *The Uncorrupted Heart: Journal and Letters of Frederick Julius Gustorf, 1800–1845.* Columbia: University of Missouri Press, 1969.

Kamphoefner, Walter D., Wolfgang Helbich, and Ulrike Sommer, eds. *News from the Land of Freedom: German Immigrants Write Home.* Ithaca, NY: Cornell University Press, 1991.

Missouri: The WPA Guide to the "Show Me" State. St. Louis: Missouri Historical Society Press, 1998; reprint of 1941 edition.

Schroeder, Adolf E., and Carla Schulz-Geisberg, eds. *Hold Dear as Always: Jette, a German Immigrant Life in Letters.* Columbia: University of Missouri Press, 1988.

Wilson, Woodrow. "Americanism and the Foreign-Born." Address to Naturalized Citizens at Philadelphia, Pennsylvania, May 10, 1915. http://douglassarchives.org /wils_b02.htm.

Letters and Interviews

Garstang, Phyllis. To Petra DeWitt, January 15, 2004.

Holterman, Martina. To Petra DeWitt, September 29, 2003.

Schulte, Martin. Interview by Petra DeWitt and John Viesman, July 2, 2003, Victory Gardens, Vienna, Missouri. Department of Natural Resources, Capitol Museum, Jefferson Landing, Jefferson City, Missouri.

Sellenschutter, Ralph. To Petra DeWitt, July 9, 2003.

Smith, Marylin Shaw. To Petra DeWitt, September 24, 2002.

Newspapers

ENGLISH LANGUAGE (CITY OF PUBLICATION)

Advertiser-Courier (Hermann), 1914–18

Bland Courier, 1914–16

Columbia Daily Tribune, 1914–17

Concordian (Concordia), 1917–18

Daily Capital News (Jefferson City), 1917–18

Daily Post (Jefferson City), 1917–18

Franklin County Tribune (Union), 1917–18

Franklin County Observer (Washington), 1914–18

Fulton Daily Sun, 1918

Gasconade County Republican (Owensville), 1910–18

Joplin News-Herald, 1914–18

Kansas City Journal, 1914–18

Kansas City Star, 1917–18

Kansas City Times, 1914–18

Kirksville Daily Express, 1914–18

Lexington News, 1918
Missouri Republican (St. Louis), 1887
Moberly Democrat, 1914–18
New Era (Rolla), 1914–17
New York Times. 1914–18
Osage County Enterprise (Chamois), 1902
Osage County Observer (Linn), 1979
Osage County Republican (Linn), 1910–18
Sedalia Democrat, 1914–18
Springfield Leader, 1914–17
St. Joseph News Press, 1914–18
St. Louis Globe-Democrat, 1914–18
St. Louis Post-Dispatch, 1914–18
St. Louis Republic, 1914–18
St. Louis Times, 1909
Sweet Springs Herald, 1918
Tipton Times, 1917–18
Unterrified Democrat (Linn), 1914–18, 1982, 1998
Weekly Democrat-News (Marshall), 1918
Weekly Graphic (Kirksville), 1914–18
Weekly Republican (Cape Girardeau), 1914–18
Weekly Saline Citizen (Marshall), 1918
Wentzville Union, 1918

GERMAN LANGUAGE (CITY OF PUBLICATION)

Amerika (St. Louis), 1900–1918
Deutscher Volksfreund (Jackson), 1914–18
Hermanner Volksblatt (Hermann), 1900–1918
Kansas City Presse, 1914–18
Missouri Staatszeitung (Kansas City), 1914–18
Missouri Thalbote (Higginsville), 1914–18
Missouri Volksfreund (Jefferson City), 1914–18
Osage County Volksblatt (Westphalia), 1914–17
Sedalia Journal, 1914–17
Tägliche Deutsche Tribüne (St. Louis), 1850
Warrenton Volksfreund, 1914–18
Westliche Post (St. Louis), 1900–1918
Wöchentlicher Anzeiger des Westens (St. Louis), 1858

Secondary Sources

Books

Albrecht, Erich A., and J. Anthony Burzle, eds. *Germanica-Americana: Symposium on German-American Literature and Culture.* Lawrence: University of Kansas, 1976.

Arndt, Karl J. R., and Mary E. Olson, eds. *German-American Newspapers and Periodicals, 1732–1955: History and Bibliography.* Heidelberg, Germany: Quelle & Meyer Verlag, 1961; reprint, New York: Johnson Reprinting, 1965.

Auburger, Leopold, Heinz Kloss, and Heinz Rupp, eds. *Deutsch als Muttersprache in den Vereinigten Staaten: Teil I, Der Mittelwesten.* Wiesbaden: Franz Steiner Verlag, 1979.

Auchincloss, Louis. *Woodrow Wilson.* New York: Penguin Putnam, 2000.

Bade, Klaus J., ed. *Auswanderer—Wanderarbeiter—Gastarbeiter: Bevölkerung, Arbeitsmarkt und Wanderung in Deutschland seit der Mitte des 19. Jahrhunderts.* Ostfildern, Germany: Scripta Mercaturea Verlag, 1984.

———. "German Emigration to the United States and Continental Immigration to Germany in the Late Nineteenth and Early Twentieth Centuries." In *Labor Migration in the Atlantic Economies: The European and North American Working Classes during the Period of Industrialization,* edited by Dirk Hoerder, 117–42. Westport, CT: Greenwood Press, 1985.

Baepler, Walter A. *A Century of Grace: A History of the Missouri Synod, 1847–1947.* St. Louis: Concordia, 1947.

Bek, William G. *The German Settlement Society of Philadelphia and Its Colony, Hermann, Missouri.* Edited by Dorothy Heckmann Shrader. Hermann, MO: American Press, 1984.

Bodnar, John. *The Transplanted: A History of Immigrants in Urban America.* Bloomington: Indiana University Press, 1985.

Buschan, Georg. *Das deutsche Volk in Sitte und Brauch.* Stuttgart, Germany: Union Deutscher Verlagsgesellschaft, 1922.

Chambers, John Whiteclay. *To Raise an Army: The Draft Comes to Modern America.* New York: Free Press, 1987.

Child, Clifton James. *The German-Americans in Politics, 1914–1917.* Madison: University of Wisconsin Press, 1939.

Christensen, Lawrence O., William E. Foley, Gary R. Kremer, and Kenneth H. Winn, eds. *Dictionary of Missouri Biography.* Columbia: University of Missouri Press, 1999.

Christensen, Lawrence O., and Gary R. Kremer. *A History of Missouri.* Vol. 4: *1875 to 1919.* Columbia: University of Missouri Press, 1997.

Conzen, Kathleen Neils. "Ethnicity as Festive Culture: Nineteenth-Century German America on Parade." In *The Invention of Ethnicity,* edited by Werner Sollors, 44–76. New York: Oxford University Press, 1989.

———. *Immigrant Milwaukee, 1836–1860: Accommodation and Community in a Frontier City.* Cambridge: Cambridge University Press, 1976.

Crighton, John Clark. *Missouri and the World War, 1914–1917: A Study in Public Opinion.* Columbia: University of Missouri Press, 1947.

Detjen, David W. *The Germans in Missouri, 1900–1918: Prohibition, Neutrality, and Assimilation.* Columbia: University of Missouri Press, 1985.

Dinnerstein, Leonard, Roger L. Nichols, and David M. Reimers. *Natives and Strangers: A Multicultural History of Americans.* New York: Oxford University Press, 1996.

Dow, James R., ed. *Language and Ethnicity Focusschrift in Honor of Joshua A. Fishman on the Occasion of His 65th Birthday.* Philadelphia: John Benjamin, 1991.

Ehrlich, Walter. *Zion in the Valley: The Jewish Community of St. Louis.* 2 vols. Columbia: University of Missouri, 2002.

Faherty, William B. *Dream by the River: Two Centuries of Saint Louis Catholicism, 1766–1967.* St. Louis: Piraeus, 1973.

———. *The St. Louis German Catholics.* St. Louis: Reedy Press, 2004.

Feuerlicht, Roberta Strauss. *America's Reign of Terror: World War I, the Red Scare, and the Palmer Raids.* New York: Random House, 1971.

Feurer, Rosemary. *Radical Unionism in the Midwest, 1900–1950.* Urbana: University of Illinois Press, 2006.

Fink, Gary M. *Labor's Search for Political Order: The Political Behavior of the Missouri Labor Movement, 1890–1940.* Columbia: University of Missouri Press, 1973.

Ford, Nancy Gentile. *The Great War and America: Civil-Military Relations during World War I.* Westport, CT: Praeger Security International, 2008.

Forster, Walter O. *Zion on the Mississippi: The Settlement of the Saxon Lutherans in Missouri, 1839–1841.* St. Louis: Concordia, 1953.

Frizzell, Robert W. *Independent Immigrants: A Settlement of Hanoverian Germans in Western Missouri.* Columbia: University of Missouri Press, 2007.

Gabaccia, Donna, ed. *Seeking Common Ground: Multidisciplinary Studies of Immigrant Women in the United States.* Westport, CT: Greenwood Press, 1992.

Garcés, Laura. "The German Challenge to the Monroe Doctrine in Mexico, 1917." In *Confrontation and Cooperation: Germany and the United States in the Era of World War I, 1900–1924,* edited by Hans Jürgen Schröder, 281–313. Providence, RI: Berg, 1993.

Gerlach, Russel L. *Immigrants in the Ozarks: A Study in Ethnic Geography.* Columbia: University of Missouri Press, 1976.

———. *Settlement Patterns in Missouri: A Study of Population Origins.* Columbia: University of Missouri Press, 1986.

Gibbs, Christopher C. *The Great Silent Majority: Missouri's Resistance to World War I.* Columbia: University of Missouri Press, 1988.

Gjerde, Jon. *The Minds of the West: Ethnocultural Evolution in the Rural Middle West, 1830–1917.* Chapel Hill: University of North Carolina Press, 1997.

Gordon, Milton M. *Assimilation in American Life: The Role of Race, Religion, and National Origins.* New York: Oxford University Press, 1964.

Hardy, Richard J., Richard R. Dohm, and David A. Leuthold, eds. *Missouri Government and Politics.* Rev. ed. Columbia: University of Missouri Press, 1995.

Hawgood, John A. *The Tragedy of German America.* New York: Arno Press, 1970.

Hernon, Peter, and Terry Ganey. *Under the Influence: The Unauthorized Story of the Anheuser-Busch Dynasty.* New York: Simon & Schuster, 1991.

Higham, John. *Strangers in the Land: Patterns of American Nativism, 1860–1925.* 2nd ed. New Brunswick, NJ: Rutgers University Press, 1988.

Hoerder, Dirk. "The German-American Labor Press and Its Views of the Institutions in the United States." In *The German-American Radical Press: The Shaping of a Left Political Culture, 1850–1940,* edited by Elliott Shore, Ken Fones-Wolf, and James P. Danky, 182–99. Urbana: University of Illinois Press, 1992.

Hoerder, Dirk, ed. *Labor Migration in the Atlantic Economies: The European and North American Working Classes during the Period of Industrialization.* Westport, CT: Greenwood Press, 1985.

Hoerder, Dirk, and Jörg Nagler, eds. *People in Transit: German Migration in Comparative Perspective, 1820–1930.* New York: Cambridge University Press, 1995.

Hough, Emerson. *The Web.* Chicago: Reilly & Lee, 1919. Reprint, New York: Arno Press, 1969.

Huffins, Marion Lois. "Pennsylvania German: 'Do they love it in their hearts?'" In *Language and Ethnicity Focusschrift in Honor of Joshua A. Fishman on the Occasion of His 65th Birthday,* edited by James R. Dow, 9–22. Philadelphia: John Benjamins, 1991.

Jackson, William Rufus. *Missouri Democracy: A History of the Party and Its Representative Members—Past and Present.* Vol. 2. Chicago: S. J. Clarke, 1935.

Jacobson, Matthew Frye. *Whiteness of a Different Color: European Immigrants and the Alchemy of Race.* Cambridge: Harvard University Press, 1998.

Jensen, Joan M. *The Price of Vigilance.* Chicago: Rand McNally, 1968.

Kamphoefner, Walter D. "'Entwurzelt' oder 'verpflanzt'? Zur Bedeutung der Kettenwanderung für die Einwandererakkulturation in Amerika." In *Auswanderer—Wanderarbeiter—Gastarbeiter: Bevölkerung, Arbeitsmarkt und Wanderung in Deutschland seit der Mitte des 19. Jahrhunderts,* edited by Klaus J. Bade, 321–49. Ostfildern, Germany: Scripta Mercaturae Verlag, 1984.

———. "Learning from the 'Majority-Minority' City: Immigration in Nineteenth-Century St. Louis." In *St. Louis in the Century of Henry Shaw: A View beyond the Garden Wall,* edited by Eric Sandweiss, 79–99. Columbia: University of Missouri Press, 2003.

———. "Paths of Urbanization: St. Louis in 1860." In *Emigration and Settlement Patterns of German Communities in North America,* edited by Eberhard Reichmann, LaVern J. Rippley, and Jörg Nagler, 258–72. Indianapolis: Indiana University Press, 1995.

———. *The Westfalians: From Germany to Missouri.* Princeton: Princeton University Press, 1987.

Kazal, Russell A. *Becoming Old Stock: The Paradox of German-American Identity.* Princeton: Princeton University Press, 2004.

Keil, Hartmut. "A Profile of Editors of the German-American Radical Press." In *The German-American Radical Press: The Shaping of a Left Political Culture, 1850–1940,* edited by Elliott Shore, Ken Fones-Wolf, and James P. Danky, 15–28. Urbana: University of Illinois Press, 1992.

Keith, Jeanette. *Rich Man's War, Poor Man's Fight: Race, Class, and Power in the Rural South during the First World War.* Chapel Hill: University of North Carolina Press, 2004.

Keller, Phyllis. *States of Belonging: German-American Intellectuals and the First World War.* Cambridge: Harvard University Press, 1979.

Kennedy, David M. *Over Here: The First World War and American Society.* New York: Oxford University Press, 1980.

Keyssar, Alexander. *The Right to Vote: The Contested History of Democracy in the United States.* New York: Basic Books, 2000.

Kirschbaum, Erik. *The Eradication of German Culture in the United States, 1917–1918.* Stuttgart, Germany: Akademischer Verlag, 1986.

Kirschten, Ernest. *Catfish and Crystal.* New York: Doubleday, 1965.

Knobel, Dale T. *"America for the Americans": The Nativist Movement in the United States.* New York: Twayne, 1996.

Laskin, David. *The Long Way Home: An American Journey from Ellis Island to the Great War.* New York: Harper Collins, 2010.

Laswell, Harold D. *Propaganda Technique in World War I.* Cambridge, MA: MIT Press, 1971.

Levine, Bruce. *The Spirit of 1848: German Immigrants, Labor Conflict, and the Coming of the Civil War.* Urbana: University of Illinois Press, 1992.

Luebke, Frederick C. *Bonds of Loyalty: German-Americans and World War I.* DeKalb: Northern Illinois University Press, 1974.

———. *Ethnic Voters and the Election of Lincoln.* Lincoln: University of Nebraska Press, 1971.

———, ed. *Germans in the New World: Essays in the History of Immigration.* Urbana: University of Illinois Press, 1990.

Malešević, Siniša, and Mark Kaugaard, eds. *Making Sense of Collectivity: Ethnicity, Nationalism and Globalization.* Sterling, VA: Pluto Press, 2002.

March, David D. *The History of Missouri.* Vol. 2. New York: Lewis Historical, 1967.

Marshall, Howard Wight, and James W. Goodrich, eds. *The German-American Experience in Missouri: Essays in Commemoration of German Immigration to America, 1683–1983.* Columbia: University of Missouri Press, 1986.

McCaffery, Robert Paul. *Islands of Deutschtum: German-Americans in Manchester, New Hampshire, and Lawrence, Massachusetts, 1870–1942.* New York: Peter Lang, 1996.

Meier, Everette, and Herbert T. Mayer. "The Process of Americanization." In *Moving Frontiers: Readings in the History of the Lutheran Church–Missouri Synod,* edited by Carl S. Meyer, 344–85. St. Louis: Concordia, 1964.

Mezger, Werner. *Das große Buch der schwäbisch-alemannischen Fasnet: Ursprünge, Entwicklungen und Erscheinungsformen organisierter Narretei in Südwestdeutschland.* Stuttgart, Germany: Theiss Verlag, 1999.

Mikkelsen, Robert Lewis. "Immigrants in Politics: Poles, Germans, and the Social Democratic Party of Milwaukee." In *Labor Migration in the Atlantic Economies: The European and North American Working Classes during the Period of Industrialization,* edited by Dirk Hoerder, 278–93. Westport, CT: Greenwood Press, 1985.

Miller, Sally M. "Germans on the Mississippi: The Socialist Party of St. Louis." In *Race, Ethnicity, and Gender in Early Twentieth-Century American Socialism,* 73–94. New York: Garland, 1996.

Mock, James R. *Censorship 1917.* Princeton: Princeton University Press, 1941.

Mock, James R., and Cedric Larson. *Words That Won the War: The Story of the Committee on Public Information.* Princeton: Princeton University Press, 1939. Reprint, New York: Russell & Russell, 1968.

Mormino, Gary Ross. *Immigrants on the Hill: Italian-Americans in St. Louis, 1882–1982.* Urbana: University of Illinois Press, 1986.

Nagler, Jörg. *Nationale Minoritäten im Krieg: Feindliche Ausländer und die amerikanische Heimatfront während des Ersten Weltkriegs.* Hamburg: Hamburger Edition HIS, 2000.

———. "Pandora's Box: Propaganda and War Hysteria in the United States during World War I." In *Great War, Total War: Combat and Mobilization on the Western Front, 1914–1918,* edited by Roger Chickering and Stig Förster, 73–93. Cambridge: Cambridge University Press, 2000.

Neth, Mary. *Preserving the Family Farm: Women, Community, and the Foundation of Agribusiness in the Midwest, 1900–1940.* Baltimore: Johns Hopkins University Press, 1995.

O'Leary, Cecilia Elizabeth. *To Die For: The Paradox of American Patriotism.* Princeton: Princeton University Press, 1999.

Olson, James S. *Catholic Immigrants in America.* Chicago: Nelson-Hall, 1987.

Olzak, Susan. *The Dynamics of Ethnic Competition and Conflict.* Stanford: Stanford University Press, 1992.

Park, Robert E. *The Immigrant Press and Its Control.* New York: Harper & Brothers, 1922. Reprint, St. Clair Shores, MI: Scholarly Press, 1970.

Peterson, H. C., and Gilbert C. Fite. *Opponents of War, 1917–1918.* Madison: University of Wisconsin Press, 1957.

Pickle, Linda Schelbitzki. *Contented among Strangers: Rural German-Speaking Women and Their Families in the Nineteenth-Century Midwest.* Urbana: University of Illinois Press, 1996.

Piott, Steven L. *Joseph W. Folk and the Missouri Idea.* Columbia: University of Missouri Press, 1997.

Primm, James Neal. *Lion of the Valley: St. Louis, Missouri, 1764–1989.* 3rd ed. St. Louis: Missouri Historical Society Press, 1998.

Rex, John. "The Fundamentals of the Theory of Ethnicity." In *Making Sense of Collectivity: Ethnicity, Nationalism, and Globalization,* edited by Siniša Malešević and Mark Haugaard, 88–121. Sterling, VA: Pluto Press, 2002.

Rippley, LaVern J. "Ameliorated Americanization: The Effect of World War I on German-Americans in the 1920s." In *The Relationship in the Twentieth Century,* vol. 2 of *German-Americans in the Twentieth Century,* edited by Frank Trommler and Joseph McVeigh, 217–31. Philadelphia: University of Pennsylvania Press, 1985.

———. "The German-American Normal Schools." In *Germanica-Americana: Symposium on German-American Literature and Culture,* edited by Erich A. Albrecht and J. Anthony Burzle, 63–71. Lawrence: University of Kansas, 1976.

———. *The German-Americans.* Boston: G. K. Hall, 1976.

———. *The Immigrant Experience in Wisconsin.* Boston: G. K. Hall, 1985.

Robinson, Edgar Eugene. *The Presidential Vote, 1896–1932.* Stanford: Stanford University Press, 1947.

Roediger, David R. *The Wages of Whiteness: Race and the Making of the American Working Class.* Rev. ed. New York: Verso, 1999.

Ross, Stewart Halsey. *Propaganda for War: How the United States Was Conditioned to Fight the Great War of 1914–1918.* Jefferson, NC: McFarland, 1996.

Ross, William G. *Forging New Freedoms: Nativism, Education, and the Constitution, 1917–1927.* Lincoln: University of Nebraska Press, 1994.

Rothensteiner, John. *History of the Archdiocese of St. Louis: In Its Various Stages of Development from AD 1673 to AD 1928.* 2 vols. St. Louis: Blackwell Wielandy, 1928.

Sauer, Carl O. *The Geography of the Ozark Highland of Missouri.* Chicago: University of Chicago Press, 1971.

Schiavo, Giovanni. *The Italians in Missouri.* New York: Italian American, 1929.

Schroeder, Adolf E. "Deutsche Sprache in Missouri." In *Deutsch als Muttersprache in den Vereinigten Staaten: Teil I, Der Mittelwesten,* edited by Leopold Auburger, Heinz Kloss, and Heinz Rupp, 125–59. Wiesbaden: Franz Steiner Verlag, 1979.

———. "The Persistence of Ethnic Identity in Missouri German Communities." In *Germanica-Americana: Symposium on German-American Literature and Culture,* edited by Erich A. Albrecht and J. Anthony Burzle, 29–41. Lawrence: University of Kansas, 1976.

———. "The Survival of German Traditions in Missouri." In *The German Contribution to the Building of the Americas: Studies in Honor of Karl J. R. Arndt,* edited by Gerhard K. Friesen, Wilfried Laurier, and Walter Schatzberg, Hanover, NH: Clark University Press, 1977.

———. "To Missouri, Where the Sun of Freedom Shines: Dream and Reality on the Western Frontier." In *The German-American Experience in Missouri: Essays in Commemoration of the Tricentennial of German Immigration to America, 1683–1983,* edited by Howard Wight Marshall and James W. Goodrich. Columbia: University of Missouri Press, 1986.

Schroeder, Walter A. "Rural Settlement Patterns of the German-Missourian Cultural Landscape." In *The German-American Experience in Missouri: Essays in Commemoration of the Tricentennial of German Immigration to America, 1683–1983,* edited by Howard Wight Marshall and James W. Goodrich, 25–43. Columbia: University of Missouri Press, 1986.

Shell, Marc. "Hyphens: Between Deitsch and American." In *Multilingual America: Transnationalism, Ethnicity, and Languages of American Literature,* edited by Werner Sollors, 258–71. New York: New York University Press, 1998.

Shoemaker, Floyd C. *Missouri and Missourians: Land of Contrast and People of Achievements.* Chicago: Lewis, 1943.

Sinke, Suzanne. "The International Marriage Market and the Sphere of Social Reproduction: A German Case Study." In *Seeking Common Ground: Multidisciplinary Studies of Immigrant Women in the United States,* edited by Donna Gabaccia, 67–83. Westport, CT: Greenwood Press, 1992.

Sollors, Werner, ed. *The Invention of Ethnicity.* New York Oxford University Press, 1989.

———, ed. *Multilingual America: Transnationalism, Ethnicity, and Languages of American Literature.* New York: New York University Press, 1998.

Sterba, Christopher M. *Good Americans: Italian and Jewish Immigrants during the First World War.* New York: Oxford University Press, 2003.

Sullivan, Margaret LoPiccolo. *Hyphenism in St. Louis, 1900–1921: A View from the Outside.* New York: Garland, 1990.

Thelen, David. *Paths of Resistance: Tradition and Democracy in Industrializing Missouri.* Columbia: University of Missouri Press, 1986.

Thernstrom, Stephan, Ann Orlov, and Oscar Handlin, eds. *Harvard Encyclopedia of American Ethnic Groups.* Cambridge: Harvard University Press, 1980.

Tippens, Matthew D. *Turning Germans into Texans: World War I and the Assimilation and Survival of German Culture in Texas, 1900–1930.* Lexington, KY: Kleingarten Press, 2010.

Tischauser, Leslie V. *The Burden of Ethnicity: The German Question in Chicago, 1914–1941.* New York: Garland, 1990.

Tolzmann, Don Heinrich. *The German-American Experience.* New York: Humanity Books, 2000.

Towne, Ruth Warner. *Senator William J. Stone and the Politics of Compromise.* Port Washington, NY: Kennikat Press, 1979.

Trefousse, Hans L. *Carl Schurz: A Biography.* New York: Fordham University Press, 1998.

Troen, Selwyn K. *The Public and the Schools: Shaping the St. Louis System, 1838–1920.* Columbia: University of Missouri Press, 1975.

Trommler, Frank, and Elliott Shore, eds. *The German-American Encounter: Conflict and Cooperation between Two Cultures, 1800–2000.* New York: Berghahn Books, 2001.

Vaughn, Stephen. *Holding Fast the Inner Lines: Democracy, Nationalism, and the Committee on Public Information.* Chapel Hill: University of North Carolina Press, 1980.

Von Hippel, Wolfgang. *Auswanderung aus Südwestdeutschland: Studien zur Württembergischen Auswanderung und Auswanderungspolitik im 18. und 19. Jahrhundert.* Stuttgart, Germany: Klett-Cotta, 1984.

Walker, Mack. *Germany and the Emigration, 1816–1885.* Cambridge: Harvard University Press, 1964.

Weinberg, Carl R. *Labor, Loyalty & Rebellion: Southwestern Illinois Coal Miners & World War I.* Carbondale: Southern Illinois University Press, 2005.

Wittke, Carl. *German-Americans and the World War: With Special Emphasis on Ohio's German-Language Press.* Columbus: Ohio State Archaeological and Historical Society, 1936.

———. *The German-Language Press in America.* Lexington: University of Kentucky Press, 1957; reprint, New York: Haskell House, 1973.

———. *Refugees of Revolution: The German Forty-Eighters in America.* Philadelphia: University of Pennsylvania Press, 1920.

Wüstenbecker, Katja. *Deutsch-Amerikaner im Ersten Weltkrieg: US-Politik und Nationale Identitäten im Mittleren Westen.* Stuttgart, Germany: Franz Steiner Verlag, 2007.

Yinger, J. Milton. *Ethnicity: Source of Strength? Source of Conflict?* New York: State University of New York Press, 1994.

Zeidel, Robert F. *Immigrants, Progressives, and Exclusion Politics: The Dillingham Commission, 1900–1927.* DeKalb: Northern Illinois University Press, 2004.

Zelinsky, Wilbur. *The Cultural Geography of the United States.* Englewood Cliffs, NJ: Prentice Hall, 1992.

Zucker, A. E., ed. *The Forty-Eighters: Political Refugees of the German Revolution.* New York: Columbia University Press, 1950.

Bethany United Church of Christ, Big Berger, Missouri. *125th Anniversary, 1825–1977.* Vertical File, Gasconade County Historical Society, Hermann, Missouri.

Cole Camp, Missouri: Area History, 1839–1976. Cole Camp: Cole Camp Area Historical Society, 1986.

Evangelischen St. Pauls Gemeinde, Hermann, Missouri. Festprogramm zum Diamanten Jubiläum. Hermann: Graf, 1919.

Gasconade County Historical Society. *Gasconade County History,* vol. 1. Dallas: Taylor, 1979.

Graue, Evelyn. *A History of St. Paul's Church, Hermann, Missouri, 1844–1994.* St. Paul's United Church of Christ, 1994.

Harrison, Samuel F. *History of Hermann, Missouri.* Hermann: Historic Hermann, 1983.

History of Cole, Moniteau, Benton, Miller, Maries and Osage Counties, Missouri. Chicago: Goodspeed, 1889. Reprint, Easely, SC: Southern Historical Press, 1978.

History of Franklin, Jefferson, Washington, Crawford, and Gasconade Counties, Missouri. Chicago: Goodspeed, 1888; reprint, Cape Girardeau, MO: Ramfre Press, 1958.

Kishmar, George. *History of Chamois, Missouri.* New and rev. ed. Jefferson City: Jeff City, 1985.

Miller, Jessie C., ed. *Lawrence County, Missouri, History.* Mt. Vernon, MO: Lawrence County Historical Society, 1974.

Saint Boniface Church, Koeltztown, Missouri. Souvenir of the Diamond Jubilee of 1877–1952 (1952). Located in vertical file, Osage County Historical Society, Linn, Missouri.

St. Paul United Church of Christ, Hermann, Missouri. Records located in Parsonage.

Scharf, J. Thomas. *History of St. Louis and County.* Philadelphia: Louis H. Everts, 1883.

Standard Atlas of Gasconade County, Missouri. Chicago: George A. Ogle, 1913.

Standard Atlas of Osage County, Missouri. Chicago: George A. Ogle, 1913.

The One-hundredth Anniversary: St. Paul Evangelical and Reformed Church, Hermann, Missouri. Hermann, MO, 1944.

Vaughan, C. J. *Osage County Directory and Statistical Compendium.* Jefferson City, MO: Hugh Stephens, 1915.

Welschmeyer, Joe. *Freeburg, MO: Holy Family Parish Centennial History, 1904–2004.* Linn, MO: Observer, 2004.

———. *Sacred Heart Sesquicentennial, 1838–1988.* Linn, MO: Unterrified Democrat, 1988.

Zion–St. Peter's United Church of Christ, Pershing, Missouri. Microfilm, M72. State Archives of Missouri, Jefferson City, Missouri.

Articles

Barrett, James R. "Americanization from the Bottom Up: Immigration and the Remaking of the Working Class in the United States, 1880–1930." *Journal of American History* 79 (December 1992): 996–1020.

Bek, William G. "The Followers of Duden." *Missouri Historical Review* 14 (October 1919–July 1920): 29–73.

———. "The Followers of Duden: Fifteenth Article." *Missouri Historical Review* 18 (April 1924): 415–37.

———. "The Followers of Duden: Sixteenth Article." *Missouri Historical Review* 18 (July 1924): 562–84.

———. "The Followers of Duden: Seventeenth Article." *Missouri Historical Review* 19 (October 1924): 114–29.

———. "The Followers of Duden: Eighteenth Article," *Missouri Historical Review* 19 (January 1925): 338–52.

———. "Nicholas Hesse, German Visitor to Missouri, 1835–1837." *Missouri Historical Review* 41 (October 1946): 19–44.

———. "Survivals of Old Marriage Customs among the Low Germans of West Missouri." *Journal of American Folklore* 21 (January–March 1908): 60–65.

Bigham, Darrel E. "Charles Leich and Company of Evansville: A Note on the Dilemma of German Americans during World War I." *Indiana Magazine of History* 70 (June 1974): 95–121.

Burchell, R. A. "Did the Irish and German Voters Desert the Democrats in 1920? A Tentative Statistical Answer." *Journal of American Studies* 6 (January–March 1972): 153–64.

Burton, Shirley J. "The Espionage and Sedition Acts of 1917 and 1918: Sectional Interpretations in the United States District Courts of Illinois." *Illinois Historical Journal* 87 (Spring 1994): 41–50.

Christensen, Lawrence O. "Missouri's Response to World War I: The Missouri Council of Defense." *Midwest Review* 12 (1990): 34–43.

———. "Popular Reaction to World War I in Missouri." *Missouri Historical Review* 86 (July 1992): 386–95.

———. "Prelude to World War I in Missouri." *Missouri Historical Review* 89 (October 1994): 1–16.

———. "World War I in Missouri: Part I." *Missouri Historical Review* 90 (April 1996): 330–54.

Conzen, Kathleen Neils. "The Paradox of German-American Assimilation." *Yearbook of German-American Studies* 1 (1982): 153–60.

Conzen, Kathleen Neils, David A. Gerber, Ewa Morawska, George E. Pozzetta, and Rudolph J. Vecoli. "The Invention of Ethnicity: A Perspective from the U.S.A." *Journal of American Ethnic History* 12 (Fall 1992): 3–41.

Cortinovis, Irene E. "The Golden Age of German Song." *Missouri Historical Review* 68 (July 1974): 437–42.

Cott, Nancy F. "Marriage and Women's Citizenship in the United States, 1830–1934." *American Historical Review* 103 (December 1998): 1440–74.

Cozzens, Arthur B. "Conservation in German Settlements of the Missouri Ozarks." *Geographical Review* 33 (April 1943): 286–98.

Daum, Andreas. "Celebrating Humanism in St. Louis: The Origins of the Humboldt Statue in Tower Grove Park, 1859–1878." *Gateway Heritage* 15 (Fall 1994): 48–58.

DeChenne, David. "Recipe for Violence: War Attitudes, the Black Hundred Riot, and Superpatriotism in an Illinois Coalfield, 1917–1918." *Illinois Historical Journal* 85 (Winter 1992): 221–38.

Dorpalem, Andreas. "Mühlenberg and Schurz: A Comparative Study of Two Periods of German Immigration into the United States." *American German Review* 5 (June 1939): 16–17, 35.

Efford, Alison Clark. "Race Should Be as Unimportant as Ancestry: German Radicals and African American Citizenship in the Missouri Constitution of 1865." *Missouri Historical Review* 104 (April 2010): 138–58.

Frizzell, Robert W. "The Low German Settlements of Western Missouri: Examples of Ethnic Cocoons." *Yearbook of German-American Studies* 33 (1998): 103–25.

Gibbs, Christopher C. "The Lead Belt Riot and World War One." *Missouri Historical Review* 71 (July 1977): 396–418.

Glenn, Bess. "Private Records Seized by the United States in Wartime—Their Legal Status." *American Archivist* 25 (Fall 1962): 399–405.

Grant, H. Roger. "The Society of Bethel: A Visitor's Account." *Missouri Historical Review* 68 (January 1974): 223–31.

Gross, Stephen J. "Perils of Prussianism: Main Street German America, Local Autonomy, and the Great War." *Agricultural History* 78 (Winter 2004): 78–116.

Hegi, Benjamin Paul. "'Old Time Good Germans': German Americans in Cooke County, Texas, during World War I." *Southwestern Historical Quarterly* 109 (April 2006): 235–58.

Heming, Carol Piper. "*Schulhaus* to Schoolhouse: The German School at Hermann, Missouri, 1839–1955." *Missouri Historical Review* 82 (April 1988): 280–98.

Hickey, Donald R. "The Prager Affair: A Study of Wartime Hysteria." *Journal of the Illinois State Historical Society* 62 (1969): 117–34.

Hilton, O. A. "Public Opinion and Civil Liberties in Wartime, 1917–1919." *Southwestern Social Science Quarterly* 28 (December 1947): 201–24.

Kamphoefner, Walter D. "German-Americans and Civil War Politics: A Reconsideration of the Ethnocultural Thesis." *Civil War History* 37 (September 1991): 232–46.

———. "The German Agricultural Frontier: Crucible or Cocoon." *Ethnic Forum* 4, no. 1/2 (1984): 21–35.

Kaplan, Jeffrey. "Islamophobia in America?: September 11 and Islamophobic Hate Crime." *Terrorism & Political Violence* 18 (Spring 2006): 1–33.

Kazal, Russell A. "Revisiting Assimilation: The Rise, Fall, and Reappraisal of a Concept in American Ethnic History." *American Historical Review* 100 (April 1995): 437–71.

Khoudour-Castéras, David. "Welfare State and Labor Mobility: The Impact of Bismarck's Social Legislation on German Emigration before World War I." *Journal of Economic History* 68 (March 2008): 211–43.

Kretzmann, Paul E. "The Saxon Immigration to Missouri, 1838–1839." *Missouri Historical Review* 33 (January 1939): 157–70.

Kremer, Gary. "Persistence and Change in the German Ozarks." *Ozarks Watch* 3 (Summer 1989): 8–10.

Kupsky, Gregory. "'We, Too, Are Still Here': German Americans in St. Louis, 1919–1941." *Missouri Historical Review* 103 (July 2009): 212–25.

Mormino, Gary Ross. "Over Here: St. Louis Italo-Americans and the First World War." *Bulletin of the Missouri Historical Society* 30 (October 1973): 44–53.

Muehl, Sigmar. "Eduard Mühl: Hermann's Brave Fighter for Truth and Human Rights." *Der Maibaum* 11 (December 2003): 30–32.

———. "Shock of the New: Advising Mid-Nineteenth-Century German Immigrants to Missouri." *Yearbook of German-American Studies* 33 (1998): 85–101.

Muller, Jerry Z. "Us and Them." *Foreign Affairs* 87 (March/April 2008): 18–35.

Ramsey, Paul J. "The War against German-American Culture: The Removal of German-Language Instruction from the Indianapolis Schools, 1917–1919." *Indiana Magazine of History* 98 (December 2002): 285–303.

Schroeder, Adolf E. "The Contexts of Continuity: Germanic Folklore in Missouri." *Kansas Quarterly* 13 (Spring 1981): 89–102.

Schwartz, E. A. "The Lynching of Robert Prager, the United Mine Workers, and the Problems of Patriotism in 1918." *Journal of the Illinois State Historical Society* 96 (2003): 414–37.

Shoemaker, Floyd C. "Hermann: A Bit of the Old World in the Heart of the New." *Missouri Historical Review* 51 (April 1957): 235–44.

———. "Missouri and the War." *Missouri Historical Review* 12 (October 1917): 22–31.

———. "Missouri and the War: Second Article." *Missouri Historical Review* 12 (January 1918): 90–110.

———. "Missouri and the War: Sixth Article." *Missouri Historical Review* 13 (July 1919): 319–60.

Willibrand, W. A. "When German Was King: The FLES Program around 1900." *German Quarterly* 30 (November 1957): 254–61.

Theses and Dissertations

Anderson, Timothy Gene. "Immigrants in the World System: Domestic Industry and Industrialization in Northwest Germany and the Migration to Osage County, Missouri, 1835–1900." PhD diss., Texas A&M University, 1994.

Apprill, Arthur William. "The Culture of a German Community in Missouri." Master's thesis, University of Missouri, 1935.

Balgenorth, John D. "A History of Vincennes, Indiana, during World War I: With Special Emphasis on the German-American Population." Master's thesis, Eastern Illinois University, 1967.

Busen, Leonard John. "A History of the Newspapers of Gasconade County, Missouri, from 1843 to 1960." Master's thesis, University of Missouri, 1960.

Churchwell, Thomas Everett. "The Founding, Growth, and Decline of the German Religious Colony at Bethel, Missouri." Master's thesis, Northeast Missouri State University, 1959.

De Bres, Karen Jean. "From Germans to Americans: The Creation and Destruction of Three Ethnic Communities." PhD diss., Columbia University, 1986.

DeWitt, Petra. "Searching for the Roots of Harassment and the Meaning of Loyalty: A Study of the German-American Experience in Missouri during World War I." PhD diss., University of Missouri, 2005.

Dippold, Doris. "'It Just Doesn't Sound Right': Spracherhalt und Sprachwechsel bei Deutschen Kirchengemeinden in Cole County, Missouri." Master's thesis, University of Kansas, 2002.

Forsythe, Edwin James. "The St. Louis Central Trades and Labor Union, 1887–1945." PhD diss., University of Missouri, 1956.

Gleason, John Philip. "The Central Verein, 1900–1917: A Chapter in the History of the German-American Catholics." PhD diss., University of Notre Dame, 1960.

Graebner, Alan Niehaus. "The Acculturation of an Immigration Lutheran Church: The Lutheran Church–Missouri Synod, 1917–1929." PhD diss., Columbia University, 1965.

Janes, Franziska P. "The St. Louis German Press and World War I, 1914–1917." Master's thesis, Saint Louis University, 1969.

Kellner, George Helmuth. "The German Element on the Urban Frontier: St. Louis, 1830–1860." PhD diss., University of Missouri, 1973.

Kuyper, Susan Jean. "The Americanization of German Immigrants: Language, Religion, and Schools in Nineteenth-Century Rural Wisconsin." PhD diss., University of Wisconsin–Madison, 1980.

Marquard, Mary Beth. "Americanization in Dispersed and Clustered German Settlements in Osage County, Missouri: 1860–1910." Master's thesis, University of Missouri, 1997.

Northwick, Byron. "The Development of the Missouri Synod: The Role of Education in the Preservation and Promotion of Lutheran Orthodoxy, 1839–1872." PhD diss., Kansas State University, 1987.

Nussmann, Oscar Cornelius. "The Town of Concordia, Missouri: A Study in Cultural Conflict." Master's thesis, University of Missouri, 1933.

Olson, Audrey L. "St. Louis Germans, 1850–1920: The Nature of an Immigrant Community and Its Relation to the Assimilation Process." PhD diss., University of Kansas, 1970.

Rüdiger, Helmut. "Die Geographische Bedingtheit der Besiedlung Missouris." Master's thesis, University of Missouri, 1946.

Saalberg, Harvey. "The *Westliche Post* of St. Louis: A Daily Newspaper for German-Americans, 1857–1938." PhD diss., University of Missouri, 1967.

Wolkerstorfer, Sister John Christine. "Nativism in Minnesota in World War I: A Comparative Study of Brown, Ramsey, and Stearns Counties, 1914–18." PhD diss., University of Minnesota, 1973.

ethnicity 2, 5, 17–22, 25, 127, 142, 164, 166
Evangelical Reformed Church (Zoar), 79

Fellonius, Paul, 10
Feuers, John, 139
Fischer, Ed, 73
Folk, Joseph W., 21, 32, 161
food conservation. *See* U.S. Food
  Administration
Franklin County, 13, 14, 69, 82, 165; county
  council of defense, 74–75, 77
Franklin County Tribune, 36
Freeburg, MO, 18, 137
Freistatt, MO, 14, 166
Frenz, Joseph, 67
Froos, Henry, 98
Fulton Township Council of Defense, 73

Gaebler, Frank, 125–26, 128, 130–32, 159
Gardner, Frederick D., 5, 47, 83, 85, 91,
  138; aggressive patriotism, 55–56, 71–72;
  creation of Missouri Council of Defense,
  63, 69; election, 49–50, 114; pro-
  Germany stance, 49, 55
Garstang, J. Richard, 133, 146–47, 161
Gasconade County, 25, 47, 50, 158; access to
  information, 121; aggressive patriotism,
  126, 131; anti-German sentiment, 131; class
  conflict, 15, 123, 126, 160; definition of
  patriotism, 115–17; disloyal county label,
  118, 120–32; economic competition, 126;
  election of 1916, 114; evidence of loyalty,
  116, 120, 122; food conservation, 118–19,
  121, 159; geographic divisions, 123, 126;
  German language, 127–29, 131; German
  settlement history, 10, 13–16; liberty loan,
  119–20, 126–27, 160; neutrality period,
  111–14; pro-German sentiment, 127, 132;
  Red Cross chapter, 119; selective service,
  117–18; War Savings Stamps, 120, 129–30.
  See also Potsdam, MO
Gasconade County Council of Defense, 111,
  116, 123–26
Gasconade County Republican (Owensville):
  defining patriotism, 115–16; on disloyalty,
  122; on war, 112–13
Gellhorn, Edna, 88
Gellhorn, George, 52
German Aid Society, 12

German-Americans: acculturation, 29–30,
  155; agricultural traditions, 9, 14, 20; class
  division, 26, 28–29; cultural traditions, 9,
  18, 25, 30, 165–67; defined, 2; economic
  competition with non-Germans, 13–15;
  identity, 8–9, 18–22, 30, 34, 40–42; labor
  union history, 26–28; lack of unity, 44,
  52; loyalty, 45–46, 54, 57, 75, 105, 117,
  135, 141–42, 159; perceived ethnic unity,
  25–26, 41–43, 48; perception as antiwar,
  43; political activity, 20–21, 31, 46–49,
  161; and prohibition, 33, 48, 166; reaction
  to disloyalty charges, 3, 58, 80, 89, 97,
  112, 158–61; support for Gardner, 49;
  support for Germany during neutrality,
  41; view on imperialism, 32. *See also* St.
  Louis German-Americans
German and Austro-Hungarian Prisoners of
  War in Siberia Fund, 41, 52
German churches, 23–24, 31; Catholics, 11,
  17, 23–25, 28, 50–51, 79, 108, 164–65;
  compulsory laws, resistance to, 24; ethnic
  identity, role in, 17, 22–25, 28, 31, 108;
  German language, efforts to ban it, 78–80,
  108–9, 151, 162; Jews, 109; loyalty, 109;
  Lutherans, 10–11, 21–24, 78–79, 82, 109,
  163–64; Methodists, 106, 165; parochial
  schools, 22–24, 162; perceived as disloyal,
  24–25, 43, 50–51, 78–79; settlement, role
  in, 17; transition to English, 23, 79, 108–9,
  162, 164–65. *See also specific congregations*
German culture: customs and festivals,
  17–18, 25, 105, 157; efforts to end, 154,
  167; praise for, 30; preservation of, 10, 14,
  17, 22, 25–26, 31, 165–67
German Day, 25, 30, 113, 136
German Evangelical Church (Chamois), 151
German Evangelical Lutheran Synod of
  Missouri, Ohio, and Other States. *See*
  Lutheran Church—Missouri Synod
German immigrants, 26, 9–18, 141
German language: bilingualism, 19–20,
  128, 164; efforts to ban, 2, 75–83, 106–9,
  127–29, 131, 150–51, 154–55, 161–63; low
  German dialect, 11, 164; natural decline,
  163–67; preservation of, 10, 16, 19, 23–25;
  in public schools, 24, 81, 162; role in
  identity, 14, 19, 21, 108; survival, 163–67;
  used to create patriotism, 67, 78

German-language newspapers: assimilation, role in, 21–22, 29, 166; cooperation with CPI, 70, 92; disloyalty, perceived, 32; efforts to suppress, 75–77, 106, 154, 161–62; on imperialism, 32–33; neutrality period, 37–40, 43–45, 112, 134–36; pro-Gardner stance, 49; pro-Germany sentiment, 38, 43; translation requirement, 70, 75, 106. *See also specific newspapers*
German Lutheran Church (Creighton), 80
German Lutheran Church (Jefferson City), 80
German Lutheran Holy Cross Church (St. Louis), 23
German Red Cross, 41, 52, 112
German religions. *See* German churches
German School Society. *See* Deutsche Schulverein
German Settlement Society of Philadelphia, 10
German Social Democrats, 21, 27
German Society, 12, 52
German spies, 55, 59
German synod. *See* Lutheran Church—Missouri Synod
Germany, 35
Gibbs, Christopher, 62
Gibbs, D. A., 146
Gießen Emigration Society, 10
Gill, S. C., 77
Gleeser, Carl C., 76, 154
Glenn, Robert, 75, 122, 126, 147, 151, 160
Glennon, John J., 43, 50–51, 108
Gordon, Milton, 161
Graebner, August L., 23
Graebner, Theodore, 23, 79–80, 163
Graegner, A., 79
Graf, Theodore, 112
Greebuer, Rev. Allen, 79
Gregory, Thomas, 58, 102
Grimes, P. J., 88
Grossman, E. M., 71

Hagedorn, Hermann, 73
Harkort, Auguste, 96
Harrison, O. S., 163
Hatton, Claudia, 118
Hayes, Rutherford B., 8
Heidbreder, August, 122, 140
Heine Safety Boiler Works, 99

Helias, Ferdinand M., 11
Helmich, Hermann, K., 164
Henry County, 69
Hensley, Walter L., 37
Hermann, MO: German culture, 18–19, 25, 30, 113, 166; German language, 20, 82, 128, 162, 164; loyalty, evidence of, 118–19; neutrality period, 37, 112; prohibition, 33, 166; registration of alien enemies, 117; settlement history, 4, 10, 14
Hermanner Volksblatt, 25, 112, 162; defining patriotism, 115–16; on food conservation, 119; Trading-with-the-Enemy Act, 116
Higham, John, 5, 153
Hilfsverein Deutscher Frauen, 41, 112
Hoehn, Gottlieb, 27
Home Guard, 61, 67, 73, 117; Osage County, 133, 146–50, 152; St. Louis, 91
Hoover, Herbert, 63, 85, 156. *See also* U.S. Food Administration
Howard County, MO, 13
Hughes, Charles Evans, 45–47

Illinois, 1, 6–7, 24, 36, 70, 99, 110; contrast with Missouri, 3–4, 27, 101, 156; Prager lynching, 59, 71, 154
Indianapolis, 89
Industrial Workers of the World (IWW), 6–7, 27, 97
influenza, 94, 118
internment, 53, 97, 104
intimidation. *See* coercion
Iowa, 2–4, 61, 89, 118, 122, 155, 161–62
Italian immigrants, 12, 94, 128, 157

Jaeger, Charles, 73
Jefferson City, MO: Alien Property Custodian, 75; German churches, 23, 80; German-language newspaper, 37–38, 74, 76, 139; Home Guard, 146; IWW threat, 7; mob activity, 1–2, 5–7, 61, 71; neutrality period, 37. *See also* Missouri Council of Defense

Kansas City Journal, 37
Kansas City Presse, 46, 76
Kansas City Star, 63
Kasmann, R. H., 128, 164
Keil, William, 11

Missouri General Assembly, 5, 56, 64, 82–83, 156, 163
Missouri National Guard, 53, 89, 145–46
Missouri Republican (St. Louis), 30
Missouri Staats Zeitung (Kansas City), 76
Missouri State Federation of Labor (MFL), 27, 57
Missouri Thalbote (Higginsville), 38, 76
Missouri Volksfreund, 2, 38, 74, 76, 139
Moberly Democrat, 37
mobilization, 5, 43, 139, 153; farmers, 64; lack of information, 62, 121; military, 53, 67, 142; national guidelines, 2, 56–57, 63–64, 124; state guidelines, 64, 69, 75. *See also* Missouri Council of Defense
mob violence 3, 6–7, 59–61, 88, 133, 150–51, 154, 157
Monat, Fritz, 1, 3, 6, 11, 61, 71
Moniteau County, 2, 13, 77
Montgomery County, 13
Morgan County, 50
Morris, Page, 102–3
Muller, A. W., 79
Mumford, Frederick, 6, 63, 83
Münch, Friedrich, 10
Murphy, M. J., 151

Nagel, Charles, 33
National Council of Defense, 5, 51, 62, 156; on German language, 80; state council instructions, 63–64, 75, 83
National German-American Alliance, 25–26, 33, 154; Cape Girardeau, 49; ethnic pride, 26, 42; Gasconade County, 126; Missouri chapter, 103–4, 113; prohibition, 48; St. Louis, 44, 45–46, 47, 52, 89, 103, 114
National Security League, 42–43, 53, 106
National War Labor Board, 98–99
nativism, 26, 32, 34, 44, 46, 110, 163
naturalization, 26, 53, 86, 89, 94, 117
Nazareth Evangelical Church, 101
New York Times, 39, 63
Nugent, Carrie, 85

Oesterlei, Theodore, 99
Ohio, 3, 10, 22, 27, 61, 71, 76, 101
Oidtmann, Frank, 149–50
Oliver, Arthur L., 94, 100–103
Omaha, NE, 89

Oncken, Frank, 124
"100 percent Americanism," 95–96, 131
opposition to war: control of, 58; in Missouri, 68–69; punishment for, 6, 58–59, 73, 141, 154; St. Louis, 42; suspected, 62. *See also* disloyalty
Osage County, 31, 47, 158; anti-German sentiment, 16, 134, 141; Benton Township Council of Defense, 147, 151; county council of defense, 139, 150–51, 156; disloyalty, 134–36, 140, 144, 148–51; food conservation, 144; Home Guard, 146, 148–50; internal divisions, 137–38, 150; language ordinance, 150–51; Liberty Loan, 144–45, 147, 160; loyalty, definition of, 134–35, 139, 142, 145, 152; military service, 142–43, 145–46; patriotism, expression of, 134, 139, 141–43, 145–46; Red Cross, 144, 146, 148; settlement history, 11, 13–17, 133–34; slacker label, 147, 152. *See also* Chamois, MO
Osage County Republican, 134, 138–39
Osage County Volksblatt, 33, 138, 158; on aggressive patriotism, 139–41; demise of, 140–41; on neutrality, 134; on Wilson, 136, 140
Overstolz, Henry C., 31
Owensville, MO, 117, 118; accusations of disloyalty, 123; Red Cross chapter, 119

Pahmeyer, William, 137
Palme, Arno B., 90
Palmer, A. Mitchell, 74, 94–95
Pardick, Edward, 100
patriotism: appeal to, 5, 24, 45, 64, 120, 153; definition of, 56–58, 67, 101, 116, 142, 155; expression of, 29, 53, 57–59, 62, 79; Gasconade County, evidence of, 115, 118, 120; German-American peer pressure, 3, 29, 73–74, 78, 80, 109, 124–25, 158; Missouri, evidence of, 68, 78, 83, 85, 115; Osage County, evidence of, 134–35, 139, 142, 145, 152; passive, 62, 155; St. Louis, evidence of, 85–86, 89, 91–92, 94. *See also* loyalty
Paulsmeyer, Paul, 148, 158
Perry County, 10, 13, 47
Pershing, MO. *See* Potsdam, MO
Petersdorf, Andrew, 99

Pettis County, 14, 50
Pfotenhauer, Frederick, 80
plattdeutsch, 11
political machine, 21, 32, 53
Potsdam, MO, 117, 129–32
Prager, Robert, 59, 71, 154
Preetorius, Emil, 30
pro-German propaganda, 68–69, 70
pro-German sentiment, 6, 42–46, 50, 57,
    59, 154; Gardner, Frederick, 50, 55, 72;
    in Gasconade County, 113, 123, 125, 127,
    130, 132, 158; German-Americans, 61–62,
    71–73; German-language press, 38, 52;
    National German-American Alliance, 44,
    46; in Osage County, 133–36, 141, 147; in
    St. Louis, 43, 87–89, 94, 96–97, 103, 110
prohibition, 21, 28, 33, 166; 1916 ballot issue,
    48–49, 114, 136
propaganda, British. *See* British propaganda

radical press, 21
Radical Republican Party, 33
Randolph County Council of Defense, 74
Red Cross, American, 6, 52, 56, 66–68, 73,
    80, 155; Gasconade County, 17, 111, 115–
    16, 119, 121–22, 130–31; Osage County,
    144, 146, 148; St. Louis, 91, 94, 97, 101,
    105–6, 108–9
Reed, James A., 47, 49, 112
Reformed Zion German Church (Potsdam),
    131
Reisinger, Kurt, 97
Relief of Widows and Orphans, 41
revolution, 9–10, 11
Richfountain, MO, 11, 15, 17, 29, 137, 165
Rippstein, Eugene F., 111, 126
Rippstein, Rose Sophia, 111, 118–19, 121,
    123–24, 127
Roosevelt, Theodore, 35, 45–46
Rose, Frank, 73
Russell, George, 61

sabotage, 52, 53, 61
Saline County, 13, 73
Saunders, William, 6, 62, 68, 73, 83, 123, 151;
    coercion, use of, 80–81; on disloyalty, 71;
    on Gasconade County, 124–25, 127, 131;
    on German language, 80–81
Saxon Settlement Society, 10

Scheunemann, Ernest, 61
Scheuring, August, 100–101
Schlomann, Fritz, 72
Schmook, Fritz, 104
Schrader, Frederick C., 71
Schramm, Ernst Prang, 88
Schroeder, Adolf, 165
Schubert, William, 100–101
Schulte, Martin, 18, 152
Schurz, Carl, 8, 11, 30, 95
Seba, John D., 112
Secret Service, 53, 61, 148, 154; threat of
    investigation, 69, 92, 94, 145
Sedalia Democrat, 70
Sedalia Journal, 38, 76, 162
Sedition Act (1918), 73, 104–5
Seifert, Oscar, 96
Selective Service, 89; draft dodgers,
    90–91, 97; exemptions from, 90, 117–18,
    142–43; interference with, 61, 100–105;
    opposition to, 69, 76; St. Louis, 90
Selph, Colin M., 91, 105
Shackleford, Dorsey W., 37, 57
Sigel, Franz, 11, 30, 116
slacker label, 69–70, 89, 111, 119, 126, 144–47,
    152, 160
Smith, Elliott Dunlap, 67
Smith, Jackson, 122
Social Democrats. *See* German Social
    Democrats
Socialist Party, 20, 21, 32; 1916 presidential
    election, 47–48; St. Louis, 27–28, 42, 51,
    88, 99, 110, 157
socialists, 6–7, 27–28, 37, 50; and Espionage
    Act, 100–103; opposition to war, 62, 90;
    Wisconsin, 64
Spencer, Seldon, 161
Springfield, MO, 50
Springfield Leader, 37
Staunton, Illinois 1, 6–7, 61
St. Charles County, 9, 13
St. Clair County, 69
Steele, Elmer E., 88
Ste. Genevieve County, 11, 13
Steichen, Clara, 148
Steinkraus, Charles, 77
Steinmann, Harry Edward, 149–50
Steinmann, Henry, 146
Stephan, Martin, 10